James

A Commentary on the Greek Text

W<small>ILLIAM</small> V<small>ARNER</small>

Fontes Press

James:
A Commentary on the Greek Text

Copyright © 2017 by Fontes Press

ISBN-10: 1-948048-01-9
ISBN-13: 978-1-948048-01-9

FONTES PRESS

www.fontespress.com

This commentary is dedicated to
Abner Chou,
a former student and current colleague,
who personifies "the wisdom from above."

CONTENTS

LIST OF FIGURES

ABBREVIATIONS

ABD	D. N. Freedman, ed., *Anchor Yale Bible Dictionary*
ASV	American Standard Version
ABRL	Anchor Bible Reference Library
acc.	accusative
ACCS	Ancient Christian Commentary on Scripture
A.D.	anno Domini
Ag. Ap.	Josephus, *Against Apion*
Ant.	Josephus, *Jewish Antiquities*
AOT	Sparks, H.F.D., *Apocryphal Old Testament*
ATR	*Anglican Theological Review*
Bar	Baruch
B.C.	Before Christ
BDAG	W. F. Bauer, W. Danker, W. F. Arndt, and F. W. Gingrich, *Greek-English Lexicon of the New Testament and Other Early Christian Literature*
BDF	F. Blass, A. Debrunner, and R. W. Funk, *A Greek Grammar of the New Testament and Other Early Christian Literature*
Bib	*Biblica*
BJRL	*Bulletin of the John Rylands University Library of Manchester*
BNTC	Black's New Testament Commentaries
BR	*Biblical Research*
BSac	*Bibliotheca Sacra*
BST	The Bible Speaks Today
Burton	Burton, *Moods and Tenses of New Testament Greek*

ca.	circa
CBQ	*Catholic Biblical Quarterly*
CBR	*Currents in Biblical Research*
CEB	Common English Bible
cf.	*confer*, compare
Col	Colossians
CSB	Christian Standard Bible
Dan	Daniel
Deut	Deuteronomy
Did	Didache
DSS	Dead Sea Scrolls
Eccl	Ecclesiastes
ed.	Edition
EDEJ	J. J. Collins and D. C. Harlow, eds. *Eerdmans Dictionary of Early Judaism*
ed(s).	editor(s)
EDNT	H. Balz and G. Schneider, eds., *Exegetical Dictionary of the New Testament*
EEC	Evangelical Exegetical Commentary
e.g.	*exempli gratia*, for example
EGT	Expositors Greek Testament
EKKNT	Evangelisch-Katholischer Kommentar zum Neuen Testament
Eph	Ephesians
esp.	especially
Esth	Esther
etc.	*et cetera*, and the rest
ESV	English Standard Version
EV	English Version(s)
ETL	*Ephemerides Theologicae Lovanienses*
Exod	Exodus
EB	Expositors Bible
EBC	The Expositors Bible Commentary
ExpT	*Expository Times*
Ezek	Ezekiel
1 Chr	1 Chronicles
1 Clem.	*1 Clement*
1 Cor	1 Corinthians

Abbreviations

1 Esd	1 Esdras
1 Kgs	1 Kings
1 Macc	1 Maccabees
1 Pet	1 Peter
1 Sam	1 Samuel
1 Thess	1 Thessalonians
1 Tim	1 Timothy
4 Macc	*4 Maccabees*
Gal	Galatians
GE	Montonari, Franco, ed. *The Brill Dictionary of Ancient Greek*
Gen	Genesis
gen.	genitive
GosThom	Gospel of Thomas
HCSB	Holman Christian Standard Bible
Hab	Habakkuk
Heb	Hebrews
Hermas	*Shepherd of Hermas*
Hos	Hosea
HTR	*Harvard Theological Review*
ICC	International Critical Commentary
i.e.	*id est*, that is
Isa	Isaiah
IJSL	International Journal of the Society of Language
Jam	James
JB	Jerusalem Bible
JBL	*Journal of Biblical Literature*
Jdt	Judith
Jer	Jeremiah
JSNT	*Journal for the Study of the New Testament*
JSNTSup	Journal for the Study of the New Testament: Supplement Series
JTS	*Journal of Theological Studies*
Jub.	*Jubilees*
Judg	Judges
J.W.	Josephus, *Jewish War*
KJV	King James Version
Lam	Lamentations

Lampe	Patristic Lexicon
LB	*Linguistica Biblica*
Lev	Leviticus
LNTS	Library of New Testament Studies
L-N	J. P. Louw and E. A. Nida, eds., *Greek-English Lexicon of the New Testament Based on Semantic Domains*
LSJ	H. G. Liddell, R. Scott, and H. S. Jones, eds., *A Greek-English Lexicon*
LXX	Septuagint version(s)
LW	*Luther's Works*, Concordia College, 1973.
Mal	Malachi
Matt	Matthew
MNTS	McMaster New Testament Studies
Mic	Micah
M-M	Moulton and Milligan, *Vocabulary of the Greek New Testament*
Moule	C.F.D. Moule, *An Idiom Book of New Testament Greek*
Muraoka	T. Muraoka, *A Greek-English Lexicon of the Septuagint*
NA^{27}	Nestle-Aland: Novum Testamentum Graece, 27th edition
NA^{28}	Nestle-Aland: Novum Testamentum Graece, 28th edition
NASB	New American Standard Bible
NCABC	New Cambridge Bible Commentary
NCBC	New Century Bible Commentary
NEB	New English Bible
Neh	Nehemiah
NETS	New English Translation of the Septuagint
NICNT	New International Commentary on the New Testament
NIGTC	New International Greek Testament Commentary
NIV	New International Version (2011 edition)
NIVAC	New International Version Application Commentary
NKJV	New King James Version
NLT	New Living Translation
NovT	*Novum Testamentum*
NovTSup	Novum Testamentum Supplements
NRSV	New Revised Standard Version
NSBT	New Studies in Biblical Theology

Abbreviations

NT	New Testament
NTG	New Testament Guides
NTL	New Testament Library
NTM	New Testament Monographs
NTR	New Testament Readings
NTS	New Testament Studies
NTTS	New Testament Tools and Studies
Num	Numbers
Obad	Obadiah
OT	Old Testament
pass.	passive
Phil	Philippians
Phlm	Philemon
PNTC	Pillar New Testament Commentary
pl.	plural
Pol.	*Polycarp to the Philippians*
Porter	S. E. Porter, *Idioms of the Greek New Testament*
Prov	Proverbs
Ps	Psalm
Pss. Sol.	*Psalms of Solomon*
Q	Qumran Dead Sea Scrolls
1QH	*Hodayot* or Thanksgiving Hymns
1QpHab	*Pesher Habakkuk*
1QS	*Community Rule*
CD	*Damascus Document*
RB	*Revue biblique*
RE	*Review and Expositor*
REC	Reformed Expository Commentary
ResQ	*Restoration Quarterly*
Rev	Revelation
RevExp	*Review and Expositor*
Robertson	A. T. Robertson, *A Greek Grammar of the Greek New Testament in the Light of Historical Research*
Rom	Romans
RSV	Revised Standard Version
Runge	S. E. Runge, *Discourse Grammar of the Greek New Testament: A Practical Introduction for Teaching and Exegesis*

SBG	Studies in Biblical Greek
SBLDS	Society of Biblical Literature Dissertation Series
SBLGNT	Society of Biblical Literature Greek New Testament
SBLSBS	Society of Biblical Literature Sources for Biblical Study
SBT	*Studies in Biblical Theology*
2 Bar.	*2 Baruch*
2 Chr	2 Chronicles
2 Cor	2 Corinthians
2 Kgs	2 Kings
2 Macc	*2 Maccabees*
2 Pet	2 Peter
2 Sam	2 Samuel
2 Thess	2 Thessalonians
2 Tim	2 Timothy
SE	*Studia Evangelica*
Sir	Sirach/Ecclesiasticus
SNTG	Studies in New Testament Greek
SNTSMS	*Society of New Testament Studies Monograph Series*
SP	Sacra Pagina
Spicq	Spicq and Ernest, *Theological Lexicon of the New Testament*
ST	Studia Theologica
TC	Tyndale Commentary
TBT	*The Bible Today*
TDNT	G. Kittel, ed., *Theological Dictionary of the New Testament*
T. Benj.	*Testament of Benjamin*
T. Iss.	*Testament of Issachar*
T. Jos.	*Testament of Joseph*
T. Nap.	*Testament of Naphtali*
T. Reu.	*Testament of Reuben*
T. Sim.	*Testament of Simeon*
T. Sol.	*Testament of Solomon*
T. Zeb.	*Testament of Zebulun*
Thayer	J. H. Thayer, *Greek English Lexicon of the New Testament*
THGNT	Tyndale House Greek New Testament
3 Macc	*3 Maccabees*
Tob	Tobit

Abbreviations

TynBul	*Tyndale Bulletin*
Trench	R. C. Trench, *Synonyms of the New Testament*
Turner 3	N. Turner, *A Grammar of New Testament Greek*. Vol. 3: *Syntax*
Turner 4	N. Turner, *A Grammar of New Testament Greek*. Vol. 4: *Style*
UBS[4]	United Bible Society: Greek New Testament, 4th edition
UBS[5]	United Bible Society: Greek New Testament, 5th edition
v(v).	verse(s)
Wallace	D. B. Wallace, *Greek Grammar Beyond the Basics*
WBC	Word Biblical Commentary
Wis	Wisdom of Solomon
WUNT	Wissenschaftliche Untersuchungen zum Neuen Testament
Young	R. A. Young, *Intermediate New Testament Greek*
Zech	Zechariah
ZECNT	Zondervan Exegetical Commentary on the New Testament
ZNW	*Zeitschrift für die neutestamentliche Wissenschaft und die Kunde der älteren Kirche*

FOREWORD

This is a thoroughly revised edition of a commentary (2014) that is no longer in print. My gratitude is extended to Lexham Press for allowing me to publish this revised edition. I have taken this opportunity, therefore, to correct some spelling errors and also some mistakes in that edition. I have removed some extraneous discussions in the Introduction as well as the homiletical outlines and the biblical theology comments. A new strength of this edition is that I call attention to the five times the NA[28] adopts different readings from the NA[27] as well as the differing readings in the SBL Greek NT and in the Greek text underlying the NIV2011. I was privileged to have early access to the Tyndale House Greek New Testament and have taken note of its readings in those verses. I have also added an Appendix with an extended explanation about a textual issue in James 3:3. I have been able to incorporate a few insights from the new edition of the Holman Christian Standard Bible (HCSB), renamed the Christian Standard Bible (CSB). I am also delighted that this edition is the first NT commentary to utilize the newly published *Brill Dictionary of Ancient Greek,* edited by Franco Montonari 2016 (GE). Along with adding additional volumes to the bibliography, the result of the above changes is a more focused commentary that simply seeks to explain the Greek text of James.

INTRODUCTION

A fter lying for four hundred years in a backwater of neglect largely influenced by the opinions of two German "Martins," the Letter of James is finally emerging into the light of serious scholarly attention. Martin Luther's pungent comments on the epistle are well known. The magisterial commentary by Martin Dibelius has been one of the main works to be consulted in academic circles. Whether it be Luther's "strawy epistle" or Dibelius' disjointed "ethical paraenesis," the opinions of these German giants have influenced negatively generations of other commentators on James. For over a century, students of James were served by the commentaries of J. B. Mayor and a few others in various series. Critical commentaries by such scholars as J. H. Ropes and Dibelius provided excellent observations on the language and style of James but lacked the theological perspective of Mayor. The last forty years, however, have witnessed a new day for Jacobean scholarship. Following is a chronological list of recent major commentaries on James, and is limited to those in English. Adamson (1976); Laws (1980); Davids (1982); Kistemaker (1986); Martin (1988); Hiebert (1992); Scaer (1993); Johnson (1995); Nystrom (1997); Richardson (1997); Wall (1997); Bauckham (1999); Moo (2000); Isaacs (2002); Hartin (2003); Brosend (2004); Guthrie (2006); Doriani (2007); Witherington (2007); Blomberg-Kamell (2008); McCartney (2009); Varner (2011); McKnight (2011); Adam (2013); and Allison (2013). So is there a need for another commentary? Recent application of fresh linguistic methods to exegetical analysis demands an occasional fresh examination of familiar biblical books and passages. After a brief discussion of its Greek text, this Introduction will examine issues related to: (1) the book's author, date, and occasion; (2) language and style; (3) treatment of wisdom and faith; (4) use of Jesus' sayings; (5) canonical role; and (6) structure and outline.

The Greek Text

The translation and interpretation in this commentary are based on the twenty-seventh edition of *Novum Testamentum Graece*. This Greek text (NA[27]) is identical with the text in the fourth revised edition of the United Bible Society *Greek New Testament* (UBS[4]). Notice will be taken of the five times when the recent editions of the NA[28] and UBS[5] make changes to the text of NA[27]/UBS[4]. In this new edition, mention is also made of the SBL Greek NT, ed. Michael Holmes, when it sides with one text at points where NA/UBS texts differ. There are also a few examples of when the Greek Text of the NIV11 differs from the NA/UBS texts.

These critical editions follow an eclectic strategy in choosing the best reading to be adopted. Rather than adopting a single manuscript tradition as the norm (a "diplomatic" text) against which other textual evidence is then compared, the eclectic method decides the text by a process of selection among witnesses, based on both the relative antiquity of the manuscripts, combined with some basic canons of textual criticism. These rules are: (1) the shorter and harder readings are usually preferred, and (2) the reading that best explains the rise of other readings is to be preferred. These canons are referred to as the internal evidence. For the external evidence, the earliest and most important Greek witnesses are the great uncial manuscripts of the fourth and fifth centuries (א, B, A, C), supplemented by fragmentary papyri: P[20] from the third century includes 2:19–3:9; P[23] from the third century includes 1:10–12, 15–18; P[54] from the fifth century has only three short passages; and P[74] from the seventh century contains around seventy verses spread throughout the entire letter. Although there are a few exceptions, the papyri and most uncial manuscripts exhibit a type of text that is often referred to as "Alexandrian."

While the text of James is relatively stable, there are still some differences between the Alexandrian, Western, and "Majority" textual traditions. I am aware that the terms Majority and Byzantine are not accepted by all. In this commentary I use both terms and view them as basically synonymous. I will generally support the reading found in the NA critical texts, although on a rare occasion I suggest a preference for another Alexandrian reading. The Appendix also contains an extended discussion of the one verse (Jas 3:3) where I defend what could be called a Majority Text reading.

Author

Serious works on the epistle that are bold enough to attribute the work to James, the half-brother of Jesus, and to date it before his death in A.D. 62, continue to appear (Davids, 2–22; Johnson, 108–14; Moo, 2000, 20–22; Witherington, 395–401; Blomberg-Kamell, 32–35; McCartney, 8–32; McKnight, 13–34). A new appreciation of James has been emerging, but what about James the man? Research on James has led me to a fresh reading of both the letter and the sparse references to the man in Acts, Galatians, and 1 Corinthians. The result of that research has led to a new perspective on James the leader and also on James the letter. There is still a need for a fresh reading of the James materials, and to that end results of my own fresh reading are offered.

A Perspective on James the Man

The information about the siblings of Jesus in the Gospels is scant but adequate to suggest some sort of role that his half-brother James played in relation to Jesus prior to the cross and resurrection.[1] The only

---

[1] Treatments of the man James by Adamson, Hartin, Painter, and Shanks-Witherington are listed in the General Bibliography. The eccentric handling of James by Robert Eisenman is radical in its conclusions, identifying James with the "Teacher of Righteousness" in the Dead Sea Scrolls (R. Eisenman, *James the Brother of Jesus* [New York: Penguin Books, 1997] and *The New Testament Code* [London: Watkins Publishing, 2006]). His proposals demand a much later dating of the scrolls and the

debate in this regard is whether James shared in the apparent unbelief or disbelief attributed to Jesus' brothers in John 7:5, and hinted at in Mark 3:21 and 31–35. There are a number of men by the name of James in the New Testament, but I know of no serious commentary on the letter that argues the author is any one of the others apart from "James, the Lord's brother," or as he was called in the early church, "James the Just" or "James the Righteous." There is no reason to question the accuracy of John 7:5, which strongly implies that James was a nonbeliever in his brother's messianic role until after the resurrection (1 Cor 15:7). Furthermore, in this writer's opinion there is no solid reason to doubt that James along with his sisters and brothers were all the uterine siblings of Jesus, born of a common mother at least.

What are some other ideas about the meaning of "brother" as applied to James? The three views that emerged in the fourth century A.D. about the question of Jesus' brothers and sisters are as follows:

1. The Hieronymian view (espoused by Jerome, late fourth century) holds that the "brothers" of Jesus were actually his cousins.

2. The Epiphanian view (proposed by Epiphanius of Salamis, early fifth century) proposes that the brothers were from a previous marriage of Joseph.

3. The Helvidian view (named after Helvidius of late fourth century) says that the brothers and sisters were children born to Mary and Joseph after Jesus' birth.

Some may be perplexed that there is any discussion on the matter,

Qumran settlement than the consensus of DSS scholars allow. I cite here the observation of McCartney, 2009, 11 n 17: "The suggestion that James was the central figure of the Qumran community caused a brief sensation in the popular media, but virtually all other scholars have rightly rejected it because it is built on too many speculative leaps and historical improbabilities." For an evaluation of Eisenman's ideas, see Painter, 1999: 230–34, 277–88; and the articles by Myllykoski in the Bibliography.

because of the clear implications that they can draw from passages like Matt 1:25: "[Joseph] knew her not *until* she had given birth to a son," and Luke 2:7: "Then she gave birth to her *firstborn* Son." It was Mayor who pointed out that Tertullian in the late second century simply accepted without discussion that James was Jesus' younger half-brother. Because Tertullian showed no knowledge of any contradictory tradition in the second century, it is likely that the Epiphanian and Hieronymian views were driven by a later theological desire to maintain the perpetual virginity of Mary (Mayor, x).

There is simply no clear evidence in the New Testament that Joseph was previously married with children (Epiphanian view), and there is no evidence in that regard in the first century and a half of Christianity. Furthermore, the idea that the brothers and sisters mentioned in the Gospels were cousins of Jesus (Hieronymian view) flounders on the fact that the Greek word for "cousin" (ἀνεψιός) appears later in the NT (Col 4:10) but is never used of those who are called His brothers and sisters in the Gospels. As important as this discussion has been, let us turn rather to how James, being the "brother" of Jesus, may be viewed in a new light.

A Perspective on James the Leader[2]

What was the role and ministry that James performed in the early church? My proposal is simple, but its implications are profound. A careful reading of Luke's account in Acts and Paul's comments in Galatians supports the idea that James was not merely a significant leader in the early church and not just the leader of the Jerusalem church, but that he was *the* leader of *the* church. The implications of this fact are significant not only for the Roman Catholic attitude toward Peter, but also for the Protestant evangelical attitude toward Paul.

Ironically, it was a chapter written by still another "German Martin"

---

[2] The following is an adaptation and expansion of Appendix One in my discourse commentary on the book (Varner, 199–207).

(Martin Hengel) that raised the possibility of a new perspective on James. British and American scholars have largely neglected this chapter, published in German.[3] An even more neglected article by Richard Bauckham in an obscure European journal reviews much of the same evidence.[4] The evidence from Hengel and Bauckham combined with a renewed personal investigation has led me to adopt similar conclusions.

The argument is that after the Pentecostal effusion James rose quickly to a parity of leadership with the traditional apostles and by the early forties was *the* leader, although as a *primus inter pares* ("first among equals"), not only of the Jerusalem church (a point usually recognized) but of the entire Jesus movement. If a stranger arrived in Jerusalem or in Antioch between the years A.D. 40–62 and asked, "Who is the person in charge of this movement?" any knowledgeable Christian, including Peter or John or Paul, would have answered without hesitation, "James." Moreover, he would not have needed to add "the brother of Jesus" because everyone would have known that there was only one person who would be instantly recognized by that single name without any additional description or qualifier. "James" was the one known in his lifetime as "the brother of Jesus" and by later generations by the title "James the Just." The adjective is best rendered in English not by "just" but by "righteous." Such a conclusion is the clear implication of the canonical statements about James, and it is also supported by a large number of writers, both Christian and non-Christian, from the second through the fifth centuries.

The evidence for James' rise to leadership in the church is found not only in Acts but also in Galatians and 1 Corinthians. Paul mentions that James received a special appearance of the risen Lord, which would have led to a radical reassessment of his brother's person and

---

[3] M. Hengel, "Jakobus der Herrenbruder—der erste 'Papst'?" in *Glaube und Eschatologie*, ed. E. Grasser and O. Merk (Tübingen: JCB Mohr, 1985) 71–104.

[4] R. Bauckham, "James at the Centre," *EPTA Bulletin* (1995) 23–33. Bauckham elaborated his ideas about the role of James in "James and the Jerusalem Church," *The Book of Acts in its First Century Setting*, ed. R. Bauckham, vol. 4: *Palestinian Setting* (Grand Rapids, MI: 1995) 415–480.

role (1 Cor 15:7). It is possible that he had already come to recognize Jesus and that this was an appearance to commission James as a leader, but the evidence is too scant to be dogmatic. James is simply mentioned as being with the apostles and Mary in Acts 1:14, where he is probably processing the new information that the one whom he previously thought was "beside himself" (Mark 3:21) was actually the Son of God and Lord of creation! Paul mentions that during his first visit to Jerusalem after his conversion he saw only two of the "apostles," Peter and James (Gal 1:19). From his statements about James in 1 Cor 15:7 and Gal 1:19, it appears that Paul at least classed James along with the apostles. This is an important fact to recognize about James' rise to leadership.

This information is crucial for the argument that James became the leader of the entire church, because of what Luke and Paul later record about James. When Paul and Barnabas visited Jerusalem as described in Galatians 2:1–10 (probably the famine relief visit of Acts 11–12), they met privately with the Three Pillars—James, Peter, and John (Gal 2:9). The order of these "pillars" should not be overlooked. James was first in order and his primacy is illustrated in Peter's attitude toward James from at least this point onward. After "the pillars" affirm Paul's Gentile ministry they remind him to "remember the poor." Paul was eager to add that he had done that and would continue to do so. *Paul did what James requested that he do.* Around the same time, during the dramatic episode in Acts 12 when Peter was released miraculously from prison, Peter made a special effort to ask the people in John Mark's mother's prayer meeting to inform "James and the brothers" about his release. Peter here acknowledged the leadership role of James and may indicate Peter's transferal of the leadership of the Jewish mission to James. This action would parallel James' transferal of the leadership of the Gentile mission to Paul.

The events in Acts 15 surrounding what is called the Apostolic Council make it obvious that James had by then risen to be *the* leader of the church. The crucial decision about whether believing Gentiles would have to convert to Judaism was clearly made. No, circumcision would not be required of them, even if there was a group (not including James) who pushed for it. The text is clear that James rendered the final decision as the moderator of the council, to which the apostles and brethren agreed as also being the guidance of the Holy Spirit! Peter had first related his experience with Cornelius that was accompanied by the Spirit's work (15:7–11). Then Paul and Barnabas related their experience with Gentile conversions accompanied by signs (15:12). The point of these testimonials was that God had bestowed the blessings of His Spirit on these Gentile believers without their being circumcised and joining the family of Israel. When James presents his opinion, however, he does not base his argument on experience but on how the prophets had affirmed this future Gentile conversion with citations from Amos 9:11–12 and Isa 45:21. The words of these prophets agree with the experiences of Paul and Peter in that when Gentiles come into the kingdom, they will come in as Gentiles, not as converts to Judaism. It is very important to note the language attributed to James as he introduces his concluding decision in 15:19a: διὸ ἐγὼ κρίνω. We should not blunt the force of these words that to any Greek reader would mean, "Therefore, I decide." The transitional conjunction διὸ introduces the conclusion to the argument. This is followed by the pronoun ἐγὼ, which is not needed in Greek so it must be added for particular prominence and emphasis (Therefore, I ...). Then the verb κρίνω describes James' action in rendering the verdict. Greek lexicons (e.g., BDAG, 568.5) inform us that this verb often carries the sense of a judicial verdict or decision. The verb is often used in the NT of a decision in a judicial process (John 7:51; Luke 12:57; 19:22; 1 Cor 5:12). Most important is its appearance in Acts in what are clearly judicial contexts (Acts 13:27; 23:3, 6; 25:10, 20; 26:6). Therefore, this meaning should not be softened by an idea like, "Well, let me sum up our discussion."

In Acts 15:19 James makes the final decision and everyone agrees with it. He is not a pope (in the later sense of that term), but again he is serving as the "first among equals." Both Peter and Paul acknowledge that authority and then proceed to do what he requests them to do. When James adds that certain practices particularly offensive to Jews should be observed by the Gentile believers and composes a letter requesting such, Paul delivers the letter as he was instructed to do (see Acts 16:4). For the second time, *Paul did what James requested that he do.*

In Acts 21:18–26 Paul exemplified what he calls elsewhere "becoming all things to all men" (1 Cor 9:22), by again doing what James asks him to do in regard to ending the Nazirite vows of four young Jewish men. Paul probably thought that such an action was not necessary, but out of deference to James, he does it. He perhaps even used some of the offerings from the Gentile believers that he had brought with him to pay for this action in the temple (2 Cor 8–9; Rom 15:25–29). For at least the third time, *Paul did what James requested that he do.*

"In Jerusalem 49 AD James appears to have been the world head of Christianity."[5] This bold statement by Paul Barnett is accurate and is supported by some strong evidence. This assertion is not an overstatement but is in accord with the facts as they emerge from Acts and Galatians.

An important question also arises. If this leadership role of James was the real situation reflected in the NT writings, did the early church in later centuries recognize James' primacy? The answer is yes, and it is witnessed by writers, Jewish and Christian, from the second through the early fifth centuries.

The martyr death of James took place in A.D. 62 and is vividly described by the Jewish historian Josephus. "Festus ... assembled the Sanhedrin of judges, and brought before them the brother of Jesus, who was called Christ, whose name was James, and some others, and when he had formed an accusation against them as breakers of the law, he delivered them to be stoned" (*Ant.* 20.200). The passage is widely accepted as an essentially genuine description of the demise of James. Josephus never mentions any other prominent leaders of the early Christian movement, such as Peter, John, or Paul, seems to have been overlooked in previous scholarship. Apart from a statement

---

[5] Paul Barnett, *Jesus and the Rise of Early Christianity* (Madison, WI: IVP, 1999), 314.

about "the tribe of Christians" in the controversial *Testimonium Flavianum* ("Flavian Testimony") about Jesus, the only early Christian that Josephus mentions is James! This recognition of his death is because of James' leading role in the fledgling Jesus movement, a role that was recognized even outside the movement!

Clement of Alexandria records a tradition that the risen Jesus had actually appointed James to be the leader of the apostles, something affirmed by Eusebius' citation of the Jewish-Christian historian Hegessipus and even attested by Jerome. Statements by such orthodox leaders as these are also echoed in a number of pseudepigraphal "gospels" such as *The Gospel of Thomas* 12: "The disciples said to Jesus, 'We know that you will depart from us. Who is to be our leader?' Jesus said to them, 'Wherever you are, you are to go to James the Just, for whose sake heaven and earth came into being.'" This quotation is included, although probably not genuine, because it reflects an attitude that prevailed in the early church despite the growing authority of Peter's so-called successors in Rome! How did this universal recognition of James develop if it did not reflect something like the actual state of affairs? While no one claimed a continuing primacy for the bishop in Jerusalem in the succeeding centuries, everyone acknowledged James' original role.

Hesychius of Jerusalem in the fifth century preached in the church founded by James on Mount Zion, where the chair supposedly used by James was still displayed. In a sermon on Acts 15, Hesychius said the following about his predecessor: "How shall I praise the servant and brother of Christ, the commander in chief of the new Jerusalem, the prince of the presbyters, the leader of the apostles, among the heads the highest, among the shining lights the one who shines brightest, among the stars the most illustrious? Peter speaks, but James makes the law. [Here he cites Acts 15:19]. 'I judge,' whose judgment neither the law of custom nor the decree of an assembly can challenge. For in me speaks the one who is judge of all, the living and the dead.'" Even after acknowledging a strong measure of rhetorical hyperbole by Hesychius, this description must clearly indicate four centuries after his death a view about the position that James held.

If James was *the* leader of the early church, there are some implications of this fact both for Roman Catholicism and also for Protestant evangelicalism. In other words, Peter was not the original primate of the church. He was in his place under James, and he even yielded to his leadership. Readers can draw their own conclusions why James the brother of our Lord has been marginalized by Rome and written out of the history of the early church. It is interesting that among the so-called saints in Romanism, "Saint James" usually refers to the "James the Less" among the apostles, not James the brother of the Lord. This is a clear indication of his marginalization and is most probably intentional so as to blunt the role of James the brother of Jesus in favor of the supposed role of Peter.

There are also some implications for those in Protestantism. In evangelical circles Paul has often been exalted above the role that he actually played in the early church. Although most will not acknowledge it, many have an unofficial pope whose name is Paul. While there is a NT canon of twenty-seven books, the thirteen epistles of Paul often serve unofficially as a sort of "canon within a canon." This discussion is in no way an attempt put down or criticize Paul or even to deconstruct the description about him in the NT. I only desire to portray Paul and his role as it is actually indicated in the NT and also *by his own words*. We should not miss the fact that Paul himself told us something about his role when he called himself "the least of the apostles" (1 Cor 15:9). Richard Bauckham reminds us: "If for once we displace Paul from the central position he occupies not only in the New Testament contents page but also in the perceptions of early Christian history, and instead place James at the centre, the exercise will not diminish Paul's stature but will expand our horizons."[6]

Recipients

Most "introduction" issues can only be addressed in the exegesis of the book itself, so we will deal with this issue in our study of 1:1. The

---

[6] Bauckham, "James at the Centre," 25.

following assertions are a fair assessment of the circumstances of the original receivers. James, the uterine brother of Jesus and the undisputed leader during the first generation of the Christian movement (at least from A.D. 44–62), is writing a sort of "Diaspora encyclical" from Jerusalem to groups of primarily Jewish-Christian congregations. His writing most likely took place during the mid-to-late forties A.D., and the original recipient communities were probably located somewhere in or around Syria. As leader of the church, it is reasonable to conclude that this James resided in Jerusalem at this time. James' letter thus joins the early chapters of Acts as unique canonical witnesses, and together they comprise unique firsthand testimonies to the earliest period of Jewish Christianity. This is the essential conclusion of a number of recent commentators (McCartney, 30–33; McKnight, 23–28). Another even concludes: "In short, these are our roots!" (Blomberg-Kamell, 35). I refer the reader to these excellent discussions for more details, until we examine the meaning of "the twelve tribes in the Diaspora" (1:1).

Dating

Along with a number of evangelical interpreters, I propose that the book we call the Letter of James is probably the first NT document written and the first Christian writing of any kind, at least any of which we know. James, the half-brother of Jesus and leader of the church in Jerusalem, who also led the entire Jesus movement from around A.D. 44 until his death in 62, wrote to a group of Jewish Christians outside Israel most likely in the mid- to late forties (46–48?). We assume, because we have no evidence otherwise, that James wrote from Jerusalem. Thus this encyclical from James "joins the early chapters of Acts as a unique canonical witness, and the lone firsthand testimony, to very early Jewish Christianity" (Blomberg-Kamell, 35).

The arguments of John A.T. Robinson have never been adequately answered by exponents of a late date for James. Robinson was well known outside academic circles for his writings in which he rejected Christian doctrine and even traditional theism. Despite being very much in the camp of liberal theology, in *Redating the New Testament,* Robinson assaulted the academic guild of NT scholarship by arguing that the evidence points to the documents of the NT being written prior to A.D. 70, a position rejected by liberal NT scholarship since the nineteenth century. What Robinson offered was evidence within the books themselves and also evidence from the books' silence (like the destruction of the temple) that the books were written early, although he stopped short of arguing that the books were actually written by their traditional authors.

For James, however, Robinson concluded as follows: "It can take its natural place, alongside other literature in the process of formation in the second decade of the Christian mission, as the first surviving document of the church."[7] Robinson argued that what is left out of the book argues for the early date as well as what is found in the book. Agreeing with what is now becoming the dominant view, Robinson reminds us that there is no clearly discernible polemic against Paul in the epistle. Therefore, it must have come into existence before Paul's written ministry, which everyone agrees did not commence until at least A.D. 48.

Furthermore, there is not only no reference to the climactic fall of Jerusalem, but there is no reference to the final break between church and synagogue. The epistle also makes no reference to the Gentile mission. That does not mean that there had been no such mission, but the controversy surrounding that mission dating from at least A.D. 48 (Acts 15:1) is telling in its absence. There are also no references to the controversies over circumcision, the Sabbath, and the ritual law that dominated matters from A.D. 48 and later.

The above arguments illustrate how an early date for the letter is not simply a fallback on traditional conservative ideas. Robinson felt the force of these arguments, despite his own theology and the higher critical tendency toward later dating in the "academy" of which he was a part.

---

[7] J. A. T. Robinson, *Redating the New Testament* (London: SCM Press, 1976), 139.

A powerful argument about the intriguing similarities of language between the canonical letter and James' speech as well as his letter in Acts 15 should also be considered. These similarities become even more striking if both were written by the same author around the same time. The intriguing parallels between the two letters are as follows:

1. The letters have similar beginnings:

> James 1:1–2: James, a servant of God and of the Lord Jesus Christ, to the twelve tribes in the Dispersion: *Greetings*. My *brothers* ...

> Acts 15:23: The *brothers* ... to the believers of Gentile origin in Antioch and Syria and Cilicia, *greetings*.

2. The letters each express the need to "keep" oneself from sins:

> James 1:27: to care for orphans and widows in their distress, and to *keep* oneself unstained by the world.

> Acts 15:29: that you ... *keep* yourselves from these.

3. The words of James each connect "listen" to "brothers":

> James 2:5: *Listen*, my beloved *brothers* ...

> Acts 15:13: My *brothers*, *listen* to me.

4. The words of James each use the "name" invoked by the believers:

> James 2:7: Do they not blaspheme the excellent *name* invoked over you?

> Acts 15:17: ... all the Gentiles over whom my *name* has been called.

5. The letters use distinctive vocabulary:

"Care for" or "visit" pastorally (James 1:27; Acts 15:14).
"Turning" as conversion (James 5:19–20; Acts 15:19). See
McKnight (24) for further elaboration of these parallels.

It is possible that two different authors can employ a shared vocabulary. In a letter as short as the one in Acts 15:23–29, however, the parallels to the language in the book of James are remarkable and seem more than coincidental.

There are a number of additional arguments supporting an early date for the letter. (1) The author's simple self-description in 1:1, without any reference to his relationship to Jesus or to his leadership office, contrasts with later apocryphal works that always stress that he was the "brother of the Lord" or was "bishop" of the Jerusalem church. (2) The way in which the author loosely utilizes the "Jesus sayings" would be less likely after the *logia* were written in the canonical Gospels. (3) Although clearly acknowledging the Lordship of Jesus, the otherwise simplicity of the letter's Christology is consistent with a time before the development of a more fully matured Pauline theology. (4) The lack of any reference to persecution of Jewish Christians in the Diaspora argues that the "sect" was still under the protection of the Roman *religio licita* legislation. That is, the Jesus movement was still viewed by Rome as a conventicle within Judaism. (5) The ruthlessness of Jewish landlords toward their day laborers reflected in James 5 would have been relevant only prior to the events of A.D. 70.

It will never be possible to conclude absolutely that the author of this epistle is the one known as "James the Just," the brother of Jesus. The above evidence, however, is compelling and also significant. He was the very James who attained such recognizable stature in the early church so that the author did not need to add any further descriptors to his name. In light of this, the burden of proof should lie with those who question the Jacobean authorship and first century dating of the book.

Introduction

Origin

While no one can be dogmatic about the specific location of the letter's origin, the city of Jerusalem is at least consistent with a number of factors. There is no reason to believe that James ever left the Holy City from A.D. 44 until his death in 62. Bauckham has argued that Jerusalem was the "centre" of the ancient Jewish and Christian vision of the world. This writing, therefore, would be viewed as an authoritative Diaspora encyclical emanating from the city that was viewed both as the center of the world and as the center of the new Jesus movement, Jerusalem. In this manner, it is part of a tradition of Diaspora letters sent from authorities in Jerusalem during the Second Temple Period to Jewish communities in the Diaspora (Bauckham, 25–28).

Furthermore, the color and tone of the letter are consistent with it emanating from Jerusalem and Judea. Take, for example, the reference to the "early and later rains," a phenomenon peculiar to the Levant (5:7); the reference to the scorching and withering wind from the desert, known as the *sharav* in Hebrew, or *hamsin* in Arabic (1:11); and the familiarity of the author with fresh and salty springs near to Jerusalem at the Dead Sea (3:11). The letter is the only other place in the NT that refers to hell as γέεννα (3:6), also referred to by Jesus in Mark 9:43–45. If the early Christian community was located, as strong tradition has it, on Mount Zion, it should not be overlooked that immediately to the south of Mount Zion is the Valley of Hinnom (Gehenna), which lent its name to the Greek word.[8]

None of these points by itself proves that the letter originated in Israel, but their consensual testimony certainly offers an explanation that is hard to explain away if a second-century, non-Judean origin is posited for the book. All of these facts are consistent with an early date

---

[8] For examples of language and culture in the epistle that point to a provenance within the land of Israel, see D. Y. Hadidian, "Palestinian Pictures in the Epistle of James," *ExpTim* 63 (1952) 227–28; and P. H. Davids, "Palestinian Traditions in the Epistle of James," in *James the Just and Christian Origins*, eds. Bruce Chilton and Craig A. Evans (NovTSup 98; Leiden: Brill, 1999) 47–48.

(A.D. 46–48) and a Jerusalem origin.

Language

One of the classic commentators on James offered the following opinion about the author's style: "If we are asked to characterize in a few words the more general qualities of St. James' style, as they impress themselves on the attentive reader, perhaps these would be best summed up in the terms, energy, vivacity, and, as conducive to both, vividness of representation" (Mayor, ccxxix). No one familiar with the Greek text of James would disagree with Mayor's remark about the way our author employs the Greek language in this letter, but nothing is as simple as it appears. Some have questioned that a "Galilean peasant" with no formal education could have written at the level of Greek in the book (Dibelius, 34–38).

What exactly do writers mean when they affirm that James used a more literary Greek than would be expected of a Galilean? And why do we think that a Galilean would write in a less literary style than a Jerusalemite? The labors of scholars like Martin Hengel have showed conclusively that all of first-century Israel, from Judea to the Galilee, was Hellenized. It was not a question about which residents in first-century Israel were Hellenized and which ones were not. All were Hellenized. The only question was how far along the continuum a person was considered as Hellenized.

J. N. Sevenster's 1968 work *Do You Know Greek?* settled the question in many minds about whether a first-century Galilean could have written at the level of the Greek language found in James.[9] Alas, some writers still occasionally bring forward the old idea about James and the Greek language that we should expect him to use. The arguments of Sevenster, Hengel, and more recent scholars have established the

---

[9] J. N. Sevenster, *Do You Know Greek? How Much Greek Could the First Jewish Christians Have Known?* (NovTSup 19; Leiden: Brill, 1968). Sevenster illustrated how first century Galilee and even Judea were thoroughly Hellenized in language and culture and how it would be normal for a Galilean to be capable in the Greek language.

point that there is nothing in James that a first-century Galilean who had any contact with the world around him would not be expected to know.[10]

Many of these critics seem to forget that Nazareth, although a small town, was only a couple of miles north of the ancient *Via Maris*, the most important international highway in the Middle East, and one of the most important thoroughfares in the entire ancient world! Recent excavations at Sepphoris, just two miles distant from Nazareth in the other direction, reveal that this town was a thoroughly Hellenistic center where Gentile Roman/Greeks with their theaters and mosaics of pagan scenes coexisted with a flourishing Jewish culture. Nazareth existed in the hub of a very thorough Hellenistic milieu. Who are we moderns to conclude anything about the literary knowledge of a skilled craftsman family who no doubt had business contacts within this culture? To express it colloquially, it should be stated clearly that Joseph and Jesus and James were not country bumpkins!

Nevertheless, we should question what writers actually mean when they speak of the higher literary or even classical style of James. The first thing that strikes the Greek beginner in translating James is the larger vocabulary of the book, but if we recognize the peculiar register of the Greek, the larger vocabulary makes perfect sense. Probably more than any writer after the Synoptics, James constantly uses examples and illustrations from nature and the mercantile arts. This would demand a specialized vocabulary, but that does not mean that the vocabulary is somehow higher in its literary style! Different and even rare vocabulary words need only imply that the subjects discussed are simply different.

---

[10] For additional studies of the Greek in James and in first-century Galilee, see A.W. Argyle, "Greek among the Jews of Palestine in New Testament Times," *NTS* 20 (1973–74) 87–89; Martin Hengel, *Judaism and Hellenism: Studies in Their Encounter in Palestine during the Early Hellenistic Period*. Trans. J. Bowden. Philadelphia: Fortress Press, 1974; and S. E. Porter, "Jesus and the Use of Greek in Galilee," in *Studying the Historical Jesus: Evaluations of the State of Current Research*, eds. B. D. Chilton and C. A. Evans (NTTS 19; Leiden: Brill, 1994), 123–54.

Some comments about James' elevated, and even classical, style simply betray a misunderstanding of the difference between Classical Greek and literary Koine Greek. One of the characteristics that distinguish Classical Greek from Koine Greek is the former's preference for using the periodic sentence—a complex sentence that involves more than the expected, or even required, number of subordinate clauses. Students who have translated the most classical of the NT books, Hebrews, know the unbelievably complex sentences they have to unravel. A personal favorite example is Hebrews 7:1–3, where the subject introduced at the beginning—"For this Melchizedek ..." (Οὗτος γὰρ ὁ Μελχισέδεκ)—is then followed by more than a dozen subordinate clauses and appositional statements (7:1b–3a) before the predicate of that subject appears at the end of verse 3: "abides as a priest continually" (μένει ἱερεὺς εἰς τὸ διηνεκές). This characteristic of literary Greek, whether Attic or Hellenistic, is almost totally lacking in James.

To the contrary, the Letter of James is known for simple sentences with few subordinate clauses that are combined with a large use of asyndeton (lack of conjunctions). Out of the total number of 108 verses in the entire work, the author uses approximately 140 sentences that contain not a single finite subordinate verb. He employs only forty sentences that contain a single subordinate clause. He also employs only seven sentences that contain two subordinate clauses, plus only three sentences with more than two subordinate clauses. "James makes small use of subordinating particles, never doubles the relative, never uses genitive absolute, does not accumulate prepositions, or use the epexegetic infinitive—in a word, he never allows his principal sentence to be lost in the rank luxuriance of the subordinate clauses" (Turner 4, 118). This pales in comparison with the large number of complex sentences utilized by the author of the Letter to the Hebrews. Such a comparison is quite justified since both works share a common hortatory thrust. The clipped style of James would strike horror in an Attic rhetorician, but it is that very forceful, direct style that has endeared James to so many readers.

This simple and straightforward style, however, is anything but pedantic and boring. James can employ such tropes as alliteration (the use of π- in 1:2, 11, 17, 22) and wordplay (the use of ἔργων over against ἀργή [ἀ + ἔργων] in 2:20). Although obviously it is a written document, this colorful and rhetorically vibrant message seems more like an impassioned homily than the polished deliverance of an Attic Greek rhetorician.

Another word to describe the Greek style of James is its "energy" (Mayor, 277, to whom I am indebted for some of the following points). What James writes, he writes forcibly, with the style of one who is absolutely convinced of the truth and of the importance of his message. There is a great economy in his words with little or no circumlocution. Yet he often displays a poetic imagination (such as his description of the tongue in chapter 3). His tirades against sin (5:1–6) can be compared to the most powerful of the OT prophetic diatribes. These attacks, however, can be softened but not blunted by the gentler influence of that wisdom that is from above (3:13–18). In its rugged abruptness and brevity of its phrases, however, James' language is almost unique among the writings of the NT. Note the biting irony in the words he uses to confront those who trust only in an orthodox creed: σὺ πιστεύεις ὅτι εἷς ἐστιν ὁ Θεός· καλῶς ποιεῖς· καὶ τὰ δαιμόνια πιστεύουσιν καὶ φρίσσουσιν ("You believe that God is one? You are doing well. Even the demons believe—and shudder!"). The well-known irony utilized by Paul in 2 Corinthians is the only real comparison with the energy of the language of James. For example, in James 5:1–6 the tarnishing of precious metals witnesses to the defrauding of the day laborer and they eat as a canker at the very heart of these landed oppressors of the poor. While we may still be uncertain of its exact meaning, who can resist the energy in the abrupt yet powerful end to the passage: κατεδικάσατε, ἐφονεύσατε τὸν δίκαιον· οὐκ ἀντιτάσσεται ὑμῖν? ("You have condemned; you have murdered the righteous person. Does He not oppose you?").

Perhaps this almost contradictory combination of simplicity of language with profundity of style is what has contributed to making this epistle such a favorite among lay Christian readers.

Genre

It is important to recognize a salient literary feature in the book: namely, its heavily hortatory character. Our author's language is heavily marked on its surface level by a large number of Greek imperative verb forms. James delivers these exhortations by a total of fifty-five imperative verb forms (both in the second and third persons) plus four imperatival future forms. These imperatival forms in James form a higher ratio of imperative forms to total words than in any other NT book. James' fondness for the imperative mood, as compared with other New Testament authors, can be visually demonstrated by Figure 1.

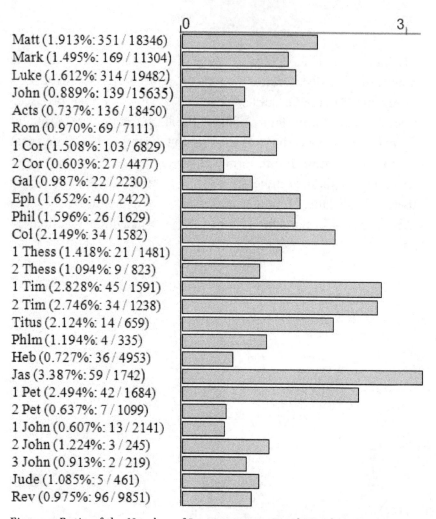

Figure 1: Ratio of the Number of Imperatives to Total Words in Each New Testament Book

Not only is there a higher number and also a higher ratio of these imperatives in James than in any other NT book, but the imperatives are also distributed throughout the five chapters rather than grouped in one hortatory section. The relatively balanced distribution of imperatives in James is unlike some other NT books in which the hortatory sections are clearly separate from the indicative sections, e.g., Romans 1–11/12–16; Ephesians 1–3/4–6, and Colossians 1–2/3–4. This distribution further demonstrates the pervasive hortatory nature of the document. The rhetoric of exhortation found in James, however, does not consist of random or unconnected commandments (a characteristic of paraenesis). These imperatives are usually accompanied by explanations or reasons. James uses participles (1:3, 14, 22; 2:9, 25; 3:1), γὰρ clauses (1:6, 7, 11, 13, 20, 24; 2:11, 13, 26; 3:2, 16; 4:14), and ὅτι clauses (1:12, 23; 2:10; 3:1; 4:3; 5:8, 11) in connection with these exhortations. The commandments are also often connected to purpose clauses (1:3; 5:8) and sometimes occur in the context of an implied argument signified by the use of οὖν (4:4, 7; 5:7, 16), διὸ (1:21; 4:6), or οὕτως (1:11; 2:12, 17; 2:26; 3:5). These grammatical features must be taken into consideration when addressing the question of genre. The discourse is heavily hortatory in whatever final form is utilized to convey these exhortations.

A Circular Encyclical?

By being associated from the early days of canon-consciousness with the other "catholic" or "general" epistles, the nature of James as a sort of circular epistle must also be recognized. This is reflected not only in its salutation to "the Diaspora of the twelve tribes" (1:1), but is also evidenced by the fact that the situations addressed are general and typical, rather than specific and local. This contrasts with the majority of the Pauline epistles where specific situations inside a specific community are addressed. The Letter of James has the most essential characteristics of an ancient letter: (1) a sender; (2) recipient(s); and (3) a greeting—all of which can be found in 1:1. The contents of the letter neither offer personal greetings nor mention any personal circumstances. Consistent with the first distinctive feature, only commands are issued and no requests are made. These last features distinguish the letter from ancient letters and are consistent with what might be called a general letter, and because it is written to more than one recipient, they indicate its general encyclical nature.

However, there simply exists nothing else in the ancient world to compare it with equivalently, at least in terms of genre. What is clear is that James is hortatory and that it is in the form of a letter while sounding like a homily that addresses the behavior of the readers. That much is evident and we should be satisfied with that and cease trying to genre-type the document. James has surprises to any literary critic who insists on identifying it with an accepted genre. And if we must conclude that it represents a new genre, what really have we gained in trying to understand its message? That effort may work with many if not most of ancient literature. Fortunately our frustration in this area does not mean that we cannot appreciate this document and read it with comprehension. Our efforts to find its overall message, however, should lie in our discovering its linguistic, structural, and semantic features that help communicate that message. The discipline of discourse analysis offers some real hope and help in that regard.

Themes

Dibelius, as he was apt to do, puts it bluntly: "First, Jas has no theology" (Dibelius, 21). This is an unfortunate inference because James desires us to live out our Christian profession, not just to "be moral" without any foundation from which to construct that morality. Although the letter is short, it displays knowledge of a number of OT books, possibly some extrabiblical writings, and certainly a wide acquaintance with the teachings of Jesus. The intensely practical matters that he affirms about life proceed from a rather firm theological substructure that is often more implied than expressed. Douglas Moo has remarked perceptively about the supposed lack of theology, particularly Christology:

> More serious is the charge that James fails to ground his teaching
> in Christology. Indeed, James mentions Jesus explicitly only
> twice (1:1; 2:1). So if by "theology" one means a system of beliefs
> explicitly built on the person of Christ, then, indeed, the letter of
> James lacks a "theology." But such a definition of theology is
> much too narrow. If we expand the definition to include
> teaching grounded in an understanding of God and his purposes
> in the world, then James is thoroughly "theological." Appeal to

God's person, the values taught in his Word, and his purpose in history undergirds virtually everything in the letter. And while Jesus' person and work might be generally absent, his teaching is not. No NT document is more influenced by the teaching of Jesus than James (Moo, 27).

It is expected that a commentary have a section on the theology of the book, but I have chosen rather to address two of the main themes that permeate James, wisdom and faith. The reader can pursue the theology of James in a number of books and articles.[11]

James and Wisdom

Is the Letter of James to be included in the Jewish wisdom literature found in both the canonical and the later Jewish writings? Some of this literature was read and enjoyed by James and his contemporaries. While the literature on this subject is extensive, exact parallels and explanations differ greatly. The German scholar Ernst Baasland has surveyed the different ideas and suggested a creative solution to the tension between James' similarity and differences with traditional Jewish wisdom. Baasland calls James the "wisdom writing of the NT which connects the closest to Old Testament wisdom literature."[12] Although only once does he clearly quote Proverbs (4:6), the ethos of that wisdom book, along with that of Sirach, has left footprints throughout the book.

However, the Letter of James also has its own uniqueness in this wisdom tradition because of its evident debt to the wisdom teaching of James' brother. In Baasland's words, "The same thing that

---

[11] A. Chester and R.P. Martin (eds.), *The Theology of the Letters of James, Peter, and Jude*. Cambridge: CUP, 1994; P. Davids, "Theological Perspectives on the Epistle of James," *JETS* 23 (1980) 97–103; and S. Laws, "The Doctrinal Basis for the Ethics of James," *SE* 7 (1982) 299–305. Also see J.B. Adamson, *James: the Man and his Message* (Grand Rapids: Eerdmans, 1989) 259–471.

[12] Ernst Baasland, "Der Jakobusbrief als Neutestamentliche Weisheits- schrift," *ST* 36 (1982) 119, my translation.

differentiates James from Jewish wisdom writing is what connects James with the proclamation of Jesus."[13] To James wisdom has received a new center, the starting point of which is belief in the "glorious Messiah, the Lord Jesus" (2:1), and the manifestation of which is that the poor will inherit the kingdom (2:5). While there seems to be no dependence on Paul, neither are they alien, with Paul taking wisdom further into more ontological realms. Baasland concludes:

> The lines of wisdom can be traced back to the wisdom literature of the OT. On the other hand, we see a line in the NT, which originates in Jesus and stretches over the parts of the proclamation of Paul (Rom. 2:6, 12; 1 Cor. 1–4, etc.) and which continues over James and other NT letters up to the Apostolic Fathers (the Clements and Origen).[14]

Some writers have described the approach of James as "subverting" the traditional wisdom tradition and preferring a descriptive title like "apocalyptic wisdom."[15] James would probably not have viewed his approach as subversive. He simply approaches the two ways tradition in Hebraic literature as echoed by Jesus and then applies it to the new kingdom inaugurated by his more famous brother. The poor, for example, had a definite role in the social message of the Hebrew prophets. Jesus and James simply focus their role as being more central to the purposes of God and the Messiah in this phase of the kingdom plan. This may be more accurately described as an extension of wisdom rather than a subversion of wisdom.[16]

---

[13] Baasland, 120.

[14] Baasland, 139.

[15] See Hartin, "Who is wise," and Penner, *James and Eschatology* in the bibliography.

[16] For wisdom in James, see also B. R. Halson, "The Epistle of James: Christian Wisdom?" *SE* 4 (1968) 308–14; Kirk, "Meaning of Wisdom," 24–38; and J. M. Reese, "The Exegete as Sage: Hearing the Message of James," *BTB* 12 (1982), 82–85.

James (and Paul) on Faith

No treatment of James can avoid the controversial subject of the relationship between faith and works in the epistle and how his teaching relates to Paul's teaching on the same subject(s). The problem for many can be stated by asking how the Reformation distinctive of *sola fide*, derived primarily from Paul, can be squared with Jas 2:24: "You see that a person is justified by works and not by faith alone." But by even framing the problem within a later Reformation context, or even in a Pauline context, we may be wrongly approaching this so-called problem. Rarely has reading James apart from its being a foil for Pauline theology ever really taken place. An effort will be made to do just that in the subsequent analysis of James 2. Although an adequate treatment of this issue can only arise from a full exegesis of 2:14–26, the following should provide a context in which the issues can be explored in a more in-depth analysis.

If, as some suppose, either Paul or James is opposing the other, neither does a very good job, because neither addresses the central argument of their supposed "opponent." Paul certainly stresses the importance of faith with such statements as "A person is justified by faith without works of the law" (Rom 3:28), the verse most often cited as opposing James 2:24. But if we focus on isolated statements like these, we may wrongly conclude that there is a clear contradiction between the writers. In actuality, the two authors are not discussing the same subject and thus can never contradict each other!

James never belittles faith and Paul actually refers to "good works" far more than James and always to commend them, not to criticize them (Rom 2:6; 2 Cor 9:8; Eph 2:10; Col 1:10; 2 Thess 2:17; 1 Tim 2:10; 5:10, 25; 6:18; Titus 2:7, 14; 3:8, 14). What does James really say about faith, and what does he mean by works? If we can answer those questions, we can better determine what it is about "works" that Paul negates. James says that the believing poor are "rich in faith" (2:5). He links faith with prayer (1:6; 5:15). He refers to faith being demonstrated by works (2:18). He assumes that faith is vital, and his concern is not "Should a person have faith?" but rather "When is faith dead and when is it alive?" The kind of faith James rejects is a faith like the demons display (2:19) – to no avail for themselves! Such faith only causes them to shudder. A faith that does not transform the believer's life is not faith as James describes it. It is dead. It is the kind of faith that responds to the needs of the poor by some "pious" remark but actually does nothing to meet their felt needs (2:15–16).

That James is not teaching salvation by works is shown by his clear teaching on universal sinfulness (3:2). Sin is not only an act of wrongdoing; to know to do good and not do it is also sin (4:17). To fail in one point of the law is to be guilty of all (2:10). An author with this deep understanding of sin does not expect people to save themselves by their good deeds. James looks for deliverance through God's mercy (2:13), and that mercy originates in the divine will that determines our spiritual birth (1:18). James is firmly insisting that real faith is more than a barren intellectualism but is fruitful in its deeds of love and mercy. Like Paul he expects a faith that works through love (Gal 5:6). Both Paul and James agree that salvation comes through divine grace, not through human merit, and that salvation is appropriated by a faith that must be demonstrated in obedient lives.

Another solution to the conundrum of their similar language is that when these two speak of justification, they are describing different stages in the life of the believer. While they both appeal to Abraham, Paul stresses the statement in Gen 15:6 about the patriarch's initial step of faith that was reckoned to him as righteousness (Rom 4:3, 9–10). James speaks of a time years later when Abraham was willing to offer his son (2:21; Gen 22:2–18). Some authors also stress that Paul uses justification language that refers to the beginning of the Christian life, while James, along with Jesus in Matthew, uses the term for final justification, which will be displayed on judgment day (see Moo, 1985, 114).

Another factor to keep in mind is the different ways in which James and Paul use the word *works*. To Paul, the expression "works of the law" refers primarily to the badges of national Jewish identity—namely, circumcision, Sabbath keeping, and ritual purity. James uses "works" to refer not to those badges but to the deeds of kindness that must accompany those who say they have faith. This is particularly seen in the lack of love shown to the needy poor in 2:15–17. Paul would equally have been horrified by such a callous attitude by one who professed to have faith (Eph 2:8–10). Paul would say, in agreement with James, that we should have "a faith that works through love" (Gal 5:6).

An often overlooked way that James and Paul approach the subject of faith is the actual way in which each one utilizes a common text about Abraham: "And he [Abraham] believed in the Lord, and He accounted it to him for righteousness" (Gen 15:6; cited by James in 2:23 and by Paul in Rom 4:3 and Gal 4:6). Each writer applies the text by referring to different events after the statement recorded in that chapter. Paul makes the point that the Gen 15:6 event took place before Abraham's being circumcised (Gen 17). To Paul this is evidence that the patriarch was a true believer in his so-called "Gentile" period *before* he was circumcised. Thus it is not necessary for Gentiles to be circumcised to become true believers. Like Father Abraham, Gentiles can have a saving faith and a righteous standing before God. This is exactly the context of the problem being faced in Romans and Galatians—namely, can Gentiles be genuine believers without circumcision? Yes, affirms Paul, because Abraham was just such a believer. James, on the other hand, mentions Abraham's attempted sacrifice of Isaac at God's command (Jas 2:21–22; Gen 22). God tested Abraham's faith by this difficult command (Gen 22:1), but Abraham's faith passed the test and thus the statement in Gen 15:6 was "fulfilled" (found its full meaning) in the *Akedah*, or the "binding" of Isaac. Thus Abraham showed that his faith was genuine by his "work," and that is the point that James is making to his readers: faith becomes evident as true by one's deeds.

There is one final observation that may help us to understand that James was not consciously referring to any Pauline writing about justification in Galatians or Romans. If we are correct in assigning a date to the Letter of James around A.D. 46–48, then he could not refer to those Pauline letters that had not yet been written. If someone responds that such dating does not prevent Paul from criticizing

James, a valid response would be that such an attitude of correcting James is totally unlike the Paul in Acts and Galatians who did what James told him to do on at least three separate occasions (Acts 16:4; Acts 21:23–26; Gal 2:10).

In light of the above evidence, it is not necessary to see a conflict between these two great leaders on the subject of faith. They each should be read in their own contexts. When that is done, their letters make perfect sense and complement rather than contradict each other.

James and the Sayings of Jesus

With the above conclusion that James' approach to wisdom must be pursued through Jesus' approach to the subject, this is the appropriate place to explore the issue of the *logia* of Jesus that may be found in the book. To date the most thorough treatment of the question is the published dissertation by David Deppe, who analyzes in detail the twenty-five most common sayings in James that writers have referred back to Jesus. He applies a very conservative set of standards and concludes that there are only eight firm allusions to Jesus' teaching, as we know them in the Synoptic Gospels. Those allusions are set out in Figure 2.[17]

James Reference	Synoptic Reference	Subject
Jas 1:5	Matt 7:7//Luke 11:9	ask and you will receive
Jas 2:5	Luke 6:20b//Matt 5:3	kingdom belongs to poor
Jas 4:2c–3	Matt 7:7//Luke 11:9	ask and you will receive
Jas 4:9	Luke 6:21, 25b	those who laugh will mourn
Jas 4:10	Matt 23:12//Luke 14:11; 18:14b	humble will be exalted

---

[17] Dean B. Deppe, *The Sayings of Jesus in the Epistle of James* (Chelsea, MI: Bookcrafters, 1989). The chart was constructed from data in Deppe and the author's analysis of the sayings of Jesus in James.

Jas 5:1	Luke 6:24	woe to the rich
Jas 5:2–3a	Matt 6:19, 20//Luke 12:33b	do not treasure up wealth
Jas 5:12	Matt 5:33–37	oaths

Figure 2: Firm Allusions by James to Jesus' Teaching

Despite the large number of shared expressions and themes, not one of them qualifies as a direct verbal quotation of the *logia* of Jesus as we have them in the Synoptic Gospels. The closest example is James' warning about oaths in 5:12 with its striking verbal similarities to Matthew 5:33–37. But even there James is not quoting exactly the words of Jesus as we have them in Matthew. Perhaps we have not approached this issue in the best way when we try to find undoubted allusions based on the standards of exact quotations. Richard Bauckham has provided an excellent solution to this problem (Bauckham, 74–108). He compares James' use of Jesus material to *Sirach*'s use of the canonical Proverbs. In no place does *Sirach* quote that canonical book, but any reader recognizes the large amount of shared themes and expressions in the two books. Bauckham suggests that *Sirach* adapts and reshapes hundreds of individual verses from Proverbs without ever actually quoting any of them. He argues that James approaches the sayings of Jesus in the same way. Without ever clearly quoting a saying of Jesus, James adapts for his purpose dozens of those sayings and reshapes them for his own specific purpose.

Bauckham's suggestion, therefore, frees us from the need for a painstaking verbal comparison between James' statements and the *logia* of Jesus. Another aspect of the question is that we need not even suppose that James had a written Gospel in front of him. James may have simply recalled the oral traditions of Jesus' sayings before Matthew, Mark, or Luke ever wrote them down. The voice of Jesus, therefore, is heard distinctly in the Letter of James, but not in the form of direct citations. Consequently, we may safely conclude that in James we may not have the *ipsissima verba* ("very words") of Jesus, but we do hear loudly the *ipsissima vox* ("very voice") of Jesus.

Some authors have criticized James as being one of the least

"Christian" books of the NT.[18] When we realize, however, the thorough way in which Jesus' teachings permeate the writing, we could conclude that, after the Gospels, James is the most Jesus-centered book in the NT canon. While Paul theologizes about Jesus, James displays a measured interest in the teachings of Jesus (Acts 20:30). However, almost every point that James makes is grounded in or illustrated by an adapted saying or aphorism that echoes in some way a *logion* of his brother. An attempt will be made in the commentary to point out these specific uses. Finally, when we recognize how James uses the orally transmitted sayings of Jesus, it becomes probably the strongest argument for the early dating of the book.

In conclusion, to illustrate the thoroughness of James' use of Jesus material, the following table includes James' additional echoes of the teachings of Jesus. Notice that his brother's teaching in some way influences every paragraph of the book.

James	Jesus	Theme
Jas 1:2	Matt 5:11, 12	joy in tribulation
Jas 1:5	Matt 7:7//Luke 11:9	ask and you will receive
Jas 1:6	Matt 21:21	faith and doubting
Jas 1:12	Matt 5:11–12 // Luke 6:22, 23	blessing on those who endure trials
Jas 1:19, 20	Matt 5:22	against anger
Jas 1:22–25	Matt 7:24–27 // Luke 6:46–49	doers of the word
Jas 2:5	Luke 6:20b // Matt 5:3	kingdom belongs to poor
Jas 2:8	Matt 22:39	the love commandment

---

[18] Dunn writes: "The letter of James is the most Jewish, the most undistinctively Christian document in the NT." J. D. G. Dunn, *Unity and Diversity in the New Testament* (3rd ed.; London: SCM Press, 2006), 271.

Jas 2:13	Matt 5:7, 13; 9:13	results of mercy
Jas 2:14–17	Matt 25:31–46	helping the disadvantaged
Jas 3:6	Matt 15:18–19; 5:22	the tongue defiles
Jas 3:12	Matt 7:16 // Luke 6:44	fruit from the tree
Jas 3:18	Matt 5:9	being peacemakers
Jas 4:2–3	Matt 7:7; Luke 11:9	and you will receive
Jas 4:4	Matt 6:24; Luke 16:13	serving God vs. loving the world
Jas 4:9	Luke 6:21, 25b	those who laugh will mourn
Jas 4:10	Matt 23:12 // Luke 14:11; 18:14	humble will be exalted
Jas 4:11–12	Matt 7:1–2 // Luke 6:37	against judging others
Jas 4:13–16	Luke 12:18–21	boasting of successful businessman
Jas 4:17	Luke 12:47	knowing master's will and not doing it
Jas 5:1	Luke 6:24	woe to the rich
Jas 5:2–3a	Matt 6:19–20 // Luke 12:33b	do not treasure up wealth
Jas 5:10–11	Matt 5:11–12; 10:22	persevere in trials/receive blessing
Jas 5:12	Matt 5:33–37	oaths
Jas 5:17	Luke 4:15	Elijah: three and a half years
Jas 5:19–20	Matt 18:12–14 // Luke 17:3–4	restoring lost sheep/brother

Figure 3: Echoes by James to Jesus' Teaching

This use by James of an abundant amount of "Jesus material" in the Gospels has led one author to call James "The Fifth Gospel."[19]

Canonical Role

Every commentator must make some hard choices due to the limits of their commentary. Therefore, I do not include a discussion of how James found his way into the accepted canon of the NT over the centuries following its writing. I refer the reader to the magisterial treatment of this question by Johnson (124-40). I will only mention here the location of the letter in early copies of the New Testament. Pride of place in our modern editions of the New Testament has gone to Paul's epistles coming after the Book of Acts and heading the other writings of the apostles. However, this was not the case for over one thousand years of church history. One of the two oldest copies of the NT that we possess (Codex Vaticanus) has James, the two Peters, the three Johns and Jude immediately after Acts, then followed by the Pauline Epistles and Hebrews. Codex Alexandrinus also has this order and ends with the Apocalypse. Furthermore, the Eastern Orthodox Church still has maintained this order in their Bibles and the earliest editions of the Greek NT (Tischendorf, Tregelles, and Westcott/Hort) also adopted this ancient order. English versions in the West and the current critical Greek texts (NA/UBS) changed the ancient order to that in the Vulgate, which has been reflected in our New Testaments since the sixteenth century. The ancient recognition of the three "pillars" (Gal 2:9) can also be seen in the order of the general epistles: James' letter is followed by those of Peter and John. Throughout the Middle Ages, manuscripts of the Greek NT placed James and the general epistles after Acts. There are hundreds of manuscripts, each referred to as *Praxapostolos* (comprised of Acts and the General Epistles), with James as the first of the epistles after Acts. The ancient and medieval manuscripts witnessed to James at the head with Paul always included, but in his proper place—after the epistles of the "pillar

---

[19] R. S. T. Haslehurst, "The Fifth Gospel," *Theology* 35 (1937) 96–103.

apostles." Paul would have heartily agreed with this order as well, in light of his repeated deference to James and in his describing himself as "the least of the apostles." One of the few authors to recognize the implications for this canonical role of the epistle is John Painter, who argues that the epistles attributed to James and Jude, the brothers of the Lord, were intentionally placed to bracket what he refers to as the "Jerusalem Epistles."

An important question, however, remains to be answered. Why does this matter? If we recognize that James wrote to the whole church (as did Peter and John) while Paul wrote to individual churches and individuals, this does not diminish Paul's significance. It simply enhances the role of this Diaspora encyclical written by the church's leader in Jerusalem. To put it in lay terms, this recognition adds a bit of octane to our reading of this little letter. As James the leader should not be marginalized, so James the letter should not be marginalized either.

Structure

Many have called attention to Martin Luther's infamous statements about the book of James. In his Preface to the NT of 1522, Luther says James is "really an epistle of straw," for "it has nothing of the nature of the gospel about it." In his Preface to the epistle itself he writes, "James throws things together in such disorderly fashion that it seems to me he must have been some good, pious man, who took some sayings of the Apostles' disciples and threw them thus on paper."[20] Luther's frustration over James' lack of order (at least to him) further demeaned the epistle in his eyes. It should be clearly noted, however, that John Calvin did not share this pessimism about the Letter of James but expounded the book at length and published a commentary on it essentially composed of his lectures on James delivered in the Academy of Geneva. Luther thought that the organization of the book was as bad as its doctrine. As will be seen, a fresh recognition of the

---

[20] *LW* 35:397; see also *LW* 54: 425.

structure of the epistle, formed around the call to be "whole" and not divided, with the positing of 3:13–18 as its peak and its call to follow wisdom from above and not below is an overlooked aspect of the book that will contribute the key to its seemingly disparate order. Following the segments introduced with "brothers" plus an imperative or question also suggests that there is a structure and progression in this epistle that Luther somehow missed. Perhaps his vision was clouded by his indebtedness to Paul and by his own deliverance from a works-righteousness, which he (wrongly) supposed James to be advocating. Let us explore that structure in more detail.

The two biggest internal issues that have engaged scholars studying the book are: (1) discovering its main theme, and (2) discovering its structure, if there is any. A new perspective on James the Letter must answer those challenges. The way to answer those challenges is by studying how authors show prominence in their writings and how they provide cohesive ties that lead to the segmenting of their discourses.

Authors will often indicate the most important section in their writing by means of what is called the "peak" of their discourse. The peak is the paragraph that stands out above the rest of the paragraphs due to its difference in structure and grammatical features. It will also sum up the macro-theme of the entire work. Space does not allow examples of how this occurs in other writings. The following ideas point to the prominent role of the thematic peak of James, found in 3:13–18.

> Who is wise and understanding among you? By his good conduct let him show his deeds with the gentleness of wisdom. But if you have bitter jealousy and selfish ambition in your hearts, do not boast and be false to the truth. This is not the wisdom that comes down from above, but is earthly, unspiritual, demonic. For where jealousy and selfish ambition exist, there will be disorder and every vile practice. But the wisdom from above is first pure, then peaceable, gentle, open to reason, full of mercy and good fruits, impartial and sincere. And a harvest of righteousness is sown in

peace by those who make peace.

This paragraph is different than the others in the book in that it is introduced by a rhetorical question that asks what a wise person looks like. A wise person is marked by a behavior that accords with *wisdom*. That word appears four times in this paragraph, only occurring once elsewhere in 1:5. This paragraph justifies James being called *"the wisdom writing of the NT"*—an accolade that not many would dispute, although James' wisdom has an apocalyptic focus that is lacking in Jewish wisdom writings. The many other unique features of this paragraph (larger ratio of adjectives, the only virtue and vice lists, more ideas here that appear elsewhere) justify its prominent role. The paragraph also provides the main theme that permeates the entire writing: *follow heavenly wisdom (from above) rather than earthly wisdom (from below)*. Thus the meta-theme is an exhortation to follow God's wisdom in one's behavior. This is the theme that is stamped on every other paragraph by means of the old "two ways" exhortation so prevalent in Old Testament and Jewish literature.

The choice between the two wisdoms is conveyed by means of the use of polar opposites consistent with the Jewish "two ways" approach to ethics. To those of his readers who think they can have it both ways, James issues the scathing denunciation of being "double-minded" or literally "double-souled"—an adjective he may have coined (1:8; 4:8). In the paragraph following his thematic peak (4:1–10, which I argue is the hortatory peak of the book and also introduced by a rhetorical question), James calls for a change from being double-minded to purifying our hearts (4:8). As Søren Kierkegaard said in his work so-entitled, "Purity of heart is to will one thing." This is consistent with another of James' themes, that of *perfection*. Early in his letter he tells us that our goal in all of this is to be "perfect and entire, lacking nothing" (1:4). To be perfect (τέλειος) is not to be sinless but to be *whole*. In other words, we are not to be divided people marked by doubleness but rather to exhibit singleness. *Maturity* is another word that conveys this goal.

Now, how does James then organize his message? Does he just

throw these words on paper, willy-nilly, as Luther thought? No, he uses a cohesive device that cements his hortatory written discourse together much like a good preacher organizes and presents his material in a progressive manner by a coherent outline, sometimes with a repetitive device like alliteration. That cohesive device is his use of the direct address word "brothers" accompanied by either an imperative command or by a rhetorical question.

The chart below that accompanies the outline of James indicates where those paragraphs begin, each of which introduces a new topic as well. The two topics introduced, not by "brothers" but by a rhetorical question, serve as the two peaks (thematic and hortatory) that convey the main themes of the letter in the prominent way. The task of the student/teacher/preacher of James is to discern how each paragraph develops its topic along the lines of the behavior condemned (which follows earthly wisdom) and the behavior commended (which follows heavenly wisdom). The task is to recognize that wholeness, completeness, maturity, and their consequent peace (3:18) will be the result of his hearers and readers making the wise choice of heavenly wisdom.

Outline

To better enable the reader to see the segmentation of the book that results from the above analysis, there follows an outline of the epistle as a whole in the chart below. It visually displays the divisions of the epistle based on the cohesive devices mentioned above. The coupling of a nominative of address with a command or a rhetorical question is the key discourse marker. Note also the effort to identify the thematic peak and the hortatory peak in 3:13–18 and in 4:1–10 respectively.

Section	Nominative of Address	Imperative Command/ Rhetorical Question
1:2–15	ἀδελφοί μου	πᾶσαν χαρὰν ἡγήσασθε
1:16–18	ἀδελφοί μου ἀγαπητοί	Μὴ πλανᾶσθε
1:19–27	ἀδελφοί μου ἀγαπητοί	ἴστε plus ἔστω
2:1–13	ἀδελφοί μου	μὴ ἐν προσωπολημψίαις ἔχετε
2:14–26	ἀδελφοί μου	τί τὸ ὄφελος,
3:1–12	ἀδελφοί μου	μὴ πολλοὶ διδάσκαλοι γίνεσθε
3:13–18	ἐν ὑμῖν THEMATIC PEAK	τίς σοφὸς καὶ ἐπιστήμων
4:1–10	ἐν ὑμῖν HORTATORY PEAK	Πόθεν πόλεμοι καὶ πόθεν μάχαι 10 imperatives in 4:7–10
4:11–12	ἀδελφοί	μὴ καταλαλεῖτε ἀλλήλων
4:13–17	οἱ λέγοντες	ἄγε νῦν
5:1–6	οἱ πλούσιοι	ἄγε νῦν ... κλαύσατε
5:7–11	ἀδελφοί	μακροθυμήσατε plus 4 imperatives
5:12–18	ἀδελφοί μου	μὴ ὀμνύετε
5:19–20	ἀδελφοί μου	γινωσκέτω

Figure 4: Sections in James

The following is a simplified outline with the main points expressed by an imperative command that communicates the gist of each section.

Introduction

Prescript 1:1

1. Be Joyful in Trials 1:2–15
2. Do Not Be Deceived about God's Goodness 1:16–18
3. Become a Good Hearer/Doer of the Word 1:19–27
4. Do Not Show Favoritism 2:1–13
5. Show Your Faith by Your Works 2:14–26
6. Be Consistent in Your Speech 3:1–12
7. *Follow the Wisdom of God* 3:13–18
8. *Become a Friend of God* 4:1–10
9. Do Not Speak Against One Another 4:11–12
10. Do Not Plan Presumptuously 4:13–17
11. You Rich Should Treat the Poor Justly 5:1–6
12. Wait Patiently for the Lord's Coming 5:7–11
13. Do Not Swear but Pray 5:12–18
14. Convert the Erring Brother 5:19–20

As we work through the text of James section by section, it will become clear how each of these paragraphs relates to the peak meta-theme in 3:13–18. Commentators have not always attended to how James structures his argument by the surface features of his text. What an author *does* with the words he *speaks* or *writes* has been amply illustrated by the philosophy and hermeneutics associated with speech-act theory. I believe that what James does with his words, as seen in the above formal analysis of his linguistic features, suggests that hearing his "voice" means heeding his call to a unified ("perfect") life that consistently follows divine wisdom, set apart from and distinct from the wisdom of this world.[21]

Detailed Outline

Based on the above structure of James, the following is a more detailed exegetical outline of the book that will form the pericopes for the

---

[21] For further elaboration of the theme and structure of James, see W. Varner, "The Main Theme and Structure of James," *TMSJ* 22 (Spring, 2011) 115–32.

exegetical comments.

I. Salutation (1:1)

II. Be Joyful in Trials (1:2–15)
    A. Trials and Maturity (1:2–4)
    B. Wisdom and Faith (1:5–8)
    C. Poor Man, Rich Man (1:9–11)
    D. Blessing for Those Who Pass the Test (1:12–15)

III. Do Not Be Deceived about God's Gifts (1:16–18)

IV. Become Good Hearers and Doers (1:19–27)
    A. Hearing and Doing (1:19–21)
    B. Deceived or Blessed? (1:22–25)
    C. Real Religion (1:26–27)

V. Do Not Show Favoritism (2:1–13)
    A. Partiality in Practice (2:1–4)
    B. Honoring Those God Honors (2:5–7)
    C. The Royal Law (2:8–9)
    D. The Whole Law (2:10–13)

VI. Show Your Faith by Your Deeds (2:14–26)
    A. A Parable of the Poor (2:14–17)
    B. A Debate about Deeds (2:18–19)
    C. Patriarchal Proof (2:20–23)
    D. Matriarchal Proof (2:24–26)

VII. Be Consistent in Your Speech (3:1–12)
    A. Taming the Tongue (3:1–2)
    B. Small but Powerful (3:3–5)
    C. A Wildfire and a Wild Beast (3:6–8)
    D. A Strange Mixture (3:9–12)

VIII. Follow the Wisdom of God (3:13–18) (*Thematic Peak*)
    A. Wisdom is Shown by Behavior (3:13)
    B. Unwise Behavior That Comes from Below (3:14–16)
    C. Wise Behavior That Comes from Above (3:17–18)

IX. Become a Friend of God (4:1–10) (*Hortatory Peak*)
    A. A War in the Members (4:1–3)
    B. Adultery and Bad Friendships (4:4–6)

Commentary Bibliography

While there are some excellent German and French commentaries on James, this bibliography is limited to commentaries in English that pay special attention to the original text.

Adam, A.K.M. *James: A Handbook on the Greek Text.* Waco: Baylor University Press, 2013. Adamson, J.B. *The Epistle of James.* NICNT. Grand Rapids: Eerdmans, 1976.

Alford, H.A. "Epistle of James." In H. A. Alford. *The Greek Testament.* Vol. IV. Chicago: Moody Press, 1958, 274–330.

Allison, Dale A. *James.* ICC. London/New York: Bloomsbury T&T Clark, 2013.

Bauckham, R. *James: Wisdom of James, Disciple of Jesus the Sage*. NTR. London and New York: Routledge, 1999.

———. "James." *Eerdmans Bible Commentary*, eds. James D.G. Dunn and J. W. Rogerson. Grand Rapids: Eerdmans, 2003.

Bede, V. *Commentary on the Seven Catholic Epistles*, trans. by David Hurst. Kalamazoo: Cistercian Publications, 1985, 1483–92.

Bengel, J. A. *Bengel's New Testament Commentary*, trans. C. Lewis and M. Vincent. 2 vols. Grand Rapids, MI: Kregel, 1887.

Blomberg, C.L. and Kamell, M. J. *James*. ZECNT. Grand Rapids: Zondervan, 2008.

Brosend II, W. F. *James and Jude*. NCABC. Cambridge: CUP, 2004.

Davids, P. *The Epistle of James*. NIGTC. Grand Rapids: Eerdmans, 1982.

Dibelius, M. *Commentary on James*, trans. Michael Williams. Hermeneia. Philadelphia: Fortress Press, 1976.

Hartin, P. J. *James*. SP 14. Collegeville: Liturgical, 2003.

Hodges, Z. C. *The Epistle of James: Proven Character through Testing*. Irving, TX: Grace Evangelical Society, 1994.

Hort, F.J.A. *The Epistle of James*. London: Macmillan, 1909.

Huther, J. E. *Critical and Exegetical Handbook to the General Epistles of James, Peter, John, and Jude*. New York: Funk & Wagnalls, 1887.

Johnson, L. T. *The Letter of James*. AB 37A. New York: Doubleday, 1995.

Kistemaker, S. *Exposition of the Epistle of James and the Epistles of John*. New Testament Commentary. Grand Rapids: Baker, 1986.

Knowling, R. J. *The Epistle of James*. 2nd ed. London: Methuen, 1910.

Laws, S. *A Commentary on the Epistle of James*. HNTC. San Francisco: Harper & Row, 1980.

Martin, R. *The Epistle of James*. WBC. Waco, TX: Word Books, 1988.

Mayor, J. B. *The Epistle of St. James: The Greek Text with Introduction, Notes, and Comments*. 3rd ed. London: MacMillan & Co., 1910.

McCartney, D.G. *James*. BECNT. Grand Rapids: Baker Academic, 2009.

McKnight, S. *The Letter of James*. NICNT. Grand Rapids: Eerdmans, 2011.

Moo, D. J. *The Letter of James*. PNTC. Grand Rapids: Eerdmans, 2000.

———. *The Letter of James*. TC. Grand Rapids: Eerdmans, 1985.

Oesterley, W.E. *The General Epistle of James.* EGT. Vol. 4. London: Hodder & Stoughton, 1910.

Plummer, A. *General Epistles of St. James and St. Jude.* EB. Vol. 46. New York: Funk and Wagnalls, 1900.

Varner, W. *The Book of James: A New Perspective. A Linguistic Commentary Applying Discourse Analysis.* Woodlands, TX: Kress Biblical Resources, 2011.

Wall, R. W. *The Community of the Wise: The Letter of James.* Valley Forge, PA: Trinity Press International, 1997.

Witherington, B. *Letters and Homilies to Jewish Christians.* Downers Grove, IL: Intervarsity Press, 2007.

1

SALUTATION (1:1)

Greek Text

ᵃἸάκωβος ᵇθεοῦ καὶ κυρίου Ἰησοῦ Χριστοῦ δοῦλος ταῖς δώδεκα φυλαῖς ταῖς ἐν τῇ διασπορᾷ χαίρειν.

Textual Notes

1.a. The earliest complete NT manuscripts, א and B, as well as a few uncials, include the inscription (title) Ιακωβου Επιστολη, but the earliest manuscript of James (P⁷⁴) is untitled.

1.b. A few manuscripts (429, 614, 630) also insert πατρος after θεου. The variant readings are late, the first simply reflecting a scribal effort to title the book, and the second an effort to distinguish clearly the divine Father from the Son.

Sentence Flow and Translation

Ἰάκωβος θεοῦ καὶ κυρίου Ἰησοῦ Χριστοῦ δοῦλος
James, a slave of God and of the Lord Jesus Christ

45

ταῖς δώδεκα φυλαῖς
to the twelve tribes

ταῖς ἐν τῇ διασπορᾷ
who are in the Diaspora

χαίρειν.
Greetings

Context

The salutation included at the beginning of first-century letters followed the standard formula in James 1:1, which included an introduction of the author, the recipients of the letter, and a greeting. A papyrus letter discovered in Egypt and dated 4 August A.D. 41, contains the following salutation:

Πλάτων Νεχθύρει χαίρειν.
Platon to Nechthyres greetings.[1]

Each of the three elements in these salutations could be expanded, as in the following example.

Ἀπίων Ἐπιμάχῳ τῶι πατρὶ καὶ κυρίῳ πλεῖστα χαίρειν.
Apion to Epimachos, his father and lord, very many greetings.[2]

This expansion of one of the three elements was a prevalent practice among the NT letters, especially those attributed to Paul (Rom 1:1–7, when all three are greatly expanded). The form of the salutation in James 1:1 follows the simple formula of three elements: sender, addressee, and greeting. In the book of Acts we find

---

[1] P. Bour. 10. Cited in John L. White, *Light from Ancient Letters* (Philadelphia: Fortress Press, 1986), 95.

[2] This papyrus letter is analyzed in Hans Joseph Klauck, *Ancient Letters and the New Testament* (Waco, TX: Baylor University Press, 2006), 9–14.

salutations similar to this Hellenistic model in the so-called apostolic letter associated with James (Acts 15:23) and also in a Greek letter from a Roman centurion to the Roman procurator (Acts 23:26).

Exegetical Comments

1:1 Ἰάκωβος: The author immediately identifies himself as Jacob, the transliterated form of his name which is the Graecized form of the Hebrew name for the OT "Jacob" (Gen 27:36). Jacob was a common name, appearing among three leaders in the early church: James the brother of John; James the Apostle, and James the brother of Jesus. The James referred to here was the uterine brother of Jesus (1 Cor 15:7; Gal 1:19; 2:9, 12). Although at first James was skeptical of his brother's status as Son of God (John 7:3–5) he would later become, along with Peter and John, one of the three original pillars of the earliest church (Acts 15; Gal 2:9). The English name "James" reveals no clear indication that it is derived from the Hebrew "Jacob." The Latin is a straight transliteration from the Greek (*Iakōbos*). The combination of simplicity and authority that is found in this superscription suggests that this name can only refer to James, the "brother of the Lord," who alone in the early church could expect such immediate recognition.

θεοῦ καὶ κυρίου Ἰησοῦ Χριστοῦ: The fronting of the genitive prior to its head noun δοῦλος, which is placed at the end of the self-designation, is striking. James only departs from the default order of "head noun plus genitive" two other times in the letter (1:17: τροπῆς ἀποσκίασμα; 3:3: τῶν ἵππων τοὺς χαλινοὺς). It is interesting also to note that Jude the brother of James also utilizes this order in his greeting (Jude 1). This usage differs from the default order used in other salutations by Paul and Peter (Rom 1:1; Titus 1:1; 2 Pet 1:1). James wished to give prominence to the origin of his authority (God/Jesus) over his authoritative function (slave). The textual variant after θεοῦ, πάτρος, added here by some MSS, is probably not original but does represent an accurate interpretive reading. By calling himself a slave of both God and Lord,

James acknowledges equality of essence and dignity among the divine persons but does so by establishing a distinction between them: "Slave of God, namely the Father, and also of the Lord Jesus Christ."

δοῦλος: This appositional noun denotes literal ownership by another person (BDAG, 260.1; GE, 551-52). An abundant amount of evidence in Greek literature clearly describes a δοῦλος as a person who was owned by another free person (NIDNTTE, 1:767-68). This is illustrated in the NT when δοῦλος is opposite ἐλεύθερος as in 1 Cor 12:13: εἴτε δοῦλοι εἴτε ἐλεύθεροι (also Gal 3:28; 4:22–31; Eph 6:8; Col 3:11; Rev 6:15; 13:16; 19:18). The Israelites were very much "slaves (not "servants") in the land of Egypt in the house of Pharaoh" (LXX 1 Sam 2:27). They could not buy their way out of this slavery.

There is another way, however, of viewing the semantics of δοῦλος in Jas 1:1. In canonical Jewish literature, עֶבֶד (regularly translated δοῦλος in the LXX) often indicates a special relationship between God and a person defined in terms of possession by God and service by the δοῦλος. Religious "slavery" as complete dedication to God is mentioned in the Psalms (LXX Pss 118:38, 76; 122:2; 133:1). Isa 42:19 utilizes the plural οἱ δοῦλοι τοῦ θεοῦ ("slaves of God") to convey the singular "servant of the Lord," the only occurrence of this Greek phrase in the LXX. The term δοῦλος also was applied to those leaders who mediated between God and His people, such as Joshua (Josh 24:30), David (2 Sam 7:8, 25, 29), and Moses (Ps 104:26; Mal 3:24). It is often used of the prophets as messengers of the Lord (Amos 3:7; Joel 3:2; Jonah 1:9; Zech 1:6; Jer 7:25). In addition to "slave" Muraoka defines this other LXX usage of the noun as a "submissive and respectful person" to his master even if the δοῦλος was not a victim of "slavery" (177).

In the NT *it also appears as a title for Christians who minister publicly*, either in the expression "slave of Jesus Christ" (Rom 1:1; Phil 1:1; 2 Pet 1:1) or "slave of Christ" (Gal 1:10). In light of this usage, especially in the OT, the functional sense of the word should be viewed against its Jewish background (a "servant/slave" like the prophets and other Israelite leaders), rather than against its Greco-

Roman background. The Jewishness of James and his readers should point us toward this context. The term here in 1:1, therefore, stresses more the role of a prophet/apostle/δοῦλος rather than that of an ignominious slave with no rights. Actually it is best to understand the self-title as both (1) an indication of humility and (2) a description of a prophetic ministry.[3]

ταῖς δώδεκα φυλαῖς ταῖς ἐν τῇ διασπορᾷ: The first article ταῖς is in the dative case because it is an address, a variant of an indirect object of the unexpressed verb. The second article ταῖς is used as a relative pronoun, a usage appearing often in the NT and also occasionally in James (2:7). The location of the "twelve tribes" is *in* the Diaspora—the lands outside the land of Israel. James, in his role at the center of the Jerusalem church, is writing a Diaspora encyclical to believing Jewish communities, as he did also in Acts 15:23–31 to believing Gentiles.

While many commentators identify "the twelve tribes" as a reference to the church composed of believers from all ethnic backgrounds, this approach ignores the literal use of διασπορά in John 7:35 and Acts 26:7. Furthermore the early Christian use of the word is entirely in a literal sense in our earliest Christian literature outside the NT (*1 Clem.* 55:6; *Prot. Jas.* 1:3).[4] It is best to understand in James 1:1 a

---

[3] Johnson (168-69) has a helpful discussion of δοῦλος, which has informed my own comments. He adds the following interesting observation. "The odd designation of James as *OBLIAS* by Hegesippus (in Eusebius, *HE* II, 23,7) is due to a scribal error, mistaking the Greek Δ for the Λ, thus yielding *OBLIAS* rather than the original *OBDIAS*. The name Obadiah, furthermore, means "slave of Yahweh" in Hebrew. Such an explanation would make sense of Eusebius' otherwise inexplicable supplying of the "Greek meaning" of *OBLIAS* as "rampart (*perioche*) of the people and righteousness," for the beginning of the prophecy of Obadiah ("slave of Yahweh") in the LXX says that the Lord set out a "rampart" (*perioche*) for the nations (*ethne*)." The link to our author's self-designation is tenuous but possible.

[4] W. C. Van Unnik, "*Diaspora* and *Church* in the First Centuries of Church History," *Sparsa Collecta*, vol. 3 (NovTSup 31; Leiden: Brill, 1983), 95–105. Van Unnik adds further examples from later Greek Christian writers such as Clement of Alexandria, Basilides of Caesarea, Chrysostom, and the Apostolic Constitutions that "twelve tribes" and "diaspora" were understood in a Jewish or Jewish Christian sense.

literal use of "*the* twelve tribes" and "*the* Diaspora" as describing Jewish believers living outside the land of Israel.

While the address does not identify the readers as believers in Jesus, 1:1 and 2:1 clearly imply that the readers acknowledge the messiahship of Jesus. James makes no reference in his book to the Gentile mission, because Gentiles at this time were not a significant part of the congregations he addressed. The Pauline Gentile mission apparently was yet to emerge as it is especially described in Acts 16–28.

Χαίρειν: This use of the present active infinitive, standing apart from the syntax of the sender and addressee, is the standard form in the salutation of a letter and is attested since the classical period. Wallace (608) refers to this special use of the Present Infinitive as an "Infinitive Absolute." A word like λέγει was intentionally suppressed so the infinitive χαίρειν would function here as an infinitive in indirect discourse that often follows a verb like λέγει. This yields the following sense: "James tells (those in the Diaspora) to feel greeted." The Greek verb χαίρω means to "rejoice, be glad" but the word had probably acquired the sense of the English equivalent of "greetings." The imperative singular of the word (χαῖρε) is used for a greeting directed to Jesus (Matt 26:49; 27:29) and the imperative plural (χαίρετε) is used by the resurrected Jesus directed to his disciples (Matt 28:9). Although the infinitive form of the word in Jam 1:1 does not appear in other NT letter salutations, in the only other letter that we have from James, also an encyclical, he utilizes this same word for the greeting (Acts 15:23).

Additional examples of the literal use of the word διασπορά are also mentioned by Lampe, 359. Johannes Weiss affirmed "that the use of the twelve tribes as Christians in general is nowhere attested" (*Earliest Christianity* [New York: Harper and Row, 1959], 2:743).

BE JOYFUL IN TRIALS (1:2–15)

Trials and Maturity (1:2–4)

Greek Text

2 Πᾶσαν χαρὰν ἡγήσασθε, ἀδελφοί μου, ὅταν πειρασμοῖς περιπέσητε ποικίλοις, 3 γινώσκοντες ὅτι τὸ ᵃδοκίμιον ὑμῶν τῆς πίστεως κατεργάζεται ὑπομονήν· 4 ἡ δὲ ὑπομονὴ ἔργον τέλειον ἐχέτω, ἵνα ἦτε τέλειοι καὶ ὁλόκληροι, ἐν μηδενὶ λειπόμενοι.

Textual Notes

3.a. There is only one significant variant reading in 1:3. The critical text has δοκίμιον ("testing") while several witnesses (110, 431, 1241) have δόκιμον ("approval"). These later scribes were perhaps influenced by a variant reading in 1 Peter 1:7. James speaks of the "testing" of one's faith, while the variant reading found in 1 Peter speaks of the "approval" of one's faith after it is tested.

Sentence Flow and Translation

2a Πᾶσαν χαρὰν ἡγήσασθε, ἀδελφοί μου,
   Consider it entirely joy, my brothers,

    2b ὅταν πειρασμοῖς περιπέσητε ποικίλοις,
       when you encounter all types of trials,

3 γινώσκοντες ὅτι τὸ δοκίμιον ὑμῶν τῆς πίστεως κατεργάζεται
   ὑπομονήν·
   because you know that the testing of your faith produces
   endurance.

    4a ἡ δὲ ὑπομονὴ ἔργον τέλειον ἐχέτω,
       And endurance should bring about its perfect work,

    4b ἵνα ἦτε τέλειοι καὶ ὁλόκληροι,
       so that you may be perfect and complete,

    ἐν μηδενὶ λειπόμενοι.
       lacking in nothing.

Context

The first major division of the letter is 1:2–15. This decision is based on the conviction that the coupling in 1:2 of a nominative plural of direct address (ἀδελφοί) with an imperative command (ἡγήσασθε) signals a new section. This combination of a nominative plural (most often ἀδελφοί) plus a command appears again in 1:16. This pattern continues throughout the letter, the special exception being where the imperative command is replaced by rhetorical questions like those that open 3:13 and 4:1. Not only do the presence of these formal discourse markers confirm that 1:2–15 is the first main paragraph, but the theme that runs throughout this section (trials) indicates that it is to be viewed as a discrete unit. Although it functions as a self-contained section, the paragraph can be broken down into four smaller subparagraphs, each of which will be handled separately in the commentary below.

A number of commentators have also noticed the intentional use of "catchwords" (Dibelius, 70–71; Davids, 66–67). The most often mentioned examples of this linkage are: (1) the χαίρειν that concludes the greeting in 1:1 linked with the χαρὰν as the second word of 1:2; and (2) the λειπόμενοι and λείπεται joining the end of 1:4 with the beginning of 1:5. These proposed word linkages, however, may have been overly stressed. While James does engage in some intentional rhetorical flourishes, they are usually in the form of alliteration, as he does in the repetition of three consecutive π-words in 1:2 (πειρασμοῖς περιπέσητε ποικίλοις). As part of the larger paragraph (1:2–15), four subparagraphs can be discerned (1:2–4; 1:5–8; 1:9–11 and 1:12–15). Evidence for this fourfold segmenting of 1:2–15 will be presented in the analysis of each of the four following pericopes.

Exegetical Comments

1:2 Πᾶσαν: This does not mean strictly *totality of joy*, as though there were no joy besides, but it denotes an even higher degree than μεγάλην or πολλήν. This sense of "whole" or "complete" can be witnessed as early as Plato, *Laws* §708B: πασα πόλις, "a whole city" as well as the LXX of 2 Maccabees 2:22, μετὰ πάσης ἐπιεικείας, "with all gentleness." The expression may have originated in a contraction of πᾶν εἶναι χαράν, and is equivalent to "entire, unmixed joy," as in Phil 2:29: μετὰ πάσης χαρᾶς. The same use of πᾶς can be seen in 1 Peter 2:18 (ἐν παντὶ φόβῳ) and 1 Timothy 2:2 (ἐν πάσῃ εὐσεβείᾳ).

χαρὰν: The word χαρά echoes the preceding χαίρειν not just by a formal word-linkage, but because the verb and the noun share the same field of meaning. Χαρά is here the ground of rejoicing, as in Luke 2:10. James proceeds to show that these very trials are grounds for joy. For this thought, see also Matthew 5:10–15 and 1 Peter 4:12–14, where the teaching is that suffering is not strange or foreign to the Christian life, but is a part of the training for glory. Therefore, χαίρετε! The idea is exemplified by the disciples in Acts 5:41: "… rejoicing (χαίροντες) that they had been considered worthy to suffer shame for the name." "This joy, however, is not the detachment of the Greek philosopher (4 Macc 9–11), but the eschatological joy of those expecting the intervention of God in the end of the age (Jude 24)" (Davids, 67–68).

ἡγήσασθε: Aorist Middle Imperative of the verb ἡγέομαι, which appears in the NT in two senses, "regard" and "lead" (BDAG, 434; GE, 901). Here the meaning is *regard* or *consider* as in its other occurrences in the Epistles (except Heb 13:7, 17, 24). In Phil 2:3 we are to *regard* one another higher than ourselves (ἀλλήλους ἡγούμενοι ὑπερέχοντας ἑαυτῶν), and in 2:6, Jesus did not *regard* equality with God as something to be grasped: οὐχ ἁρπαγμὸν ἡγήσατο τὸ εἶναι ἴσα θεῷ). Thus ἡγέομαι in the indicative and imperative denotes some sort of mental judgment, such as "regarding" (1 Thess 5:13; 2 Thess 3:15) or "reckoning" (Phil 2:25; 3:7, 8; Heb 10:29; 11:26). In every usage there is the element of a value judgment. James does not say that trial *is* all joy, but he asks us to *consider* it joy, which means to look at the trial as capable of being turned to our highest good. Aorist imperative verbs appear twenty-three times in James, while present imperative verbs appear thirty-one times. An analysis of these verses bears out that the aorist imperative is usually accompanied by a limiting circumstance within which the specific command is to be obeyed ("consider it joy *when you encounter trials*"), while the present imperative does not have a qualifying circumstance but works as a general command ("do not be deceived" 1:16).

ἀδελφοί μου: While many grammars call this a "Vocative Plural," I prefer the label, "Nominative Plural of Direct Address," since there is no separate ending for the vocative plural. In the LXX this plural noun is used of Israelites generally (Lev 25:46; Deut 15:3), as it also can be used in the NT (Acts 2:29, Rom 9:3). In James, however, the sense is clearly metaphorical and intended to describe a spiritual brotherhood not based on any blood relationship. Jesus disavowed the physical family and used this type of language to describe his "true" spiritual family, namely his disciples (Matt 12:50//Mark 3:35). In James the word basically is equivalent to the later term, "Christians," or "brothers in Christ." He frequently makes use of this affectionate address (2:1, 14; 3:1, 10, 12; 5:12, 19), sometimes omitting the accompanying μου (4:11, 5:7, 5:9, 5:10), and at other times adding ἀγαπητοί (1:16, 19: 2:5). The simple ἀδελφοί is the most frequent use in the Pauline epistles (seventy-seven times, only eight times with μου). In the other general epistles ἀγαπητοί is used only by itself (16 t.). The use of μου is an indication that James is joining with his readers, rather than pontificating to them.

ὅταν ... περιπέσητε: The aorist subjunctive of περιπίπτω combined with the adverb ὅταν is a temporal clause that does not simply convey general time (*when*), but implies "at all times" (*whenever*). For this use of the verb, see also Luke 10:30: λῃσταῖς περίεπεσεν, "he fell among [or 'encountered'] bandits."

πειρασμοῖς: This dative direct object of περιπέσητε has been interpreted in two ways. Some argue that James sets up a contrast between internal sin and external temptation regarding trials (Dibelius, 71; Davids, 67). Martin (14–15), by contrast, views it specifically as persecution. Both meanings are possibly present. The noun is almost entirely confined to biblical usage (BDAG, 793; GE, 1603), although the cognate verb πειράζω has a long history. In the LXX πειράζω stands almost always for נָסָה and πειρασμός for the derivative מַסָּה. The word group is used for various kinds of testing, but especially of man by God and God by man. The most famous case is that of Abraham (Gen 22:1), and so πειρασμός usually refers to a test of men by God, and also the probations of Pharaoh (Deut 4:34; 7:19; 29:3). The noun is here used in 1:2 of *outward* trials, and examples of such are in the persecutions that followed the martyrdom of Stephen and of James, and in Paul's description of his own sufferings (1 Cor 4:9–13; 2 Cor 11:23–29). The *inner* trial ("temptation") is expressed in 1:13 by the verb πειράζω. Riches, as we will see in 1:10 and 1 Tim 6:9, can be just as much a πειρασμός as poverty. This verse brings out the externality of the temptation rather than the internal temptation arising from "your own desire" (ἰδία ἐπιθυμία), as in 1:14.

ποικίλοις: This dative adjective modifying πειρασμοῖς is used in the LXX of various types of tests and trying experiences (3 Macc. 2:6; 4 Macc. 15:8). It is also used in the NT of various desires and diseases (2 Tim 3:6; Matt 4:24), which of course answers "the varied grace of God" (ποικίλη χάρις Θεοῦ) in 1 Pet 4:10. The closest verbal parallel is 1 Pet 1:6: ἐν ποικίλοις πειρασμοῖς).

The view that the trials here refer to persecutions for the faith seems to unnecessarily restrict the verbal field of the word πειρασμοῖς, without any contextual justification. Furthermore, the adjective "various" (ποικίλοις) that modifies "trials" points away from the specific trial of persecution toward general and various trials encountered by believers in their daily lives. Some of the readers were certainly encountering seriously unfair treatment by the more affluent in their synagogues (2:1–4), and some day laborers were being deprived of their wages by the landowners (5:1–6). There does not, however, appear to be any clear or implied reference in the letter to the readers being persecuted specifically for their faith in Jesus.

1:3 γινώσκοντες: Present active participle of γινώσκω. The causal participle provides the reason for the reader's commended attitude—that their ability to perceive trials as joy comes from a conviction that adversity strengthens character. This appeal to a shared knowledge is a common feature of ethical admonition in the NT (Rom 6:6; Heb 10:34; 2 Pet 3:3). The participle also introduces the rhetorical figure known as a *gradatio* or *sorites*, in which one clause builds on another. A *gradatio* is a staircase building to a climax by the use of repetition and interlinking of phrases by keywords (Witherington, 424). It ascends through 1:4 when it reaches the top step: τέλειοι καὶ ὁλόκληροι (being "mature and complete"). See 1 Pet 1:6–7 and Rom 5:2b–5 for additional examples of *gradatio*.

ὅτι: This conjunction introduces the complement of the following content clause, which is the direct object of γινώσκοντες.

τὸ δοκίμιον: The accusative noun functions in the embedded ὅτι clause as the subject of the following verb κατεργάζεται. The majority of manuscripts from different family types read δοκίμιον, which is undoubtedly to be preferred to the reading δόκιμον ("approved character") found in a few manuscripts. This specific word meaning "testing" appears in the NT only here and in an almost parallel expression in 1 Pet 1:7: ἵνα τὸ δοκίμιον ὑμῶν τῆς πίστεως. This is one of the many evidences that Peter was familiar with the letter of James.

ὑμῶν τῆς πίστεως: The genitive πίστεως receives the action implied in the verbal head noun δοκίμιον and thus is an objective genitive (Wallace 116-19). This is the first of fourteen occurrences of the term πίστις in James, who ironically is often viewed as the exponent of works. Here it conveys a human attitude that both can be threatened and can grow. James will later (2:22–24) recall the example of Abraham, who became the classic exemplar of one who had his faith tested.

κατεργάζεται: Present middle Indicative third singular of κατεργάζω. This verb in its same form occurs also in 1:20 as one of the new readings adopted in NA28. The word prepares the reader for the use of the cognate noun ἔργον in the next line.

ὑπομονήν: The accusative direct object of κατεργάζεται. The construction shows how James will connect "faith" with its "work/deed" in chapter two, as the effective result and expression of faith. A clear parallel is provided by Rom 5:3: ὑπομονήν κατεργάζεται. "Endurance" (to be preferred over "patience" which is conveyed more by μακροθυμία) is a quality subject to testing elsewhere in the NT (Luke 8:15; 21:19; Rom 2:7; 8:25; 15:4–5; 2 Cor 1:6; Col 1:11; Heb 12:1). It will be seen again in James with the example provided by Job (5:11), as well as in the statements utilizing the verb form in 1:12 and 5:11. The overall meaning of 1:3 is that testing our faith will determine whether it is genuine or not. What is genuine will then produce endurance.

1:4 ἡ δὲ ὑπομονὴ: The particle δὲ signals a development from what has preceded and is appropriate to express the transition to the next stage of the *gradatio*. For the meaning of the noun as "endurance" see the previous verse.

ἔργον: Accusative singular direct object of ἐχέτω. This is the first of the 15 appearances of this noun in James and will be one of the main subjects in 2:14-26. BDAG (390) defines its meaning here as *"manifestation, practical proof,"* unlike its negative nuance in some Pauline examples such as the *"works of the law"* (Rom 3:20; Gal 2:16) or the human *works* that do not save (Eph 2:9).

τέλειον: This accusative adjective modifying ἔργον is a key word in James (1:17, 25; 3:2), and expresses the idea of that which is finished, complete, or mature (see "perfect love" in 1 John 4:18). Here it is the effect of endurance that is "perfect." Note the parallel in James' statement in 2:22 about Abraham: "from deeds (ἔργων) his faith (πίστις) was perfected (ἐτελειώθη)."

ἐχέτω: Present active imperative, third person singular of ἔχω. There is no evidence that the third person imperative lessens the force of a second person imperative. The usual translation of "let" should be stronger like "should." The present tense command conveys the verbal aspect of continuing process, rather than behavior in a specific situation. The verb ἔχω has an extensive usage in the NT beyond the simple "have." Among its eleven definitions in the NT, here the meaning with the accusative is "bring about, cause" (BDAG, 422a).

ἵνα ἦτε: This present active subjunctive second plural of εἰμί coupled with ἵνα introduces a purpose clause, although sometimes it is difficult to discern the exact difference from a result clause. This clause is the clearest attempt by James to express an overall *general* purpose statement anywhere in the book.

τέλειοι καὶ ὁλόκληροι: The nominative plurals are predicate adjectives describing the embedded subject (you) of the verb ἦτε. The term "perfect" now shifts from the action to the person: "*you* are the perfect work." The adjective ὁλόκληρος ("complete") has the nuance of "wholeness" or "soundness" as, e.g., in contrast to disease (Acts 3:16). As τέλειος can also means "complete," so ὁλόκληρος means "complete with no part missing." The two words together give a fuller phrase, as in a similar way in Col 4:12: τέλειοι καὶ πεπληροφορημένοι.

ἐν μηδενὶ λειπόμενοι: This present middle result participle may appear redundant, but it makes explicit what is implicit in ὁλόκληρος—that to be whole means to lack nothing. Result participles follow the main verb (Wallace 638). The "lacking" here has nothing to do with material realities (as in 2:15) but rather with moral and spiritual realities. This concluding clause helps to define the essence of "perfection"— namely, being mature and whole and complete.

Summary of How the Syntax of James 1:2-4 Conveys Its Message

Each main clause is anchored by a command expressed with a second person plural imperative and a third person singular imperative (ἡγήσασθε and ἐχέτω). The first two of the three subordinate clauses then indicate: (1) *when* a joyful attitude should be displayed— "whenever you encounter various trials" (ὅταν πειρασμοῖς περιπέσητε ποικίλοις); and (2) *why* you should maintain such an attitude—

because you know that the outcome of your trials will achieve a greater level of endurance (γινώσκοντες ὅτι τὸ δοκίμιον ὑμῶν τῆς πίστεως κατεργάζεται ὑπομονήν·). The second main clause continues to press the exhortation to each person undergoing the trials to allow this resulting endurance to complete its purpose for them (ἡ δὲ ὑπομονὴ ἔργον τέλειον ἐχέτω). Then the conclusion consists of a purpose clause and a result clause to encourage the readers that if you have the correct attitude toward your trials, it will lead to greater maturity and you will be a complete person (ἵνα ἦτε τέλειοι καὶ ὁλόκληροι, ἐν μηδενὶ λειπόμενοι).

Wisdom and Faith (1:5–8)

Greek Text

5 Εἰ δέ τις ὑμῶν λείπεται σοφίας, αἰτείτω παρὰ τοῦ διδόντος θεοῦ πᾶσιν ἁπλῶς καὶ ᵃμὴ ὀνειδίζοντος, καὶ δοθήσεται αὐτῷ. 6 αἰτείτω δὲ ἐν πίστει, μηδὲν διακρινόμενος, ὁ γὰρ διακρινόμενος ἔοικεν κλύδωνι θαλάσσης ἀνεμιζομένῳ καὶ ῥιπιζομένῳ· 7 μὴ γὰρ οἰέσθω ὁ ἄνθρωπος ἐκεῖνος ὅτι λήμψεταί τι παρὰ τοῦ κυρίου, 8 ἀνὴρᵇ δίψυχος, ἀκατάστατος ἐν πάσαις ταῖς ὁδοῖς αὐτοῦ.

Textual Notes

5.a. The variants are not significant, one in 1:5 being a clearly ungrammatical replacing of the negative μὴ with ουκ, plus a few editorial clarifications in only a few late manuscripts.

8.b. There is an interesting postpositive insertion of γάρ after ἀνὴρ by some later uncials and some Byzantine manuscripts. A possible scribal motive for this insertion will be discussed in the commentary on that verse.

Sentence Flow and Translation

5 Εἰ δέ τις ὑμῶν λείπεται σοφίας,
   Now, if anyone of you is lacking wisdom,
αἰτείτω παρὰ τοῦ διδόντος θεοῦ πᾶσιν ἁπλῶς
   he should ask from God, the one who gives without reservation

      καὶ μὴ ὀνειδίζοντος,
      and does not reproach

   καὶ δοθήσεται αὐτῷ.
   and it will be given to him.

6 αἰτείτω δὲ ἐν πίστει,
   But he should ask in faith,

      μηδὲν διακρινόμενος,
      without doubting,

   ὁ γὰρ διακρινόμενος ἔοικεν κλύδωνι θαλάσσης ἀνεμιζομένῳ καὶ
   ῥιπιζομένῳ.
   for the one who doubts is like a wave of the sea tossed and
   turned by the wind.

7 μὴ γὰρ οἰέσθω ὁ ἄνθρωπος ἐκεῖνος
   For that person should not expect

      ὅτι λήμψεταί τι παρὰ τοῦ κυρίου.
      that he will receive anything from the Lord.

8 ἀνὴρ δίψυχος, ἀκατάστατος ἐν πάσαις ταῖς ὁδοῖς αὐτοῦ.
   A double-minded individual is unstable in everything he pursues.

Context

This section is linked to the previous section by the word λείπεται which connects the thought with the closing word of 1:4, λειπόμενοι. The virtue of wisdom (σοφίας) is necessary to help complete, perfect, and make whole the individual facing trials, which is the main concern of the previous paragraph. The verb αἰτείτω ("he should request") introduces the subject of prayer, which dominates the rest of the section since each clause explains both how one should pray for wisdom and what are the hindrances to praying for wisdom. The concept of wisdom certainly runs through the paragraph, but it is the effective praying for wisdom that is its permeating theme. No definition of wisdom is given, but in 3:13–18, the thematic peak of the letter, heavenly wisdom from above is contrasted with earthly human wisdom from below by their binary-opposite behaviors. This subsection of 1:5–8 then concludes with a brief description of the "double-souled" person in 1:8, before James continues an exhortation to two opposite examples in 1:9–11, the "lowly brother" and the "rich man."

Exegetical Comments

1:5 Εἰ δέ: The particle δὲ signals a development from the preceding sentence and, coupled with the conditional particle εἰ, introduces a first class conditional sentence. The protasis extends through σοφίας and assumes the reality of the condition (Wallace 706).

τις ὑμῶν: The indefinite prounoun is followed by a partitive genitive, sometimes referred to as the "wholative genitive" (Wallace 84-86).

λείπεται: Third singular present active indicative of λείπω. The λειπόμενοι from the previous verse is taken up again like τέλειος and ὑπομονὴ were before.

σοφίας: As it does also in 2:15, the verb λείπω takes the genitive singular noun as its direct object. Earlier usage of the word group σοφία/σόφος indicates that a shift took place in its meaning. "In the early Greek period any practical skill of this kind counted as wisdom, then during the classical period the range of meaning was strongly restricted to theoretical and intellectual knowledge, and finally in the usage of the philosophical schools of Hellenism and later antiquity the practical element was united again with the theoretical in the ideal picture of the wise man" (U. Wilckens, "σοφία," *TDNT* 7:467). Biblical writers, including James, tend toward the practical definition as they seek more to *describe* rather than *define* the word group. James will later describe wise behavior as "pure, then peaceable, gentle, open to reason, full of mercy and good fruits, impartial and sincere (3:17). Wisdom is "that endowment of heart and mind which is needed for the right conduct of life" (Hort, 7). To James, as in OT wisdom writings, wisdom is the principal thing, to which he gives the same prominence as Paul to faith, John to love, and Peter to hope.

αἰτείτω: This third person imperative introduces a clause that is the apodosis of the preceding conditional protasis in the first class conditional sentence. "The imp. may be (James 1:5) the apodosis of an expressed condition and the implied protasis of another conclusion"—namely, the imperative αἰτείτω in 1:6 (Robertson 1023). The translation "should ask" rather than the traditional "let him ask" avoids the idea of permission associated with the English word "let." The greatest example of this request is Solomon (1 Kgs 3:9–12; see also Prov 2:3 and James 3:17: ἡ ἄνωθεν σοφία).

παρὰ τοῦ διδόντος θεοῦ: The adjectival participle is in the genitive case because it is the object of the preposition. The article τοῦ preceding the διδόντος is in the first attributive position modifying θεοῦ. One would expect that an article plus the participle would follow the noun (in the second attributive position) and describe what God does for those who are the recipients of His giving (πᾶσιν), as is the case with the following participle, ὀνειδίζοντος. Most commentators ignore this apparent grammatical anomaly. This unexpected order is also found in 2 Peter 3:2 and Matt 25:34. The reason for this different word order involving unexpected intervening words may be that James wished to land greater prominence to God's manner of giving and to those who are the recipients of His gracious act of giving: "without hesitation to all" (πᾶσιν ἁπλῶς). Although it may sound a bit redundant, the sense of this construction could be expressed as follows: "Ask from the giving God, *who gives* to all without reservation."

ἁπλῶς: This adverb occurs only here in the NT and signifies simplicity as opposed to complexity. In connection with the verb "giving," the adverb should be seen in the light of the use of the noun ἁπλότης in other contexts to signify "generosity" or "liberality" (Josephus, *Ant.* 7:332). The adjective ἁπλοῦς, "single-fold" (Matt 6:22), and the noun ἁπλότης are more common in the NT (2 Cor 8:2; 9:11, 13; Rom 12:8).

There are two ways in which ἁπλῶς can be taken: (1) in a logical sense as "unconditionally," or (2) in a moral sense as "generously." The latter sense is in accordance with the use of ἁπλότης = "liberality," which is common in the NT. This use of ἁπλότης seems to come from the idea of frankness and openheartedness conveyed by ἁπλοῦς. The word describes the manner in which God gives to all people the wisdom they request. English versions throughout the last five hundred years have generally translated this adverb as "generously" (NRSV, NAU, NIV, ESV) or "liberally" (Geneva, KJV). However, the first sense of the word, "without hesitation," may be more appropriate in the context. The adverb is nonexistent in classical sources, but the adjective ἁπλοῦς is a moral epithet that denotes the absence of guile or duplicity. BDAG defines this *hapax legomenon* only as "without reservation" and cites patristic sources (e.g., *Herm.* 27.4: "give without hesitation to those in need"). This meaning certainly fits with James' call for singleness and his aversion to doubleness throughout his discourse. In other words, God's willingness to give "without hesitation" contrasts vividly with the unanswered prayers of the person who prays "with hesitation." With this support from sources outside the NT and also from the context, it is difficult to understand why the versions still cling to the "generously" translation.

καὶ μὴ ὀνειδίζοντος: The present participle parallels the previous participle διδόντος but with the negative particle μή. BDAG perceptively defines the verb's usage here as: "*charge* or *reproach* someone with someth. a kind of verbal extortion, with the purpose of obtaining someth. from a pers.... God does not do this" (710; see also GE, 1461). See also its use as "rebuke" or "reproach" in the LXX (Prov 25:8–9) and in the NT (Matt 5:11; Rom 15:3; 1 Pet 4:14). This is not intended to mean that God never reproaches someone (Mark 16:14: ὠνείδισεν τὴν ἀπιστίαν αὐτῶν), but that where there is repentance, He freely gives and forgives whatever may have been their past sin(s).

καὶ δοθήσεται: Following the participle διδόντος in the previous conditional clause, this future passive indicative of the same root (δίδωμι) says that what has been requested will be given. The same form of the verb with the same sense is found in Matt 7:7 (αἰτεῖτε καὶ δοθήσεται ὑμῖν), which makes this verse one of James' adapted *logia* of Jesus. See also the variations of Jesus' words expressing the same idea in Matt 7:11; 21:22; Luke 11:9; and John 16:23.

αὐτῷ: Dative singular of the personal pronoun as an indirect object.

1:6 αἰτείτω δέ: Again the δέ implies a development from what precedes. James again references a preceding word, namely, the third person imperative verb αἰτείτω in 1:5. For a similar pattern, note εὐχὴ τῆς πίστεως in 5:15, and for αἰτείτω, see 4:3, where there is also a limitation on the prayer that is sure of an answer. "The ἁπλότης of the Giver must be met by a corresponding ἁπλότης of the suppliant, as in the case of Solomon, who asked simply for wisdom, without a thought of material good things" (Mayor, 40).

ἐν πίστει: The dative with ἐν expresses that the manner of asking refers not to initial belief, but to that continuing trust in God's goodness and generosity.

μηδὲν διακρινόμενος: A present middle participle followed by the negated accusative direct object. The sense of the active voice of this verb is to "divide." While this specific use of the verb as "doubting" has not been found in writings earlier than the NT, it is seen in early Christian literature like *1 Clem.* 2.40. It is sometimes used in the NT of quarrelling (Acts 11:2; Jude 23), and of internal division and is contrasted with faith (Matt 21:21; Mark 11:23; Rom 4:20; James 2:4; Acts 10:20; Rom 14:23). As was mentioned, this use is apparently confined to the NT and some later Christian writings. The active voice of the verb also appears in the sense of *distinguishing* (Matt 16:3; Acts 15:9; 1 Cor 11:29—not distinguishing the body of Christ from common food); and 14:29 (discerning of spirits). The force of the word can be illustrated by the attitudes expressed later in James 4:4 ("whoever is a friend of the world is an enemy of God") and by Matt 6:24 ("no one is able to serve two masters").

ὁ γὰρ διακρινόμενος: The γὰρ introduces the reason why one should ask in faith without wavering. The present middle participle is the substantival subject of the following verb ἔοικεν.
ἔοικεν: The word is found in the NT only here and in 1:23, both times in the third person perfect tense form, and both conveying the timeless state of affairs of the respective analogies (Porter, *Verbal Aspect* 254). The doubter is compared to a leaf floating on the wave, now carried toward the shore, now away from it.

κλύδωνι θαλάσσης: The dative head noun follows the verb ἔοικεν and the genitive θαλάσσης is partitive. The expression in extra Biblical literature can also mean "rough seas" (Philo, *Creation* 58; Josephus, *Ant.* 9.210).

ἀνεμιζομένῳ καὶ ῥιπιζομένῳ: These two present passive adjectival participles modify the dative noun κλύδωνι. Mayor remarks that ἀνεμίζω "is perhaps coined by the writer," and adds that "James has a fondness for verbs in -ιζω, e.g. ὀνειδίζω, ῥιπίζω, παραλογίζομαι, φλογίζω, ἐγγίζω, καθαρίζω, ἁγνίζω, ἀφανίζω, θησαυρίζω, θερίζω, στηρίζω, μακαρίζω" (Mayor, 39). The second present passive participle ῥιπιζομένῳ means literally "turned." The word "wind" is supplied as it is in every English version consulted. The verb ῥιπίζω was frequently used in contemporary writers about the action of wind on the sea (Dio Chrysostom, *Or.* 32; Philo, *Gig.* 11). This verb is another of those colorful words in James that is found only here in the NT. A fondness for analogies from nature is characteristic of James (James 1:1, 17; 3:3–12; 5:3–4, 7).

1:7 γὰρ: As with its use in 1:6, the γὰρ introduces the reason that αἰτείτω δὲ ἐν πίστει, μηδὲν διακρινόμενος.

μὴ ... οἰέσθω: Present middle imperative third singular of οἴομαι. This is one of the three appearances of the verb in the NT, "δοκέω having taken its place (cf. Mt. 3:9 μὴ δόξητε)" (Ropes, 132). He notes also that the verb appeared often both in earlier and contemporary Greek literature (Job 11:2; 1 Macc 5:61; 2 Macc 5:21; P. Oxy. 1666, 2), usually "with the collateral notion of wrong judgment or conceit." See its appearance in John 21:25 and οἰόμενοι in Phil 1:17.

ὁ ἄνθρωπος ἐκεῖνος: The nominal phrase is the subject of οἰέσθω. Since the word for "male" (ἀνήρ) is used in the next line, the suggested translation is "person." and the demonstrative pronoun ἐκεῖνος generally. The pronoun (ἐκεῖνος) also connotes a sense of disdain. The 'man' or 'person' (ὁ ἄνθρωπος) here is clearly gender inclusive, for doubting is not something that only men do!" (Blomberg-Kamell, 53).

ὅτι λήμψεταί: The conjunction introduces a noun clause that is the direct object of οἰέσθω. The verb λήμψεταί, future middle indicative of λαμβάνω, alludes to another of Jesus' sayings on prayer: "for everyone who asks, receives" (Matt 7:8; Luke 11:10).

τι: The indefinite pronoun (without an accent as compared to the interrogative pronoun τίς) is in the accusative case as the direct object of λήμψεταί.

παρὰ τοῦ κυρίου: The prepositional phrase "from the Lord" matches "from God" in 1:5 (παρὰ τοῦ ... θεοῦ). Here and later (4:15, 5:10, 11), the word κυρίου is used of God, but it is used specifically of Jesus in 1:1 and 2:1, and probably also in 5:8, 14, 15.

This entire primary clause complex, although introduced also by γὰρ, boldly declares that such a wavering "person" (ἄνθρωπος) should never even suppose (μὴ ... οἰέσθω) that they will receive anything from the Lord. James begins and ends his letter with references to prayer (1:6–7; 5:13–18). Ancient letters, especially those composed by Christians, often contained both, even if they are doxological prayers (Rom 1:8–10; 16:25–27; 1 Cor 1:3–4; 16:22–24; 1 Thess 1:2–3; 5:23–25).

1:8 The following extended notes will focus on the meaning of the adjective δίψυχος and justify taking this verse as a straightforward sentence rather than the way it is usually punctuated and translated.

ἀνὴρ: There is a switch from the use of ἄνθρωπος in the previous verse to ἀνήρ here in 1:8. "James commonly uses ἀνήρ with some characteristic word like μακάριος 1:12, κατανοῶν 1:23, χρυσοδακτύλιος 2:2, and τέλειος 3:2, reserving ἄνθρωπος for more general expressions like ἐκεῖνος, πᾶς, and οὐδείς" (Mayor, 42). The word functions as the subject of an unexpressed verb in the sentence.

δίψυχος: English versions usually translate this nominative adjective modifying ἀνήρ as "double-minded," with Tyndale rendering it as "waveringe mynded." This is the first appearance of this adjective in Greek literature, and it is used in the NT only here and in 4:8. While δίψυχος may be a neologism, the practice conveyed by the word was not novel to the reader of Israel's scriptures. The concept of "doubleness" is found in Psa 12:2: "with a double heart [ἐν καρδίᾳ καὶ ἐν καρδίᾳ] do they speak," as well as in 1 Chron 12:33 and 1 Kgs 18:21. It is the opposite of what is commanded in Deut 4:29: "You shall seek there the Lord your God and you shall find Him when you seek Him with your heart and with all your soul (ἐξ ὅλης τῆς ψυχῆς σου)." Although introduced by James, the word was quickly taken up by subsequent writers, because it appears more than forty times in *Shepherd of Hermas*. The word adjective also appears three times in *1 Clem.* 11.2; 23:3 and *2 Clem.* 11.2, while *Did.* 4:4/*Barn.* 19:5 condemn being double-souled with the cognate verb (οὐ διψυχήσεις).

The most recent critical texts (NA[28] and UBS[5]) place a comma after δίψυχος and read the rest of the verse as a further elaboration of the person mentioned in 1:6–7. "He is a double-minded man, unstable in all his ways." The verse/clause does not contain an expressed verb and requires that the readers supply either a copulative verb or both a pronoun and a copulative verb. On the other hand, Westcott-Hort's punctuation of the text with no intervening comma considers ἀνὴρ δίψυχος as the subject of λήμψεται. The Vulgate, with its addition of the verb *est*, also makes 1:8 an entire sentence: *vir duplex inconstans est*. I recommend, therefore, that we follow the punctuation of these earlier textual traditions and editions and read this as a primary clause/sentence that is independent in structure from the previous verse. Then by including the understood copula and by removing any partial stop following δίψυχος, the complete sentence would translate: "A double-minded man is unstable in all his ways." The HCSB followed this option: "An indecisive man is unstable in all his ways" (although the CSB changes to "being double-minded and unstable in all his ways").

This punctuation should be preferred for additional reasons. (1) Verse 8 read this way sounds like a concise aphoristic saying. James will often round off one of his paragraphs by adding such a stand-alone aphorism that illustrates his main point. This suggestion would better explain the sudden switch to the masculine ἀνὴρ in 1:8 from the more generic ἄνθρωπος in 1:7. The aphorism must have contained the masculine term and James faithfully reproduces it, although the uncertainty he condemns would apply to both men and women. (2) The initial English versions (Tyndale, Geneva, KJV, and Douay preferred this approach to the verse by recognizing a full stop before 1:8 and inserting no comma after "a double-minded man." (3) Support from antiquity for reading 1:8 as an independent clause is in the fourth-century manuscript B (Vaticanus), which indicates a full stop before 1:8. (4) Many Medieval Greek manuscripts inserted a γάρ after ἀνὴρ, indicating that these scribes recognized that 1:8 provides the reason that the person in 1:7 will not receive anything from the Lord: "*For* a doubled-souled man is unstable in all his ways." Thus 1:8 should stand by itself as the concluding judgment on the man who prays while still doubting the effectuality of his prayer.

ἀκατάστατος: In our reconstruction of the syntax in this clause, this word is a predicate adjective describing the ἀνὴρ δίψυχος. The word appears once in the LXX of Isa 54:11: "O humbled and "unsteady one" (ἀκατάστατος), you have not been comforted." In James we see it later in 3:8 to describe the tongue: "a restless evil" (ἀκατάστατον κακόν). The cognate noun ἀκαταστασία is found in 3:16 where wisdom from below is characterized as "disorder." In 1 Cor 14:33 it is opposed to εἰρήνη, and in the plural as "rebellions" in Luke 21:9 and as "riots" in 2 Cor 6:5. Its translation, therefore, should be "unsettled" or "unstable."

ἐν πάσαις ταῖς ὁδοῖς αὐτοῦ: This locative dative phrase describes a person who walks not on *one* path, but as in Sir 2:12: ἐπιβαίνει ἐπὶ δύο τρίβους ("he treads on two paths"). The noun "way" (ὁδος) was used of one's behavior or way of life (LXX Ps 1:1, 6; 15:11; 118:1, 32; Prov 1:15; Wis 5:6). Compare the use of the noun in James 5:20 ("the error of his way") and in Rom 3:16 ("miseries are in their way"). The same comparison of life to a journey is implied in the verbs πορεύομαι and περιπατέω.

Conclusion

In conclusion, as expressed in one complete independent clause, 1:8 should be as follows:

ἀνὴρ δίψυχος ἀκατάστατος ἐν πάσαις ταῖς ὁδοῖς αὐτοῦ
A double-souled man is unstable in everything he pursues.

Poor Man, Rich Man (1:9–11)

Greek Text

9 Καυχάσθω δὲ ὁ ἀδελφὸς ὁ ταπεινὸς ᵃἐν τῷ ὕψει αὐτοῦ, 10 ὁ δὲ πλούσιος ἐν τῇ ταπεινώσει αὐτοῦ, ὅτι ὡς ἄνθος χόρτου παρελεύσεται. 11 ἀνέτειλεν γὰρ ὁ ἥλιος σὺν τῷ καύσωνι καὶ ἐξήρανεν τὸν χόρτον καὶ τὸ ἄνθος ᵇαὐτοῦ ἐξέπεσεν καὶ ἡ εὐπρέπεια τοῦ προσώπου ᶜαὐτοῦ ἀπώλετο· οὕτως καὶ ὁ πλούσιος ἐν ταῖς πορείαις αὐτοῦ μαρανθήσεται.

Textual Notes

There are no significant textual variants in 1:9–11 that affect translation or interpretation.

9.a. After ὁ ταπεινὸς in 1:9, P74 alone omits the qualifying expression ἐν τῷ ὕψει αὐτοῦ.

11.b. A handful of minuscule and Vulgate mss omit the first αὐτοῦ.

11.c. B strangely omits the second αὐτοῦ.

Sentence Flow and Translation

9 Καυχάσθω δὲ ὁ ἀδελφὸς ὁ ταπεινὸς ἐν τῷ ὕψει αὐτοῦ,
   The lowly brother should rather boast in his exaltation,

10 ὁ δὲ πλούσιος ἐν τῇ ταπεινώσει αὐτοῦ,
   but the rich in his humiliation,

   ὅτι ὡς ἄνθος χόρτου παρελεύσεται.
   because like a flower of the grass he will pass away.

11 ἀνέτειλεν γὰρ ὁ ἥλιος σὺν τῷ καύσωνι
   For the sun rises with its scorching heat

   καὶ ἐξήρανεν τὸν χόρτον,
   and withers the grass,

   καὶ τὸ ἄνθος αὐτοῦ ἐξέπεσεν
   and its flower falls,

   καὶ ἡ εὐπρέπεια τοῦ προσώπου αὐτοῦ ἀπώλετο·
   and the beauty of its appearance perishes.

   οὕτως καὶ ὁ πλούσιος ἐν ταῖς πορείαις αὐτοῦ μαρανθήσεται.
   So also the rich man will fade away in the midst of his pursuits.

Context

This sub-paragraph reveals a clear linkage with the two preceding paragraphs (1:2–4 and 5–8). The postpositive δὲ connects and contrasts the humble brother with the double-minded person in 1:8. I have translated it as "rather" to bring out its contrasting function. There is also a semantic link with 1:2 where the "brothers" are exhorted to "consider it all joy" when they encounter trials. In 1:9 an example of one of those brothers is exhorted to boast (positively) in an example of those trials, i.e., being lowly. Just as it may sound strange to exhort someone to be joyful in trials, so it is also strange, or at least counterintuitive, to exhort someone when he is being lowered to boast (καυχάσθω), and also to exhort someone in a higher status to boast when they are lowered. This is a graphic illustration of the countercultural attitude displayed by one who holds to "the faith of the glorious Lord Jesus Christ" (2:1).

Another link with the preceding verses appears in the last clause of the little pericope, where it is said that "the rich man will fade away *in the midst of his pursuits.*" This statement parallels both in structure and in thought what is affirmed at the conclusion of 1:8: "a double-minded man is unstable *in all his ways.*" Although the words for "ways" are different, some versions translate πορείαις αὐτοῦ in 1:11 as "his ways," thus indicating a parallelism to the ὁδοῖς αὐτοῦ ending 1:8. More will be mentioned about these inner-textual connections in the Exegetical Comments.

Exegetical Comments

1:9 Καυχάσθω δὲ: The postpositive δὲ signifies a development from the preceding verse by contrasting the humble brother with the double-minded person in 1:8. The third person imperative καυχάσθω has been rendered by a number of different words and expressions, from the more literal "boast" (ESV, NRSV, ESV, NLT, CSB) to "rejoice" (TNT, KJV), "glory" (NASB, NKJV), and "take pride" (nab, NET, NIV). BDAG defines the word as "take pride in something" (536), with the context deciding whether the action is viewed as good (here and Phil 3:3) or bad (Gal 6:13). See also GE, 1106: "to exult, rejoice." James will return to the subject of *inappropriate* boasting in 3:14 and 4:16.

ὁ ἀδελφὸς ὁ ταπεινός: The adjective is in the second attributive position (article-noun-article-adjective). The characteristics embodied in the word group ταπεινός/ταπεινοφροσύνη were not particularly admired by the ancient Greeks. Even considering the possibility of overstatement, the passage from Trench conveys well that attitude. "The instances are few and exceptional in which ταπεινός signifies anything for them which is not groveling, slavish, and mean-spirited" (Trench 149). In contrast, the NT references draw upon the self-designation of Jesus in Matt 11:29: πραΰς εἰμι καὶ ταπεινὸς τῇ καρδίᾳ ("I am gentle and humble in heart"). Whatever be one's outward circumstances, it is the lowliness of heart that becomes one of the distinguishing Christian virtues. And if we choose "meekness" as the translation, it should be remembered that meekness does not equate with weakness.

ἐν τῷ ὕψει αὐτοῦ: Dative of "sphere" within which one should boast. The term ὕψος can denote any kind of "height," whether it is one of physical stature (Herodotus 1:50) or of social rank (1 Macc 1:40; 10:24). This exaltation can be understood as describing the future reward of the one who endures, which is promised by 1:12, and therefore can be seen as eschatological. A currently realized eschatological exaltation is in view when we recognize God's choice of the poor to be "rich in faith" as heirs of His kingdom (2:5).

1:10 ὁ δὲ πλούσιος: The δὲ again signals development from the ταπεινός in 1:9 to the πλούσιος. There is an intended suppression of the word "boast," which must be supplied from 1:9. The rich should cease to pride himself on his wealth, but rather (δὲ) rejoice that he has learned the emptiness of all worldly distinctions and has learned that they are valuable only when they are regarded as a trust to be used for the service of God and the good of others. The graphic language of Jeremiah, where he is also discussing the characteristics of a wise man, is the probable intertextual link. "'But let him that boasts, boast [καυχάσθω] in this, that he understands and knows me' ... says the Lord" (Jer 9:24).

ἐν τῇ ταπεινώσει αὐτοῦ: The opposite reason for boasting contrasts the rich man in 1:10 from the humble man in 1:9. Commentators are divided over whether the πλούσιος is a believer or not. The "fading away" language that follows fits the description of an unbeliever, but the overall structure of 1:9–10 seems to view the "rich person" also as a "brother." It is obvious that at least one expression from the first clause (καυχάσθω) is suppressed in the second clause, a fact that is readily recognized. Thus we might expect that the word "brother" in 1:9 is also intentionally suppressed and thus understood when referring to the rich person in 1:10. Since the letter is addressed to Jewish believers and the beginning of the paragraph (1:2) addresses "brothers," the argument is blunted somewhat if this rich man is an unbeliever. The difference with the exhortation to the rich in 5:1–6 is that in that passage they are not addressed as brothers (5:1), and they have no eschatological hope at all because of the way in which they have treated their poor employees. It seems clear that the rich ones in 5:1–6 are outside the community of faith. In 1:10–11, however, it is not clear that the rich person will experience eternal punishment. See following comments.

ὅτι ὡς ἄνθος χόρτου: This ὅτι-causal clause is the one subordinate clause in 1:9–11 and offers the reason why the rich man should rejoice in his humbling. In the LXX the ἄνθος was a figure for the transient quality of life (Job 14:2; Ps 102:15; Zeph 2:2). This is a definite allusion to Isa 40:6, which will become evident in the next verse.

παρελεύσεται: The subject of the verb (third person future middle from παρέρχομαι, "fade away") is difficult to determine. Is it the rich man or his wealth that will disappear? Grammatically, the closest possible antecedent is the rich man, but larger semantic issues can take precedence. These words effectively announce in what the "humbling" of the rich consists, and in which he should "boast." It should be noted that the verbs (παρελεύσεται in 1:10; μαρανθήσεται in 1:11) are not used of eternal punishment in other biblical passages. In light of all these factors, including it is best to take "it will pass away" as referring to the wealth rather than to the person.

1:11 ἀνέτειλεν γὰρ ὁ ἥλιος σὺν τῷ καύσωνι καὶ ἐξήρανεν τὸν χόρτον, καὶ τὸ ἄνθος αὐτοῦ ἐξέπεσεν καὶ ἡ εὐπρέπεια τοῦ προσώπου αὐτοῦ ἀπώλετο· Because 1:11a is a mini-parable that should be read as a whole, the comments will focus on the structure of this extended sentence with its four clauses rather than on its individual parts. There are four phases in this withering process. First, "the sun rises with its scorching heat." Second, the sun's heat "withers the flower." Third, "its flower falls." Fourth, "its beauty perishes."

The vivid imagery that James utilizes requires a special vocabulary to adequately communicate it. Note the one *hapax legomenon* in this passage (εὐπρέπεια). Furthermore, there are two words that appear only once elsewhere (ἄνθος, 1 Pet 1:24; πορεία, Luke 13:22). Finally, there is another word (καύσων) that occurs only once in Matthew (20:12) and once in Luke (12:55). This analogy from nature suggests fragility and transience. The noun χόρτος is used of field plants such as hay and ἄνθος is used of a flower or bloom. Taken together, the terms suggest fragile wildflowers of the field that are exposed to the sun. The elegance of the KJV rendering of the fourth clause in 1:11, although sorely dated, should not be ignored because of its quaint beauty: "and the grace of the fashion of it perisheth." See the excellent treatment of this verse by McKnight (103–04).

James' careful use of verb tenses in 1:10–11 illustrates an aspectual approach to verb tenses. In this analogy drawn from nature, he utilizes in 1:10 the future tense when the rich man "will pass away" (παρελεύσεται, future middle of παρέρχομαι), and in 1:11 he describes with the future tense that the rich man "will fade away" (μαρανθήσεται, future middle of μαραίνω). Between these two future tense forms, he employs a string of aorist indicative forms to describe the symbiotic relationship in nature between the sun's shining and earth's vegetation. "The sun rises (ἀνέτειλεν) with its scorching heat and withers (ἐξήρανεν) the grass, and its flower falls (ἐξέπεσεν), and the beauty of its appearance perishes (ἀπώλετο)" (1:11). Grammarians have referred to this exceptional usage of the aorist tense as a *gnomic* aorist. The aorist verb forms do not refer to an event that occurred in past time but rather refer to events that occur during many occasions and thus are not bound to any past occurrence. An aspectual approach to the aorist tense argues that it is used to convey *perfective* aspect, which views the action as a whole event that is not related to time, unless the surrounding context demands that it be viewed as taking place in the past. Most examples of the gnomic aorist are used to describe processes of nature. The present tense (as above) is still the best translation, as long as we do not think that the Greek tense is equivalent to it.

οὕτως καὶ ὁ πλούσιος ἐν ταῖς πορείαις αὐτοῦ: The adverb οὕτως introduces the transition from the nature analogy to the lesson for the rich person who trusts in his riches. He will fade away (μαρανθήσεται) in "his pursuits" (πορείαις αὐτοῦ). This last clause is fully integrated into the preceding verses, as it balances the semantic parallel to the ὁδοῖς αὐτοῦ ending 1:8. James skillfully employs it as a statement to round off his argument, something that he often does in the book (1:8; 3:18 and 4:17). The noun πορεία derives from the verb πορεύομαι ("I go") and is used to describe literal journeys (Num 33:2; Luke 13:22) as well as a "way of life" (Prov 2:7; Jer 10:23). This word also anticipates the development of the theme of the transience of business pursuits apart from God's will in 4:13–16. If so, the translation "journeys" would also be appropriate. A reference to the lifestyle of travel is supported by Luke 13:22, where the same expression (πορείαν ποιούμενος) is used for Jesus' travel. Along with James 4:13–17, the parable of the rich fool (Luke 12:13–21) is close enough in content to suggest that James has in mind the overall lifestyle of the rich man, who plans and plots how to increase riches instead of living each day before God.

μαρανθήσεται: See the above discussion about the use of the future tense of this verb. BDAG defines it as "wither" (616).

Conclusion

This paragraph is not isolated from its context. It links with the two preceding paragraphs (1:2–4 and 5–8), not only semantically but also syntactically. There is a semantic link with 1:2 where the "brothers" are exhorted to "consider it all joy" when they encounter trials. In 1:9 an example of one of those brothers is exhorted to boast (positively) in an example of those trials, i.e., being lowly. Although the language varies, the meaning is still quite clear—namely, that neither the one who doubts and is double-souled nor the one who is rich and proud will finally emerge as successful in what they do.

Blessing for Those Who Pass the Test (1:12–15)

Greek Text

12 Μακάριος ªἀνὴρ ὃς ὑπομένει πειρασμόν, ὅτι δόκιμος γενόμενος λήμψεται τὸν στέφανον τῆς ζωῆς ὃν ᵇἐπηγγείλατο τοῖς ἀγαπῶσιν αὐτόν. 13 Μηδεὶς πειραζόμενος λεγέτω ὅτι ᶜἀπὸ θεοῦ πειράζομαι· ὁ γὰρ θεὸς ἀπείραστός ἐστιν κακῶν, πειράζει δὲ αὐτὸς οὐδένα. 15 εἶτα ἡ ἐπιθυμία συλλαβοῦσα τίκτει ἁμαρτίαν, ἡ δὲ ἁμαρτία ἀποτελεσθεῖσα ᵈἀποκύει θάνατον.

Textual Notes

12.a. First, A and a few minuscule manuscripts prefer the more generic ἄνθρωπος to the much stronger attested ἀνὴρ. Some scribes probably desired to stay away from the more limited masculine sense of ἀνὴρ. "Since James was writing to Jewish Christians, who still met in synagogues (2:2), and since synagogues were attended only by males, it is very likely that James was addressing his comments specifically to men. Indeed, James specifically uses the masculine term ἀνὴρ several times throughout this epistle (see 1:7–8, 19–20, 23; 2:2; 3:2)" (Comfort 724).

12.b. Second, the earlier and better witnesses (P²³ ℵ A B Ψ 81 206* 323 it^ff cop^sa), following a Jewish tendency to suppress the divine name, support the reading ἐπηγγείλατο in 1:12 without a subject being expressed. Later witnesses complete what may have seemed to be a lacuna by adding either κύριος (C 1829) or ὁ κύριος (K L P most minuscules syr) or ὁ θεός (33^vid 322 323 463 547 945 1241 1739 2492 vg syr eth) as the subject of the verb. It is difficult to imagine why a later scribe would omit the divine name, and the fact that there is evidence of three different efforts to supply a name supports the absence of the name as original.

13.c. Instead of the widely supported ἀπό before θεοῦ, a few mss have απο του while ℵ along with a few late minuscules replace the word with ὑπό, which is clearly an effort to "improve" the idea of divine agency being denied.

15.d. Scribes of some later uncials (L, Ψ, 181, 323, 1739) understood the present tense of the heavily supported ἀποκύει as a future tense ἀποκυεῖ, which is inconsistent with the rest of the tense usages in 1:14–15.

Sentence Flow and Translation

12 Μακάριος ἀνὴρ
　Blessed is a man

　　　ὃς ὑπομένει πειρασμόν,
　　　who remains steadfast under a trial

　　ὅτι δόκιμος γενόμενος λήμψεται τὸν στέφανον τῆς ζωῆς,
　　for when he has stood the test he will receive the crown of life,

　　　　　ὃν ἐπηγγείλατο τοῖς ἀγαπῶσιν αὐτόν.
　　　　　which he has promised to those who love him.

13 μηδεὶς πειραζόμενος λεγέτω ὅτι Ἀπὸ θεοῦ πειράζομαι·
Let no one say when he is tempted, "I am being tempted by God,"

ὁ γὰρ θεὸς ἀπείραστός ἐστιν κακῶν,
for God cannot be tempted with evil things,

πειράζει δὲ αὐτὸς οὐδένα.
and he himself tempts no one.

14 ἕκαστος δὲ πειράζεται ὑπὸ τῆς ἰδίας ἐπιθυμίας
But each person is tempted by his own desire

ἐξελκόμενος καὶ δελεαζόμενος·
when he is lured and enticed

15 εἶτα ἡ ἐπιθυμία ... τίκτει ἁμαρτίαν,
Then desire ...   gives birth to sin

συλλαβοῦσα
when it has conceived

ἡ δὲ ἁμαρτία ... ἀποκύει θάνατον.
and sin   ...   gives birth to death.

ἀποτελεσθεῖσα
when it is fully grown

Context

James 1:12–15 is the fourth subparagraph in the first main section of the letter: 1:2–15. Some commentators attach 1:12 to the previous section and view the trials as describing those that are experienced by the poor and the rich. It is more likely that he has never abandoned the topic of being tested and learning to respond properly. While affirming the shared themes of the overall pericope, it is also best to view 1:12 as introducing the fourth section of 1:12–15. This is because of the many occurrences of the πειρα-word group that bind them together with the preceding verses. The passage is introduced in 1:12 by the first of two uses of μακάριος in the chapter (see also 1:25), and concludes with a climactic reference to death at the end of 1:15. Then 1:16 opens with the second of the "brothers-plus-imperative" combinations which begin each new section. While able to thus stand alone, 1:12–15 also has clear affinities with the beginning of the section (1:2–4) which has its own references to "testing" (six examples of πειρα-words). Other verbal connections with 1:3–4 are the ὑπομένει and δόκιμος in 1:12. Furthermore, the description of one who shows constancy under trial as "blessed" completes the thought expressed in 1:2—namely, that we must count it "entirely joy" when we encounter all kinds of trials. An additional way of viewing the strategic role of 1:12 is to recognize it as a bridge that spans 1:2–11 and 1:13–15. Thus the passage functions independently and also anaphorically and cataphorically as the introduction of an *inclusio* that begins in 1:2 and ends in 1:15.

Exegetical Comments

1:12 Μακάριος ἀνὴρ: The nominative singular functions as the predicate adjective of the following ἀνὴρ with an understood equative verb (εστιν). A *macarism*, (Greek for the Latin "beatitude"), is pronounced on the one who endures trial, followed by a causal clause with ὅτι, providing the explanation of the blessing—namely, that the one who endures will be blessed by receiving the crown of life. Μακάριος ἀνὴρ in the LXX occurs six times in Psalms (1:1; 31:2; 33:9; 39:5; 83:6; 111:1) and twice in Proverbs (8:34; 28:14). Some translations prefer the translation "happy" but in the OT the term is applied to a person in a right relationship with God (Deut 33:29; Ps 1:1; 2:12; 32:1), and so the translation "blessed" is to be preferred. The same singular *macarism* (μακάριος ἀνὴρ) occurs also in Romans 4:8, a quotation from Psalm

32:2, but does not appear elsewhere in the NT. It is clear that James is adapting in the same form the blessing employed by his older brother in the Gospels (Matt 5:3–12; Luke 6:20–26). The plural adjective μακάριοι appears 26 t. in the NT and describes in the Revelation (14:13; 19:9; 22:14) the blessedness of believers in death and in the eschaton.

ὃς ὑπομένει πειρασμόν: This subordinate clause is introduced by the nominative relative pronoun ὅς which functions as the subject of the third person present tense form of the verb ὑπομένω. The clause refers to the ἀνὴρ in the previous clause. This is the first of six occurrences of the πειρα-word group in these four verses that bind together the overall section with 1:2. The verb is best rendered by "endures" or "remains steadfast." This same blessing for enduring trial is mentioned again in 5:11 of Job (and the prophets) who was tested and endured. It is not the one who experiences the trial, but the one who patiently endures the trial who is pronounced "blessed."

ὅτι δόκιμος γενόμενος: The causal ὅτι introduces a temporal clause anchored by the aorist middle participle γενόμενος. The nominative δόκιμος is a predicate adjective modifying the unexpressed subject of the participle which of course is the original ἀνὴρ. While the participle γενόμενος can be understood as conditional ("if he stands the test"), it is better translated as temporal ("after he is approved"). The word δόκιμος therefore contains not only the notion of trial, but also trial and approval (2 Cor 10:18; 13:7; 2 Tim 2:15). This temporal clause complex points to the *testing* nuance of the πειρα-word group rather than the *tempting* aspect, which clearly is its meaning in 1:13. Saying that one *has stood the test* or that he *has been approved* is actually another way of saying that he *endures*.

λήμψεται: Future middle indicative of the irregular verb λαμβάνω.
τὸν στέφανον: Accusative singular direct object of λήμψεται. The word στέφανον is used in the NT for the wreath of victory in the games (1 Cor 9:25, 2 Tim 2:5). While well known in the Greek mainland (Isthmus

and Olympus), these games were also conducted across the Greco-Roman world. Greek games were also common in Judea in the days of Herod the Great, and were practiced even in Jerusalem itself (Josephus, *Ant.* 15.8.1). In the LXX στέφανος appears also as a symbol of royal or priestly dignity (Muraoka, 636). "David took their king's crown (στέφανον) from off his head, the weight of which was a talent of gold with the precious stones" (2 Sam. 12:30). In Prov 1:9 the instruction of father and mother "shall be a crown (στέφανον) of grace unto your head" (also 4:9). The word also appears in Sir 15:6 as "a crown of gladness," and in *T. Lev.* 8.2 as "crown of righteousness." The echo of the combination of "crown" and "enduring" in Zech 6:14 may be intentional: ὁ δὲ στέφανος ἔσται τοῖς ὑπομένουσιν, "the crown shall be for those who endure." This usage also is in the NT: "Upon the thrones I saw 24 elders ... and upon their heads gold crowns (στεφάνους)" (Rev 4:4). In Rev 5:10 the same elders praise the Lamb for making kings and priests to God out of every nation (also Rev 14:14). In Matt 27:29, the στέφανος and κάλαμος stand for the crown and scepter as Jesus' kingly role was mocked. It is true, however, that διάδημα was more commonly used in this royal sense, as in the LXX of Isa 62:3 (Muraoka, 150) and Rev 19:12: "and upon his head were many crowns (διαδήματα)."

τῆς ζωῆς: It is best to see this phrase as a Genitive of Apposition or Epexegetical Genitive, namely "the crown which consists of eternal life" (Wallace 95-100; see also 1 Pet 3:7).

ὃν ἐπηγγείλατο: The relative pronoun in the accusative case, relating back to στέφανον. The verb is aorist middle indicative of ἐπαγγέλομαι.

τοῖς ἀγαπῶσιν αὐτόν. The final clause consists of an adjectival substantive participle in the dative case serving as the indirect object of ἐπηγγείλατο and an accusative αὐτόν as the direct object of the participle. Apart from Rev 2:10, which was written later, we do not find the precise words τὸν στέφανον τῆς ζωῆς in any specific scriptural passage. We may have here an allusion to a *logion* of Jesus that is not preserved in which he makes such a promise. The other possibility is that it is an instance of loose quotation, representing one of the verses cited above that mention στέφανος.

1:13 μηδεὶς πειραζόμενος: The present middle participle πειραζόμενος is temporal with the negative noun μηδεὶς the subject of the following λεγέτω. While James has employed the noun πειρασμός twice (1:2, 12), he now uses the verb πειράζω four times in 1:13 and 14. Πειράζω can mean "put to the test" i.e., "to discover the nature or character of someth." (BDAG, 792.2) or, as it is used here, "to tempt" i.e., "to entice to improper behavior" (793.4). In the LXX the verb always translates the piel of the Hebrew נָסָה. In its "religious" uses, it is a trial of virtue by means of affliction or adversity, or even by Satan's intervention (Job 1:9). In this perspective, God is its author and its purpose is to instruct. Two memorable examples are (1) when God tested Abraham by asking him to sacrifice Isaac (Gen 22:1), and (2) when God tested the chosen people in the wilderness (Exod 15:25). These trials are tests that allow Yahweh to assess the quality of his servants ("I test the people *to find out* if they will walk according to my law or not" [Exod 16:4]). Though trial in itself is ordered by God for our good, the inner solicitation to evil aroused by the outer trial is from ourselves. The substantive πειρασμός denotes the objective trial, while the verb πειράζομαι denotes a more subjective temptation (NIDNTTE 3, 694-303).

λεγέτω: Present active imperative third person singular. There is no lessening of the imperatival force the third person of the imperative mood.

ὅτι: The conjunction ὅτι can introduce both a direct and an indirect quotation. Here it introduces a direct quotation so the ὅτι is not translated and functions like an initial quotation mark (Wallace 454-55).

Ἀπὸ θεοῦ πειράζομαι· The preposition is capitalized because this is a hypothetical direct quotation that serves as the direct object of λεγέτω. While we might expect the preposition ὑπό at this point, it is ἀπό, which expresses a remoter source, compared with the personal agency conveyed by ὑπό (cf. Harris 59, 222).

ὁ γὰρ θεὸς: The causal γὰρ gives the reason why the previous statement is wrong. The nominative θεὸς is the subject of an unexpressed copulative verb.

ἀπείραστός ... κακῶν: The predicate adjective ἀπείραστός is not found elsewhere in NT nor in the LXX. The Vulgate gives it an active sense, "God is not one who tempts to evil" (Deus enim intemptator malorum est). This interpretation, however, would make the next clause (πειράζει δέ) contradictory. The force of a verbal adjective ending in -τος can express possibility. Coupled with the alpha privative prefix the form then connotes the idea of impossibility. For the genitive κακῶν, Wallace (125) suggests a Genitive of Means, "not tempted with evil things." The meaning of the rare word ἀπείραστος must also be determined from the general force of πειράζω in the NT, and especially from the following clause, which is evidently intended to be its corresponding meaning in the active voice (ἀπείραστος: πειράζει δὲ αὐτός). BDAG, 83: "certainly passive, *cannot be tempted.*" See also the discussions in GE, 1603; *TDNT* 6.23–26; and *NIDNTT* 3.798–799, 802, 809.

πειράζει δὲ αὐτὸς οὐδένα: The δὲ signals a development from the previous statement that God cannot be tempted. "Nor" probably conveys the sense well. The expressed personal pronoun αὐτός refers back to θεὸς, expressed probably to avoid any confusion about the subject. It also may intensify the subject ("and he himself"). The direct object of πειράζει is the accusative οὐδένα. This declarative clause, however, apparently conflicts with OT statements where God actually does test/tempt His followers (see Gen 21:1). The lexicons reveal that the semantic field of the entire word group includes both concepts of testing and tempting (BDAG, 792–93; L-N, fields 27 and 88). James utilizes that shared semantic field by moving from one shade of the meaning (testing for a good purpose) in 1:2–4, 12 to the other shade of meaning (enticement for an evil purpose) in 1:13–15. This semantic shift is possible because of the arrangement of the chapter is influenced by word linkage. Thus 1:12 and 1:13–16 are linked by the words πειρασμός and πειράζω rather than by their semantic equivalence. God is immediately behind the idea of a "test," which has clearly been implied earlier in 1:2–4. But while He is ultimately behind all things as a providential ruler, God is not the immediate seducer to sin. The one who is that seducer is Satan/the Devil, and has been described by those terms in the Chronicler's handling of David's sin (cf. 1 Chron 21:1 with 2 Sam 21:1). While Satan/the devil is not mentioned by name in this passage, his role as a solicitor to evil should not be discounted. The "devil" actually is mentioned later in that very role (Jas 4:7).

To summarize the teaching of this challenging verse, James commands in the third person ("No one") rather than in the second person ("You"). The accent, therefore, falls on "No one." Even one exception would besmirch God's character. Nothing in His character makes him succumb to temptation, so there is nothing in His character that would make him tempt anyone else to sin. Therefore, no one should blame him for a temptation or excuse their yielding because God wanted him to yield.

1:14 ἕκαστος: Nominative singular subject of πειράζεται. The choice of this more specific substantival adjective (BDAG, 298b "each one") rather than a general pronoun like αὐτός is deliberate.

δὲ: Signals development from the wrong source of temptation in 1:13 to the correct source here.

πειράζεται: Present passive indicative third singular of πειράζω (see previous discussion of the semantics of this verb).

ὑπὸ τῆς ἰδίας ἐπιθυμίας: The preposition ὑπὸ "with the genitive of the thing personifies the thing" (Harris 220). See this also in Matt 14:24; Rom 3:21; and Col 2:18. The possessive pronoun ἰδίας is genitive feminine modifying ἐπιθυμίας. The noun ἐπιθυμία basically means desire, and by itself is neutral, gaining its moral sense from the worth of the object desired. In the LXX, ἐπιθυμία and ἐπιθυμέω are defined by their object (Muraoka, 272). The Decalogue forbids any ἐπιθυμία for a neighbor's wife or property (Exod 20:17; Deut 5:21). Yet the ἐπιθυμία of a righteous person is acceptable (Prov 10:24). Its use for sexual desire, however, enables the term easily to slide into the meaning of "lust" (BDAG, 372). If God is not the source of temptation, James points deep within our inner persons: our own desires.

ἐξελκόμενος καὶ δελεαζόμενος: Both verbs are present passive participles nominative singular. The first verb (ἐξέλκω, "drag away," BDAG, 347; "pull away," GE, 720) is another *hapax legomenon* in James, while the second verb (δελεάζω, "lure, entice," BDAG, 217; "to bait," GE, 464) is used elsewhere only in 2 Pet 2:14, also in a metaphorical sense of the snare of false teachers. Some commentators (Mayor, 51; Witherington, 434) see the temporal participles as fishing and hunting terms applied to the snares of temptation. The desire, like a creature, is drawn out of its "normal" sphere and then seduced by the bait.

1:15 εἶτα: This adverb appears 16 times in the NT, but only here in James, and always initiates a clause.

ἡ ἐπιθυμία: The article ἡ has an anaphoric function pointing back to the mention of ἐπιθυμίας in 1:14. The noun here functions as the subject of the following τίκτει. For the meaning of ἐπιθυμία, see the previous verse.

συλλαβοῦσα: Aorist active participle, nominative feminine singular of συλλαμβάνω, "conceive" (BDAG, 955.3). The participle is temporal. The verb appears 16 times in the NT, but only 5 times with the meaning of "conceive" and only here in a metaphorical sense (Lk 1:24, 31, 36; 2:21).

τίκτει: While the verb τίκτω means to literally give birth (Matt 1:21; John 16:21; Rev 12:4), it had been used metaphorically by Plato (*Symp.* 212A; GE, 2116) as well as in earlier Jewish literature (*Sib. Or.* 3.235; Prov 10:23).

ἁμαρτίαν: This accusative direct object of τίκτει is the first of 7 appearances of this noun in James (see also 2:15b; 2:9; 4:17; 5:15, 16, 20). A popular argument is that ἁμαρτία is best understood by the original meaning of the cognate verb ἁμαρτάνω as "to miss the mark." Silva cautions that "the actual usage of this word group in extrabib. writers does not indicate that Gk. speakers typically attached to it the specific sense "miss the mark" (NIDNTTE, 1, 256). GE (102) mentions this literal meaning in only a couple of writers. Silva adds: "The only (NT) passage where perhaps it could be argued that the vb. reflects the notion "miss the mark" is Rom 3:23, but even here the clause 'fall short of the glory of God' clearly refers not to the *nature* of sin but rather to its *consequences*. Instead, the actual images associated with the concept of sin incl. rebellion, corruption, violation, trespassing, disobedience, etc." (259).

ἡ δὲ ἁμαρτία: The δὲ does not signal contrast but further development from the preceding clause. See above for ἁμαρτία.

ἀποτελεσθεῖσα: Aorist passive participle nominative feminine singular of ἀποτελέω, "bring to completion, finish" (BDAG, 123). There are seven circumstantial participles in 1:13–15, comprising the most intense concentration of participles in the book. The four vivid temporal participles in vv. 14 and 15 colorfully convey the sequential drama of the analogy in 1:14–15 ("lured," "enticed," "conceived," "finished").

ἀποκύει: Present active indicative third singular. This verb means literally "give birth to" (BDAG, 1004) and was rarely used, even in Attic

Greek (GE, 255). Here and in 1:18 it has a metaphorical meaning. There is more than one birth here, and it is better to view the analogy as describing the birth of both a child (sin) and a grandchild (death). "The focus of James is not a technical analysis of the process of sin but a rhetorical laying of blame on the individual for succumbing in various ways to desire" (McKnight, 120). The verb will be used again of *God* in 1:18. Two different words used in this verse of the actual "birth" event—τίκτει and ἀποκύει—but efforts to find what distinguishes them seem at times a bit strained. James often creatively uses synonyms for language variety.

θάνατον: Accusative direct object of ἀποκύει. Death occurs at the end of life and for non-Christians results not only in physical death but in eternal punishment, which elsewhere is called "the second death" (Rev 2:11; 20:6, 14; 21:8). We should probably see here a current sense of death as spiritual separation (cf. Gen 2:16–17; Rom 6:23). James' only other use of the word in 5:20 points to this meaning here.

The verse displays a rhetorical balance with two independent clauses connected by δὲ, with each clause having an articular subject followed by a participle plus a verb and direct object.

ἡ ἐπιθυμία   συλλαβοῦσα   τίκτει   ἁμαρτίαν,
ἡ ἁμαρτία   ἀποτελεσθεῖσα   ἀποκύει   θάνατον.

Conclusion

The rhetorical device of *gradatio,* noted earlier in 1:2–4, can also be seen here in the description of a progression from temptation on to desire on to conception on to birth and finally on to death in 1:14, 15. If so, it is a reversed *gradatio,* leading toward death, not toward maturity as in 1:2–4. There are ten words in this passage found in the Louw and Nida Semantic Domain 88: "Moral/Ethical Qualities and Related Behavior" and thus dominate the paragraph. These are the six πειραcognates, κακῶν, δελεαζόμενος and ἁμαρτία/ν (twice). This repetition of semantically related words creates a "semantic chain." The chain begins with the topic statement, "Blessed is the man who remains steadfast under a trial (πειρασμόν)," and continues through the passage until the final comment clause: "and sin (ἁμαρτία) when it is fully grown brings forth death." The reader should also recognize that this chain reaches back to 1:2.

3

DO NOT BE DECEIVED ABOUT GOD'S GOOD GIFTS (1:16-18)

Greek Text

16 Μὴ πλανᾶσθε, ἀδελφοί μου ἀγαπητοί. **17** πᾶσα δόσις ἀγαθὴ καὶ πᾶν δώρημα τέλειον ἄνωθέν ἐστιν καταβαῖνονἀπὸ τοῦ πατρὸς τῶν φώτων, παρ' ᾧ οὐκ ἔνι παραλλαγὴ ἢ τροπῆς ἀποσκίασμα. **18** βουληθεὶς ἀπεκύησεν ἡμᾶς λόγῳ ἀληθείας εἰς τὸ εἶναι ἡμᾶς ἀπαρχήν τινα τῶν αὐτοῦ κτισμάτων.

Sentence Flow and Translation

16 Μὴ πλανᾶσθε, ἀδελφοί μου ἀγαπητοί.
   Do not be deceived, my beloved brothers.

17 πᾶσα δόσις ἀγαθὴ καὶ πᾶν δώρημα τέλειον ἄνωθέν ἐστιν
   Every good act of giving and every complete gift is from above,

   καταβαῖνον ἀπὸ τοῦ πατρὸς τῶν φώτων,
   coming down from the Father of the lights

παρ' ᾧ οὐκ ἔνι παραλλαγὴ ἢ τροπῆς ἀποσκίασμα.
with whom there is no variation or shadow due
to change.

18 βουληθεὶς ἀπεκύησεν ἡμᾶς λόγῳ ἀληθείας
When he decided, he gave birth to us by the word of truth

εἰς τὸ εἶναι ἡμᾶς ἀπαρχήν τινα τῶν αὐτοῦ κτισμάτων.
that we should be a first portion of his created beings.

Context

The paragraph opens with the collocation of a nominative of direct
address (or vocative plural), ἀδελφοί μου ἀγαπητοί, and a negated
imperative, πλανᾶσθε that is fronted for emphasis. Other such negated
commands accompanying ἀδελφοί are in 2:1; 3:1; 4:11; and 5:9. With this
repeated pattern, James provides cohesion to his composition and also
advances the subjects by successive shifts in topics. While this
linguistic marker does introduce a new paragraph, the semantic links
between these paragraphs should also not be ignored. Some
commentators have seen this command as linking closer to what was
previously written than to the following verses (Blomberg-Kamell, 72).
Others have preferred to view this little paragraph as the closing
section of 1:2–18 (Dibelius, 99). Combining the address with the
imperative, however, introduces enough of a semantic shift that
strongly suggests the beginning of a separate paragraph, with 1:19–27
as the closing paragraph. James desires that his readers not be led
astray from their faith commitment that God only gives good gifts. But
since an overall theme (trials and God) does overlap these sections, it
is also appropriate to view 1:16 as a bridge between 1:2–15 and 17–18.

Exegetical Comments

1:16 Μὴ πλανᾶσθε: This is the negated present passive imperative of

92

πλανάω (BDAG, 821). It opens another section of James as is so often the case in the book (see above). It appears 126 times in the LXX with the sense of "wander about, not knowing whither heading" (Muraoka, 56, and often in diatribal Greek literature (e.g., Epictetus). The verb can mean either "to wander" or "to err" (GE, 1673; see e.g., Matt 18:12– 13), and it is used in that sense later in James 5:19. In the passive, it can mean "to be led astray" (Deut 11:28) or "to be deceived/in error" (Deut 4:19; Luke 21:8). This specific command conveyed by the negated aorist imperative appears elsewhere in the NT (1 Cor 6:9; 15:33; Gal 6:7) and also in Ignatius (*Eph.* 5:2; 16:1; *Phld.* 3:3). In each of these examples the writer is calling attention to a decisive statement about God expressed in the form of a proverbial saying. Furthermore, these admonitions refer not to some intellectual error about divine ways, but to a serious error that strikes at the heart of faith itself. This is also the case here, since what follows are statements about God's goodness.

ἀδελφοί μου ἀγαπητοί: For the first time, the brothers addressed are also called *beloved* (ἀγαπητοί), an affectionate term that James later includes in the openings of paragraphs in 1:19 and 2:5. Would James deliberately choose this substantival adjective to address the brothers or is this addition simply a change for stylistic reasons? In using similar terms for being deceived in 1:19 (πλανᾶσθε) and in 1:22 (παραλογιζόμενοι), James is concerned that his readers not be deceived into wrong thinking about God (1:17), His word (1:22), and what He says about the poor (1:27 and 2:5). There is a common concern in each of these instances where he uses the term ἀγαπητοί. The deep concern that he has about his readers being deceived and led astray by wrong thinking in each of these three paragraphs evidently leads James to employ the more pastoral expression, "beloved brothers."

1:17 πᾶσα δόσις ἀγαθὴ καὶ πᾶν δώρημα τέλειον: The main idea of 1:17a is quite clear. It is that the good God always gives good gifts. There are, however, two important linguistic issues involved in that simple affirmation. The first relates to the use of two synonyms, δόσις and δώρημα. Did James intend to make a fine distinction between these two terms, both of which can simply mean "gift"? Many commentators, heeding some recent cautions about the abuse of synonyms, conclude that more likely the terms are synonymous (Moo, 77; Blomberg-Kamell, 73). Even with these warnings in mind, we are still justified in seeing here a careful difference in nuance between these two words. Both of these words rarely appear in the NT, with δόσις only occurring elsewhere in Matt 6:1 and Phil 4:15. Furthermore, while δόσις describes the human actions of giving and receiving, it can also refer to gift-giving by God (Sir 26:14). It is used elsewhere in the LXX only once (Sir 34:18), and appears only once among the Apostolic Fathers (*Hermas* 34:2). The second word for "gift," δώρημα, occurs elsewhere in the NT only in Rom 5:16 but is used in the LXX 21 t. and again in Apostolic Fathers only twice (*Hermas* 27:4; 51:7). A third more common word is δῶρον which appears 19 t. in the NT and 170 t. in the LXX. This last word is the one that is most often used for human gifts to God. The two words in James 1:17, however, are describing divine gifts. A general morphological observation is that nouns ending in -σις express the action of the verbal root while nouns ending in -μα stress the result of the action implied in the verbal root.

James desires his readers to know that every action of God's giving is "good" (ἀγαθή) and every result of God's giving is "complete" (τέλειον). A further confirmation of this distinction is the repetition of the little adjective, πᾶσα/πᾶν, with each of the two nouns. It is certainly true that we should be careful about imagining distinctions based on a too simple approach to lexical analysis. On the other hand, we should not ignore such choices when the evidence from the context points to a possible reason for his choice. The possibility of an appropriate choice between these nuanced definitions of "good" in the context (the repetition of πᾶσα/πᾶν) should not be overlooked. James is telling us that just as the good and complete God gives us only good and complete gifts, so He also desires that His new creations be good and complete persons!

ἄνωθέν ἐστιν καταβαῖνον: The second linguistic challenge in 1:17 is to determine if the copula ἐστιν is related directly to the adverb ἄνωθέν that precedes it, or to the participle καταβαῖνον that follows it. The latter choice makes the participle periphrastic ("is coming down"), and the first choice makes the participle simply adverbial ("is from above, coming down"). The similar use of the copula-adverb-participle in 3:14 (ἔστιν αὕτη ἡ σοφία ἄνωθεν κατερχομένη) seems to point to the periphrastic use, although the word order there is different. Commentators are divided over the issue, as well as grammarians. Wallace sees a periphrastic participle as "possible" and Moule writes that "it need not be periphrastic at all." I view the participle as adverbial, because of a need to repeat the "is" and add an "and" to make better sense ("the gift is from above *and is* coming down"). The choice here is based more on a smooth translation rather than on some clear grammatical "rule."

ἀπὸ τοῦ πατρὸς τῶν φώτων: God is termed as "Father" and more specifically as the "father of *the* lights" (τοῦ πατρὸς τῶν φώτων, note the article). This use of "Father" as expressing "source" is quite Hebraic and Jewish readers would recognize the reference to God as the creator of the heavenly luminaries that give us light. As a divine title, it naturally refers to the stars, which are called "lights" (φῶτα) in the LXX of Jer 4:23 and Ps 135:7. The *Assumption of Moses* (36, 38) describes God as "Father of lights" (ἐνώπιον τοῦ φωτὸς τῶν ὅλων, τοῦ πατρὸς τῶν φώτων). With biblical texts also describing God as the creator of the heavenly bodies (Ps 136:7, τῷ ποιήσαντι φῶτα μεγάλα μόνῳ; Jer 4:23, ἐπέβλεψα ... εἰς τὸν οὐρανόν, καὶ οὐκ ἦν τὰ φῶτα αὐτοῦ), and as the ultimate source of all light and blessings (Ps 36:9, ἐν τῷ φωτί σου ὀψόμεθα φῶς), it is evident that James is utilizing a very recognizable Jewish metaphor. All of this is quite appropriate to James' point that all gifts, whether they be natural or supernatural, come down to us from a loving and giving Father.

παρ' ᾧ οὐκ ἔνι: The verb ἔνι here is the short form of ἔνεστιν from ἔνειμι (BDAG, 316; GE, 697), used in the NT elsewhere only in negative constructions like this one (1 Cor 6:5; Gal 3:28; Col 3:11).

παραλλαγὴ ἢ τροπῆς ἀποσκίασμα: In this elegant expression, the noun παραλλαγὴ signifies "change" or "alteration" (BDAG, 768). The noun τροπή occurs frequently in astrological contexts, usually for solstices (Deut 33:14; Job 38:33; Wis 7:18; BDAG, 1016; GE, 1556). Finally, the noun ἀποσκίασμα literally means "shadow" (BDAG, 120). Here, it is the shadow cast by the alteration of a heavenly light.

The placing of the genitive τροπῆς before its head noun ἀποσκίασμα is unusual although not improper. It is difficult to properly classify the function of this genitive. Robertson calls it an "objective genitive" ("a shadow 'cast by' turning"). It may simply be a descriptive genitive (NIV's and CSB's "shifting shadows" or ESV's "shadow due to change"). Why is there such an abrupt introduction of a divine attribute at this point? Furthermore, why is this particular attribute—namely, the immutability of God—utilized in the argument? The answers to these questions lie in recognizing that James' desire in this encyclical is to direct his readers to become whole and complete persons (1:4). The God who has gifted "us" to become his spiritual creation by the word of truth (1:18) is also Himself undivided and complete! It is not necessary to see this as an abstract theological description of divine immutability, although that attribute is certainly true! Consistent with his concern expressed throughout his writing, the purpose of James is more ethical than metaphysical.

1:18 βουληθείς: While the use of the aorist passive participle βουληθείς is not irregular, its passive voice and its being fronted prior to the main verb merits some reflection. The verb is a θη middle because a passive translation makes no sense. The participle form of βούλομαι appears thirteen times in the NT, but everywhere apart from James 1:18 it is in the present middle form βουλόμενος in its various cases (e.g., Mark 15:15; Acts 12:4; 22:30; 23:28; 27:43; 2 Cor 1:17; Heb 6:17; 2 Pet 3:9). This specific form does not appear in the LXX, but Philo employs it twenty times of the divine will, and always in a temporal sense. Typical of these uses is *Virtues* 188: "For when God decided [βουληθείς] to establish this in us out of his own exceeding mercy..." Most English versions translate the participle here in an "instrumental" sense. Typical is the KJV and ESV's "Of his own will," or the CSB's "By his own choice." However, since the only other use of βουληθείς in Judeo-Christian literature is in a temporal sense, a temporal rather than an instrumental force should be preferred. Closer examination reveals that a clear instrumental dative later in the verse conveys that the divine word is the means by which he gave birth to us. Therefore, we should render the verse: "*When he decided*, he gave birth to us *by* the word of truth [λόγῳ ἀληθείας]." The Maker of the lights was sovereign in His creation of his natural "children" in the heavens. He was also sovereign in the timing of the creation of His supernatural children on earth.

ἀπεκύησεν ἡμᾶς λόγῳ ἀληθείας: For the aorist verb ἀπεκύησεν, see the discussion in 1:15 and the previous discussion of βουληθείς. The specific nature of this "word" (λόγῳ) of truth will be explored further in 1:21–23, and also in the references to the "law of liberty" in 1:25 and 2:12, and finally the reference to the "royal law" in 2:8. James follows his mention of "the word" here with a reference to the "implanted word" which "saves your souls" in 1:21. Therefore, the "truthful message" (descriptive genitive ἀληθείας) is the message that contains the truth about the Messiah (2:1). The other references to this expression also supports this "gospel" interpretation (2 Cor 6:7; Eph 1:13; Col 1:5; 2 Tim 2:15).

εἰς τὸ εἶναι ἡμᾶς: The infinitive with εἰς τὸ plus the accusative subject of the infinitive ἡμᾶς conveys God's purpose for these believers. The use of the indefinite enclitic τινα has the effect of heightening the metaphorical nature of the analogy with agriculture and with sacrificial offerings.

ἀπαρχήν τινα τῶν αὐτοῦ κτισμάτων. In the LXX, the word ἀπαρχή translates a number of different Hebrew terms for the offering to God of the first animals or vegetation from either field or flock (Exo 22:28;

25:2–3; Lev 2:12; Num 15:20–21; Deut 18:4). In Exod 23:19, it is defined as the "first produce of the earth." In the NT, however, the term is always used as a figure for the pledge of the Spirit (Rom 8:23); for the first one to rise from the dead (1 Cor 15:20, 23); for the founding of the early Christian communities (Rom 16:5; 1 Cor 16:15); for the elect in heaven (Rev 14:4); and for the remnant of believing Israel (Rom 11:16; see Johnson, 198). Commentators have identified the firstfruits here as a general reference to believers in the apostolic period (McCartney, 112–13). However, since James is writing specifically to Jewish believers, it is better to interpret the first fruits as referring to the Jewish messianic community (McKnight, 131). These Jewish believers in Jesus as Messiah (2:1) composed the earliest group of all those who later would accept the gospel. In keeping with the OT concept that the firstfruits were a pledge of the harvest to come, these Jewish believers are the "down payment" or first installment of the later harvest that would eventually include the many Gentile believers in the body of the Messiah (see also Rom 8:19–23).

Conclusion

This semantically rich paragraph is an eloquent transition between 1:2–15, which describes God's gracious giving of wisdom for the trials, and 1:19–27, which stresses God's gracious giving of His word to bring forth new life within His children.

4

BECOME GOOD HEARERS
AND DOERS (1:19-27)

Hearing and Doing (1:19-21)

Greek Text

19 ᵃ῎Ιστε, ἀδελφοί μου ἀγαπητοί· ἔστω δὲ πᾶς ἄνθρωπος ταχὺς εἰς τὸ ἀκοῦσαι, βραδὺς εἰς τὸ λαλῆσαι, βραδὺς εἰς ὀργήν· 20 ὀργὴ γὰρ ἀνδρὸς δικαιοσύνην θεοῦ ᵇοὐκ ἐργάζεται. 21 διὸ ἀποθέμενοι πᾶσαν ῥυπαρίαν καὶ περισσείαν κακίας ἐν πραΰτητι, δέξασθε τὸν ἔμφυτον λόγον τὸν δυνάμενον σῶσαι τὰς ψυχὰς ὑμῶν.

Textual Notes

The relative stability of the Greek text in James is again illustrated by the fact that there are only two important textual variant issues in 1:19–27, one in 1:19 and the other in 1:27. More important than variations in wording is a punctuation issue regarding a comma placement in 1:21, which will be dealt with in the commentary.

19.a. Instead of the abrupt ῎Ιστε opening 1:19, the Byzantine family of manuscripts and the Textus Receptus connect the following ἔστω δὲ (dropping δὲ) more closely with 1:18 by substituting ὥστε, which is supported by a variety of later witnesses (K Π Ψ 614 *Byz* syrᵖ; Metzger, 115). The reading adopted as the text, however, is strongly supported by both Alexandrian and Western witnesses (ℵᶜ B C 81 1739 it vg). Furthermore, it is to be preferred as the more difficult reading because the later reading looks like a scribal attempt to smooth out what was considered as a rarely used form followed by an awkward word order. There is probably no clearer example of the Byzantine scribal effort to smooth over some of the perceived roughness of the Greek than these variant readings in 1:19.

1:20.b. NA27: ὀργὴ γὰρ ἀνδρὸς δικαιοσύνην θεοῦ <u>οὐκ ἐργάζεται</u>.

1:20 MAJ: ὀργὴ γὰρ ἀνδρὸς δικαιοσύνην θεοῦ <u>οὐ κατεργάζεται</u>.

1:20 NA28: ὀργὴ γὰρ ἀνδρὸς δικαιοσύνην θεοῦ <u>οὐ κατεργάζεται</u>.

NA28 now agrees with MAJ. NIV, SBLGNT, and THGNT follow NA27.

Sentence Flow and Translation

19 Ἴστε, ἀδελφοί μου ἀγαπητοί·
   Know this, my beloved brothers:

ἔστω δὲ πᾶς ἄνθρωπος ταχὺς εἰς τὸ ἀκοῦσαι,
So every person must be quick to hear,

βραδὺς εἰς τὸ λαλῆσαι,
slow to speak,

βραδὺς εἰς ὀργήν·
slow to anger;

20 ὀργὴ γὰρ ἀνδρὸς δικαιοσύνην θεοῦ οὐκ ἐργάζεται.
   for a man's anger does not produce the righteousness God requires.

21 διὸ ἀποθέμενοι πᾶσαν ῥυπαρίαν καὶ περισσείαν κακίας
Therefore putting away all filthiness and rampant wickedness

ἐν πραΰτητι δέξασθε τὸν ἔμφυτον λόγον
receive with meekness the implanted word

τὸν δυνάμενον σῶσαι τὰς ψυχὰς ὑμῶν.
which is able to save your souls.

Context

James 1:19–27 is introduced by the combination of a nominative plural of direct address (ἀδελφοί) with an imperatival command (Ἴστε). In agreement with the UBS5, we discern three subparagraphs within this larger section (1:19–21; 22–25; 26–27). The διὸ clause-complex in 1:21 concludes the first section (1:19–21). The repeated beatitude pronounced in 1:25b (οὗτος μακάριος ἐν τῇ ποιήσει αὐτοῦ ἔσται) concludes the second section (1:22–25). The third section (1:26–27) consists of three life-related examples of what it means to be the "doer of the word" described in 1:22–25. The first subparagraph (1:19–21) is composed of five clauses, four of which are primary and two of which are secondary participial clauses, along with three embedded infinitive clauses, as can be seen in the above sentence flow analysis.

Exegetical Comments

1:19 Ἴστε: The first question is how to translate Ἴστε, which in its form can be either the perfect imperative or the perfect indicative of the verb οἶδα. It is a rare form, appearing only twice elsewhere in the NT (Eph 5:5; Heb 12:17). Earlier commentators preferred the indicative here (Mayor, 65; Hort, 35; but also Reicke, 19–20). There have, however, always been commentators who have preferred the imperative (Ropes, 168; Dibelius, 108–09; Davids, 91; Moo, 2000, 82; Blomberg-Kamell, 85; McCartney, 114), although the indicative also has its recent advocates (McKnight, 135). Generally those favoring an indicative say that James is appealing to the readers' knowledge of what he has just written, while advocates of the imperative say that he is calling attention to what follows.

The imperative is preferred for a number of reasons. (1) It is consistent with the style of James, who uses the imperative more than any other NT writer, especially when opening a new paragraph. (2) The other two occurrences of the form (Eph 5:5; Heb 12:17) may be indicative, but each is introduced by a causal γάρ, which is not the case here with its absolute, standalone appeal for the readers to know what follows. (3) In the other uses of "beloved brothers," James calls attention to what follows, which is more consistent with the imperative usage (1:16; 2:5). (4) In these passages James is fond of using what linguists call a "meta-comment"—an orienter that is not necessary to the sentence but calls attention to what is about to be said ("do not be deceived"; "listen"; see also "above all things" in 5:12).

This is the only time that a perfect, and not a present or aorist imperative, opens a new paragraph. Why? It is becoming recognized that the perfect tense conveys greater prominence in a sentence than do the other tense forms. The word functions as a meta-comment to call attention to the imperative ἔστω that is then followed by three infinitives. Specifically how those infinitives convey the message in this paragraph will now be examined.

ἀδελφοί μου ἀγαπητοί: See comments on this address in 1:16.

ἔστω δὲ πᾶς ἄνθρωπος: The third person imperative of εἰμί is as strong as any of the second person imperatives in the book ("must be"). Any translation that leaves an impression of permission and not of a command reflects an English phenomenon and does not reflect the Greek imperatival force. It is the imperative ἔστω that introduces what the readers need to "know."

The postpositive δὲ may seem out of place and unnecessary in the flow of the sentence. Hort's explanation makes sense of its presence.

Here St James repeats positively what he has said negatively in *v.* 16. In *vv.* 13–15 he was combating error; and then he finally says Μὴ πλανᾶσθε as introductory to his fundamental doctrine of 17, 18. That doctrine being now set forth, he a second time calls attention to it on the positive side, as the basis of what he is going to say. 'Know it well, my beloved brethren (the old address repeated). And on the other hand' (δὲ, with tacit reference to the acquiescence in evil hinted at in *v.* 13) (Hort, 35).

ταχὺς εἰς τὸ ἀκοῦσαι, βραδὺς εἰς τὸ λαλῆσαι, βραδὺς εἰς ὀργήν: What the reader should know is conveyed by two adjectives (ταχὺς and βραδὺς twice), each of which is followed by εἰς plus two articular infinitives and one noun. Commentators query why there are two infinitives plus a noun. The infinitives are usually described as epexegetical, explaining further the adjectives that precede them (Wallace 607). The preposition εἰς that precedes all three expressions, however, may be the key. Every person (the generic ἄνθρωπος) must be swift *with reference to* hearing, slow *with reference to* speaking, slow *with reference to* wrath. Thus the infinitive verbal nouns parallel better the final noun as objects of the preposition εἰς. This use of εἰς is attested in BDAG, 291: "marker of a specific point of reference, *for, to, with respect to, with reference to.*" The third completer of the imperative, "slow to anger" (βραδὺς εἰς ὀργήν), slightly breaks the grammatical pattern of adjective plus infinitive, perhaps for rhetorical effect.

The adjectives ("swift" and "slow") and the infinitives that complete the imperative ἔστω actually convey the expected imperatival commands in the paragraph rather than the initial imperative Ἴστε, which only calls attention to them. These expressions also function to introduce the topics of the entire paragraph. The three commands, "every person must be quick to hear, slow to speak, slow to anger," are then further developed in various ways in the entire passage through 1:27. The subject of being "quick to hear" is developed further in 1:22–25. The subject of being "slow to speak" is developed further in 1:27. The subject of being "slow to wrath" is developed further in 1:20–21.

This triad also introduces three prominent themes in the book. These three themes are: 1) becoming swift to hear and do; 2) becoming slow to speak; and 3) becoming slow to anger. The rare perfect form Ἴστε, therefore, raises to greater prominence these themes that James is about to elaborate.

That "hearing" God's will cannot be separated from "doing" sounds a distinctive chord in James and he will pick up on that point very soon (1:22). The repetition of the adjective βραδὺς in the second and third of these commands is intentional. It is striking how often anger and speech go together, and the implication that believers should not be quick to follow their own desires and designs is a common theme in the wisdom literature (Prov 10:9; 13:3; 15:1; 29:11, 20; Eccl 9:18; Sir 1:22–24).

1:20 ὀργὴ γὰρ ἀνδρός: The causal conjunction γὰρ introduces the reason why the anger just mentioned is to be avoided. James turns first to the third member of that triad of behaviors he has just commended and condemned. He describes the negative consequences of anger first because he just mentioned it last. But if we are correct in our analysis of the entire paragraph, he will then turn his attention to the first one, hearing, in 1:22–25, and then the second one, speaking, in 1:27. As he did earlier (1:7–8), James moves from the use of the more generic ἄνθρωπος in 1:19 to the more masculine word ἀνδρός here. Recent commentators either ignore this switch of terms or see both terms as generic, as they appear to be in 1:7–8 (Blomberg-Kamell, 86). Older commentators often discerned an intentional distinction with the male person in view in 1:20 (Mayor, 65). Johnson (200) maintains a balance in this regard while still drawing a distinction between the words: "Although in antiquity, anger was associated more with men than with women ... the maxim obviously applies to all humans."

δικαιοσύνην θεοῦ οὐκ ἐργάζεται: It is better to translate ἐργάζεται as "produce," as in 2 Cor 7:10, where it alternates with κατεργάζεσθαι ("to produce"). What does James specifically mean by the genitive expression "righteousness of God" that cannot be "produced" by the angry man? If the genitive θεοῦ conveys "source," it is easy to read into this familiar expression the Pauline meaning of a right standing before God (Rom 3:21–22). But it is wrong to think that James must always use the phrase in the same way that Paul does, which is a common mistake that leads to confusion at many points. James is writing before Paul had written any of his letters and probably has no direct knowledge of Paul's teaching. James must be read rather against the background of the OT and the teaching of Jesus. To be sure, James shares with Paul the use of Gen 15:6, with its reference to "righteousness" (2:23). But the word "righteousness" in 1:20 must be understood in light of the verb that governs it (cf. Acts 10:35; Heb 11:33). The translation "produce righteousness" makes it very difficult to think that James could be referring to God's gift of a righteous standing—the sense in which Paul most often uses it. James uses the phrase "produce righteousness" with the meaning it normally has in the Bible: to do what God requires of his people. Jesus used the word "righteousness" this way when he called on his followers to exhibit a "righteousness" that exceeds that of the Pharisees (Matt 5:20; see also Matt 5:6, 10; 6:33). This usage of θεοῦ, which may be called the "objective genitive" (McCartney, 115), makes the best sense in this verse. We may compare with this idea the phrase δίκαιοι ἐνώπιον τοῦ Θεοῦ in Luke 1:6 (Zechariah and Elizabeth); in Acts 4:19; 8:21; and in 1 Pet 3:4.

1:21 διὸ ἀποθέμενοι: The διὸ introduces a further application of the warnings in 1:19–21. The aorist middle participle ἀποθέμενοι assumes the mood of the imperative δέξασθε in the following clause, as is expected with attendant circumstance participles (Wallace 640). The verb ἀποτίθημι (BDAG, 123.1) is used for removing clothes in Acts 7:58 and this meaning is applied metaphorically in the NT for the "stripping off" a non-Christian lifestyle from the walk of a believer (Rom 13:12; Eph 4:22, 25; Col 3:8; Heb 12:1; 1 Pet 2:1).

πᾶσαν ῥυπαρίαν καὶ περισσείαν κακίας: The colorful word ῥυπαρίαν applies to this spiritual sphere the literal meaning of "dirtiness" (see the literal use of the cognate adjective for physical "filthiness" of clothes in 2:2). We have rendered the expression περισσείαν κακίας as "rampant wickedness" despite my sentimental fondness for the quaint expression in the KJV, "superfluity of naughtiness." Thus we see that anger, filthiness, and wickedness each can impede the beneficial reception of the word and are the attitudes that one must "put off." This colorful analogy drawn from one's clothing has its best commentary in the familiar Pauline dynamic of "putting off" and "putting on" in Eph 4:17–24. While recognizing the colorful language in the verse, it is also possible to take note of a rhetorical punch that only those listening to the oral recitation of this book could appreciate. A deliberate alliteration on the p *or* π sound characterizes this verse in the Greek, with five of its six main words featuring the sound in a prominent syllable (ἀποθέμενοι, πᾶσαν, ῥυπαρίαν, περισσείαν, πραΰτητι). "This alliteration thereby punctuates the exhortation and makes it memorable to the listener" (Witherington, 441).

ἐν πραΰτητι δέξασθε τὸν ἔμφυτον λόγον: A punctuation issue is whether to place a comma before or after the ἐν πραΰτητι. The current critical texts place the comma after the πραΰτητι, so that the phrase is related to the participle ἀποθέμενοι by indicating the way in which we are to put off anger (i.e., "put away wickedness with meekness"). No English version that I have been able to find, however, translates ἐν πραΰτητι with the previous clause. The NA28/UBS5 texts remove the comma and leave the decision to the reader. Perhaps the earlier editors were uncomfortable with placing a prepositional phrase like ἐν πραΰτητι before the imperative δέξασθε in the following clause. James does this again, however, in 2:1 when he places ἐν προσωπολημψίαις before the imperative ἔχετε! The fronting of the phrase, rather than being ungrammatical, actually lends a greater prominence on the attitude required of the brothers when they receive the word, namely with humility and not with anger.

Some commentators suggest that the "ingrafted word" (τὸν ἔμφυτον λόγον) refers to the reception of a word already implanted within us, as in Luke 21:19: "possess your souls" (Hort, 37). This is doubtful, however, because of the command to receive the word, for how could we receive the word if it is innately implanted within us? The command is probably proleptic—namely, as we receive the word it becomes implanted. Or the command to receive the word given to believers is to pay attention closely to the word that has been implanted. The colorful expression is the second link in a semantic chain that extends from the λόγῳ ἀληθείας in 1:18 to the third link, ποιηταὶ λόγου, in 1:22 and then to the final νόμον τέλειον in 1:25. Receiving, responding to, and obeying the word is the theme that dominates the entire paragraph.

τὸν δυνάμενον σῶσαι τὰς ψυχὰς ὑμῶν. The attributive participle clause includes a complementary infinitive (δύναμαι normally is followed by such an infinitive) with a direct object. This expression "to save your souls" does not refer to the initial experience of salvation, as in the idea that we should "save souls." The expression actually refers to the ongoing and continuous (note the imperfective aspect of δυνάμενον) work of restoring and rescuing the inner life of believers. This is obvious when one recognizes that James is addressing "brothers" (1:19) who have already been "birthed" through a supernatural word from God (1:18). To save "your souls" by no means excludes the salvation of the body, but no contrast between soul and body is even implied. This perspective is reflected also in 5:20, which promises that one rescuing a brother will "save his soul from death." The "soul" may thus be used as a metonymy for the entire person (BDAG, 1099.3), a usage that is quite common in James and in both testaments (see Acts 2:41: "about three thousand souls").

Deceived or Blessed? (1:22-25)

Greek Text

22 Γίνεσθε δὲ ποιηταὶ λόγου καὶ μὴ μόνον ἀκροαταὶ παραλογιζόμενοι ἑαυτούς. 23 ὅτι εἴ τις ἀκροατὴς λόγου ἐστὶν καὶ οὐ ποιητής, οὗτος ἔοικεν ἀνδρὶ κατανοοῦντι τὸ πρόσωπον τῆς γενέσεως αὐτοῦ ἐν ἐσόπτρῳ· 24 κατενόησεν γὰρ ἑαυτὸν καὶ ᵃἀπελήλυθεν καὶ εὐθέως ἐπελάθετο ὁποῖος ἦν. 25 ὁ δὲ παρακύψας εἰς νόμον τέλειον τὸν τῆς ἐλευθερίας καὶ παραμείνας, οὐκ ἀκροατὴς ἐπιλησμονῆς γενόμενος ἀλλὰ ποιητὴς ἔργου, ᵇοὗτος μακάριος ἐν τῇ ποιήσει αὐτοῦ ἔσται.

Textual Notes

There are no textual variants in this section that affect interpretation, with a few medieval readings that attempt to smooth out the apparent roughness of James' grammar.

In 1:22 the SBLGNT, following Codex B and Westcott-Hort, reverses the order of μόνον ἀκροαταὶ in the NA28 and in the Majority Text.

24.a. Some Byzantine scribes also apparently struggled with the perfect tense of ἀπελήλυθεν in 1:24. A few manuscripts have απεληλυθει (43 330 1441), while one adds the aorist απηλθεν (621), and a few change the verb prefix to παρεληλυθεν (38 104 459 1838 1842). The TR has ἀπελήλυθεν.

25.b. P[74] omits the "unnecessary" οὗτος in 1:25b, making the preceding ποιητὴς ἔργου the subject of the following verb ἔσται. This attempt, however, ignores the style of James.

Context

In this paragraph, James develops another one of the triadic virtues that he mentioned in 1:19. Having further developed the expression, "slow to anger" in 1:20–21, he now draws out the command to be "quick to hear" in this section. That conjunction δὲ again links 1:22 with the preceding verses by developing the idea that the one who truly receives the word which is able to save him (1:21) is also the one who should become a "doer" of the word, not just one who "hears" it. The two primary clauses (1:22, 25) serve to bookend the paragraph and function as its inclusio with a cognate noun and verb (1:22, ποιηταί; 1:25, ποιήσει). The secondary clauses between comprise a parable from life about a person who forgets what he looks like in the mirror (1:23–24). The parable serves also to illustrate from real life the meaning of "deceiving yourselves" (1:22b). It also contrasts this self-deception with the hearer/doer who will ultimately be blessed because of his obedience to the word (1:25). This structure can be visualized in the following clausal analysis of 1:22–25. Note the underlined cognate words at the beginning and the end of the passage that serve as an inclusio.

Sentence Flow and Translation

22 Γίνεσθε δὲ <u>ποιηταὶ</u> λόγου καὶ μὴ μόνον ἀκροαταὶ
   But become doers of the word, and not hearers only,

> παραλογιζόμενοι ἑαυτούς.
> deceiving yourselves.

23 ὅτι εἴ τις ἀκροατὴς λόγου ἐστὶν καὶ οὐ ποιητής,
   Because if anyone is a hearer of the word and not a doer,

> οὗτος ἔοικεν ἀνδρὶ κατανοοῦντι τὸ πρόσωπον τῆς γενέσεως αὐτοῦ
> ἐν ἐσόπτρῳ·
> this one is like a man who looks intently at his natural face
> in a mirror.

24 κατενόησεν γὰρ ἑαυτὸν

For he looks at himself

καὶ ἀπελήλυθεν
and goes[1] away

καὶ εὐθέως ἐπελάθετο ὁποῖος ἦν.
and at once forgets what he was like.

25 ὁ δὲ παρακύψας εἰς νόμον τέλειον τὸν τῆς ἐλευθερίας
But the one who looks carefully into the perfect law of liberty,

καὶ παραμείνας,
and perseveres in it,

οὐκ ἀκροατὴς ἐπιλησμονῆς γενόμενος ἀλλὰ ποιητὴς
ἔργου,
being not a forgetful hearer but one who does
the deed,

οὗτος μακάριος ἐν τῇ <u>ποιήσει</u> αὐτοῦ ἔσται.
this one will be blessed in his doing.

Exegetical Comments

1:22 Γίνεσθε δὲ: The imperative γίνεσθε means not simply "be" but in the more dynamic nuance of "become" or "show yourselves to be" (Mayor, 69; Hort, 38; Johnson, 206). BDAG (197) defines γίνομαι as "to experience a change in nature and so indicate entry into a new

---

[1] There is remarkable agreement among the versions in their rendering of this passage. The practice of the NASB to pedantically include "has" in its translation of the aorist and perfect tenses in 1:25 ("He has looked at himself and (has) gone away, he has immediately forgotten") simply betrays a misunderstanding of the stative aspect conveyed through the perfect tense, as will be examined further in the commentary.

condition, *become something*"). The imperfective aspect of the present verb further supports this dynamic idea of process (McKnight, 146). This is consistent with the imperatival function of the verb in 3:1: "do not many of you become (γίνεσθε) teachers," and is also the way James uses the verb in 1:12, 25; 2:4, 10, 11. The issue in 1:22 is one of *becoming* rather than *being*—namely, turning profession into action. The postpositive δέ again signals development from the negative behaviors described in 1:21.

ποιηταὶ λόγου: This noun plus genitive construction is a clear example of an "objective genitive" in which the genitive word receives the action of the verbal idea contained in its head noun. The construction is thus unpacked as "those who do the word." This phrase is clearly a Semitism, for the phrase in classical Greek meant a "wordsmith" or even a "poet" (LSJ 149). The same idea is in Matt 7:24: "Everyone who hears these words [λόγους] of mine and does [ποιεῖ] them" (see also Luke 6:46, 11:28, and John 13:17). The word ποιητής occurs only six times in NT, of which four are in James (1:23, 25; 4:11). A similar sense is a "doer of the Law" (ποιητής τοῦ νόμου) in Rom 2:13. Semantic parallels are found in a number of the Jesus *logia*, including Matt 7:26–27 and Luke 11:28.

καὶ μὴ μόνον ἀκροαταί: This noun was used in classical Greek to describe an attendant at a lecture. The modern term would be an "auditor." We first should think of the reading and hearing of the Scriptures in the synagogue, on which Jewish leaders laid great importance. The word appears three times in this paragraph, and only once elsewhere in the NT. For the entire expression, note that similar construction in Rom 2:13: "not the hearers [ἀκροαταί] of the law are righteous before God but the doers [ποιηταί] of the law will be declared righteous." The difference in our verse, particularly with the δέ again introducing it, is that the "word" is not just Torah but must refer back to the "word of truth" that was the theme of 1:18–21. James' use of μόνον here has a similar function later in 2:24: "You see that a person is justified not by faith only [μόνον]." The hearing parallels faith, while the doing parallels deeds.

παραλογιζόμενοι ἑαυτούς. This present middle participle expresses the result that takes place when one hears but does not act upon what he heard by obeying it: self-deception. In the LXX, the colorful verb appears in 1 Sam 28:12 where the woman of Endor says to Saul: "Why have you deceived [παρελογίσω] me?" The only other passage in which this verb appears in the NT is Col 2:4: "so that no one fraudulently deceives [παραλογίζηται] you." The same idea is found here—namely, that those who hear but fail to do are also "deceiving themselves" into thinking that some sort of passive reception of the message is enough. The result is that they are "defrauding themselves" by missing the path to maturity through the doing of the word.

1:23 ὅτι εἴ τις ἀκροατὴς λόγου ἐστὶν καὶ οὐ ποιητής: The causal ὅτι introduces a conditional clause with the indefinite pronoun τις the subject of the verb ἐστὶν in the protasis. The ἀκροατὴς λόγου is another example of the head noun plus objective genitive construction (cf ποιηταὶ λόγου in 1:22). The first class conditional sentence, assuming the reality of the protasis for the sake of the argument, repeats the words of 1:22 to emphasize the point. There is a parallel in thought with Jesus' condemnation of those who only listened to his words (Matt 7:24–27), but James does not utilize Jesus' parable of the two houses. The assumption of such a person's hearing and not doing in the protasis of the clause leads to James' own effective parable in the apodosis.

οὗτος ἔοικεν: The use of demonstrative pronoun οὗτος is a rhetorical move that calls attention to the problem of this "nondoer." He will also apply the parable with the same demonstrative pronoun in 1:25 with the opposite point when it refers to the "hearer and doer" who will be blessed, and is a characteristic of his style (see also 1:26, 27; 3:2, 10). James has previously used the perfect active indicative ἔοικεν in 1:6 when he had introduced another parable about nature, the only times the form appears in the NT (only twice also in the LXX: Job 6:3, 25). GE (731) documents its extensive use in Plato, Herodotus and Aristophanes while BDAG, (355) calls the form an "old pf. of εἴκω *be like, resemble.*"

ἀνδρὶ κατανοοῦντι: The dative noun and present attributive participle follow the verb as also in 1:6. "James commonly uses ἀνήρ with some characteristic word like μακάριος 1:12, κατανοῶν 1:23, χρυσοδακτύλιος 2:2, and τέλειος 3:2, reserving ἄνθρωπος for more general expressions like ἐκεῖνος, πᾶς, and οὐδείς" (Mayor, 42). It is striking that he uses the word for a male when females are often teased about the time they spend in front of a mirror!

τὸ πρόσωπον τῆς γενέσεως αὐτοῦ: This elaborate expression, "the face of his birth," is used to contrast the reflection of a face in the mirror that belongs to this passing life. The noun γένεσις is used, as in 3:6, in the sense of "nature," to mean the created world (including man) as distinguished from God, and with a suggestion of its character as seen and temporal. The reflection of the character is being shaped here by that contrasting look into the word which he is about to mention. For the word γενέσεως as meaning "birth," see the LXX of Genesis 31:13; Ruth 2:11; and also Matt 1:18).

ἐν ἐσόπτρῳ· The "mirror" made out of polished metal was referred to quite often in secular literature, especially in the papyri. Its use was limited in biblical Greek, appearing only twice in the LXX, on both occasions in wisdom books (Wis 7:26; Sir 12:11). The noun appears in the NT elsewhere only in 1 Cor 13:12, where imperfect knowledge gained through reflection is contrasted with the perfect knowledge of the reality. In 2 Cor 3:18 the verb (κατοπτριζόμενοι: "reflecting as in a mirror") alludes to the glory in the face of Moses.

1:24 κατενόησεν γὰρ ἑαυτὸν καὶ ἀπελήλυθεν καὶ εὐθέως ἐπελάθετο ὁποῖος ἦν. The γὰρ introduces an explanation of what James means by the man looking in the mirror. It is best to examine the triple compound clauses as a whole to take notice of the verb forms. James displays here a skillful variety through the different tenses of his verbs that vividly highlight the forgetful actions of the mirror-gazer in 1:24. He looks (κατενόησεν—aorist tense) at himself; he departs (ἀπελήλυθεν—perfect tense), and then at once forgets (ἐπελάθετο—aorist tense) what he looked like. Is there more here than simple verbal variety? Some commentators simply ignore the change in tense from the aorist to the perfect and back to the aorist. Many of the standard grammars and also many commentators refer to the "gnomic aorist" and suggest some sort of similar function for the perfect (proleptic perfect?). Moo and Davids explain the purpose in using different tense forms as solely an example of stylistic variety (Moo, 2000, 125; Davids, 98). Porter, on the other hand, prefers the category "omnitemporal" for these aorists that grammaticalize the "perfective" aspect. The perfective aspect of the aorist deals with observed processes, and an example of this would be the aorist tense used to describe a natural process (Jas 1:11), conceiving the process as complete. Porter also defines the aspectual function of the perfect tense as "stative" (Porter, *Verbal Aspect*, 245–90; 318–19). In his later grammar he further describes the stative aspect of the perfect tense form as describing a "state of affairs" (Porter, *Idioms*, 40). This is the best approach to understanding James' use of the perfect tense in this passage, particularly when one recognizes the function of the perfect tense as bringing to greater prominence this action in the narrative. In other words, what James wants the reader to focus on is the state of forgetful looker having departed from his gazing in the mirror.

It is interesting that a well-known and respected nineteenth-century commentator, Henry Alford, called attention to this stative function of the perfect tense in the following way.

> We might have had all aorists, but seeing that the *departing* begins a permanent state of absence from the mirror, that is chosen to be designated by a perfect. The forgetting is also a permanent state, but the Apostle rather chooses in this case to bring out the act itself, as one *immediately* (εὐθέως) and

suddenly taking place (Alford, 288).

James' fondness for using the perfect tense in this stative role while being juxtaposed with an aorist can also be seen in 2:10: "For whoever keeps [aorist τηρήσῃ] the whole law, yet stumbles [aorist πταίσῃ] in one point, he has become [perfect γέγονεν] guilty of all." This man "took cognizance of himself," and then "has gone away and immediately forgot what kind [of man] he was." This is what made him a hearer only: he saw, he went off, he forgot. His hearing netted him nothing as far as the real purpose and the power of the Word are concerned.

1:25 This long sentence is probably the closest that James ever comes to what is called a classical "periodic sentence." The three aorist participles (παρακύψας, παραμείνας, γενόμενος) in the opening clause complex set up the future tense (ἔσται) in the last clause. While not containing the normal features of a conditional clause, the sentence functions that way because the participles form the protasis to which the future tense responds as the apodosis.

ὁ δὲ παρακύψας: The δὲ signals development for the negative behavior (1:24) to the positive. For the meaning of this aorist substantival participle, see the comments on its counterpart παραμείνας below.

εἰς νόμον τέλειον τὸν τῆς ἐλευθερίας: The intense gaze into the law is to be associated with freedom (ἐλευθερία) James sees a continuity between the "word of truth" (1:18); the "implanted word" (1:21); the "perfect law" and "law of liberty" (1:25; 2:12); and even the "royal law" (2:8). Each modifier brings out a different nuance of that word from God that has become embodied in the "faith of our Lord Jesus Christ" (2:1).

καὶ παραμείνας: It is important to understand clearly see what James is actually contrasting in this parable with its accompanying application. Some commentators stress that James is contrasting two types of "looking"—namely, a casual glance in the mirror with a studied peering into the word (Bengel, 11). Such fine distinctions between the meanings of these two verbs, with the verb κατανοέω in 1:23, 24 apparently conveying a more casual glance and the participle form of παρακύπτω conveying a more intent gaze, actually misunderstand the real purpose of the intended analogy. Other appearances of the first verb, κατανοέω, simply not to imply any less serious "glance" (Acts 11:16; 27:39; Rom 4:19; esp. Heb 3:1; 10:24). The contrast in this parable is not between the way in which the two verbs look at their respective objects. The real difference between the two is that the first person forgets what he saw and the second person perseveres (παραμείνας) in his look and does not forget what he saw. The contrasting idea seems to be as follows. When one gives careful attention to what the Word teaches by not forgetting what it teaches, then this person will be blessed both in his hearing and his doing. The blessed one is he who does not forget what he has heard and who will obey the Word. The person condemned is he who does not allow the Word to affect his "doing."

οὐκ ἀκροατὴς ἐπιλησμονῆς γενόμενος ἀλλὰ ποιητὴς ἔργου: This subordinate participial clause, anchored by the middle participle γενόμενος, almost serves as a modern parenthesis in the verse, clarifying what he means by looking into the law and continuing to do so. The genitive ἐπιλησμονῆς is simply descriptive of its head noun ἀκροατὴς. The ἀλλὰ is a strong adversative that points to the ideal hearer who is a doer of the work, ποιητὴς ἔργου, another head noun and objective genitive.

οὗτος μακάριος ἐν τῇ ποιήσει αὐτοῦ ἔσται. The comparison between the two different types of hearers is brought into sharp relief by the effective use of the demonstrative pronoun οὗτος in 1:23 and 1:25. The use of this pronoun to emphasize the apodosis after a relative, a condition, or a participle, has been noted as a characteristic of the writer's style elsewhere in 1:25 and 3:2. In 1:23 the conditional clause proposes a forgetful hearer and then adds: "this one" is like a person who forgets what he looks like in the mirror. On the other hand (δὲ), 1:25 describes a hearer who obeys and then concludes with the important beatitude: "this one" will be blessed in his deed (ἐν τῇ ποιήσει αὐτοῦ). Note the final word of the inclusio, the noun ποιήσει, answering to the cognate noun ποιηταὶ in 1:22a. It is also possible to see another inclusio at work with the two *macarisms*, or beatitudes: μακάριος initiating a new section and in 1:12 and ending one here in 1:25.

Conclusion

The semantic theme of the divine "word," introduced in 1:21 with λόγος, continues to permeate this paragraph with the repetition of the lexemes λόγος (1:22) and νόμος (1:25). As here and throughout the book (2:8: the "royal law" and the "scripture"), these separate words are not intended by James to convey different functions of the divine "word/law/scripture." Their use suggests that they represent the same revelation from the one God. Sometimes that "word" was delivered through the writings of the Torah and the Nevi'im, and sometimes it was delivered through the wisdom teaching of the Messiah whose word was a faithful communication of the divine will (1:1; 2:1). To artificially separate the "word" into various distinct components would simply be a strange bifurcation to James. Our author viewed all of these different but similar expressions as part of one "word," namely, the revelatory word from the one true God faithfully conveyed through His servants. At the appropriate places, further explanation will be offered about how the teaching of Jesus also forms part of that wisdom continuum of word/law, especially in the comments on 2:5–6.

Real Religion (1:26-27)

Greek Text

26 Εἴ τις δοκεῖ θρησκὸς εἶναι ᵃ μὴ χαλιναγωγῶν γλῶσσαν αὐτοῦ ἀλλὰ ἀπατῶν καρδίαν αὐτοῦ, τούτου μάταιος ἡ θρησκεία. **27** θρησκεία καθαρὰ καὶ ἀμίαντος παρὰ τῷ θεῷ καὶ πατρὶ αὕτη ἐστίν, ἐπισκέπτεσθαι ὀρφανοὺς καὶ χήρας ἐν τῇ θλίψει αὐτῶν, ᵇἄσπιλον ἑαυτὸν τηρεῖν ἀπὸ τοῦ κόσμου.

Textual Notes

26.a. The Majority Text inserts εν υμιν at this point, while all uncials and early versions omit it. The internal evidence also supports its absence, since James apparently reserves this expression for the latter half of his letter when he addresses more communal concerns (3:13; 4:1; 5:13, 14, 19).

27.b. Instead of the text that is supported by the overwhelming bulk of the witnesses in 1:27: ἄσπιλον ἑαυτὸν τηρεῖν, P⁷⁴ reads ὑπερασπίζειν αὐτούς ("to protect them"). This reading, although probably not original, focuses on protecting the weak ones rather than just visiting them. Plural words also are in several late minuscules (ἀσπίλους ἑαυτοὺς τηρεῖτε), where the third person singular τις δοκεῖ in 1:26 is shifted to a more direct second person plural imperatival command.

Sentence Flow and Translation

26 Εἴ τις δοκεῖ θρησκὸς εἶναι
    If anyone thinks he is religious

      μὴ χαλιναγωγῶν γλῶσσαν αὐτοῦ ἀλλὰ ἀπατῶν καρδίαν αὐτοῦ,
      while not bridling his tongue but deceiving his heart,

τούτου μάταιος ἡ θρησκεία.
this person's religion is worthless.

27 θρησκεία καθαρὰ καὶ ἀμίαντος παρὰ τῷ θεῷ καὶ πατρὶ αὕτη ἐστίν,
   A religion pure and undefiled before God the Father is this:

   ἐπισκέπτεσθαι ὀρφανοὺς καὶ χήρας ἐν τῇ θλίψει αὐτῶν,
   to visit orphans and widows in their affliction,

   ἄσπιλον ἑαυτὸν τηρεῖν ἀπὸ τοῦ κόσμου.
   to keep oneself unstained from the world.

Context

The third subparagraph (1:26–27) of the larger section (1:19–27) is the concluding elaboration on the threefold command delivered at the beginning of the main paragraph in James 1:19: "every person must be quick to hear, *slow to speak,* slow to anger." James has commented and elaborated on being "slow to anger" in 1:19–21. He expanded and applied the idea of being "quick to hear" in 1:22–25. Now he applies further (among other matters) what it means to be "slow to speak" here in 1:26–27.

This compact exhortation also introduces themes that are further discussed in the next three chapters. In chapter 2 James further develops how we must be "quick to hear" what the Torah and the Lord Jesus both say about the poor in 2:1–5 and to put what we have "heard" to "work" in 2:12–26. Then in 3:1–12, he vividly illustrates how we should be "slow to speak" by means of numerous analogies illustrating the dangers of an uncontrolled tongue. In 3:13–4:10, James also warns that the failure to be "slow to wrath" displays devilish wisdom and is the root cause of conflicts that he knows about among his extended flock. Through this intentionally strategic method James 1:26–27 functions both anaphorically (looking back), as it recalls 1:19, and then functions cataphorically (looking forward) as it prepares the reader for chapters 2 through 4 (adapted from Witherington, 447).

Exegetical Comments

1:26 Εἴ τις δοκεῖ θρησκὸς εἶναι: The conditional particle εἴ poses the "question" in the form of a first class conditional sentence, a grammatical move that is also used frequently by Paul (1 Cor 3:18; 8:2; 11:16; 14:37; Gal 6:3; Phil 3:4). The verb δοκεῖ ("think/consider") is often used in the NT for a false opinion, as it is here (Matt 3:9; 6:7; 26:53; Mark 6:49; Luke 8:18; 12:51; 13:2; 19:11; 24:37; Acts 12:9; John 5:39). This is a continuation of the theme of self-deception referred to in 1:22. The predicate adjective θρησκὸς is a NT *hapax legomenon*, and does not appear in previous Greek literature. Its meaning, however, is easily determined from the common noun θρησκεία that appears later in this verse and in 1:27. It is best translated simply as "religious," and denotes a relationship with the Deity, but there is more to be considered in the noun cognate in 1:27. The term here likely refers to religious observance—rites and rituals, prayer and fasting, the elements of worship and devotional practice—while the term θρησκεία in 1:27 probably refers to religion in its more cultic aspects (Wis 14:18, 27; Acts 26:5), something that is reinforced by the further use of the term ἄσπιλος ("undefiled, spotless") in the same verse (1 Tim 6:14). The complementary infinitive εἶναι is a good example of indirect discourse. In other words, we can imagine that the "direct discourse" spoken by this hypothetical person is "I am religious."

μὴ χαλιναγωγῶν γλῶσσαν αὐτοῦ: The colorful participle χαλιναγωγῶν apparently is the first known usage of the verb and occurs again in relation to the tongue in 3:2 and later in the Apostolic Fathers, especially in the *Hermas* 44.1, which reflects a dependency on James at this and at many other points (see also Pol. *Phil.* 5:3). The present participle is probably temporal, conveying the sense of "while he is not bridling his tongue" (Blomberg-Kamell, 93). Some, however, see it as concessive, with the sense being "although not bridling his tongue"

(Dibelius, 121). A good periphrastic rendering of the verb might be "a tongue as loose as an unbridled horse."

ἀλλὰ ἀπατῶν καρδίαν αὐτοῦ: The present participle, ἀπατῶν, could also be temporal but its sense is conveyed better because of the adversative ἀλλὰ preceding it. The theme of self-deception has been running through the chapter (1:6–7, 14, 16, 22). This stress on the self-deception of the "heart" - the first of five references to this inner seat (3:14; 4:8; 5:5, 8) - is a reminder that the ethical, praxis-laden James is no mere moralist. He constantly traces both the behavioral problems and their solutions to that which is within us, not just in a change of our observed actions (cf. 1:15–17; 4:1–3).

τούτου μάταιος ἡ θρησκεία: James again utilizes the near demonstrative pronoun τούτου to specifically focus on his subject (1:23, 25, 26). He will soon state that the religion that is pure and undefiled is characterized by "this [αὕτη]. The negative use of the adjective θρησκός ("religious") in the protasis now is balanced by the positive stress of the noun θρησκεία ("religion") in the apodosis. The word group was not owned by either Jews or Christians, since it was widely used in the Greek world. The noun here focuses on the outward manifestation of one's religious practices. The use of predicate adjective μάταιος ("worthless") in the LXX often has an idolatrous context (Zech 10:2; Jer 2:5; 8:19; Wis 13:1; Esth 4:17). This meaning of μάταιος for describing the futility of idolatry is also witnessed in the NT (Acts 14:15; Rom 1:21; 8:20; Eph 4:17). It is striking that this assertion by James associates the uncontrolled use of the tongue as a practice that is in the same rank of pagan worship. We would be fair to conclude that James describes a religion of uncontrolled speech and self-deception as a form of idolatry.

1:27 θρησκεία καθαρὰ καὶ ἀμίαντος: The language of 1:27 features a number of cultic terms that were associated with outward manifestations of "worship" both of Jews and of pagans. For example, καθαρά, ἀμίαντος, τηρεῖν and ἄσπιλον echo Jewish cultic purity laws. The term καθαρός is associated in Judaism with ceremonial/cultic objects and persons that are in a condition fit to approach the deity (Gen 7:3; 8:20; Lev 4:12; 7:19; 11:32; 15:13; Num 8:7; Deut 12:15; see also the Jewish cultic associations in Luke 11:41; Rom 14:20; Titus 1:15; Heb 10:22). The adjective ἀμίαντος has similar associations, since μιαίνω is used in the LXX for making someone or something ritually impure (Lev 5:3; 11:24; 18:24; Num 5:3; Deut 21:23). It also carries the figurative sense of moral or religious purity in the NT in such places as Heb 7:26; 13:4; 1 Pet 1:4. But James does not apply these terms to any examples of Jewish ritual purity either in the required worship regulations or in the family purity laws, which were so important to his Jewish contemporaries. "James subverts these cultic associations by applying the terms not to ceremonial religious observances but to ethical praxis" (Varner, 82). The focus is rather on ethical and spiritual purity that is manifested by one's behavior. Since James is writing to Jewish believers, one might expect that this would be the opportunity to apply his message by emphasizing ritual purity. He does not, but chooses to make an ethical application of the words.

παρὰ τῷ θεῷ καὶ πατρὶ αὕτη ἐστίν: While James employs asyndeton (not using connective conjunctions) in this verse, his use of the conjunction καὶ in 1:27 is important to note: "A religion pure *and* undefiled before God *and* the Father is this...." It is pointless to discern some fine distinction in meaning between the first two adjectives. Furthermore, the article preceding God and Father (τῷ θεῷ καὶ πατρὶ) identities as the same "person" the one described by these two substantives, an example of the Granville-Sharp Rule. It appears that James is employing the linguistic trope called *hendiadys* in both expressions. The sense would be: "A completely pure religion before our divine Father is as follows." In the OT God is pictured as a Father to the "fatherless" (Ps 68:5), which is also why James is careful to mention God's role here as a Father.

ἐπισκέπτεσθαι ὀρφανοὺς καὶ χήρας ἐν τῇ θλίψει αὐτῶν: While

commentators identify these two infinitives as "epexegetical," Wallace (606) prefers to identify the usage of the infinitive here as "appositional"—namely, *to visit* ... The sense conveyed by both uses, however, is still the same. James begins his definition of true religion by turning toward the internal concerns in the community of the faithful. To visit orphans and widows may be literally to go and spend time with them (Matt 25:36, 43), but such "visiting" also is for the purpose of making provision for their needs. The word "visit" in both Testaments involves tangible actions as well as presence, especially when God is the "visitor" (Gen 21:1; 50:24–25; Exo 3:16; 4:31; Luke 1:68; 7:16).

James singles out the special objects for compassionate care those who were often the chronically impoverished, the widows and the orphans. James continues an important theme in the Torah (Exod 22:20–21; 23:9; Lev 19:9–10; 19:33; 23:22; Deut 10:17–19; 14:28–29), the prophets (Isa 3:5, 14–15; Jer 22:3; Amos 2:6–8; 3:2; Hos 12:8–9; Mic 3:1–4; Zech 7:8–10; Mal 3:5), the writings (Prov 19:17; 21:3; 31:9); and also in the NT examples and exhortations (Acts 6:1–6; 1 Tim 5:3–16). True piety helps the helpless. By placing the assistance of the disadvantaged at the heart of true religion, James prepares the reader for his rebuke of those who favor the rich over the poor in 2:1–7, and is furthered by his insistence on helping the needy in 2:14–16, as well as by his condemnation of the oppressive rich landowners in 5:1–6.

ἄσπιλον ἑαυτὸν τηρεῖν ἀπὸ τοῦ κόσμου: The second infinitive clause that defines true religion turns outward from the community, toward the dangers found in the external world. This is James' first use of the term κόσμος, and it appears in binary opposition to God (παρὰ τῷ θεῷ / ἀπὸ τοῦ κόσμου), the way it functions later in the letter (2:5; 3:6; 4:4). "The world (κόσμος) in James is moral: a widespread disposition and power in mankind for evil in opposition to God" (Davids, 103). It is clear that "keeping oneself unstained from the world" at this point has nothing to do with ritual observance, or the lack of it, and everything to do with moral attitudes and behavior.

Conclusion

1:27 is another example of the Jacobean penchant for asyndeton (lack of conjunctions connecting the clauses). Most translations recognize this and insert the conjunction "and" before the complement in the first clause and then also between the parallel infinitive clauses. This asyndetic style results in a staccato-like manner that appears at times to be abrupt and straightforward, something for which James is well known. An explanation for some of these peculiar uses of language in 1:26–27 may also be found in the special transitional function of these verses. For example, notice the ideas that are repeated from the previous paragraph (anaphorically). The expression, ἀπατῶν καρδίαν αὐτοῦ, recalls the παραλογιζόμενοι ἑαυτούς in 1:22. These verses also provide some concrete examples of what James exhorted us about in 1:22: to be "doers" not just "hearers" of the word. These verses, however, also look forward (cataphorically) with their first mention of the word χαλιναγωγῶν, which is also repeated in 3:2. The stern and straightforward admonition about the spiritual dangers in the "world" also anticipates the mention again of the enemy in 4:4. Therefore, the summary of these transitional themes join together with the other special linguistic features that we noticed to indicate that 1:26–27 is a prominent high point in chapter 1.

5

DO NOT SHOW FAVORITISM (2:1-13)

Partiality in Practice (2:1-4)

Greek Text

1 Ἀδελφοί μου, μὴ ἐν προσωπολημψίαις ἔχετε τὴν πίστιν ᵃτοῦ κυρίου ἡμῶν Ἰησοῦ Χριστοῦ τῆς δόξης. 2 ἐὰν γὰρ <u>εἰσέλθῃ</u> εἰς συναγωγὴν ὑμῶν ἀνὴρ χρυσοδακτύλιος ἐν ἐσθῆτι λαμπρᾷ, <u>εἰσέλθῃ</u> δὲ καὶ πτωχὸς ἐν ῥυπαρᾷ ἐσθῆτι, 3 ἐπιβλέψητε δὲ ἐπὶ τὸν φοροῦντα τὴν ἐσθῆτα τὴν λαμπρὰν καὶ εἴπητεᵇ·σὺ κάθου ὧδε καλῶς, καὶ τῷ πτωχῷ εἴπητε·ᶜσὺ στῆθι ἐκεῖ ἢ κάθου ὑπὸ τὸ ὑποπόδιόν μου, 4 οὐ διεκρίθητε ἐν ἑαυτοῖς καὶ ἐγένεσθε κριταὶ διαλογισμῶν πονηρῶν;

Textual Notes

1.a. A few late manuscripts (630, 105, 1505), possibly influenced by some early versions (sy sa bo) transpose the order of the seven words in 2:1 that follow by placing τῆς δόξης before τοῦ κυρίου, thus clearly leading to the translation "the glory of our Lord Jesus Christ." A few other minuscules, including the significant 33 plus a few Latin manuscripts completely omit τῆς δόξης. The order in the text is supported, however, by the vast majority of both early and later Greek manuscripts and Fathers.

3.b. The Majority Text and the Clementine Vulgate insert in 2:3 a personal pronoun (αυτω in Greek) to make the address more specific. The context, however, is clear that the rich visitor is being addressed.

3.c. In 2:3, the reading that best explains the origin of the others is the one supported by A C* Ψ 33 81 614 630 2495 vg syr[h]: σὺ στῆθι ἐκεῖ ἢ κάθου ("'Stand there' or 'Sit'"). Obviously secondary is ἐκεῖ ἢ κάθου ὧδε (P[74] ℵ C[2] K P and most minuscules), where ὧδε creates a better parallelism and expresses explicitly what is otherwise implied—namely, that the place ὑπὸ τὸ ὑποπόδιόν μου is thought of as nearer to the speaker than the place indicated by the command στῆθι ἐκεῖ. Not recognizing this, B and several other witnesses transposed ἐκεῖ so as to produce a parallelism of two references to places.

Changes in NA28

2:3 NA27: ἐπιβλέψητε δὲ ἐπὶ τὸν φοροῦντα τὴν ἐσθῆτα τὴν λαμπρὰν καὶ εἴπητε· σὺ κάθου ὧδε καλῶς, καὶ τῷ πτωχῷ εἴπητε· σὺ στῆθι ἐκεῖ ἢ κάθου ὑπὸ τὸ ὑποπόδιόν μου,

2:3 NA28: ἐπιβλέψητε δὲ ἐπὶ τὸν φοροῦντα τὴν ἐσθῆτα τὴν λαμπρὰν καὶ εἴπητε· σὺ κάθου ὧδε καλῶς, καὶ τῷ πτωχῷ εἴπητε· σὺ στῆθι ἢ κάθου ἐκεῖ ὑπὸ τὸ ὑποπόδιόν μου,

SBLGNT follows the word order in NA28. MAJ reading is ἐκεῖ ἢ κάθου ὧδε. NIV and THGNT follow NA27.

2:4 NA27: οὐ διεκρίθητε ἐν ἑαυτοῖς καὶ ἐγένεσθε κριταὶ διαλογισμῶν πονηρῶν;

2:4 MAJ: καὶ οὐ διεκρίθητε ἐν ἑαυτοῖς, καὶ ἐγένεσθε κριταὶ διαλογισμῶν πονηρῶν;

2:4 NA28: <u>καὶ</u> οὐ διεκρίθητε ἐν ἑαυτοῖς καὶ ἐγένεσθε κριταὶ διαλογισμῶν πονηρῶν;

NA28 now agrees with MAJ. SBLGNT, NIV, and THGNT follow NA27.

Context

This paragraph (2:1–4) is bracketed by its opening and closing with two independent, primary clauses, the first conveying a command (2:1) and the second asking a rhetorical question (2:4). The first of those clauses opens with the now-familiar nominative of direct address, "my brothers," followed by a negated imperative, "do not hold." This combination is one of the devices most utilized by James to introduce a new paragraph or subject. When this combination signals a new topic, as is the case in 2:1, it serves as one of the twelve main divisions of the letter (e.g., 1:2, 16, 19). The second primary clause (2:4) is actually the apodosis (the "then" clause) of a long conditional clause (2:2–4). The protasis (the "if") of the conditional clause contains five secondary clauses, each containing a subjunctive verb introduced by the single ἐάν that initiates 2:2 (see the sentence flow analysis below, where the subjunctive verbs are underlined and are in parallel). This approach is also quite typical of our author's style, since he often opens a paragraph with a primary clause consisting of what could be called "mainline material" (usually a command), and then he employs a series of clauses serving as "supporting material" for that initial command (see 1:19). Sometimes the command is replaced by a rhetorical question that further expands his topic (3:13; 4:1). The sentence flow analysis helps to visualize this structure.

Sentence Flow and Translation

1 Ἀδελφοί μου
  My brothers,

μὴ ἐν προσωπολημψίαις ἔχετε τὴν πίστιν
do not hold to the faith ... while committing acts of partiality.

τοῦ κυρίου ἡμῶν Ἰησοῦ Χριστοῦ τῆς δόξης.
of our glorious Lord Jesus Christ,

2 ἐὰν γὰρ εἰσέλθῃ εἰς συναγωγὴν ὑμῶν ἀνὴρ χρυσοδακτύλιος
For if a man wearing a gold ring ... comes into your synagogue,

ἐν ἐσθῆτι λαμπρᾷ,
and fine clothing

εἰσέλθῃ δὲ καὶ πτωχὸς ἐν ῥυπαρᾷ ἐσθῆτι,
and a poor man in shabby clothing also comes in,

3 ἐπιβλέψητε δὲ ἐπὶ τὸν φοροῦντα τὴν ἐσθῆτα τὴν λαμπρὰν
and if you pay attention to the one who wears the fine clothing

καὶ εἴπητε· σὺ κάθου ὧδε καλῶς, καὶ τῷ πτωχῷ εἴπητε·
and say, "You sit here in a good place," and you say to the poor man,

σὺ στῆθι ἐκεῖ ἢ κάθου ὑπὸ τὸ ὑποπόδιόν μου,
"You stand over there," or, "Sit down at my feet,"

4 οὐ διεκρίθητε ἐν ἑαυτοῖς
have you not made distinctions among yourselves

καὶ ἐγένεσθε κριταὶ διαλογισμῶν πονηρῶν;
and become judges with evil thoughts?

Exegetical Comments

2:1 Ἀδελφοί μου: This nominative of address opens a new paragraph and introduces a change in the topic. A fact often overlooked is that here and in its final appearance in 5:19 are the only times when ἀδελφοί μου initiates the clause in which it is found. In the comments on 1:26–27, it was shown that the themes introduced at that point may serve as a bridge to span what was initially mentioned back in 1:19 to what is about to be developed in the way those themes are elaborated in chapters 2–5. Thus 1:26–27 appears to function both anaphorically and cataphorically in the literary strategy of the author. The two examples of the fronting of ἀδελφοί μου in 2:1 and 5:19, therefore, serve a discourse function as a sort of *inclusio* initiating the first and last paragraphs of the main body of the letter (chapters 2–5).

μὴ ἐν προσωπολημψίαις ἔχετε τὴν πίστιν: In its form, ἔχετε can be either present imperative or indicative. At least one version (NRSV) and an occasional commentator (Hort, 46) view it as indicative and translate it as a question ("do you have the faith?"). Why would James question that they are showing partiality when he proceeds to give examples of their partiality in 2:2–4? To interpret it as a question would imply a negative response, which is also contradictory to the following context. Consistent with other paragraph openings accompanied by ἀδελφοί, it is best to take the verb here as an imperative (see 1:2, 16; 3:1; 4:11; 5:7, 12, 19).

The abstract noun "partiality" (προσωπολημψίαις) appears in 2:1 in this specific nominal form for the first time in Greek literature (like δίψυχος in 1:8). The noun also appears in Rom 2:11; Eph 6:9; and Col 3:25. Along with the cognate verb προσωπολημπτέω (only in Jas 2:9) and the personal noun προσωπολήμπτης (only in Acts 10:34), this word group represents the expression πρόσωπον λαμβάνειν in the LXX, which in turn is an attempt to render the Hebrew נָשָׂא פָנִים (see Mal 1:8). This conveys the literal idea of "receiving" or "regarding" the "face" of someone when making a judgment. These three related words "have so far been found only in Christian writers" (BDAG, 887), and GE (1835) affirms this observation. The substantive προσωπολημψία (without the μ) is mentioned as a sin in Polycarp, *Phil.* 6:1, and is not a divine quality in *T. Job* 43.13. The broader semantic theme of showing partiality, however, is often mentioned in the OT (see the thought expressed in LXX Lev 19:15: οὐ λήμψῃ πρόσωπον; and in Deut 1:17: οὐκ ἐπιγνώσῃ πρόσωπον ἐν κρίσει). This use of this noun is either an allusion to Lev 19:15 or at least a prominent NT echo of that verse. Leviticus 19:15 is again alluded to in 2:8 and that chapter from Leviticus is a key intertextual link throughout the book. The preposition ἐν has a temporal force here and, with its object being plural in form, probably refers to "acts of partiality." Hence a permissible translation is: "while committing acts of partiality." The use of other plural abstract substantives to describe outward manifestations of the corresponding behavior can also be seen in 2 Cor 12:20, Gal 5:20, and 1 Pet 4:3.

James is effectively declaring that one cannot hold to the faith of Jesus while at the same time practicing acts of favoritism or discrimination. Another lexicographer summarizes the word group in the following way: Partiality is "the fault of one who when called on to requite or to give judgment has respect to the outward circumstances of men and not to their intrinsic merits, and so prefers, as the more worthy, one who is rich, high-born, or powerful, to another who is destitute of such gifts" (Thayer, 551). James will soon provide a vivid example of such partiality in 2:2–4.

μὴ ... ἔχετε: Some would argue for an indicative see this as implying a question: "Can you have the faith?" This would imply a negative response and also involve a bit of rhetorical sarcasm by James. James is certainly not averse to asking his readers confrontational rhetorical questions. He will follow his diatribe in this chapter with such questions (2:5, 6, 7, 14, 16, 20, 21, 25), but those questions are not in the same form as the grammar of 2:1 (ἀδελφοί plus a present imperative verb). The present tense of the command has occasionally led some interpreters to conclude that James is telling his readers to stop practicing partiality (Burdick, 177). This expected sense is based on a view of the present tense that was often conveyed in some older standard grammars.[1] This also raises the questionable issue of "mirror hermeneutics"—namely, that what a writer condemns is actually a mirror of what he knows is being done by the readers. More recent grammars have acknowledged that while the present imperative with μὴ *could* refer to the cessation of an activity in progress, it can also convey a "general precept." This usage "makes no comment about whether the action is going on or not"[2] The general/encyclical nature of James' letter also points to a general command here. Furthermore, the use of the imperative does not imply that such sinful favoritism is possible to exist alongside Jesus-faith. Thus, a tendential use may express the idea even better. "'Do not *try* to combine faith in Christ with (let us here say) worship of wealth.' To translate otherwise, 'Do not combine,' would leave men to imagine it would be possible" (Adamson, 123).

τὴν πίστιν τοῦ κυρίου ἡμῶν Ἰησοῦ Χριστοῦ: This entire phrase is the direct object of the previous negated command. What is meant by τὴν πίστιν? Also what is the function of the genitive τοῦ κυρίου ἡμῶν and the following titles of the Lord (Ἰησοῦ Χριστοῦ)? The first question is whether the genitive case of "Lord" (κυρίου) functions as an object in relation to the head noun ("faith *in* Christ") or as a subject of the action implied in the head noun ("Christ's faithfulness" or simply "the faith of Christ"). The more recent English translations usually view it as an objective genitive expressed by "faith *in* our Lord ..." Older English versions render it as "*the* faith *of* our Lord ..." Most commentators agree with the recent versions and either argue for an objective genitive here or simply do not comment on the issue (Blomberg-Kamell, 106; McCartney, 135–36; and McKnight, 176–77). Later in the chapter, James does employ the noun to refer to an

---

[1] D.M. 301.

[2] Wallace adds: "It is not safe to say that when an author uses the present prohibition the audience is being indicted for not heeding the command. Other factors—especially the context and *Sitz im leben* of the book—must be taken into account" (Wallace, 724–25). See also Young, 143–44 and Porter, 224–26.

individual's faith, but the specific object of that faith is not mentioned in those verses (2:14, 17, 18, 20, 22, 24, and 26).

I suggest that the article τὴν before πίστιν should cause us to return to the older versions for the translation/interpretation of Ἰησοῦ Χριστοῦ as a subjective genitive: "the faith of ... Jesus Christ." The article before the substantive (τὴν πίστιν) has led James Dunn, who is a known defender of the "objective genitive" view in the Pauline corpus, to argue that the presence of the article is evidence in this verse of the subjective genitive.[3] Thus, the translation of the arthrous head noun τὴν πίστιν combined with the imperative ἔχετε would be: "My brothers do not *hold to the faith of our glorious Lord Jesus Christ*, while showing acts of partiality."

What particularly, then, is conveyed by the phrase, "the faith of Jesus"? It is *the* faith that is to be displayed in the Jesus *logion* in 2:5 and also in the "royal law" of 2:8, which law was reaffirmed by Jesus in Matt 22:39. It is *the faith that comes from Jesus* that would never show such partiality exhibited by the behavior that is about to be exemplified in 2:2–4. Therefore, the following context also supports the presence of a subjective genitive in 2:1. It is not necessary to resort to the translation "faithfulness," a rare meaning of that word in any case. Johnson also points the best way forward in this debate. "The use of Jesus' sayings throughout the composition suggests a meaning like 'the faith of Jesus in God as reflected in his teaching,' or perhaps 'the faith that is from Jesus Christ,' in the sense 'declared by Jesus' " (Johnson 220).

τῆς δόξης: The genitival "glory" has been taken adjectivally by a number of versions and commentators—"our glorious Lord Jesus Christ" (NASB, NIV, NLT, NAB, NET, NRSV, ESV, CSB. Ropes, 187; Dibelius, 128; Davids, 106; Martin, 60). If the latter words in the genitive chain all modify Lord, however, we can also have a translation as follows: "our Lord Jesus Christ, *the Lord of glory*." Another view is that the

---

[3] Dunn, 252–53. See also the presence of the article in Rev 2:13 and 14:12, as well as Rom 3:3.

articular τῆς δόξης is in apposition to the "our Lord Jesus Christ," namely "the Glory" (Bengel, 13; Hort, 47–48; Mayor, 81; Laws, 95–96). This view is grammatically possible, would certainly agree with the high Christology reflected elsewhere in the NT, and is possibly supported by the use of the noun δόξα in such texts as Luke 2:32; John 1:14; Eph 1:17; and Heb 1:3. The problem is that James 2:1 would be the only place in the NT where the Messiah is directly called "the Glory," a reference to the Hebrew כָּבֵד. Even if this last view may not be preferred, the implication in this statement of a high Christology and even soteriology should not be overlooked. In the NT, the word δόξα is often used as a sort of shorthand for Jesus' resurrection (Luke 24:26; John 17:5; Acts 22:11; 1 Cor 2:8; 15:43; 2 Cor 4:6; Phil 2:11; 3:21; Col 1:11; Heb 2:7; 1 Pet 1:11). This clear pointer to the resurrection should also be considered when one responds to James' apparent lack of clear references to the redemptive acts of Jesus in his book.

In the end, the phrase should best be understood adjectivally: "our glorious Lord Jesus Christ" (Huther, 99; Ropes, 187; Dibelius, 128). The article τῆς before δόξης indicates that the expression is in the "second attributive" position, because an article also precedes the previous genitive title: τοῦ κυρίου ἡμῶν Ἰησοῦ Χριστοῦ (Wallace 239). Furthermore, James himself in Acts 15:26 uses the exact title, τοῦ κυρίου ἡμῶν Ἰησοῦ Χριστοῦ, as a single unit. This translation is both grammatically sound and it also supports the theological idea of accenting Jesus' resurrected "glory."

As was mentioned in the Introduction, when combined with these two verses (1:1 and 2:1), the abundant allusions to Jesus' teaching and the later references to "Lord" (5:7, 14) illustrate that James is one of the most "Jesus-filled" NT books after the Gospels.

2:2 ἐὰν γὰρ εἰσέλθῃ εἰς συναγωγὴν ὑμῶν ἀνὴρ χρυσοδακτύλιος ἐν ἐσθῆτι λαμπρᾷ, εἰσέλθῃ δὲ καὶ πτωχὸς ἐν ῥυπαρᾷ ἐσθῆτι: As mentioned, 2:2–3 composes an elaborate protasis of a conditional clause, of which 2:4 is its corresponding apodosis. The intensity of the five subjunctive verbs is increased by two embedded clause-quotations in 2:3 conveying by direct discourse the directions to the rich person and to the poor person about their respective seating assignments. We should read all the subjunctive clauses as part of one large protasis rather than break them up into separate sentences. This type of protasis is usually called a third class conditional clause. Porter states, "A third class conditional with ἐάν and the subjunctive, in distinction to a first class conditional, is more tentative and simply projects some action or event for hypothetical consideration" (262). While this grammatical observation cannot be the deciding factor, it does support the suggestion that James is simply raising a hypothetical situation and that he is not necessarily describing a scene that he has witnessed or that he has heard to have taken place in their assemblies. It should not be overlooked that in the immediately preceding paragraph (1:26–27), he used a first class conditional clause introduced in its protasis by: Εἴ τις δοκεῖ θρησκὸς εἶναι ... This type of conditional clause assumes the reality of the action in the protasis in 1:26a for the sake of the argument, and this consequently fits the rhetorical force of his admonition in the apodosis of 1:26b. Elsewhere James will often make an assertion or issue a command and then follow it with a parable or some other hypothetical situation (1:22–25; 2:14–17). This careful use of the grammar supports the suggestion that the scene that is portrayed in their "synagogue" *may* have taken place, but it is not necessarily a scene that actually *has* taken place.

The language of 2:2 sharply contrasting the two characters reminds us of the parable of Lazarus and the rich man (Luke 16:19–31). The wealthy (πλούσιος) man there dined "splendidly" (λάμπρος) every day as he ignored the poor man (πτωχός) lying at his gate. The colorful word χρυσοδακτύλιος (literally "gold-fingered") does not appear in earlier Greek sources, but Epictetus does refer to a hypothetical scene where a gray old man enters having "many gold rings on his fingers" (χρυσοῦς δακτυλίους ἔχων πολλούς) (Epictetus, *Diatrib.* 1.18.22). In some Latin sources, the wearing of a gold ring was evidently the mark of equestrian rank (Reicke, 27; Laws, 27). Such a specific identification of the parties involved is not necessary, however, in light of the broad contrast expressed here between the rich and the poor. The appropriate connection with the glorious description of the Messiah's person mentioned in 2:1 should not be overlooked. The glory of Jesus alludes to the brightness of His heavenly exaltation and so outshines the gold ring and lustrous clothing of the proposed rich man that it would also insult the Messiah to show him favoritism.

The scene is in "your synagogue" (συναγωγὴν ὑμῶν), which adds to the authenticity of the scene even if it does not prove that an actual case is being described. In Classical Greek, the rare word συναγωγή could signify any gathering or bringing together of persons or things, the same meaning it acquired in the LXX. In its 228 LXX occurrences it not once in the canonical books has the meaning that it later acquired clearly by NT times. In the LXX we read about a συναγωγὴ ὑδάτων (Gen 1:9) and even a συναγωγὴ ἐθνῶν (Gen 48:4). It did, however, often render the Hebrew עֵדָה (Exod 12:3; Lev 4:13; Num 1:2 and more than a hundred times). It was during the time between the testaments that συναγωγή began to acquire the technical meaning of a building set apart for the purposes of worship and the reading of the Torah, the familiar transliterated word in English, the "synagogue." Philo witnessed that every significant Jewish community in Palestine and the Dispersion had a synagogue, and larger cities had more than one. Of Alexandria, he wrote: πολλαὶ ... καθ' ἕκαστον τμῆμα τῆς πόλεως (*Laws* 132). The Gospels and Acts alone mention the συναγωγὴ as a place of Jewish worship fifty-three times.

But this συναγωγὴ has congregants who hold to the faith of Jesus the Messiah (2:1). This building is not synonymous with the "church" (ἐκκλησία) in 5:13, which refers to the body of people. The context is Jewish, and the use of the word elsewhere in the NT affirms that is a worship center for Jewish believers. There have been commentators who have viewed this word as referring not to a building, but to the assembly of persons (Ropes, 188; Davids, 108; Moo, 2000, 103), but the physical references to "entering" and "sitting" and "footstool" point, however, to some sort of building. This is the only place in the NT where this specific term is used for gatherings of Jesus-followers, although a similar cognate noun (ἐπισυναγωγή) is used in a parallel function in Hebrews 10:25. While this is another indication of the Jewish-Christian nature of the letter, it may also illustrate the possible measure of continuity between the Torah-based communities and the Jesus-based communities in these early days of the movement. When in 5:14 we read of the prayer and healing ministry of the elders from the "assembly" (τοὺς πρεσβυτέρους τῆς ἐκκλησίας), the word is consistent with its usage elsewhere in the NT—namely, the ἐκκλησία is the *gathering* of believers, while the term συνάγωγη is used for their gathering *place*. It is difficult to find an example of the term ἐκκλησία referring to a church building until late in the second century. The use of the word συναγωγή for a place of worship that included Jewish believers, and possibly even for mixed congregants, continued also into the second century (Justin, *1 Apol.* 134.3; Ign. *Pol.* 4.2; *Trall.* 3.1).

2:3 ἐπιβλέψητε δὲ ἐπὶ τὸν φοροῦντα τὴν ἐσθῆτα τὴν λαμπρὰν καὶ εἴπητε· σὺ κάθου ὧδε καλῶς, καὶ τῷ πτωχῷ εἴπητε· σὺ στῆθι ἐκεῖ ἢ κάθου ὑπὸ τὸ ὑποπόδιόν μου: The verb ἐπιβλέψητε is the plural aorist subjunctive of ἐπιβλέπω which is used in LXX Psalms for looking on someone favorably (Pss 12:4; 24:16; 32:13; 68:17; 73:20). This is the sense in the only other NT uses of the verb (Luke 1:48; 9:38). Here the favorable look is based solely on the outward appearance of the rich man. The adjective λαμπρός ("luminous, shining, radiant" GE, 1212) was often used to describe a "bright" heavenly body (Philo, *Som.* 2.282; Rev 22:16), but could also be applied to the "bright" clothing of a human (Philo, *Jos.* 105; Josephus, *Vit.* 334; *Ant.* 8.72), of an angel (Luke 23:11; Acts 10:30), or of the glorified saints (Rev 19:8).

Mr. "Goldfinger" is ushered to "sit here in a good place" (κάθου ὧδε καλῶς). The RSV renders the adverb as a request to "sit here, *please.*" The main verbs of 2:3 are actually plural in form, following the plurality of the opening address in 2:1. In the illustration, one person would presumably do the directing of people to their seats, although he would no doubt do so to reflect the usual practice of the meeting. James is concerned with a general warning to his readers against the attitude of favoritism thus illustrated.

In contrast the poor man is directed to sit in the shadow of the discriminator's footrest (ὑποπόδιόν). The use of the image in LXX Ps 109:1—as well as in other NT and LXX passages (Ps 98:5; Isa 66:1; Matt 5:35)—subordinates one person to another. In contrast to the proximity of the rich person ("sit here in a good place"), the closeness here is even more humbling than being made to stand at a distance. It is in reality a form of mockery. To these very different people, different treatment is wrongly given.

2:4 οὐ διεκρίθητε ἐν ἑαυτοῖς καὶ ἐγένεσθε κριταὶ διαλογισμῶν πονηρῶν: The apodosis of the conditional clause (2:4) is actually a question that (with the negative particle οὐ) expects a positive answer. The question is asked: "Have you not made distinctions among yourselves....?" The answer is expected: "Yes, we have." The verb διεκρίθητε is the aorist passive of διακρίνω and with the phrase ἐν ἑαυτοῖς, it can be a bit ambiguous. On a literal level, the passive of the verb expresses an internal dividedness (Mayor, 85; Ropes, 192; Martin, 63), in the sense of trying to live by two standards at once and thus "divided in opinion" (Matt 21:21; Mark 11:23; Acts 10:20; Rom 4:20; 14:23). At the same time, the active sense of the verb ("to make distinctions/discriminate") is conveyed in Matt 16:3; Acts 11:12; 15:9 (Dibelius, 136; Laws, 102; Davids, 110).

The verb was used earlier of making distinctions between persons where preeminence was then allowed for certain ones (Herodotus 3:39; Philo, *Op.* 137). This is the same verb used in 1:6 of doubting in prayer (διακρινόμενος). It means literally "to divide," and in 1:6 it was characteristic of the double-souled man (1:7) who is so very unstable. The divisiveness here in 2:4 ("made distinctions among yourselves") is displayed by a divided attitude toward the rich and the poor, instead of a whole and "perfect" attitude that treats each in one consistent way—fairly! The divided leaders have become "judges *with* evil motives" (διαλογισμῶν πονηρῶν), in the sense of judges characterized by evil motives, or "judges who make evil decisions." This is best identified as a genitive of description, the most essential use of the genitive case.[4] These leaders are wrong because they regard only external appearances and do not take account of the unmatched glory of our Lord Jesus Christ.

This passage has been applied by most commentators to acts of discrimination in seating privileges within a public worship service (e.g., Mayor, 82–83; McCartney, 139–40; McKnight, 185–87). The context of the passage and its intertextual OT links, however, may point to another explanation. In an influential article, R. B. Ward has argued that the scene in this passage should not be viewed as describing the gathering of a congregation for a worship service but rather as describing a congregational "court" session to render judgment on a case brought before its leaders.[5] James condemns the sinful partiality displayed so openly by those who are "judges" (κριταί) who "made discriminatory distinctions" (διεκρίθητε). The paronomasia (wordplay) is evident in the original language with such words as διακρίνω and κριταί. The reference in 2:6 to the poor being drawn into "courts" (κριτήρια) continues a chain in the passage consisting of the κρι-words' semantic field and further supports this view from the context. Furthermore, the OT warning about showing partiality was addressed to Israel's judges (Deut 1:17; Lev 19:15).

A legitimate application of the passage can certainly still be made

---

[4] Wallace, 88. This is also called an "adjectival genitive" (Moule, 175).

[5] R. B. Ward, "Partiality in the Assembly," *HTR* 62 (1969) 87–97. Although some commentators have taken notice of Ward's suggestion, they often treat his article as introducing something new to the interpretation of James. Actually, the "legal" interpretation was quite popular among commentators in the seventeenth and eighteenth centuries. I personally found this view expressed by Daniel Whitby prior to 1727 (D. Whitby, *A Paraphrase and Commentary on the New Testament* [5th ed.; London, 1727]). Dale Allison traces the interpretation back to the Puritan Thomas Manton (1620–1677). He cites a total of sixteen English and French commentators who expounded it. He also mentions that, for some strange reason, it completely dropped out of sight in the nineteenth and twentieth centuries until Ward's Harvard dissertation and subsequent article. D.A. Allison, "Exegetical Amnesia in James," *ETL* 76 (2000) 162–66.

by preachers concerning the discriminatory favoring of rich people in their seating privileges or in their social positions of authority. It appears, however, that the context of the passage makes better sense if readers and hearers can imagine the assembly leaders gathering to decide discriminatory issues between believers (Matt 18:15–17; 1 Cor 6:1–6). There are some recent commentators who are also persuaded about the "judicial gathering" interpretation (Davids, 109–10; Martin, 57–58; Johnson, 223–27; Hartin, 117–18; Blomberg-Kamell, 110–11). Perhaps the unjust practice of rich landowners withholding pay to their day-laborers, which will be so strongly condemned in 5:1–6, was the kind of legal complaint that was possibly being handled in such a scene. As is so true today, it is in legal proceedings where poor people often suffer discrimination because they do not have an adequate recourse available to them. While that may happen in some secular contexts, James insists that it must not happen among those who believe in the glorious Lord who became poor for all of us. Jesus' specific contribution to this issue and James' application of it is seen in the next section.

Honoring Those God Honors (2:5–7)

Greek Text

5 Ἀκούσατε, ἀδελφοί μου ἀγαπητοί· οὐχ ὁ θεὸς ἐξελέξατο τοὺς πτωχοὺς ᵃτῷ κόσμῳ πλουσίους ἐν πίστει καὶ κληρονόμους τῆς ᵇβασιλείας ἧς ᶜἐπηγγείλατο τοῖς ἀγαπῶσιν αὐτόν; 6 ὑμεῖς δὲ ἠτιμάσατε τὸν πτωχόν. οὐχ οἱ πλούσιοι καταδυναστεύουσιν ὑμῶν καὶ αὐτοὶ ἕλκουσιν ὑμᾶς εἰς κριτήρια; 7 οὐκ αὐτοὶ βλασφημοῦσιν τὸ καλὸν ὄνομα τὸ ἐπικληθὲν ἐφ' ὑμᾶς;

Textual Notes

5.a. The dative τῷ κόσμῳ in 2:5, the reading of the critical text, is strongly supported by a number of important witnesses (ℵ A* B C*).

The variant readings εν τω κοσμω (322 323 *pc*) and του κοσμου (A² C² P Ψ m) are most likely attempts by later scribes to smooth out the reading.

5.b. Alone among the entire manuscript tradition, the original scribes of ℵ and A replace βασιλείας with επαγγελιας, possibly under the influence of Hebrews 6:17.

5.c. Two mss from the twelfth (1505) and the fifteenth (2495) centuries add ο θς and one from the eleventh century (1243) adds ο κς to provide an expressed subject of the verb ἐπηγγείλατο, which is unnecessary in the relative clause because θεὸς has already been expressed as the subject of the main verb.

Context

This section begins with the familiar nominative of direct address, ἀδελφοί μου, combined with the fronted imperative verb, ἀκούσατε. This combination, however, does not justify a too-quick decision that an entirely new paragraph of James is now being initiated. Actually, there are three linguistic features that must be present to signal that beginning of a new paragraph in James: first, a nominative of address (sometimes called a vocative plural); second, an imperative command or a rhetorical question; and third, a new semantic theme. Without a new topic there cannot be the introduction of a new major paragraph. This was clearly seen previously at James 1:2, 16, 19, and 2:1. It will also be evidenced later at James 2:14; 3:1, 13; 4:1, 11, 13; 5:1, 7, 12 and 19. Combinations of ἀδελφοί and an imperative alone at other locations like this one only serve to intensify the portrayal of the topic introduced in 2:1 throughout the rest of the section by making an additional comment on the topic or a particular application of it within the section. This function is also clearly illustrated at James 3:10, 12; 5:9, 10. In James 2:5 the initial imperative ἀκούσατε further functions as a meta-comment that calls attention to the question that follows. Therefore, in light of this, James 2:5 is the beginning of the second subparagraph (2:5–7) within the larger unit (2:1–13).

Sentence Flow and Translation

5 Ἀκούσατε, ἀδελφοί μου ἀγαπητοί·
Listen, my beloved brothers,

οὐχ ὁ θεὸς ἐξελέξατο τοὺς πτωχοὺς τῷ κόσμῳ πλουσίους ἐν πίστει
has not God chosen those considered poor *in the eyes of* the world to
  be rich *with respect to* faith

καὶ κληρονόμους τῆς βασιλείας
and heirs of the kingdom

ἧς ἐπηγγείλατο τοῖς ἀγαπῶσιν αὐτόν;
that he promised to those who love him?

6 ὑμεῖς δὲ ἠτιμάσατε τὸν πτωχόν.
But you have dishonored the poor person.

οὐχ οἱ πλούσιοι καταδυναστεύουσιν ὑμῶν
Do not the rich oppress you,

καὶ αὐτοὶ ἕλκουσιν ὑμᾶς εἰς κριτήρια;
and do they not drag you into courts?

7 οὐκ αὐτοὶ βλασφημοῦσιν τὸ καλὸν ὄνομα
Do they not blaspheme that honorable name

τὸ ἐπικληθὲν ἐφ᾽ ὑμᾶς;
which has been pronounced over you?

Exegetical Comments

2:5 Ἀκούσατε, ἀδελφοί μου ἀγαπητοί· The aorist imperative ἀκούσατε ("listen") is used to mark emphatically the importance of what follows in the law (Deut 6:3–4; 9:1), the prophets (Amos 3:1; 5:1; Mic 1:2; 6:1; Joel 1:2; Isa 1:10; 7:13; 48:1), the writings (Ps 119:149; Prov 1:8; 4:1; 19:20), as well as other Jewish wisdom literature (Wis 6:1; Sir 6:23). It is also used this way also in Matthew 13:18; Mark 7:14; Luke 18:6; Acts 1:22; 15:13; 22:1. In the NT a meta-comment or orienter like this word is used to direct attention to a following principle of fundamental importance.[6] While it is not used in second person plural in other epistles, we find the similar but still more urgent ὁ ἔχων οὖς ἀκουέτω/ἀκουσάτω in the Gospels (Matt 11:15; 13:9, 43) and in the Apocalypse (Rev 2:7, 11, 17; 29; 3:6, 13, 22; 13:9). This is the last of three times that James will accompany one of these imperatives with ἀγαπητοί (1:16, 19). The common characteristic in each of these occurrences is that a principle is stressed that the readers know but are neglecting to do or to recognize.

οὐχ ὁ θεὸς ἐξελέξατο τοὺς πτωχοὺς τῷ κόσμῳ πλουσίους ἐν πίστει, "has not God chosen those who are considered poor in the eyes of the world to be rich with respect to faith"? After the command to listen, there are five primary clauses in 2:5-7. These clauses contain three rhetorical questions, which also provide a link with the rhetorical question asked at the end of 2:4. The hypothetical scene that he described in 2:2-3 has been concluded and James now effectively makes his point by means of these questions, each of which is conveyed with the negative particle οὐχ/οὐκ that indicates that James expects a positive answer.[7] The rhetorical effect in these questions is that they convey three declarative statements (queclaratives), which James expects his readers to then affirm. Those queclaratives are (1) that God has chosen those that are poor by the world's standards to become rich heirs in

---

[6] Runge, 101–124
[7] Mathewson-Emig, 232–33.

His kingdom, 2:5; (2) that the rich usually dishonor the poor and often oppress them, 2:6; and (3) that by doing so, the rich ironically dishonor the name that is honored by the poor, 2:7. These themes of shame and honor, which were so important in the socioeconomic scene in the ancient world, are clearly evident in these rhetorical questions. Therefore, readers and hearers should rather honor the ones whom God honors. On the other hand, they also should not show favoritism in honoring the ones who dishonor those whom God chooses to honor![8]

Those synagogue leaders in the illustration of 2:2–3 have chosen to honor the rich. God, however, has honored many poor people by choosing them to be the heirs of His kingdom. The words echo the biblical election of Israel (Num 16:5; Deut 4:37; 7:7; LXX Pss 32:12; 134:4; Isa 14:1; 43:10), which also carries over to the NT (Acts 13:17) and is applied specifically to the messianic believers (Mark 13:20; John 15:16; Eph 1:4). The emphasis on God's sovereign choice of His people as a gracious gift is consistent with what James wrote earlier about the choice that God made when he would "birth" believers (1:18). The aorist middle indicative of ἐκλέγομαι ("He chose for Himself") is the very form used by Paul three times of God's electing choice in 1 Cor 1:27–28. In that passage, the emphasis is also on God's choosing the "despised and lowly," in contrast with the "high and mighty." In choosing the poor, He has made them to be rich, although their riches do not consist in gold and fine clothing. The double accusative (πτωχοὺς ... πλουσίους) is in an object-complement relationship to the verb. He chose the poor "to be" rich in faith.

The first dative (κόσμῳ) is either a dative of respect (poor in the things of the world)[9] or an ethical dative (poor in the eyes of the world: see Acts 7:20; 1 Cor 1:18; 2 Cor 10:4). The second dative (πίστει) is governed by ἐν and is probably indicating respect ("rich in respect to

---

[8] For a thorough treatment of 2:5 and the entire letter in light of 2:5, see D. H. Edgar, *Has God not Chosen the Poor? The Social Setting of the Epistle of James* (JSNTSup 206; Sheffield: Sheffield Academic Press, 2001).

[9] Moule, 46; Turner 3, 238; Wallace, 145.

faith") or even sphere ("rich in the sphere of faith").[10] Therefore, the absence of the preposition with κόσμῳ and the references cited probably indicate an ethical dative in the first expression ("poor in the world's eyes").

The words κληρονόμους τῆς βασιλείας combine the second word of the double accusative with an objective genitive ("the ones who inherit the kingdom"). "Heirs" are persons who are appointed to receive the inheritance. This expression clearly echoes a passage like Matt 5:3: "Blessed are the poor in spirit, for theirs is the kingdom of heaven." This is indication that when James mentions the "royal" or "kingly" law in 2:8, he must be referring to the King, who promised His kingdom to poor believers. The genitive kingdom (βασιλείας) serves as the direct object of the head noun κληρονόμους. Many older commentators have viewed the "kingdom" as being the present one on earth (Mayor, 86; Oesterley, 438; Lange, 75). Consistent with the eschatological focus for the poor in the rest of the book (1:9–11; 5:1–6), it is best to see the kingdom as an eschatological promise (Huther, 107; Davids, 112; Moo, 107). The kingdom is neither further described at this point nor does James use the term again. A nuanced and balanced approach is to affirm that the kingdom denotes the great future blessing that God offers to his chosen heirs, yet which is "already" experienced in foretaste (McKnight, 195) and thus practically equivalent to salvation (Luke 12:31–32).

ἧς ἐπηγγείλατο τοῖς ἀγαπῶσιν αὐτόν: They are inheritors of a kingdom not passed on by the normal channels of inheritance. The kingdom is here thought of as still future (as is shown by ἐπηγγείλατο). They are heirs through a promise that was given to those who love Him. Later in this section that "royal law" will be expressed in terms of Lev 19:18 and its use by Jesus in Matt 22:37–39. Love for one's neighbor is stressed there, but how about the love to God command in Deut 6:5? Already James has mentioned through the very same words in 1:12 that God

---

promised the crown of life "to those who love Him" (ἐπηγγείλατο τοῖς ἀγαπῶσιν αὐτόν). Thus the twofold command of love to God and love to mankind is evident in James' message.

We should pay closer attention to two larger issues that are raised in Jas 2:5–7. They are (1) the presence of the *logia* of Jesus in James and (2) the specific identity of the "poor" and the "rich" in the letter. This divergence is in keeping with our conviction that most introductory issues can only be solved by the exegesis of the book itself. Hence they are treated here even though the issue of James' use of Jesus-sayings was discussed in the Introduction. The questions probe deeply the layers of this text beyond the important textual and ideological layers—layers at which many commentators cease exploring.

In considering the intertextuality of passages like 2:5–7, the question again emerges about James' possible utilization of the canonical or oral Jesus-sayings. This issue of intertextuality is also important in the following subparagraph (2:8–13) where citations from the OT are utilized, one of which he calls the "royal law" or the "law of freedom." Does James intentionally use what he had heard from the teaching of Jesus and, if so, in what way does he utilize these sayings? James' reference to God's choosing the poor who are rich in faith to be heirs of the kingdom share the words "poor" and "kingdom" with a saying of Jesus recorded in both Matt 5:3 and Luke 6:20. It is more than a chance similarity because both Jesus and James mention the poor as recipients and heirs of the kingdom. But James does not slavishly repeat word-for-word the Jesus *logion*, and he does not have to do so for it to be an allusion that not only shares the vocabulary but also uses the words in a similar context. In the Introduction, I shared Bauckham's insight that James uses and adapts material from Jesus in a similar way that Sirach uses and adapts material from Proverbs. Word-for-word quotation is not demanded, for other NT writers often used the OT in a similar manner.[11]

---

[11] For a thorough discussion of these ways that the NT utilizes the OT and also its relevance to James, see G. K. Beale and D. A. Carson, eds., *Commentary on the*

I repeat here the conclusions about the use of Jesus *logia* by James that we drew in the Introduction. (1) Almost every point that James makes is either grounded or illustrated by an adapted saying or aphorism that echoes in some way a *logion* of his older brother. (2) When James' use of the orally transmitted sayings of Jesus is acknowledged, it becomes probably the strongest argument for the early dating of the book.

2:6 ὑμεῖς δὲ ἠτιμάσατε τὸν πτωχόν: The δὲ indicates a development from 2:5 which stressed the teaching of Jesus. The fronting of the pronoun ὑμεῖς further intensifies the charge. The second issue, after identifying the Jesus logion is about the specific identity of the "poor" and the "rich" in James. The two groups figure prominently at key locations in his book (1:9–11; 5:1–6) as well as here in 2:1–7. Furthermore, why is specific language used about the wrongness of "dishonoring" the poor? Bruce Malina has analyzed the social conditions in the first-century society where people did not necessarily move up and down in their status but simply sought to maintain the socioeconomic status into which they had been born. "Being classified as poor was the result of some unfortunate turn of events or some untoward circumstances. Poor persons seem to be those who cannot maintain their inherited status due to the circumstances that befell them and their families, such as debt, being in a foreign land, sickness, death of a spouse, or some personal physical accident. ... The opposite of rich would not necessarily be poor. Thus, in this context, rich and poor really refer to *the greedy* and *the socially ill-fated*"[12]

It is widely acknowledged among historians of the first century that *honor* and *shame* are two of the most "pivotal values of the Mediterranean world"[13] The importance of these values has great significance for James' presentation of the favored rich and the

---

New Testament Use of the Old Testament (Grand Rapids: Baker Academic, 2007), xxiii–xxviii, and Carson, "James," 997–1013.

[12] Malina 100.

[13] Malina 27.

disfavored poor in the synagogue court context described in 2:1–4. The poor man would be dishonored while the rich man would be honored by this type of treatment. The divine standard, however, as it is communicated both in the Jesus *logion* of 2:5 and later in the "royal law" of 2:8 actually subverts the so-called accepted societal norms and reveals the radical, countercultural nature of James' ethical values for the community of those who follow Jesus as the Messiah.

οὐχ οἱ πλούσιοι καταδυναστεύουσιν ὑμῶν καὶ αὐτοὶ ἕλκουσιν ὑμᾶς εἰς κριτήρια: James employs two vivid verbs to describe the details of how the rich dishonor the poor in this particular context. The verb καταδυναστεύω conveys the sense of oppression or exploitation by abuse of power (BDAG, 516). It is found frequently in the LXX for the oppression of the poor by the rich and powerful (Ezek 18:12, 22:29; Amos 4:1; Zech 7:10). The powerful man mentioned in the OT text that James is expounding (Lev 19:15) is in the LXX referred to by the cognate noun δυνάστης (Muraoka, 179). The verb ἕλκω (BDAG, 318) is used in Acts for those who threatened to bring a form of their own perverted legal action against believers, being used "to drag" Paul away in Acts 16:19; 21:30. Wealthy Sadducees had also done this with Peter and John (Acts 4:1). Paul had once dragged (σύρω) men and women before the Sanhedrin (Acts 8:3; 22:4), and had even tried to make them blaspheme (Acts 26:11).

This judgment seat is also called a κριτήριον in Exo 21:6; Dan 7:9; 1 Cor 6:2, 4. Paul came to learn how the situation could be turned on him when he became a believer, for he also suffered what he had earlier inflicted on others (Acts 13:50). Jesus had indeed foretold that just this fate would befall his disciples before the courts of Jews and Gentiles (Matt 10:17–23). The appearance of the noun κριτήρια again supports the "legal proceedings" interpretation of the scene described earlier in 2:2–4.

2:7 οὐκ αὐτοὶ βλασφημοῦσιν τὸ καλὸν ὄνομα τὸ ἐπικληθὲν ἐφ' ὑμᾶς, Blasphemy in general is injurious speech, but in its religious context, it is to "speak irreverently/impiously/disrespectfully of or about" God or sacred things (BDAG, 178). For blasphemy from the Christian point of view, see Acts 13:45; 18:6; 26:11; 1 Tim 1:13; and 1 Cor 12:3. An interesting observation that can be made is that if the name of Jesus is blasphemed, then His deity is certainly implied.

The point that James is making in 2:7b should not be missed when seen in the above-mentioned shame and dishonor context. To slightly paraphrase it: "Do not they speak *shamefully* (βλασφημοῦσιν) of that *honorable* name (τὸ καλὸν ὄνομα) which has been pronounced over you (τὸ ἐπικληθὲν ἐφ' ὑμᾶς)?" The attributive passive participle τὸ ἐπικληθὲν modifies τὸ καλὸν ὄνομα as part of the direct object of βλασφημοῦσιν. The expression "to call a name upon someone" can be traced to the LXX, where it indicates possession, particularly in relationship to God (Amos 9:12; Deut 28:10; 2 Chron 7:14; Isa 43:7; Jer 14:9); or to a wife (Isa 4:1); or to children (Gen 48:16). That "name" that is mentioned may have been "Christian" since it had recently been used of the believers in Antioch (Acts 11:20), and it probably communicated the idea of a "Messianist." It was a term that those who belonged to the "Way" probably did not coin but that they accepted (Acts 11:26; 26:28).

James could also be referring specifically to the naming of poor believers at their baptism, indicating their new owner by taking on his "name" (Dibelius, 141; Davids, 114). Some have been quite negative toward this suggestion (Ropes, 197), and others have been hesitant (Blomberg-Kamell, 115, and Moo, 2000, 109). James' use of the aorist participle may suggest that he is deliberately alluding to the specific time when the name was received, rather than simply to the general character of his readers (Laws, 105). Whatever its original context, it soon came to be a name that was worn by these believers with honor (1 Pet 4:16; Did 12:4). James himself, during an event that was not very far distant in time from the writing of this letter, quoted the prophecy in Amos 9:15 where the LXX uses the same language to describe Yahweh's naming of Gentiles as their new owner, when they are brought into the eschatological kingdom (Acts 15:17—ἐφ' οὓς ἐπικέκληται τὸ ὄνομά μου; "upon whom my name is called").

The Royal Law (James 2:8–9)

Introduction

James 2:8–13 comprises the third and final subparagraph within the larger unit beginning at 2:1 and concluding at 2:13. The topic introduced in 2:1 was a strong warning against showing discrimination and partiality in the believing community. Throughout the larger section, this topic is especially applied to how this sinful favoritism is practiced to the disadvantage of the poor and to the advantage of the rich. The literary linkage between the sections is made clear by the use of the verb προσωπολημπτεῖτε in 2:9, which recalls the noun προσωπολημψίαις in 2:1.

In that first subparagraph (2:1–4), acts of partiality are shown to be inconsistent with a saying from the Torah (Lev 19:15) that is alluded to in 2:1. In the second subparagraph (2:5–7), acts of partiality are shown to be inconsistent with a saying from Jesus that is alluded to in 2:5 (the believing poor as heirs of the kingdom as it is expressed in Matt 5:3 and Luke 6:20). In this, the last subparagraph (2:8–13), acts of partiality are shown to be inconsistent with a saying from the Torah (Lev 19:18, regarding loving one's neighbor) that is also a saying from Jesus (Matt 22:39). James, therefore, calls it a royal or "kingly" law (2:8). James 2:1–13 is a skillful midrashic treatment of Lev 19:12–18, the use of which continues at later points in his letter as well (Jas 4:11; 5:4, 9, 12, 20). This type of creative intertextuality that utilizes both the OT and the sayings of Jesus will continue to play a major role in the argument of James about perfect and mature behavior from this point onward. We deal with 2:8–9 and 2:10–13 separately as further subsections of 2:8–13. This is for a pragmatic reason of dealing more effectively with a smaller passage by seeing the clausal analysis more clearly. But there is also a reason for the break since 2:8–9 deals with the "kingly law" (νόμον ... βασιλικὸν), while 2:10–13 deals with the "whole law" (ὅλον ... νόμον).

Greek Text

8 Εἰ μέντοι νόμον τελεῖτε βασιλικὸν κατὰ τὴν ᵃγραφήν· ἀγαπήσεις τὸν πλησίον σου ὡς σεαυτόν, καλῶς ποιεῖτε· 9 εἰ δὲ προσωπολημπτεῖτε, ἁμαρτίαν ἐργάζεσθε ἐλεγχόμενοι ὑπὸ τοῦ νόμου ὡς παραβάται.

Textual Notes

8.a. The significant variant reading is the changing of the singular "the scripture" (τὴν γραφήν) into a plural in the Vulgate and some Coptic versions plus two minuscules dating from the twelfth and fifteenth centuries. No Greek manuscript prior to the twelfth century supports this reading.

Context

We deal with 2:8–9 and 2:10–13 separately as further subsections of 2:8–13. This is for a pragmatic reason of dealing more effectively with a smaller passage by seeing the clausal analysis more clearly. But there is also a reason for the break since 2:8–9 deals with the "kingly law" (νόμον ... βασιλικὸν), while 2:10–13 deals with the "whole law" (ὅλον ... νόμον). This section consists of two first class conditional clauses that are contrasted by the author's variation on the classic μέν ... δὲ construction. A paraphrase would be as follows: "If his readers really (μέντοι) are fulfilling the royal law of loving one's neighbor, they are doing well (καλῶς ποιεῖτε). But (δὲ), if they show partiality, they are committing sin" (ἁμαρτίαν ἐργάζεσθε). He uses it again only in the contrasting statements about wisdom from above and below (3:17–18). This strongly expressed contrast serves to heighten the severity of the inconsistent behavior displayed by those who are guilty of the sin of partiality—the theme that was introduced in 2:1. James then concludes the contrast with a result participle after the second conditional clause in 2:9b showing how those who show such partiality are guilty of law breaking: "and thus are convicted (ἐλεγχόμενοι) by the law as transgressors." This result clause stresses the dangerous severity of this behavior as consisting of not simply a poor choice, but the breaking of a Torah commandment.

Sentence Flow and Translation

8 Εἰ <u>μέντοι</u> νόμον τελεῖτε βασιλικὸν κατὰ τὴν γραφήν· PROTASIS
   If you really are fulfilling the kingly law according
      to the Scripture,

     ἀγαπήσεις τὸν πλησίον σου ὡς σεαυτόν, APPOSITION
     You shall love your neighbor as yourself

καλῶς ποιεῖτε· APODOSIS
you are doing well.

 9 εἰ <u>δὲ</u> προσωπολημπτεῖτε, PROTASIS
   But if you are showing partiality,

ἁμαρτίαν ἐργάζεσθε APODOSIS
you are committing sin

   ἐλεγχόμενοι ὑπὸ τοῦ νόμου ὡς παραβάται. RESULT
   and thus are convicted by the law as transgressors.

Exegetical Comments

2:8 Εἰ μέντοι νόμον τελεῖτε βασιλικὸν κατὰ τὴν γραφήν· ἀγαπήσεις τὸν πλησίον σου ὡς σεαυτόν, καλῶς ποιεῖτε:

μέντοι, "indeed" or "really." Some commentators and translations take this particle as adversative. Indeed its limited use (five times) in the LXX may indicate this (Prov 5:4; 16, 25, 26; 22:9; 26:12; see Muraoka, 448). An adversative sense is not the case when it is combined with a δὲ like it is in 2:9. There is an implied contrast with what has gone before. Although μέντοι does perform an adversative function in John 4:27; 7:13; 12:42, in those verses it is not balanced by the δὲ as it is here. Jude 8–9 (ὁμοίως μέντοι καί, "indeed in the same way also") is a better parallel use to James 2:8–9. The μέντοι points to the next verse, not backward. It is the entire unit of 2:8–9 that contrasts with the behavior described in 2:1–7. Therefore, the best translation is "indeed" or "really."

νόμον τελεῖτε βασιλικὸν: The lack of an article does not justify the translation "a law," since James' practice is to use this word without an article (1:25; 2:11, 12; 4:11). The adjective βασιλικὸν is used of a king's official or "royal" robe (Esth 8:15) and also in the graphic scene about Herod in Acts 12:21 (described also by Josephus in *Ant.* 19, 344). Some commentators prefer the translation "supreme law" (Martin, 67; McKnight, 206), but the previous reference to "kingdom" (2:5) indicates that a rendering connecting it to royalty should be made. It is "kingly" because its source is the King and it is the law of His kingdom (Laws, 108; Davids, 114; McCartney, 147). This reference to "law" here and elsewhere in James is not restricted to the Mosaic law. When James speaks of the OT "law" (or one of its commandments), he simply uses νόμος (2:10–11). When he is referring to the Jesus-shaped understanding of that "law," he qualifies νόμος, as in 1:25 and 2:12: "the law of freedom." Here the term "law" is equally qualified, and in this case the specific "law" was mentioned by both Moses and also by Jesus! The present active indicative of τελέω is the only use of this verb in James, although common elsewhere in conjunction with νόμος (see Luke 2:39).

κατὰ τὴν γραφήν· ἀγαπήσεις τὸν πλησίον σου ὡς σεαυτόν: The specific Torah commandment he quotes is found in Lev 19:18. This is the first time James directly quotes from the OT—although he has alluded earlier to Lev 19:15 when he condemned partiality in 2:1—and he has echoed the language of the OT on a number of occasions. He will continue to utilize and adapt the message of Lev 19:12–18 to a number of the subjects he will treat. He refers to this Torah command as a "royal law," and this is the way in which it is translated by almost every English translation. This rendering, however, obscures for English readers the very point that James intends to communicate. The Greek word for "royal" (βασιλικὸν) points back to the cognate word for "kingdom" (βασιλείας) that he used in 2:5. This is the kingdom that the believing poor will inherit, and it is also an allusion to the macarism in both Matt 5:3 and Luke 6:20. This language also recalls the "faith of our glorious Lord Jesus Christ" in 2:1, whose name has been called over those same believing poor in 2:7. Thus, when "our glorious" messianic king cited Levi 19:18 as part of His program of kingdom values, it was transfigured into the royal or "kingly" law. To the English reader, the translation "royal" may blur the clear connection to 2:5, the law given by the new Davidic and messianic King. Although the adverb "kingly" is not as widely used as "royal," its cognate identity with "kingdom" enables the English reader to see better the intended semantic association, which of course was clear to the Greek reader. Some may think it is necessary to make a distinction between the various synonyms for "word" and "law" in James. I am convinced, however, that James would not intend a semantic or even theological distinction between the Torah and Jesus' teaching. James bases his argument on the Torah as it was understood, interpreted, and applied by the new King over the reconstituted twelve tribes, our glorious Lord Jesus the Messiah. Thus, although sounding awkward, it is helpful to translate the expression as the "kingly law" to make clear that James is alluding to the beatitude about the inheritors of the kingdom in 2:5.

τὸν πλησίον: This noun is generally used in the LXX for Hebrew רֵעַ, "friend", "fellow countryman," or "other person." Sentences with the subject ἕκαστος and a form of ὁ πλησίον as the object occur in Rom 15:2;

Eph 4:25; and Heb 8:11, which are quotations of the LXX Jeremiah 31:34 or 38:34. These derive from the association of the Hebrew אִישׁ with רֵעַ to indicate reciprocal behavior (Josephus, *War* 295; Philo, *Abr.* 40; *Mos.* 1.137). Under the influence of Jesus' teaching, as in Luke 10:25–37, it is equivalent to ὁ ἕτερος in the Pauline admonitions to love (Rom 13:8, 10; 15:2).

καλῶς ποιεῖτε: These two words are the apodosis of the conditional clause in 2:8. Because James uses it in a sarcastic sense in 2:19, some have thought that sarcasm was his intention here. This expression used elsewhere means simply "you are doing do well" (Mark 7:37; Acts 10:33; 1 Cor 7:37; 2 Pet 1:19; 3 John 6). Furthermore, this expression as an example of sarcasm misses the effective rhetorical use of the adverb. In 2:3, he quotes the partial leader of the synagogue who says to the wealthy attendee, "You sit here in a good place [καλῶς]." If there is sarcasm, it is directed not at the one who "fulfills" (τελεῖτε) this royal law, but at the one who is showing partiality. In other words, you are doing *well* to love your neighbor as yourself instead of seating the rich man *well*. There is another reason that Lev 19:15 is the "royal" or "kingly" law. Jesus the King cited this verse in response to a question about what is the greatest commandment in the law (Matt 22:34–40; Mark 12:28–31; Luke 10:25–27). But Jesus also included the great command to love the Lord God as part of His response (Deut 6:5). How could James omit the command from Deuteronomy in his application of the royal law to the problem of partiality? A close reading of the context indicates that he does not omit it. In 2:5 he mentioned that the kingdom is promised "to those who love Him." In our discussion of that verse we did not speculate about what specific promise James was referencing. Perhaps he was referring to the great love command in Deuteronomy. Thus love for God and for neighbor is joined together both by Jesus in the Synoptic accounts and also by James in this chapter.

2:9 εἰ δὲ προσωπολημπτεῖτε: As part of the protasis in this second conditional clause, James uses the verb of the word group he introduced at the beginning of the chapter (προσωπολημψίαις). The noun does appear three times in Paul's writings, where it indicates that there is no partiality with God (Rom 2:11; Eph 6:9; Col 3:25). In a similar context, the noun προσωπολήμπτης appears in Acts 10:34. The verb used by James is a true hapax legomenon, and may even be a neologism that is coined by James. The allusion to Lev 19:15 is even more obvious here than in 2:1. In the context of this law of love, Leviticus adds, "Do not practice wickedness in judgment. Do not accept the appearance of the poor man nor be astounded at the appearance of the powerful man. In justice, you will judge your neighbor" (Lev 19:15).

ἁμαρτίαν ἐργάζεσθε: James' two uses of the verb ἐργάζομαι are both negative. In 1:20, he asserted that human anger does not "work" the righteousness of God, and here the "working" of a sin opposes righteous judgment. Sin (ἁμαρτίαν) here does not have the personified sense that it had in 1:15. It rather points to the "transgression of the law" as disobedience to the lawgiver. It is more than an error of judgment or a breach of etiquette. It is an act of sin (ἁμαρτίαν), a missing of the mark that is fraught with grave consequences. His use of the verb ἐργάζομαι may appear unexpected ("working sin"?), but may also be appropriate to his later discussion of the "works" in 2:13ff. and contrasted with the works of faith done by Abraham and Rahab in 2:21–25. "Works can be sinful as well as faithful" (McCartney, 148).

ἐλεγχόμενοι ὑπὸ τοῦ νόμου: The present passive participle has been taken as simply restating their guilt (Davids, 115; McKnight, 210). Its tense and location, however, indicates that it more probably expresses result (Bengel, 16) since it fits all the characteristics of a result participle (Wallace 637-39). The result of one's crime is conviction! The verb ἐλέγχω means to reprove someone (Luke 3:19) or to expose them (John 3:20) or convict someone of something (John 8:46; see BDAG, 315). Here the passive voice with ὑπὸ indicates the thing by which they are convicted (1 Cor 14:24). Since breaking Lev 19:15 clearly reveals that Lev 19:18c is not being kept, the law itself exposes and convicts the sinner. The article τοῦ performs an anaphoric function, pointing back to the anarthrous νόμον in 2:8.

ὡς παραβάται: The noun παραβάτης is related to παράβασις, an "overstepping" or "transgression" as in Rom 2:23 (BDAG, 759). The noun appears in Greek literature as a "transgressor" (Aeschylus, *Eum.* 553), and a "renegade" (GE, 1542) but does not appear in the LXX, but the concept is related to παραβάσις which involves a very serious "overstepping" or "transgression" of the law (2 *Macc* 15:10; Philo, *Som.* 2.123; Josephus, *Ant.* 8.129). The severity of the transgression conveyed by both nouns in the Jewish conception of sin should not be overlooked. By "working" this sin they cross over God's established boundaries. The word is found in the NT outside of Paul (Gal 2:18; Rom 2:25, 27) only here in James 2:9 and 11. It may be that James also is speaking of the new law of 2:8, since one cannot fulfill this "supreme law" and still discriminate against the poor, as is brought out in the next verse. James, however, would probably not see that it is either the Levitical law or Jesus' law, since He viewed them both as one piece.

The Whole Law (2:10–13)

Greek Text

10 ὅστις γὰρ ὅλον τὸν νόμον ᵃτηρήσῃ πταίσῃ δὲ ἐν ἑνί, ᵇγέγονεν πάντων ἔνοχοςᵇ. 11 ὁ γὰρ εἰπών·ᶜμὴ μοιχεύσῃς, εἶπεν καί· μὴ φονεύσῃς· εἰ δὲ οὐ μοιχεύεις φονεύεις δέ, ᵈγέγονας παραβάτης νόμουᵈ. 12 Οὕτως λαλεῖτε καὶ οὕτως ποιεῖτε ὡς διὰ νόμου ἐλευθερίας μέλλοντες κρίνεσθαι. 13 ἡ γὰρ κρίσις ἀνέλεος τῷ μὴ ποιήσαντι ἔλεος· κατακαυχᾶται ἔλεος κρίσεως.

Textual Notes

10.a. A large number of variants to τηρήσῃ (τηρησει, τηρη, τελεσει, τελεση, πληρωσει, πληρωσας τηρησει) in later uncials and minuscules probably reflect an early mistake and later attempts to correct it. The early support τηρήσῃ in ℵ A B C, however, should not be questioned.

10.b...b. Ψ alone replaces γέγονεν πάντων ἔνοχος with παντων ενοχος εσται.

11.c. A handful of uncials (C, Ψ) and minuscules (primarily 614, 630, 945, 1241, 1505, 1739, 1852, 2464) seek to conform James' aorist subjunctives (μὴ μοιχεύσῃς and μὴ φονεύσῃς) to future indicatives (οὐ μοιχεύσεις and οὐ φονεύσεις) that are found in the LXX of Exod 20:13–14. This reflects an effort to change the indirect discourse found here (ὁ γὰρ εἰπών and εἶπεν καί) to convey the direct discourse of the LXX.

11.d ... d. Instead of the expression γέγονας παραβάτης νόμου in 2:11, P[74] and A have γέγενου ἀποσπάτης νόμου ("you have become an apostate from the law"). While there have been defenders of this reading (Martin, 57), it is probably later since it reflects the later meaning of παραβάτης in patristic Greek as an "apostate."

Context

This second part of the overall section of 2:8–13 is marked by a change from discussing the "royal law" to a broader discussion of "the whole law." The presence of γάρ at the beginning of vv. 10, 11, and 13 connects this section with 2:8–9 and links the section together tightly. The description of those who break the "kingly law" as transgressors (2:9b) leads to this section (2:10–11) that explains and elaborates what is intended by the expression, "transgress the law." The postpositive γάρ in 2:10 explains that even if someone could obey all the laws but one, he or she has still become guilty of all of them (γέγονεν πάντων ἔνοχος).

Then in 2:11, James will illustrate his apparently severe point by citing the sixth and seventh words of the Mosaic Decalogue, namely the prohibitions against adultery and murder. The law is a whole and breaking one command still makes a person a law transgressor. James develops further his discussion of partiality in 2:10–13 by issuing two imperatives in 2:12, with each command introduced by οὕτως. He concludes with two aphorisms conveyed by the indicative mood in 2:13, with the first clause introduced by a causal γάρ and the second standing alone.

Sentence Flow and Translation

10 ὅστις γὰρ ὅλον τὸν νόμον τηρήσῃ
   For whoever observes the whole law

      πταίσῃ δὲ ἐν ἑνί γέγονεν πάντων ἔνοχος
      but stumbles in one point is accountable for all of it.

11 γὰρ εἰπών· μὴ μοιχεύσῃς, εἶπεν καί· μὴ φονεύσῃς·
   For he who said, "Do not commit adultery," also said, "Do not murder."

      εἰ δὲ οὐ μοιχεύεις φονεύεις δέ,
      And if you do not commit adultery but you murder,

   γέγονας παραβάτης νόμου.
   you have become a transgressor of the law.

12 Οὕτως λαλεῖτε καὶ οὕτως ποιεῖτε
   So speak and so act

      ὡς διὰ νόμου ἐλευθερίας μέλλοντες κρίνεσθαι.
      as those who are to be judged under the law of liberty.

13 ἡ γὰρ κρίσις ἀνέλεος τῷ μὴ ποιήσαντι ἔλεος·
Because judgment is without mercy to one who has shown no mercy.

κατακαυχᾶται ἔλεος κρίσεως.
Mercy triumphs over judgment.

Exegetical Comments

2:10 ὅστις γὰρ ὅλον τὸν νόμον τηρήσῃ: When ὅστις takes the subjunctive it is usually joined with ἄν, as in Matt 10:33; 12:50; Luke 10:35; John 2:5; 14:13; Acts 3:23; and Gal 5:10. Regarding ὅστις: "w. ἄν whereby the indefiniteness of the expression is heightened" (BDAG, 729; see also BDF, 380). Because ἄν is omitted, there are variants of -ει replacing -η among the later manuscripts resulting in some confusion as to whether the future or aorist subjunctive is the true reading, but the aorist is strongly supported by the earlier uncials (see the previous Textual Notes). The verb for "keep" (τηρέω) is used like the Hebrew שָׁמַר ("guard") in reference to a command, the idea being guarding something against violation. The placement of the adjective ὅλον before τὸν νόμον conveys the following idea: "whoever keeps the law as a whole."

πταίσῃ δὲ ἐν ἑνί: Another aorist subjunctive following ὅστις. The verb πταίω refers to a literal stumbling (BDAG, 894.1), but this meaning lent itself easily to moral stumbling (Philo, *Alleg. Interp.* 3.66). In the indicative it appears again in 3:2 describing stumbling with the tongue. See also its figurative use in the LXX of Deut 7:25 (Muraoka, 605) and also in Rom 11:11. The picture is that of a παραβάτης stumbling over a border which marks his way, which is consistent with the famous expression in Jewish rabbinic writings about making a "hedge" or "fence" around the Torah (*m. Avot* 1.1). It does not seem that νόμος is ever used of a particular precept, the meaning of ἐντολή, but the Ten Commandments are never called οἱ δέκα νόμοι. James may unconsciously pass from the collective sense of νόμος to the particular precepts of which it consisted, without reflecting whether such a use of the term was "proper." There are many examples of the substantival use of the neuter ἕν in the nominative and accusative, but not often in the other cases (see, however, 1:4: ἐν μηδενὶ λειπόμενοι).

The specific reference is to those who fail in the one point— namely, that of committing προσωπολημψία, although they may claim to keep the rest of the law. More probably it is a general reference to the man who thinks himself to be religious (1:26) and assumes that all is right with himself, like the Pharisee in the parable (Luke 18:11). The principle affirmed by James here is also to be found in *Midrash Bemidbar*: "R. Hunna, having taught his disciples that he who committed adultery broke all the commandments, was asked by them to explain how this could be true of the fourth commandment."

γέγονεν πάντων ἔνοχος: The third singular perfect of γίνομαι describes the state of the guilty one. The adjective ἔνοχος basically means "subject to/liable to," but it has a wide range of applications (BDAG, 338.2). It can mean liable to a penalty (Aristotle, *Rhet.* 1380A), which is its use in Matt 26:66. In the NT it can also mean subject to slavery (Heb 2:15) or responsible for the body and blood of the Lord (1 Cor 11:27). The punishment with ἔνοχος is usually in the genitive (Matt 26:66; Mark 3:29, 14:46), but also in the dative (Matt 5:21). Πάντων is equivalent to ὅλου τοῦ νόμου. There are a number of passages in rabbinical writings that are in agreement with this teaching, especially *Shemot Rabbah* xxv: "The Sabbath weighs against all the precepts." In other words, if you break the Sabbath law, you have broken all of them.

But how does one become guilty of all the law by breaking one of the laws? One idea that has been suggested is that breaking one point reveals an attitude that will break the law in other points (Dibelius, 146; Davids, 117; McKnight, 215). Another approach is to view this guilt with reference to 2:11: "For he who said, 'Do not commit adultery,' also said, 'Do not murder.'" There is only one lawgiver, which is a point he will later firmly declare in 4:12. Therefore, there is one whole and entire law, not just many individual and separate laws unrelated to each other. Since the law is the expression of the will of the One who gave it, the transgression of a single portion of the law is disobedience to that one will, and consequently a transgression of the whole law. The implication is clear that followers of the Lord cannot choose to obey some laws (the "heavy" ones) and then neglect the other ones (the "light" ones) like the royal law of love to a neighbor. God is one. Therefore, His law is also unitary. This is another example of James' emphasis on being single rather than double, an emphasis that characterizes his entire message. Perhaps the translation of 2:10b, "he has become accountable for all of it," better conveys the sense of the entire expression (NRSV, ESV).

2:11 ὁ γὰρ εἰπών: The substantival participle is probably a circumlocution for God, following a Jewish practice of not directly uttering the name of God unless it was necessary to do so. The unity of the law derives from the unity of the lawgiver (see later on 4:12). The same person utters both of the commandments about adultery and murder, so a theological basis is laid for the unity of His law, which is the expression of one will. The essence of sin lies in disobedience to that will. It was by an appeal to the same principle that Jesus answered the question of the lawyer ποία ἐστὶ πρώτη πασῶν ἐντολή: "The first of all the commandments is, 'Hear, O Israel; the Lord our God is one Lord; and you shall love the Lord thy God ...'" (Mark 12:29). The citation formula of the two precepts is different from James' usual way of referencing OT passages. He normally introduces these as γραφή (2:8, 23; 4:5), but here uses a masculine article and participle, which forbids an assumed reference to the feminine γραφή. The aorist participle εἰπών suggests the definitive speaking of God on Sinai: "The one who said ... said also."

μὴ μοιχεύσῃς, εἶπεν καί· μὴ φονεύσῃς: For the order of the seventh commandment preceding the sixth, see LXX Exod 20:13, 14; Luke 18:20;

and Rom 13:9. The usual order originally given in Exod 20 is found in Deut 5:17; Matt 5:21, 27; and 19:18. A handful of uncials (C, Ψ) and minuscules (614, 630, 945, 1241, 1505, 1739, 1852, 2464) seek to conform James' aorist subjunctives to future indicatives (οὐ μοιχεύσεις and οὐ φονεύσεις) that are found in the LXX of Exod 20:13–14. This reflects an effort to change the indirect discourse found here (ὁ γὰρ εἰπών and εἶπεν καί) to convey the direct discourse of the LXX.

εἰ δὲ οὐ μοιχεύεις φονεύεις δέ: This is the second time that James directly cites the OT (Exod 20:13, 14). It is interesting to note that when James later accuses the readers of "murder" in 4:2, he then follows it up with calling them "adulteresses" in 4:4! The shift from the μή plus subjunctives to the οὐ plus indicatives evidences the shift from direct quotations in 2:11a to the indirect quotations in the conditional clause of 2:11b. There is another grammatical reason for the shift. "Condition of first class with οὐ [ou] (not μη [mē]) because of the contrast with δε [de], whereas εἰ μη [ei mē] would mean 'unless,' a different idea" (Robertson, *James*, 56).

Why does James isolate these two particular commands? Both of these are referred to by Jesus in the Sermon on the Mount, a passage with which James has numerous connections. Both the prohibition against adultery and the one against murder come from the second table of the Decalogue, whose "horizontal" commandments were closely associated in early Christian teaching with the love commandment (Matt 19:18–19; Rom 13:8–10) to which James has already referred. James does not stipulate every statute in the Mosaic covenant, but rather "the royal law" (2:8), "the law that gives freedom" (2:12). This is also in line with Jesus, who expressed unqualified endorsement of the law (Matt 5:18–19) while insisting that He is the one who fulfills it (Matt 5:17). In this fulfillment He reshapes even the prohibition against murder (Matt 5:21–30). So also does James, since he applies the point about the law's unity to the law as it is reinterpreted by Jesus. Furthermore, these are two of the laws that Jesus Himself directed toward the heart—namely, one's motives and emotions. Murder is bound up with hate and adultery with lust. Proper response to God ultimately probes the heart and motives, and a command such as "Love your neighbor as yourself" not only addresses nasty problems of favoritism but also turns out to be the crucial point on which all of God's demands hang.[14]

γέγονας παραβάτης νόμου: The perfect of γίνομαι again has in view the state of the transgressor. If a person does not break one but breaks the other he still is "a transgressor of the law." For the use of the perfect tense of γίνομαι following different tenses in both verses, see the comments on 1:24. The aspect of the verb serves to "frontground" the state of affairs in which the lawbreaker is found—he *is* a guilty transgressor. Porter also calls this the "timeless use" of the perfect (42). For his approach to the perfect tense form as "frontgrounding" the action, see Porter, 32, 302–03.

2:12 οὕτως λαλεῖτε καὶ οὕτως ποιεῖτε: The double imperative, along with the repetition of οὕτως for emphasis, propounds the idea that the readers must act in a positive way in order to be "doers of the word" (1:22; 2:14–26). The imperatives are both in the present tense, suggesting continual or habitual action; thus "You must keep on speaking and acting in every respect as ..." The exhortations again insist on the importance of one's right regulation of speech (3:1–12), as well as correct behavior (2:14–26). The repetition of οὕτως is in accordance with the style of the writer (see 1:19 on βραδύς). The double οὕτως probably looks back rather than forward.

ὡς διὰ νόμου ἐλευθερίας μέλλοντες κρίνεσθαι: The absence of the article before νόμου, which was used in 1:25, serves to lend greater prominence to the qualifying genitive. The present participle μέλλοντες ("about to") provides an eschatological frame of reference, but there is certainly nothing in James that suggests judgment will be

---

[14] For this discussion and application of 2:10-11, I have borrowed from the insightful discussion by D.A. Carson, "James," Carson and Beale, 1001–02.

in a far distant time (cf. 5:9). The verb μέλλω followed by an infinitive in the Koine Period "in a weakened sense serves simply as a periphrasis for the fut." (BDAG, 627.1.c.β). Whenever that judgment takes place, readers should recognize that those who have wrongly judged others (2:1–4) will themselves give an account. And this judgment will take place not according to the standards of the world, but according to God's standards revealed in His "perfect law."

If we are not clear about James' emphasis on the unifying nature of law as it was taught by Jesus, we may posit a different referent for the "law of liberty" under which we are to be judged. "However, the 'perfect law' (1:25), the 'law of liberty' (1:25; 2:12), the 'royal law' (2:8), the 'law' (2:9, 11), and the 'whole law' (2:10) are all in continuity with each other as the law as it is expounded by Jesus" (Varner, 101). When one recognizes this important point, they can perceive the wholeness of the entire law as James wishes us to view it. It is one law, and it is truly revealed in many aspects and characteristics. It is, however, given by the one lawgiver in heaven; conveyed by His servant lawgiver on Sinai, and then fulfilled through His messianic law-interpreter on the hills of Galilee.

2:13 ἡ γὰρ κρίσις ἀνέλεος τῷ μὴ ποιήσαντι ἔλεος: James concludes 2:1–13 and his exhortation on partiality with two parallel indicative clauses, the first introduced by γὰρ, and the second standing alone. The subtle shift from the second person used in 2:12 to the third person used in 2:13 indicates the role of these two statements as general aphorisms that apply to the problem he has been discussing. The statement introduced by the post-positive γάρ is negative in tone, concluding the exhortation against discrimination: "Because judgment is without mercy to one who has shown no mercy." The substantival infinitive clause, τῷ μὴ ποιήσαντι, is in the dative case, expressing "disadvantage" (Wallace 143-44). Mercy as a moral virtue is widely attested in Jewish wisdom writings (Sir 27:30–28:7; Tob 14:9). In Sirach, the expression "show mercy" (ποεῖν ἔλεον) becomes linked to the sharing of possessions with the poor (Sir 29:1; 18:13), thus creating a bridge to the concept of almsgiving (ἐλεημοσύνη, which translates either חֶסֶד or צְדָקָה).

When the canonical LXX books translate that Hebrew word חֶסֶד as ἔλεος, it conveys the expression of God's loving-kindness, grace, and love toward his human creations, especially conveyed through His covenant with Israel (Pss 5:8; 6:5; 39:11; 47:9; see Muraoka, 223). The focus in James, however, is not on God's mercy to his people, but mercy shown to one another. This horizontal focus of "doing mercy" also recalls many OT references combining the verb עָשָׂה ("do") with the noun חֶסֶד ("mercy"). As mentioned, this combination is translated in the LXX with ποιεῖν and ἔλεος. For the way in which this can be shown to one another, see Josh 2:12: "Swear to me before the Lord your God, 'I will show you mercy [ποιῶ ... ἔλεος/חֶסֶד],' and that you will show mercy (ποιήσετε ... ἔλεος/חֶסֶד) to my father's house." Rather than expressing the English idea of "pity," James draws on the Hebraic חֶסֶד concept of "steadfast love" as reflected in covenant relationships. Jesus also communicates this same idea by a cognate expression in Matt 6:2: ὅταν ποιῇς ἐλεημοσύνην (see also Matt 5:7; 6:14; 7:1; 18:28–35; 25:41–46).

The failure to show mercy or consideration for others forbids us to expect mercy ourselves. The perfect law of liberty produces mercy in the believer, but where no mercy is shown, no mercy can be expected—only judgment. The thought again echoes a Jesus logion such as: "For with the judgment you pronounce, you will be judged, and with the measure you use it, will be measured to you" (Matt 7:2). This strong language of Jesus and of James should not be tempered, and the severity of the verse not then diminished. Those who do not demonstrate a living faith face harsh judgment in the end.

κατακαυχᾶται ἔλεος κρίσεως: The second aphorism/statement in 2:13b, while parallel in structure as a primary clause, is more positive in tone: "Mercy triumphs over judgment." The absence of a connecting conjunction (asyndeton) is a feature in the style of James (see 5:6 κατεδικάσατε, ἐφονεύσατε τὸν δικαιον οὐκ ἀντιτάσσεται ὑμῖν and 1:19 ταχὺς εἰς τὸ ἀκοῦσαι, βραδὺς εἰς τὸ λαλῆσαι). The asyndeton also heightens the stand-alone nature of this aphorism that is specifically applied to partiality. The compound verb used here is also found in 3:14 and Rom 11:18, while the simple verb was used in 1:9. For the intertextual connections, see Hos 6:6: ἔλεος θέλω ἢ θυσίαν ("I desire mercy and not sacrifice") quoted by Jesus in Matt 9:13, where the Pharisees complain of Jesus eating with publicans and sinners, and again in Matt 12:7 when they find fault with the disciples for eating grain (see also Luke 7:47; 1 Pet 4:8; and Matt 23:23). "But the asyndeton allows the words to be taken in their widest generality, as embodying the very essence of the Christian law of liberty, affirming the universal principle of God's judgment, even when it seems to be ἀνέλεος, and supplying the rule for the believer's daily life" (Mayor, 92).

Does this expression mean that their mercy cancels out judgment (Alford, 296)? Or is it simply the other side of the preceding clause, where the unmerciful one is judged (Ropes, 202)? The best view is that those who show mercy need not fear the judgment. The boasting that is implied in the verb κατακαυχάομαι conveys the idea of triumphing over judgment (BDAG, 517: "to have a cause for boasting because of advantage in power, *triumph over*"). This does not imply that showing mercy earns God's mercy but that being merciful indicates that the person has been transformed by God's merciful grace (in which they "boast," see Rom 5:1–2) and need not fear God's judgment.

This concise but effective pair of aphorisms functions both to round off this section (2:1–13) and also to anticipate the next section (2:14–26), so the reference to mercy works both anaphorically and cataphorically. "Mercy" is that virtue that partiality denies to the poor (2:4), and "mercy" also offers practical provision for the needs of the poor (1:27; 2:15, 16).

6

SHOW YOUR FAITH
BY YOUR DEEDS (2:14-26)

A Parable of the Poor (2:14-17)

Introduction

Two distinct discourse markers set this second main paragraph of the chapter apart from the first paragraph (2:1–13). One is the use of the nominative of direct address in the words ἀδελφοί μου and the second is the introduction of a new topic, the inseparable alliance of faith and deeds (2:14). The paragraph, however, is not isolated from its previous context because it brings together three themes that were previously introduced: (1) hearing/doing (1:22–25); (2) discrimination (2:1); and (3) the poor (2:5). Although James 1:22–25 stressed the importance of not only hearing but also doing the word, it is in this passage that the theme of faith and actions finds its most complete treatment. Hearing implies faith and James uses πίστις sixteen times, eleven of them in 2:14–26. He uses ἔργον (deed) fifteen times and twelve appear here, each in the plural. Nine of these uses of ἔργον appear in close connection with πίστις—a combination that occurs nowhere else, although the theme of a behavior that must match one's profession permeates the book.

The unique association of faith and deeds in this section should not obscure the fact that this passage has many anaphoric links with what precedes. There are many semantic patterns, which are clearly parallel with themes in 2:1–13 but also advance the discussion. Consider the striking semantic themes that are repeated from 2:1–13:

1. Brothers are warned about how they should "have faith" (2:1 and 2:14).

2. A vivid and compelling example is then offered (2:2–4 and 2:15–17).

3. The non-compassionate treatment of the ill-clad poor is described (2:2 and 2:15).

4. Proofs from both logic and Scripture are offered (2:5–12 and 2:20–26).

5. An aphoristic saying rounds off and concludes each paragraph (2:13 and 2:26).

6. The comment "you do well" is used each time in an ironic sense (2:8 and 2:19).

7. His readers are "called" by a name (2:7) and Abraham was "called" by a name (2:23).

Greek Text

14 Τί τὸ ὄφελος, ἀδελφοί μου, ἐὰν πίστιν ᵃλέγῃ τις ἔχειν ἔργα δὲ μὴ ᵃἔχῃ; μὴ δύναται ἡ πίστις σῶσαι αὐτόν; 15 ἐὰν ἀδελφὸς ἢ ἀδελφὴ γυμνοὶ ὑπάρχωσιν καὶ λειπόμενοι τῆς ἐφημέρου τροφῆς 16 εἴπῃ δέ τις αὐτοῖς ἐξ ὑμῶν· ὑπάγετε ἐν εἰρήνῃ, θερμαίνεσθε καὶ χορτάζεσθε, μὴ δῶτε δὲ αὐτοῖς τὰ ἐπιτήδεια τοῦ

σώματος, τί τὸ ὄφελος; 17 οὕτως καὶ ἡ πίστις, ἐὰν μὴ ἔχῃ ἔργα, νεκρά ἐστιν καθ' ἑαυτήν.

Textual Notes

Unlike the fairly stable textual tradition of 2:1–13, there are a number of variant readings in 2:14–26. This is probably due to the various ways in which one can understand the diatribal tone of this section. Yet Metzger and the committee of the UBS4 saw no issues in 2:14–17 that merited attention, and only two others are mentioned in 2:19, 20, and 25. There are, however, some distinctively Byzantine variants.

14.a. Around a dozen late manuscripts have the indicatives λέγει and ἔχει instead of the subjunctives λέγῃ and ἔχῃ in 2:14. A few readings preserved in the Byzantine family and the Textus Receptus will be mentioned in the textual notes for 2:18–19 and 2:20–26.

Changes in NA28

2:15 NA27: ἐὰν ἀδελφὸς ἢ ἀδελφὴ γυμνοὶ ὑπάρχωσιν καὶ λειπόμενοι τῆς ἐφημέρου τροφῆς

2:15 MAJ: Ἐὰν δὲ ἀδελφὸς ἢ ἀδελφὴ γυμνοὶ ὑπάρχωσιν καὶ λειπόμενοι ὦσιν τῆς ἐφημέρου τροφῆς,

2:15 NA28: ἐὰν ἀδελφὸς ἢ ἀδελφὴ γυμνοὶ ὑπάρχωσιν καὶ λειπόμενοι ὦσιν τῆς ἐφημέρου τροφῆς

NA28 moves closer to MAJ. SBLGNT, NIV, and THGNT follow NA27.

Context

The critical Greek texts divide 2:14–26 into three sections (2:14–17, 18–19, and 20–26). This appears reasonable given the fact that they hold various linguistic characteristics in common. First, 2:14 and 2:17 bookend a parable that addresses the neglecting of the needs of the poor by the use of the rhetorical question Τί τὸ ὄφελος (What good is it?). Second, 2:18 presents an aphorism beginning with the adversative conjunction ἀλλ' which preemptively answers a possible objection that could be raised, the answer to which is immediately presented. Third, a challenge comes to the would-be objector in 2:21–25, which calls his understanding into question and provides the appropriate information through Abraham and Rahab, who serve as exemplars. Finally, in 2:26 a second aphorism is presented which summarizes his point and stresses again the inherent inseparability of faith and works. The following exegesis will develop along the lines of these three divisions of 2:14–26. Because of the large number of grammatical and semantic issues in 2:14 that need attention, we will deal with this verse in depth before we turn to the analysis of 2:15–17.

2:14 Τί τὸ ὄφελος, ἀδελφοί μου, ἐὰν πίστιν λέγῃ τις ἔχειν ἔργα δὲ μὴ ἔχῃ; μὴ δύναται ἡ πίστις σῶσαι αὐτόν; This verse contains two questions. The first rhetorical question is actually the apodosis (the "then" clause) of a third class conditional clause, with the protasis (the "if" clause) introduced by ἐὰν, which follows rather than precedes the apodosis. The protasis also has the infinitive ἔχειν to indicate "reported speech" or indirect discourse. Such infinitives follow verbs of saying or thinking and here that verb is λέγῃ. The subject of the infinitive is the same subject of the verb λέγῃ ("if someone says that he/she has faith").

The second question in the verse is an independent clause expressed negatively by the particle μή. When a question is asked with μή, it anticipates a negative response. The last important grammatical feature in the second question is the presence of the article before the noun "faith" (ἡ πίστις). The article is used anaphorically to refer back to the word "faith" (πίστιν) in the previous clause-question. The function of the article, therefore, is like the far demonstrative pronoun "that" and the expression is translated as "that faith" or "that kind of faith" in this commentary and in a number of recent English versions.[1] We will recall these grammatical features in the exegesis of the individual words and expressions in the verse.

Sentence Flow and Translation

From this point, we present a sentence flow and translation of each verse if the passage extends to over three verses.

14
Τί τὸ ὄφελος, ἀδελφοί μου,
What good is it, my brothers,

> ἐὰν πίστιν λέγῃ τις ἔχειν ἔργα
> if someone says that he has faith

> δὲ μὴ ἔχῃ;
> but he does not have accompanying deeds?

μὴ δύναται ἡ πίστις σῶσαι αὐτόν;
Can that kind of faith save him?

Exegetical Comments

Τί τὸ ὄφελος, ἀδελφοί μου: The use of ἀδελφοί without a conjunction combined with the introduction of a new topic indicates a new paragraph. The interrogative pronoun Τί appears for the first time in the book and introduces a rhetorical question, as it does also in 2:16 (the same question), and later in 3:13; 4:12; and 5:13 (twice). James has already asked rhetorical questions in 2:5, 6, and 7, and such questions continue as part of his rhetorical strategy, particularly in this section

---

[1] ESV ("that faith"); NASB ("that faith"); NIV, CSB ("such faith"); NET ("this kind of faith"); NLT ("that kind of faith"). The KJV, RSV, NRSV do not clarify this anaphoric use of the article.

(2:16, 20, 21, 25). The concentration of questions here is a clear indication that James is now thoroughly engaged in a diatribe with opponents to whom he will give a voice and then challenge that wrong opinion.

The noun ὄφελος was a common one in Jewish moral literature (Philo, *Abr.* 55; *Post.* 24; *Quod Deu.* 33; *Agr.* 30). The specific form of the word appears only once in the LXX (Job 15:3), but note the use of the similar τίς ὠφελία (Sir 20:30; 41:14; Job 21:15). The expression occurs outside James in the NT only in 1 Cor 15:32, where Paul asks, "If from human motives I fought with wild beasts at Ephesus, what does it benefit me [τί μοι τὸ ὄφελος]?" The verb ὀφείλω, however, appears often in the NT and in Matt 16:26 provides an interesting parallel to the use of the noun here in 2:14: "For what shall a person be benefited [τί γὰρ ὠφεληθήσεται ἄνθρωπος] if he gains the whole world and loses his soul?" James will use the question to end 2:16, and thus it serves as an inclusio to "bookend" his point about the necessary alliance of faith and works.

ἐὰν πίστιν λέγῃ τις ἔχειν: This "if" clause is the protasis of a third class conditional clause, which proposes a situation without assuming it has actually happened. As recent grammarians have recognized, conditional sentences can function rhetorically in a number of ways (se Young, 225-30). Here the question is used to challenge the imagined interlocutor with the lack of benefit in having a faith that is not accompanied by appropriate deeds. It is important to notice the reported speech of this imagined person. He does not necessarily have faith; he "says" (λέγῃ) that he has faith. The indirect discourse expressed by the infinitive (ἔχειν) gives voice to the imagined person who later engages with the author as a debate opponent (see Wallace, 604). That interlocutor is later directly quoted in the parable of 2:18–19 and is finally directly addressed by the second person vocative in 2:20 as "O vain person." This interpersonal dynamic, as it is so vividly portrayed through the diatribe format, progressively increases in intensity throughout the section.

ἔργα δὲ μὴ ἔχῃ: The reported speech ends before this contrasting clause is introduced by the postpositive δὲ which signals a development from James' comment on the person's statement. It is better to translate the term ἔργα as "deeds" or "actions" since the English word "works" carries a good deal of baggage from the discussions in the Reformation over meritorious religious "works." As will be seen, James and Paul are using this important term in different but very important ways. This translation of "deeds" will at least help to avoid confusion with Paul's teaching on "works of the law." We will attempt from this point to expound James' teaching in chapter 2 on its own context and not simply to read him as a foil to Pauline teaching.

μὴ δύναται ἡ πίστις σῶσαι αὐτόν; The second rhetorical question concluding 2:14 brings into doubt the nature of a faith that is professed but that is not accompanied by the appropriate actions. The accompanying negative particle μή indicates an expected negative reply. The noun πίστις has been taken to describe real Christian faith but one that does not have deeds (Dibelius, 152). It is better, however, to view the article ἡ before πίστις as serving an anaphoric function, referring back to the type of deficient faith that was described in the earlier conditional sentence. In other words, the sense conveyed is: "No. That kind of faith cannot save the person who says that he has it" (Wallace, 219). It is very important to take notice of this article, omitted in earlier translations like the KJV, RSV, and NRSV.[2] Most commentators disagree with Dibelius and recognize this anaphoric role of the article. This was the approach both of older commentators (Bede, 27–32; Alford, 297; and Mayor, 96), as well as more recent ones (Martin, 81; Moo, 2000, 123; and McKnight, 229). The importance of this more accurate translation lies in not leaving an impression on the reader that James is saying that faith does not save. This misunderstanding could possibly arise from the KJV rendering ("can faith save him?") and possibly contributed to the supposed

---

[2] An attempt by the ASV ("Can that faith save him?") was ignored by these later translations.

contradiction between James and other NT writers. James will repeat this anaphoric use of the article when he ties together the argument of this sub-section in 2:17: "So also that kind of faith (ἡ πίστις), if it is not accompanied by actions, is dead being by itself."

The reference to salvation by the complementary aorist infinitive σῶσαι echoes other passages in James. If one has followed his argument to this point, then the answer to this question is obvious. It is the "word of truth" (1:18) implanted by God that is "able to save our souls" (1:21), but that takes place only if they are "doers of the word and not hearers only" (1:22–25). It is God who both saves and destroys (4:12), as it is the concerned brother who saves the wanderer (5:20). So it is true that the right kind of faith does save (5:15)! In keeping with James' eschatological emphasis elsewhere in the letter mentioned above, the saving refers to final salvation, especially since δύναται ("is able") implies a future event (Dibelius, 152; Davids, 120; McCartney, 156; McKnight, 229). The aspect of the present verb δύναται is depicted as not yet completed, while the aspect of the aorist infinitive σῶσαι is depicted in its totality (Porter, 29–35; Young, 121–22).

Sentence Flow and Translation

15
ἐὰν ἀδελφὸς ἢ ἀδελφὴ γυμνοὶ ὑπάρχωσιν
If a brother or sister is poorly clothed

καὶ λειπόμενοι τῆς ἐφημέρου τροφῆς
and lacking in daily food,

Exegetical Comments

2:15 ἐὰν ἀδελφὸς ἢ ἀδελφὴ γυμνοὶ ὑπάρχωσιν: James again utilizes a conditional sentence as he proposes a possible scenario in 2:15–16. His fondness for parables, already seen in 1:22–25 and in 2:2–4, is illustrated again by introducing people who, like the poor person in

2:2, are inadequately dressed. This is one of the few examples in the NT where there appears the female equivalent of ἀδελφός, as describing a member of the believing community (Phlm 2; 1 Tim 5:2; 1 Cor 7:15; 9:5; Rom 16:1). Thus James clearly refers to either a "brother or sister" who lacks not only needed clothing but also the necessary food to keep them alive for that day. In the ancient world, however, people were considered "naked" (γυμνοί) if they did not have clothing that was adequate for a public appearance (BDAG, 208), or were "without a cloak" (GE, 446). The word was used of the fisherman Peter at work in John 21:7. Most commentators recognize the meaning of the word as "ill-clothed" (Ropes, 206) or lacking appropriate clothing (Oesterley, 444; Moo, 2000, 125). Rather than simply stressing a body that we see, we should associate the term with poverty (Rev 3:17) and shame (Gen 3:10; Ezek 16:7; Rev 3:18). The naked ones, therefore, are people who most obviously are in need of assistance (Tob 1:17; 4:16).

καὶ λειπόμενοι τῆς ἐφημέρου τροφῆς: The NA28 adds the present subjunctive of εἰμί, ὦσιν, following the present participle λειπόμενοι, which as a "verbal adjective" parallels the earlier adjective γυμνοί. While lacking in the 4th century majuscule texts, this ὦσιν parallels the subjunctive ὑπάρχωσιν in the first clause. The expression ἐφημέρου τροφῆς ("necessary food" or "daily food") is in the direct object genitives following the participle λειπόμενοι. The verb describes those whose need is so obvious that to refuse them is to betray the very nature of religious "faith" (Sir 4:1–6; 34:20–22). The verse again echoes a Jesus *logion* in Matt 25:36: "I was naked (γυμνός) and you clothed me."

Sentence Flow and Translation

16

εἴπῃ δέ τις αὐτοῖς ἐξ ὑμῶν·
but if one from among to you says

> ὑπάγετε ἐν εἰρήνῃ,
> Go in peace,
> θερμαίνεσθε καὶ χορτάζεσθε,
> be warmed and filled

> μὴ δῶτε δὲ αὐτοῖς τὰ ἐπιτήδεια τοῦ σώματος,
> without giving them the things needed for the body,

> τί τὸ ὄφελος;
> what good is that?

Exegetical Comments

2:16 εἴπῃ δέ τις αὐτοῖς ἐξ ὑμῶν: An aorist subjunctive third person verb εἴπῃ continues related to the original ἐάν in 2:15. Also repeated is the indefinite pronoun τις. The description of the indifferent response to the needy one mentioned in 2:15 portrays this guilty person as part of the community James is addressing. He is "from among you" (ἐξ ὑμῶν). The serious callousness conveyed by this heartless response is magnified by the fact that it is spoken by someone else in the disadvantaged person's believing community.

ὑπάγετε ἐν εἰρήνῃ, θερμαίνεσθε καὶ χορτάζεσθε: "Go (present imperative of ὑπάγω) in peace" is a familiar Jewish form of expressing a farewell. Other NT examples are in Mark 5:34; Luke 7:50; and 8:48. The Hebrew equivalent is לֵךְ לְשָׁלוֹם (1 Sam 20:42; see also Judg 18:6; 1 Sam 1:17; 2 Sam 15:9; 2 Kgs 5:19). The present verbs θερμαίνεσθε and χορτάζεσθε could be either middle or passive in form. If the former, this person would be encouraging his needy fellow-believers to provide for themselves—in other words, "to make your own way." The sense would be: "keep yourselves warm, and have plenty to eat." The NRSV, NET, and NIV also adopt a middle translation by their "keep warm." If the verbs are passive, the dismissal would take the form of a prayer: "May you be warmed and well fed." In either case, the heartless response described is the same. Faced with a seriously felt need among his own brothers and sisters, this callous and indifferent member of the community is portrayed as doing nothing but expressing his good wishes.

μὴ δῶτε δὲ αὐτοῖς τὰ ἐπιτήδεια τοῦ σώματος: The δέ signals a negative development from the previous request. The subtle shift to a plural verb (aorist subjunctive δῶτε) is easily overlooked but not a problem. "The plural is often used after an indefinite singular, such as ἕκαστος, τις, ὅστις" (Mayor, 95). The broadening of the reference is intended to apply this problem to the whole community which James is addressing. The noun ἐπιτήδεια is another of the many *hapax legomena* in James, although the word appears once in the LXX "canonical" books (1 Chr 28:2), eight times in the Apocrypha (1 Macc 4:46; 10:19; 13:40; 14:34; 2 Macc 3:37; 6:30; Wis 4:5), and as a variant reading in Acts 24:25. The substantive plural means "the things that are necessary" (BDAG, 383-84). The use of the genitive "body" (σώματος) is not discussed in the standard grammars, but is probably a simple attributive genitive: "bodily necessities," namely, the basic coverings to sustain life.

τί τὸ ὄφελος; The repetition of the rhetorical question from 2:14 provides an inclusio for this first section. But it is not used just for literary decoration. James believes his original question in 2:14 has now been answered by his illustration. It also adds a powerful rhetorical punch by reminding the reader of the serious lack of faith displayed by this outwardly pious but heartless "faith." This second conditional sentence in 2:16 inverts the apodosis from the earlier conditional sentence by ending with the repeated rhetorically-powerful question, "what good is it?" This inversion heightens the rhetorical punch of James' response. Within the illustration provided by the parable of 2:15–16, this "good" or "benefit" or "profit" refers primarily to the needy situation that has gone unmet. The words, however well intentioned, have not profited the needy people at all.

The attentive reader, on the other hand, cannot miss the way these words repeat the manner in which James introduced verse 14. Not only do the empty words of this responder do no good for the needy; they also produce no spiritual benefit for the speaker. It is appropriate as a counterbalance to quote Paul's effective semantic parallel: "And if I bestow all my goods to feed the poor, and if I give my body to be burned, but have not love, it profits me nothing" (οὐδὲν ὠφελοῦμαι, 1 Cor 13:3). James may also be alluding here to the teaching of Jesus in the parable of the sheep and the goats (Matt 24:42–43).

Sentence Flow and Translation

17

οὕτως καὶ ἡ πίστις ἐὰν μὴ ἔχῃ ἔργα,
So also that kind of faith, if it is not accompanied by actions,

νεκρά ἐστιν καθ' ἑαυτήν.
is dead being by itself.

Exegetical Comments

2:17 οὕτως καὶ ἡ πίστις, ἐὰν μὴ ἔχῃ ἔργα, νεκρά ἐστιν καθ' ἑαυτήν: The concluding verse of the section is an effective aphorism that rounds off the argument and will be repeated in various ways over the next few verses. It also adds to the already mentioned doubt over the nature of this sort of faith ("what good is it?") by openly declaring that such a faith (ἡ πίστις) is actually "dead." The consequential οὕτως with an adjunctive καί ("also") leads to an embedded third class conditional sentence with the protasis embedded between the noun phrase subject (ἡ πίστις) and its predicate (νεκρά ἐστιν), which comprises the apodosis. Rephrased would be: "If it does not have deeds, that faith is dead." The kind of faith that is isolated from its necessary companion of loving acts (it is alone) is a faith that has no life in it at all. There have occasionally been commentators and preachers that equate this faith only with a weaker form of saving faith that simply needs to be awakened from its dormancy (Hodges, 62–63). Of the 128 occurrences of νεκρός in the NT, it is difficult to find any meaning other than to be literally spiritually "without life." The analogical argument in 2:26 ("as the body without the spirit is dead") also argues that the word as used by James means "without life," or in this case, "without spiritual life." The approach to dead faith simply as something dormant also blunts the serious nature of James' rhetoric, which he repeats in the same wording of that just-mentioned aphorism that concludes this overall paragraph and the chapter (2:26). In 2:20, James will make the same statement but replace νεκρά with ἀργή ("worthless, useless"). In the comments on 2:20, we will suggest a possible reason for the change of terminology at that point in his argument.

I have chosen not to translate ἔργα in this section by its traditional rendering "works." The word in James simply refers to deeds that demonstrate Christian love and kindness that are the expected "fruit" of a faith that is alive and real. It is also important to note throughout this discussion that James is not saying that we should add "deeds" to an already existing faith. He is saying that the "faith" that does not include "deeds" is not a real faith at all. This type of faith is not really alive; it is dead.

A Debate about Deeds (2:18–19)

Introduction

There is a great irony in the interpretation of James 2:18–19. To the casual reader, the sense is clear. James is concerned that the kind of faith which is his special concern in this letter must not be separated from its appropriate accompanying deeds. That living faith is not just creedal—an affirmation of a doctrinal truth—but manifests itself in deeds. When scholars examine the details of the text, however, it bristles with some knotty problems. One scholar has observed that

James 2:18 is "one of the most difficult New Testament passages in general" (Dibelius, 154). The question is a simple one: when is James "speaking" during the brief but spirited exchange of the diatribe, and when is his "interlocutor" speaking? And when do they switch? Before we attempt to sort out the options for answering these questions, we should clearly point out what is very obvious in the text, despite its problems. James is opposing two false ideas: (1) that faith can be separated from works (or as I prefer "deeds"); and (2) that faith is defined simply by a creedal affirmation. Now how does James work that out in the diatribal form of debate that emerges in 2:18 and continues to the end of the chapter? We must first do a lexical analysis of 2:18 and then lay out the options that seek to answer those questions we have posed.

Greek Text

18 Ἀλλ' ἐρεῖ τις· σὺ πίστιν ἔχεις, κἀγὼ ἔργα ἔχω· δεῖξόν μοι τὴν πίστιν σου ᵃχωρὶς τῶν ἔργων, κἀγώ σοι δείξω ἐκ τῶν ἔργων μου τὴν πίστιν. 19 σὺ πιστεύεις ὅτι ᵇεἷς ἐστιν ὁ θεός, καλῶς ποιεῖς· καὶ τὰ δαιμόνια πιστεύουσιν καὶ φρίσσουσιν.

Textual Notes

18.a In 2:18 there is very strong support (ℵ A B C) for the presence of χωρίς: "show me your faith apart from (χωρίς) your deeds." The Byzantine tradition substitutes an ἐκ: "show me your faith by (ἐκ) your deeds." Contrary to what one commentator argues below, this is not the more difficult reading, but likely indicates a scribal error of the eye and assimilation to Pauline usage. Furthermore, it introduces an even greater problem in solving the identity of the speakers in 2:18. "According to WH and NU, the emphasis is on the collaboration of faith and works" (Comfort 727)

19.b Among the several readings of 2:19 the chief difference is the presence or absence of the article: B 614 630 1875 2412 2495 read εις θεος εστιν ("There is one God"), whereas the other readings involve ὁ θεός standing either before or after the verb ("God is one"). The reading εις ο θεος εστιν (C 33 81 syr[h]) and the reading εις θεος εστιν appear to reflect an assimilation to the style of the Christian gospel message (1 Cor 8:6; Eph 4:6; 1 Tim 2:5). On the other hand, εις εστιν ο θεος (P[74] ℵ A 2464 vg syr[p] cop[sa]) is in conformity with the familiar formula of Jewish orthodoxy. Clearly secondary is the reading of the Textus Receptus, ο θεος εις εστιν, in which ο θεος is placed first in order to give it a more emphatic position.

Sentence Flow and Translation

Because I propose a different way of identifying who the speakers are in this diatribe and when they speak, I will sort out the sentence flow analysis that I prefer and then defend it in the Exegetical Comments.

18
Ἀλλ᾽ ἐρεῖ τις·
But someone will say,

> σὺ πίστιν ἔχεις;
> "Do you have faith?"

κἀγὼ ἔργα ἔχω.
"I also have deeds.

δεῖξόν μοι τὴν πίστιν σου χωρὶς τῶν ἔργων,
Show me your faith apart from your deeds,

κἀγώ σοι δείξω ἐκ τῶν ἔργων μου τὴν πίστιν.
and I will show you my faith by my deeds.

19
σὺ πιστεύεις ὅτι εἷς ἐστιν ὁ θεός,
Do you believe that God is one?

καλῶς ποιεῖς·
You are doing well.
καὶ τὰ δαιμόνια πιστεύουσιν καὶ φρίσσουσιν.
Even the demons believe—and they shudder!

Exegetical Comments

2:18 Ἀλλ' ἐρεῖ τις: The use of the stronger adversative conjunction Ἀλλ' to introduce the verse signals an opinion that strongly differs from the point that James has made in 2:17—namely, a faith that is alone and without deeds is not a valid faith at all; it is dead.[3] James employs this conjunction only four other times and always in an adversarial way (1:25, 26; 3:15; 4:11). Combined with the indefinite pronoun τις, the expression introduces a hypothetical debate partner often referred to as the *interlocutor*.

The future verb ἐρεῖ also points to a hypothetical action. James combined the present form of this verb (λέγῃ) with τις in 2:14 when he introduced this topic. Thus, the voice of this hypothetical interlocutor has already been heard briefly in 2:14 and also in 2:16 through his apparently casual response to a real need: "Be warmed and filled." Now James allows that imagined person to have a voice of debate in 2:18–19. While he is hypothetical, this person is intended to represent an argument that must have been exemplified in the communities to which James is writing.

σὺ πίστιν ἔχεις, κἀγὼ ἔργα ἔχω, "Do you have faith?" "I also have deeds ..." The personal pronouns σύ and κἀγώ expressed with the verb ἔχω

---

[3] The milder δέ in James signals a move to a different aspect of a topic, but not to introduce a new topic. Of its thirty-nine appearances in James, it is used in this way only in chapter two (2:2, 3, 6, 9, 20, 11, 14, 16, 20, 23, 25).

serve to intensify the thrust and parry of the debate. The use of these pronouns continues throughout 2:18 and 19, with the σύ sometimes referring clearly to James (here) and sometimes to the interlocutor (2:19). The second person exchange is also evident in the vocative ὦ ἄνθρωπε κενέ in 2:20 and the βλέπεις of 2:22. The verb ἔχω has already been used with πίστιν in 2:1, 14, and 17. The difficult interpretive question is: When does the voice of the interlocutor cease? Is it after the first clause ("You have faith") or does it continue with the next clause ("and I have deeds")? Or does it extend through the rest of the verse? And when does the voice of James reenter the exchange? We will postpone a consideration of the suggested options until the end of the lexical treatment of 2:18.

δεῖξόν μοι τὴν πίστιν σου χωρὶς τῶν ἔργων: The singular aorist imperative δεῖξόν is from δείκνυμι, a verb that means "to prove or make clear by evidence or reasoning, *explain, prove*" (BDAG, 215). It is used in this way in Matt 16:1 and Acts 10:28. It also appears again in the imperative in James 3:13: "he should show (δειξάτω) by his good behavior his deeds in the gentleness of wisdom." The challenge to do this—although it is evident from the diatribe that one cannot do so—is clear enough. But who is speaking these specific words? If it is the continued voice of the interlocutor, it is strange that he would ask James to do this. It seems more likely that this is the voice of James, as well as the following words to the end of the verse. But if the interlocutor's words end in 2:18a, why does it seem that these words follow naturally in the flow of thought? These questions will be addressed after we examine the next clause.

κἀγώ σοι δείξω ἐκ τῶν ἔργων μου τὴν πίστιν: The repetition of κἀγώ is to be noted. This clause completes a chiasm from the previous clause. If we slightly rearrange the second verb, it is more evident:

A: δεῖξόν μοι τὴν πίστιν σου

B: χωρὶς τῶν ἔργων,

B': ἐκ τῶν ἔργων μου

A': κἀγώ σοι δείξω ... τὴν πίστιν.

The combination of καὶ ἐγώ by the crasis κἀγώ is, in my opinion, a deliberate rhetorical echo of how James had used the same word in 2:18 in response to the interlocutor. The contrast with the previous clause by the use of different prepositions, χωρὶς τῶν ἔργων and ἐκ τῶν ἔργων, is also important to note. One is a faith *without* deeds and the other is a faith demonstrated *by* deeds. The entire set of expressions is almost a paraphrase of another statement by the Brother of James in Matt 7:16 and 20: "By their fruits (ἀπὸ τῶν καρπῶν αὐτῶν), you shall know them." The challenge of interpreting the passage is heightened by its rapid-fire style of nine primary clauses, which again is illustrative of the diatribal style. The shorthand way in which the debate is described, combined with the obvious lack of quotation marks in the original, actually contributes to the problem of how to sort out the speakers and when they begin and switch.

These problems are exacerbated by the fact that the interlocutor's response seems to be the opposite of how we would expect him to respond. A number of commentaries explain the various possibilities about where to end the quotation that begins with "You have faith" (σὺ πίστιν ἔχεις). Solutions that recommend emendations to the text or propose questionable textual variants create more problems than they solve (Hodges, 1963, 341–50; 1994, 65). McCartney has listed eight proposed solutions to the identity of the speakers in the diatribe (McCartney, 158–60). By discounting some of the more extreme ideas like proposed emendations, doubtful textual variants, or mistakes in James' grammar, there are two main solutions to the perplexities offered by evangelical commentators. I will also offer a third possibility alluded to by McCartney and will expand it as my own proposed solution to these challenges.

Some commentators (Mayor, 96; Adamson, 14–25) propose that the interlocutor is an ally, not an opponent. He says, therefore, in support of James: "You have faith and I have works." The ἀλλά is thus viewed as conveying the idea of "yes, indeed." This sort of use in NT passages appears in contexts where a contrast between the clauses makes no sense. The problem here is that 2:18 is introduced, not only by that strong adversative conjunction, but also with the ἐρεῖ τις: "But someone will say ..." This seems to introduce an opposing point of view that will in turn be addressed by James. He does oppose this idea with his stinging address in 2:20: "O foolish man!" "The only natural way of reading 2:18 is that James is introducing a possible objection to his view" (McCartney, 158).

The suggestion most often made is that the use of the pronouns "you" and "I" are simply a way of saying, "One person says this; another says that." The statement then should be taken as: "One has faith and another has actions," with the stinging response by James that the two can't be divided but must remain together. James is thus against the notion that deeds and faith are somehow separable and that either faith or deeds is an equally acceptable approach. Since Ropes, this has been the most common approach among commentators (Ropes, 211–12; Dibelius, 156–57; Davids, 124; Moo, 129; McCartney, 160; as well as McKnight, "James 2:18a," 335–64; 2011, 236–38 who offers the most thorough defense of this view). When such minds agree, we should be hesitant to be dogmatic in disagreeing. The main problem, however, is that this view suffers from a lack of attestation elsewhere of the way in which "you" and "I" are supposed to be understood in the explanation. James could have used another Greek expression like ἄλλος ... ἄλλος ("one ... another") to convey this alternating idea, but he uses the pronouns "you" and "I" as part of the diatribe. The dominant view seems to suspend that diatribe and then pick it up again with the challenge in 2:18b to "show me."

McCartney does mention another interpretation that was

suggested by Hort, who thought that the interlocutor's words are a question that ends with the first clause in 2:18a and James' response then continues afterward (Hort, 60). The interchange would look like this:

> Interlocutor: "Do you have faith?"

> James: "I also have deeds! Show me your faith without deeds, and I will show you my faith by deeds!"

McCartney admits that "this almost convinces" but thinks the context shows otherwise and points out that the crasis of κἀγώ makes the view unlikely (McCartney, 158). Hort's view has been provided with even stronger exegetical support by the German scholar Nietzel in an article often overlooked by recent commentators.[4] He argues that σὺ πίστιν ἔχεις is a *question* standing by itself, expressing the interlocutor's doubts about the author's own faith, just as the author had done in referring to deedless faith as "dead." James then responds, "I also have deeds. Show me your faith without deeds and I will show you my faith by my deeds." This fits the context very well and also solves the problem of the unlikely response by the interlocutor in his continued response following the disputed clause. It is also more satisfying than the other forced interpretations. In this approach, the doubled κἀγώ initiating the third and fifth clauses both serve as part of James' response, and they add a rhetorical intensity to James' reply. While some have objected to the use of κἀγώ to begin a sentence, Nietzel cites a number of times in Greek literature where this takes place. This reconstruction of the dialogue resolves the problem of who is saying what in the interchange. It only suffers from the fact that few commentators and no English translations have adopted it as a

---

[4] H. Nietzel, "Eine alte crux interpretum im Jakobusbrief 2.18," *ZNW* 73 (1982): 286–93. I would like to thank David Edgar for bringing this article to my attention. D. H. Edgar, *Has God Not Chosen the Poor?* (JSNTSup 206; Sheffield: Sheffield Academic Press, 2001), 170–71.

solution. I do believe that Nietzel's suggestion, elaborated also by Edgar, is worthy of serious consideration.[5]

2:19 σὺ πιστεύεις ὅτι εἷς ἐστιν ὁ θεός; All agree that 2:19 is a frontal challenge by James to the person who thinks that "faith alone" is enough without any accompanying actions that evidence that faith. When James attributes to his debate opponent a belief in the oneness of God, he is on very Jewish ground. The expression is an adaptation of the famous Shema of Deuteronomy 6:4. Shema is a transliteration of the first word in the verse: שְׁמַע. The inclusion of the article before "God" (ὁ θεός) conforms to the practice of Jewish orthodoxy. Our translation ("God is one") is based on the reading of P[74], ℵ and A among other Greek manuscripts, as well as some early versions: εἷς ἐστιν ὁ θεός. Colwell's rule is that when two nominatives bracket a copula, the one with an article should be viewed as the subject and the other as the predicate nominative/adjective. This reading is adopted by the NA/UBS texts and among most commentators. As to the word order, the sequence εἷς θεός ἐστιν is closer to the characteristic later "Christian" ... confession (1 Cor 8:6; Eph 4:6; 1 Tim 2:5), whereas the sequence of the best reading here, εἷς ἐστιν ὁ θεός, is closer to the earlier "Jewish" version (Deut 6:4; Josephus, *Ant.* 3.91; Philo, *Decal.* 65; Matt 19:7; Mark 12:29). It gives a statement rather about God's character than simply about his existence: *God is One.*

καλῶς ποιεῖς. Some commentators take this indicative pronouncement as a favorable one (Ropes, 216, "perhaps with a slight touch of irony"), but most recognize it as purely ironic (Lange, 184; Dibelius, 159–60). Perhaps the best approach is to view the statement itself as favorable since the belief is true, but what follows introduces the irony (Mayor, 101; Davids, 125–26). This expression is "a biting comment" (Blomberg-Kamell, 135). "The next two lines pull the legs out from under the

[5] An additional monograph that advocates this punctuation and interpretation is T. Cargal, *Restoring the Diaspora: Discursive Structure and Purpose in the Epistle of James* (SBLDS 144; Atlanta, GA: Scholar's Press, 1993), 125–26.

opponent" (McKnight, 242). The irony conveyed by James' response to this supposed creedal confession echoes his earlier response in 2:8 to one who believes the law of love to his neighbor. Together they embody Jesus' summation of the law—namely, our love to God and our love to others (Matt 22:37–39). If they do not honor those who have been honored by God (2:5), they fail to demonstrate that wholehearted devotion to God that is required by the very Shema they claim to affirm (Deut 6:6–8). The intention of the allusion is not so much to indicate its inadequacy by itself, as it is to draw attention to its full consequences.

καὶ τὰ δαιμόνια πιστεύουσιν καὶ φρίσσουσιν: "Even the demons believe [that], and they tremble!" The ascensive use of the conjunction καί ("even") is preferred to maintain the irony. Commentators have devoted much attention to the meaning of exactly how the demons "shudder" (BDAG, 1065). That all created things shudder before God the Creator is a very Jewish teaching (Josephus, *War* 5.378; *Barn.* 11.2 [ἡ γῆ]; *Hermas* 2.1). The NT witnesses to the monotheism of demons (Acts 16:17; 19:15) and their fear of Christ, whom they recognize (Mark 1:23–24; 5:7). This attention, however, has often drawn away from the proper attention to the powerful sarcasm contained in the statement. It is not the specific doctrinal question that is the issue, but the bare creedal knowledge of a theological truth that even demons affirm which has no benefit for them. "Believing that there is one God (intellectual acknowledgment) is different from believing in (εἰς, *eis*, into) the God who is one" (McCartney, 160–61). There may also be a reference to that type of faith that arises out of craven fear but leads only to "shuddering" and not to peace (2 Tim 1:7a: "God has not given us the spirit of fear"). Finally, possible links with the Jesus oral and written tradition again should not be overlooked. As we have noticed before, intertextual links to Lev 19 are also present throughout this passage. It is Jesus' use of the same material, especially in what has been called "the Jesus Creed" of Matt 22:37–39, that provides the meaning and application that James further adapts and employs.

Patriarchal Proof (2:20–23)

Introduction

The passage opens with a harsh address to the author's debate partner (ὦ ἄνθρωπε κενέ). The directness of this blunt vocative connects this passage to the context of the previous diatribe. The way the question is posed effectively introduces his final argument. This involves two well-known exemplars from Israel's past history, each of whom illustrates his point that a person is justified not by a faith that is alone but by a faith that is accompanied by the appropriate deeds (2:24). The following examples are persuasive to a person who is willing (Θέλεις) to accept them. For a closer inspection of the two examples, Abraham and Rahab, we will consider them separately. Abraham is discussed in 2:20–23 and Rahab in 2:24–25, with each being introduced by a restatement of the overall topic of 2:17–26—namely, that a faith that is unaccompanied by the appropriate deeds is first "dead" (2:17), then "useless" (2:20), and finally "dead" again (2:26).

Greek Text

20 Θέλεις δὲ γνῶναι, ὦ ἄνθρωπε κενέ, ὅτι ἡ πίστις χωρὶς τῶν ἔργων ᵃἀργή ἐστιν; 21 Ἀβραὰμ ὁ πατὴρ ἡμῶν οὐκ ἐξ ἔργων ἐδικαιώθη ἀνενέγκας Ἰσαὰκ τὸν υἱὸν αὐτοῦ ἐπὶ τὸ θυσιαστήριον; 22 βλέπεις ὅτι ἡ πίστις συνήργει τοῖς ἔργοις αὐτοῦ καὶ ἐκ τῶν ἔργων ἡ πίστις ἐτελειώθη, 23 καὶ ἐπληρώθη ἡ γραφὴ ἡ λέγουσα· ἐπίστευσεν δὲ Ἀβραὰμ τῷ θεῷ, καὶ ἐλογίσθη αὐτῷ εἰς δικαιοσύνην καὶ φίλος θεοῦ ἐκλήθη.

Textual Notes

20.a. Instead of ἀργή in 2:20 the Textus Receptus reads νεκρα, with ℵ A C² K P Ψ 614 1241 *Byz* cop^[bo]. Because of a reasonable suspicion that scribes may have introduced the latter word from either 2:17 or 26, we prefer ἀργή, which is strongly supported by B C* it vg cop^[sa], and may involve a subtle play on words (ἔργων ἀργή [ἀ + ἐργή]). "The WH NU reading has good documentation and displays James' sensitivities to lexical variation and perhaps even wordplay. James argues that faith without the demonstration of works is not only dead (2:17, 26), but it is also useless in that it is unproductive" (Comfort 727-28).

Translation

The sentence flow analysis will be addressed in the comments.

20 Do you want to be shown, O foolish person, that the faith that is not accompanied by actions is barren? 21 Was not Abraham our father justified by actions when he offered up his son Isaac on the altar? 22 You see that faith was active along with his actions, and faith was completed by his actions. 23 In this way the Scripture was fulfilled that says, "Abraham believed God, and it was counted to him as righteousness"—and he was called "friend of God."

Exegetical Comments

2:20 Θέλεις δὲ γνῶναι, ὦ ἄνθρωπε κενέ, ὅτι ἡ πίστις χωρὶς τῶν ἔργων ἀργή ἐστιν: The use of the present active indicative θέλεις ("do you want") continues the confrontational diatribal style of interrogation that marks James' style throughout the book. That faith can attempt to exist without its appropriate accompanying actions is so inconceivable to James that he addresses his opponent with a vocative noun and adjective (ἄνθρωπε κενέ – "empty man") that is roughly equivalent to the modern term "blockhead" for even supposing that they can somehow be separated. The passive translation for the aorist active complementary infinitive γνῶναι ("want to be shown") is justified for rhetorical reasons. The use of this sort of question illustrated in the Greek diatribe genre can be seen as well in the NT. Compare the use of οὐκ οἴδατε in 4:4 (also Rom 6:16; 11:2; 1 Cor 3:16; 5:6; 6:2–3, 9, 15, 16, 19; 9:13, 24). James then repeats his topic statement for the second of what will be three times (2:17, 20, 26), although with a single slight but significant variation. In this second occurrence, the adjective that describes this deficient faith is ἀργή, not the νεκρά that was used in 2:17. We should not be surprised, therefore, that some later Byzantine scribes attempted to bring this verse into harmony with the wording of 2:17 and 2:26. The entire Byzantine family of manuscripts attempts this harmonization with their reading of νεκρά. Surprisingly, however, they are also joined by Sinaiticus and Alexandrinus, while P⁷⁴ has the unique reading κενή under the influence of the vocative κενέ earlier in the verse. Metzger defends the UBS⁴/NA²⁷ reading of ἀργή, which, he says, "not only is strongly supported by B C 322 323 945 1739 it vg cop arm, but may involve a subtle play on words (ἔργων ἀργή [α + εργη])." While agreeing entirely with this surface wordplay in the choice of this word, I suggest that there is another reason for the word switch by James to ἀργή, which relates to the semantics of this word in light of the author's overall rhetorical strategy. The adjective ἀργή is most often translated by "idle" or "useless" (BDAG, 128). "It is also used in the sense of 'incapable of action or of live operation'" (*TDNT*, 1:452). In 2 Pet 1:8, ἀργή is used as parallel to the adjective, ἄκαρπος ("unfruitful"). The next individual mentioned in the passage is Abraham (2:21–24). Who, therefore, could better serve as the exemplar than a respected individual who, although he once was "unfruitful" and "barren," eventually produced an unexpected heir, Isaac, and then assumes a role in this text which teaches that a faith that is accompanied by the right deeds is not "barren"?

2:21 Ἀβραὰμ ὁ πατὴρ ἡμῶν: The promise to Abraham in Gen 17:4–5 was that he would be a πατήρ. This designation was given to God in the OT (Isa 51:2); in Second Temple Period literature (Sir 44:19, 22); and throughout the NT (Matt 3:9; Luke 1:73; 3:8; 16:30; John 8:39, 56; Acts 7:2; Rom 4:1). This would be a familiar claim to Jewish readers, but Paul claimed Abraham in a spiritual sense also for Gentile believers (Rom 4:11–12, 16; Gal 3:7, 29). Perhaps he was following a precedent, since Abraham has always been considered the prototypical male proselyte (see later comments on 2:25). Clement of Rome later referred to Abraham as "our father," and he was addressing a Christian community that was certainly not exclusively made up of Jewish Christians (*1 Clem* 31:2).

Therefore, to "show" (2:20) his opponent the evidence for a faith that is appropriately accompanied by deeds, James offers not only Abraham but an additional female exemplar from Israelite history. This may seem a bit surprising, since Ruth has been the paradigmatic female Gentile convert. His use of Rahab, however, may have been for a specific purpose, which we will later examine. The parallel way in which he structures the actions of Abraham and Rahab can be seen in a sentence flow analysis of the two main verses that describe their "deed."

2:21

    Ἀβραὰμ ὁ πατὴρ ἡμῶν οὐκ ἐξ ἔργων ἐδικαιώθη
    ἀνενέγκας Ἰσαὰκ τὸν υἱὸν αὐτοῦ ἐπὶ τὸ θυσιαστήριον;

2:25 ὁμοίως δὲ καὶ

    Ῥαὰβ ἡ πόρνη οὐκ ἐξ ἔργων ἐδικαιώθη
    ὑποδεξαμένη τοὺς ἀγγέλους καὶ ἑτέρᾳ ὁδῷ ἐκβαλοῦσα;

In each sentence a rhetorical question that expects a positive answer is asked along with the subject's name (Abraham, Rahab). This is then followed by a one-word description (father, prostitute), along with the adjunct "by works" that concludes each initial primary clause. Both secondary clauses then open with a temporal participle (ἀνενέγκας, ὑποδεξαμένη) that is followed by their appropriate direct objects (Ἰσαὰκ and τοὺς ἀγγέλους) plus the appropriate prepositional phrases (ἐπὶ τὸ θυσιαστήριον and ἑτέρᾳ ὁδῷ). This parallel construction functions as more than simply an attractive linguistic ornament. The structure serves to focus the reader's (and hearer's) attention on the specific deed that illustrates the faith of its exemplar. It is very important to recognize this usage, because it is too easy to focus on the hospitality of Abraham in Gen 18 (which is so celebrated in rabbinic tradition) as a parallel to the evident hospitality displayed by Rahab in Joshua 2. While it would have been easy for James to focus on his hospitality, he chose rather to focus on the supreme deed by which Abraham displayed the evidence for his faith—the *Akedah* ("binding") of Isaac. *Akedah/Aqedah* is the Hebrew term for "binding," referred to in Gen 22:9. In Jewish tradition, it has become the title by which Jews refer to the entire incident.[6]

It is possible that the plural of ἔργων may include Abraham's earlier hospitality (as it does with Rahab). Indeed, some have taken the plural to include his "works" that preceded the *Akedah*. Perhaps the plural noun refers to all of Abraham's deeds of faith that eventually culminated in that moving scene on a hill in the land of Moriah (Gen 21:1; 1 Macc 2:52; Sir 44:19–21; Heb 11:17–19).

οὐκ ἐξ ἔργων ἐδικαιώθη: As we have seen before, a question asked with the negative οὐκ anticipates a positive response. In other words, the intended response to this question is: "yes, Abraham was justified by his deeds." It is well known that there is an apparent conflict with Paul on this issue. For Paul, justification is a sovereign, judicial act in which God, apart from any human "work," declares the sinner to be innocent before him (Rom 4:5).

There is some difficulty, however, in determining what exact meaning that James intends in his usage of this aorist passive indicative of δικαιόω. Some think that he uses it in a demonstrative sense (Adamson, 128–34), meaning that Abraham here and Rahab in 2:25 "were justified by deeds done" in the sense that they demonstrated their righteous status by performing those good deeds. But if Paul stresses that faith is the only condition for the *declaration* of righteousness, the conflict would be removed, because James is arguing that deeds/works are the only way that a righteous standing can be *demonstrated*. While this meaning is possible, it is not the usual

---

[6] See the excellent discussion of this incident as it was illustrated in Second Temple Judaism in the article, "Aqedah" (*EDEJ*, 355–57).

meaning of the word, and it is difficult to clearly discern this meaning in James 2. Here the question is not, "How can righteousness be demonstrated?" The question is, "What kind of faith secures righteousness?" It is best then to recognize that James is also using the verb in a declarative sense, as Paul also does (Rom 3:21–26; Gal 2:15–21). While James uses "justify" and "justification" to refer to God's ultimate declaration of a person's righteousness, Paul uses it to refer to the initial securing of that righteousness by faith.[7]

The use of δικαιόω in this ultimate and eschatological sense appears to be the meaning also in the teaching of Jesus. He warned his listeners on one occasion using the future tense: "By your words you will be justified, and by your words you will be condemned" (Matt 12:37). James' frequent allusions to Jesus' teaching, particularly in Matthew, accentuate this reference. James asserts that Abraham did works and that these works were used as the basis for God's ultimate pronouncement over Abraham's life. Abraham had faith and this faith was basic to his acceptance by God (2:22–23). James stresses then "that the life of the one who has been so accepted by God must show the fruit of that relationship in good works. It was what precedes and enables these works that Paul concentrates on. Paul wants to make clear that one 'gets into' God's kingdom only by faith; James insists that God requires works from those who *are* 'in'" (Moo, 1985, 114). For further discussion on how James' and Paul's teaching on faith, works, and justification are compatible, see the discussion of faith in the Introduction.

ἀνενέγκας Ἰσαὰκ τὸν υἱὸν αὐτοῦ ἐπὶ τὸ θυσιαστήριον; James draws the term θυσιαστήριον ("altar") directly from the account in Gen 22, but he

---

[7] See the nuanced discussion of this text in McCartney, 161–169. McCartney concludes that the justifying statement in Gen 15 was an *anticipatory* acquittal that integrally connected Abraham's faith in the promise with his obedient offering of Isaac in Gen 22 (167). He also wisely concludes that "his (James') overarching purpose here is not to set forth a soteriology, but to deny the viability of faith without works, to deny that a workless faith can save" (168).

uses the aorist participle of ἀναφέρω ("offer") from Gen 22:2, 13 rather than the LXX's ἐπιτίθημι ("place") for the crucial action in 22:9. The offering of Isaac was treated in Jewish literature as one of the trials by which Abraham's faith in God was tested (Sir 44:20; *Avot* 5.3; *Jub.* 17.17; 18:15–16). Hebrews 11:17–19 declares it was πίστει ("by faith") that Abraham, when he was tested (πειραζόμενος), brought forth Isaac and offered his only son. This is consistent with James' approach, as the next verse will make clear.

2:22 βλέπεις ὅτι ἡ πίστις συνήργει τοῖς ἔργοις αὐτοῦ καὶ ἐκ τῶν ἔργων ἡ πίστις ἐτελειώθη: Verses 22 and 23 further expound the undivided and singular nature of Abraham's faith and actions. Two semantically related words (συνήργει τοῖς ἔργοις αὐτοῦ) describe the inseparable nature of the two issues at hand: faith and deeds. The imperfect active verb συνήργει conveys the idea that Abraham's faith and actions "were working together." It is thus clear that James did not mean to say that Abraham had only deeds and not faith. It is his faith and his deeds that together mark Abraham, as he had earlier argued in 2:18. The imperfective aspect of the verb describes that process as taking place throughout Abraham's journey from the time he initially believed God in Gen 15:6 (2:23) until the consummation of the *Akedah* in Gen 22. The aorist passive verb, ἐτελειώθη ("was completed"), declares that his faith was completed by his accompanying deed(s). In other words, his faith was in a sense incomplete until it was perfected or completed by deeds. This is still another example of James' emphasis throughout his book on wholeness and perfection.

While we may describe Abraham's deeds as a demonstration of his faith, we should remember that the relation between his faith and his deeds is not properly one of consequence, demonstration, or confirmation. Each of these terms assumes a measure of distinction between faith and deeds. With his characteristic emphasis on wholeness, James sees faith and deeds as bound together in a necessary unity. Faith cooperated with Abraham's deeds, and by his deeds, his faith was made complete. It is not that his faith had to wait for completion during the time lapse from Gen 15 to 22. "It 'was completed' (almost 'supplemented'), and so enabled to do its proper work. If, when the test came, the faith had not been matched by works, then it would have been proved to be an incomplete faith. The works showed that the faith had always been of the right kind, and so 'completed' it" (Ropes, 220). The many "deeds" of Abraham after believing helped to fulfill that faith, and the Akedah crowned it! This statement leads directly to 2:23.

2:23 καὶ ἐπληρώθη ἡ γραφὴ ἡ λέγουσα· ἐπίστευσεν δὲ Ἀβραὰμ τῷ θεῷ, καὶ ἐλογίσθη αὐτῷ εἰς δικαιοσύνην: The quotation from Gen 15:6 does not agree exactly with the precise wording of either the LXX or the MT, but the meaning is not altered in either way.[8] Abraham's believing God (Gen 15:6) is described as being "fulfilled" (ἐπληρώθη) in the *Akedah* described in Gen 22. The word for "fulfilled" (ἐπληρώθη) is a different verb than the one in 2:22 (ἐτελειώθη). Note also that in this verse James does not say that Abraham's *faith* was fulfilled (as in 2:22), but that the *Scripture* statement was fulfilled. The English word *fulfill* often connotes the idea of a prediction and its fulfillment, but the quotation from Gen 15:6 is a past tense indicative statement, not a future prophetic prediction. The verb πληρόω here means more like "give its true or full meaning," as it also does in Matt 5:17 and Gal 5:14 (BDAG, 828.4). As was mentioned, this description of "complete" faith in 2:22–23 is also consistent with James' theme throughout his letter on a "whole" or "undivided" life. Paul's use of Gen 15:6 differs in that he associates the belief in the verse with the circumcisions among Abraham's male household in Genesis 17. His point is that Abraham believed and was declared to be in the right before he underwent the "work" of circumcision. In Paul's argument this makes perfect sense (Rom 4:9–12), especially for uncircumcised Gentiles who had believed the gospel. Yet James' use of the same text also makes sense when we

---

[8] The quotation disagrees with the LXX in using the post-positive δέ instead of a fronted καί, which agrees more with the MT. The MT, however, does not mention the name of Abraham but the LXX does.

recognize that Abraham's "works" in James were not Jewish national badges, as they appear to be in Romans and Galatians. Deeds in James are obedient deeds of love and mercy, which are the necessary accompaniment of a true saving faith. This is a classic example of how NT writers can handle an OT text in different but not contradictory ways.[9]

καὶ φίλος θεοῦ ἐκλήθη: James concludes his exposition of Abraham as exemplar by the climactic clause, "and he was called 'friend of God'." While Wallace calls φίλος a predicate nominative (40), I prefer to label it as a nominative of appellation because it follows a passive transitive verb. Predicate nominatives follow equative verbs like εἰμί. Jewish sources deal with the subject of friendship (Sir 5:15–6:17; 37:1–6) with an expected Jewish coloring. The gift of wisdom is seen as enabling friendship with God (Wis 7:14) since it creates "friends of God and prophets" (Wis 7:27). The only individual called "friend of God" in the Torah is Moses, since God spoke with him face to face as to his friend (φίλος in Exod 33:11). Surprisingly, Abraham is never directly called "God's friend." We will notice later the two references that in Hebrew call him "friend." The passage that above all would give rise to the designation of Abraham as God's friend in the Hellenistic sense is Gen 18:17, "shall I hide from Abraham my servant what I am about to do?" Philo reads the LXX text, τοῦ παιδός μου, and substitutes for it τοῦ φίλου μου (*Sob.* 56), and then interprets God's statement as an example of how "friends hold all things in common." In the *Testament of Abraham* God designates Abraham as θεοφιλής (19.9), and the designation of Abraham as "friend" occurs repeatedly in the *Testament of Abraham* (1.7; 2.3; 2.6).

The aorist passive verb ἐκλήθη indicates that someone else gave this title to the patriarch. Abraham was referred to twice by a similar

---

[9] Carson also shows how James, Paul, and the author of Hebrews each use the faith of Abraham in different ways to make their points. See Carson, "James," in Beale and Carson, *Commentary*, 1003–05, whose work I have utilized in the above comments.

name in canonical literature. On these occasions, however, the words used in both the Hebrew texts and in their LXX translations convey the idea of a "loved one." Furthermore, the Greek word in the LXX is not the noun φίλος; it is the verb ἀγαπάω (אֹהֲבִי and ὃν ἠγάπησα in Isa 41:8; אֹהַבְךָ and τῷ ἠγαπημένῳ in 2 Chr 20:7). It appears, therefore, that by using this title James is not directly referring to either the Isaiah or the Chronicles references, but rather to the noncanonical Jewish literary tradition. We recall the earlier point that in Hellenistic Jewish literature, there are a number of occasions when Abraham was referenced as God's friend by the same Greek noun, φίλος, or its equivalent in other languages. One other non-Greek (Old Slavonic) reference is in the *Apocalypse of Abraham* 10, where the angel says to Abraham, "Stand up, Abraham, Friend of God who loves you."

If we read this verse in the light of the rest of James, however, we may be able to discern two other reasons for his referring to Abraham as "friend." Hearers and readers of James' sermonic encyclical would not have to be told in detail the stories about Abraham. There are indications in the book that James assumes that they have knowledge of the biblical heroes and heroines. In this passage, he uses the words "you see" twice, with different verbs (βλέπεις in 2:22 and ὁρᾶτε in 2:24). Later he will appeal to their knowledge of the prophets and Job (5:10–11). Thus, James could assume that they knew about Abraham's hospitality to the three visitors in Genesis 18, one of whom was the Lord! The word for hospitality includes the root for friend (φιλοξενία), literally "friendship shown to strangers." If Abraham was a friend of God, he was no friend to a world that opposed God's promises that were made through him. Could this also be why James issues such a serious charge in 4:4? "O adulteresses! Do you not know that friendship with the world is enmity with God?" The choice is clear: either we will follow the world, or we will follow the footsteps of Abraham, the exemplar friend of God.

Matriarchal Proof (2:24–26)

Greek Text

24 ὁρᾶτε ὅτι ἐξ ἔργων δικαιοῦται ἄνθρωπος καὶ οὐκ ἐκ πίστεως μόνον. 25 ὁμοίως δὲ καὶ Ῥαὰβ ἡ πόρνη οὐκ ἐξ ἔργων ἐδικαιώθη ὑποδεξαμένη τοὺς ᵃἀγγέλους καὶ ἑτέρᾳ ὁδῷ ἐκβαλοῦσα; 26 ὥσπερ γὰρ τὸ σῶμα χωρὶς πνεύματος νεκρόν ἐστιν, οὕτως καὶ ἡ πίστις χωρὶς ἔργων νεκρά ἐστιν.

Textual Notes

25.a. It appears that some later scribes (C L 945 1241 1739), out of concern that readers would mistakenly understand ἀγγέλους as heavenly angels, replaced the word with κατασκόπους ("spies") which is also found in Heb 11:31. A few witnesses even added τοῦ Ἰσραήλ (61 syr).

Translation

24 You see that a person is justified by deeds and not by faith only. 25 And in the same way was not also Rahab the prostitute justified by actions when she received the scouts and sent them out by another way? 26 For just as the body apart from the spirit is dead, so also the faith that is not accompanied by actions is dead.

Exegetical Comments

2:24 ὁρᾶτε ὅτι ἐξ ἔργων δικαιοῦται ἄνθρωπος: At this point James shifts from addressing the interlocutor in the second person singular (βλέπεις in 2:22) to the second person plural (ὁρᾶτε). The author drops the dialogue with his debate partner. The address is no longer "you [sing.] see," but rather "you [pl.] see." The addressees to whom the outcome of the discussion of the Abraham example is presented are again the readers. The shift to another verb for "see" is probably due to his focus being shifted from his opponent in debate now to his readers. For the second of three times in this paragraph (see the rhetorical questions in 2:21 and 25), James declares that a "person" (ἄνθρωπος) is justified by works (ἐξ ἔργων). The choice of the generic noun for "person" may be due to the fact that he is about to introduce a "matriarch" as the second of his two prime exemplars.

καὶ οὐκ ἐκ πίστεως μόνον: The "on the basis of" translation of the preposition ἐκ/ἐξ in this verse and section, while not unknown elsewhere (BDAG, 296.3), is best explained as derived from the LXX translation of Hab 2:4 (ὁ δὲ δίκαιος ἐκ πίστεώς) which is echoed also in Rom 1:17; Gal 3:11; and Heb 10:38 (Harris, 104,107). The addition of μόνον to this verse is significant. Its use corresponds exactly to the way it was used earlier in 1:22, where the subject was the contrast between "hearing only" and "doing the word." Here, the contrast is between "faith only" and "doing the faith." The μόνον is also equivalent to the ἐστιν καθ' ἑαυτήν in 2:17. While some see a clear contradiction with the Pauline statements in Romans and Galatians, Paul never uses μόνον in this way in Rom 3–4 and Gal 2–4. Thus far James has contended vigorously for the inseparability of faith and deeds. Real faith leads to fruitful action. The function of μόνον here is clear. A confession of faith is necessary—the fact that μόνον appears shows this emphatically— but such faith in and of itself will not do, because faith must produce deeds. "This is no more than what the Jesus-tradition had taught James (cf. Mt. 7:15–21), and it would certainly have earned Paul's approval as well (Gal. 5:6, 6:4; 1 Cor. 13:2; 2 Cor. 9:8; cf. the paraenesis in Eph. 4:17ff. and Col. 3:5ff.)" (Davids, 132). The idea that faith alone saves has been misunderstood by many. James is firmly opposing here and throughout his book any such idea, without supporting any notion of "works = salvation." In reality, a truly biblical faith is never alone; it is always accompanied by love and hope (1 Cor 13:13) as well as by the other Christian virtues (2 Pet 1:5–8). Paul himself also would oppose such a bifurcation between faith and works (Eph 2:8–10; Gal 5:6). When he is not condemning a salvation that seeks to be based on the "works of the law," he uses "works" for deeds of love and kindness more than any other NT writer (Rom 2:6, 7; 13:3; 1 Cor 3:13, 14; 15:58; 2 Cor 9:8; Gal 6:4; Phil 1:22; Col 1:10; 3:17; 1 Thess 1:3, 5:13; 2 Thess 1:11; 2:17). The old cliché is still true that "faith is the root of salvation and works are the fruit of salvation." But salvation is one and the same—and includes them both! Another cliché also captures the sense very well: "A person is saved by faith alone, but not by a faith that is alone."

2:25 ὁμοίως δὲ καὶ Ῥαὰβ ἡ πόρνη οὐκ ἐξ ἔργων ἐδικαιώθη ὑποδεξαμένη τοὺς ἀγγέλους καὶ ἑτέρα ὁδῷ ἐκβαλοῦσα; Why does James particularly choose these two people (Abraham and Rahab) as his prime exemplars of faith in action? Various explanations could be conjectured, some of which have been suggested. (1) Perhaps it was because each came from a "Gentile" background and each became ideal prototypes of Gentile converts (Lenski, 596–97). (2) Perhaps it was because each was celebrated in Jewish tradition for their hospitality (Johnson, 249). (3) James himself may provide the answer by alerting us earlier in the passage to the importance of including a male and female when he departs from his use of the generic "brothers" to condemn the one who neglects either "a brother or a sister" who is in need (2:15). Or could it be a combination of all three of these reasons?[10]

ὁμοίως δὲ καὶ Ῥαὰβ ἡ πόρνη: With the second δέ in this paragraph (see 2:20), James introduces his second exemplar of faith and deeds— Rahab, the prostitute (2:25). In rabbinic lore, Rahab was celebrated as a proselyte and as a model of hospitality (*b. Meg.* 14b–15a; *Shem. Rab.* 27.4; *Bemid. Rabbah* 3.2; 8.9; 16.1; *Ruth Rab.* 2.1; Josephus, *Ant.* 5.5–30). James resists the attempts by later Jewish writers to blunt the nature of Rahab's profession as a "harlot" (πόρνη). In an effort to present the ancient stories of Israel in their best light to his Greek readers, Josephus later referred to her as an "innkeeper" in *Ant.* 5.8. He does not

---

[10] D. J. Wiseman, "Rahab of Jericho," *TynBul* 14 (1964) 8–11.

call her a πόρνη, and refers to her house as a κατἄγωγιον, or an "inn" (GE, 1048.A). The Greek word in the LXX (πόρνη) and the Hebrew word it translates (זוֹנָה), however, are both quite clear about the nature of her profession (Muraoka, 578).

ἐξ ἔργων ἐδικαιώθη: As was the case with Abraham, no mention is made of Rahab's faith. But hearers and readers of James' letter would have been aware of her confession of faith which was clearly recorded in Josh 2:9-11. That she was an evident "believer" to the readers of Joshua's account is shown by the fact that she became a heroine in Jewish religious history. Later rabbinic tradition mentions that she married Joshua and became an ancestress of Jeremiah and Ezekiel (*b. Meg.* 14b, 15a). Matthew's genealogy states with no apology about this Jericho prostitute that her husband was "Salmon" and thus she was an ancestress of Jesus (Matt 1:5). The use of the plural ἔργων is either to parallel how Abraham's faith was seen in his deeds, or it more probably refers to the two actions of Rahab that are about to be mentioned.

ὑποδεξαμένη τοὺς ἀγγέλους καὶ ἑτέρᾳ ὁδῷ ἐκβαλοῦσα: While some treat the two feminine participles ὑποδεξαμένη and ἐκβαλοῦσα as causal (njb; Adamson, 133–34), it is probably best to treat them simply as temporal (most versions; Mayor, 102; Ropes, 225). This prostitute who had come to faith in the God of Israel received "the scouts" and then sent them out another way. This translation of τοὺς ἀγγέλους has been chosen because it is hard to see how they were "messengers." James does not employ the LXX verb in Joshua (κατασκοπέω) nor the noun that is used in Heb 11:31 (κατάσκοπος). I suggest that he consciously chose this word in reflection on Abraham's earlier hospitality to the ἄγγελοι (Gen 19:1). As Abraham showed acts of kindness to those ἄγγελοι that came to him, so Rahab showed the same actions to the ἄγγελοι who came to her. Although no clear mention is made of Rahab's faith, readers would know about her faith from her confession in Josh 2:9-13. James emphasizes that no matter what she said, she acted out her faith by sending out the scouts "by another way" (ἑτέρᾳ ὁδῷ). The text in Joshua mentioned a "mountain" (Josh 2:16). It was probably the large hill directly west of Jericho, which is referred to today as the Mount of Temptation. The deeds of Rahab exemplify the "mercy" that triumphs over judgment (2:13) and effectively pull together these two sections (2:1–13 and 14–26). Furthermore, her two deeds also parallel and contrast with the condemned actions of the heartless interlocutor in 2:16: "be warmed" and "go your way." These two exemplars (Abraham and Rahab) show that faith and deeds are not opposites but are actually inseparable twins.

2:26 ὥσπερ γὰρ τὸ σῶμα χωρὶς πνεύματος νεκρόν ἐστιν, οὕτως καὶ ἡ πίστις χωρὶς ἔργων νεκρά ἐστιν: The paragraph ends in the way that James often rounds off an argument—with an aphorism conveyed in the structure of a simile. There is an interesting switch from the οὕτως / ὡς pattern used earlier (2:12) to the ὥσπερ / οὕτως construction in this sentence. "For just as (ὥσπερ) the body without a spirit is dead, so (οὕτως) also the faith that is not accompanied by actions is dead." The rhetorical figure known as σύγκρισις, or "comparison" (Aristotle, *Rhet.* 1368A), utilizes an analogy to draw conclusions based on the two things or people that are compared. As a body is not alive without its animating or life-giving principle, so no faith is alive or useful that does not necessarily entail works. The πνεῦμα without a definite article signifies "spirit" in the sense of the life principle that animates the body (BDAG, 832.2), a theme to be found in both pagan (Aristotle, *De. an.* 415B) and in Jewish writers (Judg 15:19; Ps 30:6; Ezek 37:10), and one that is also reflected in other NT passages (Luke 8:55; 23:46; 1 Cor 7:34). Here James returns to the main point that he declared in 2:17, and he also returns to the same exact wording that he had used. Although he had shifted from the adjective νεκρά to the adjective ἀργή in 2:20, his wording moves back to νεκρά here. The article ἡ before πίστις again serves an anaphoric function in pointing back to the dead and barren faith mentioned in 2:17 and 2:20. Both the similarities and the differences between the three verses can be visualized in this abbreviated sentence flow layout:

2:17 ἡ πίστις, ἐὰν μὴ ἔχῃ ἔργα, νεκρά ἐστιν καθ’ ἑαυτήν.

2:20 ἡ πίστις χωρὶς τῶν ἔργων ἀργή ἐστιν.

2:26 ἡ πίστις χωρὶς ἔργων νεκρά ἐστιν.

It is again important to stress that James is not arguing that works or deeds should be added to one's faith. "The anthropology at work in this analogy assumes that the spirit animates and gives life to the body (Gen 2:7; 6:17; Ps 31:15 [LXX 30:16]; Ezek 37:8–10; Luke 8:55; 23:46; 1 Cor 7:34)" (McKnight, 259). The analogy should not be physically pressed. A dead body, however, cannot have spirit simply added to it to make it become alive. It is alive when body and spirit are joined, and if the spirit is not present, it is a corpse. In the same way (ὥσπερ ... οὕτως), a faith that does not include deeds of love and kindness is simply a spiritual corpse.

Conclusion on James and Paul

Readers may notice that not much has been said here about the controversy over James' and Paul's differing emphases on justification. That absence has been deliberate. I wanted to make an effort to demonstrate that the argument of James makes perfect sense by itself without any reference to Paul. Too often James has been read only as a foil to Pauline theology. I argue that while James is not anti-Pauline, he should be viewed as ante-Pauline. This is not only because I see him writing prior to Galatians and Romans, but also because I believe that James and Paul are using the same words in different senses.

Furthermore, it may be helpful to see the differences between the two by looking at the views of their opponents. Without undue elaborations, I think it is clear that Paul is opposing those who desire to make "works of the law" an essential component in what makes a person right with God, in addition to the role of faith in that process. James seems to be opposing advocates of a faith-only position that does not require deeds as a part of that process. I adapt a comparison that I heard long ago. James and Paul are not opponents facing each other with swords drawn. They are standing with their backs to each other, each drawing swords as they face a different opponent.

In addition to the above, I propose the view that Paul's focus is on the "deeds of the law," while James' focus is on "deeds of love and kindness." Paul also emphasizes a believing person's entrance into justification by faith, while James emphasizes what a valid faith looks like. Any definition of the great Reformation distinctive *sola fide* should always be nuanced in light of Jas 2:24. According to Paul, NT faith is never absolutely alone since it is always accompanied by hope and love (1 Cor 13:13). In one of the two books where Paul teaches justification by faith "alone," he offers the following balanced statement, "For in Christ Jesus neither circumcision nor uncircumcision counts for anything, but only faith (πίστις) working (ἐνεργουμένη) through love" (Gal 5:6). I am sure that James would agree.

7

BE CONSISTENT IN YOUR SPEECH (3:1-12)

Taming the Tongue (3:1-2)

Introduction

All commentators agree that this pericope (3:1-12) is a separate one, being introduced by the familiar ἀδελφοί μου plus the imperative Μὴ … γίνεσθε and then concluded by a series of agricultural analogies (3:11–12). Even Martin Dibelius acknowledged that there were three consecutive sections in James that constituted self-contained "treatises" about three different subjects. Those three treatises are: (1) 2:1–13 on the evils of favoritism; (2) 2:14–26 on the inseparability of faith and works; and (3) 3:1–12 on the effects of the tongue (124). Dibelius considered 3:1–12 as only an assemblage of "school materials" whose "clauses often crash into each other" and have no connection with their context. Despite this internal lack of clear cohesion, he still viewed 3:1–12 as being a discrete section of the book with its own integrity (182).

This passage shares verbal links with both earlier and later ideas in the book. The most obvious semantic link is with 1:26, where reference is made to "not bridling" (μὴ χαλιναγωγῶν) one's tongue, in that 3:2

uses the same rare verb to describe the person who controls his tongue as "able also to bridle [χαλιναγωγῆσαι] the entire body." Other references in chapter 1 relate to the speech ethic he describes in our current chapter. It was noted earlier that a few commentators have considered that the three direct imperatives delivered in 1:19 ("be swift to hear, slow to speak, slow to wrath") serve the function of a table of contents for the rest of the book. The command to be "slow to speak" is therefore being elaborated here in 3:1–12. James also will continue his emphasis on speech ethics by his later warnings not to speak against a brother (4:11), not to speak presumptively about the future (4:13), and not to swear (5:12).

Greek Text

1 Μὴ πολλοὶ διδάσκαλοι γίνεσθε, ἀδελφοί μου, εἰδότες ὅτι μεῖζον κρίμα λημψόμεθα. 2 πολλὰ γὰρ πταίομεν ἅπαντες. εἴ τις ἐν λόγῳ οὐ ᵃπταίει, οὗτος τέλειος ἀνὴρ ᵇδυνατὸς χαλιναγωγῆσαι καὶ ὅλον τὸ σῶμα.

Textual Notes

2.a. The variant readings are mostly supported by late manuscripts, like πταίει in 3:2 replaced by the future tense (two late minuscules and a few Vulgate mss).

2.b. More important is the changing of the adjective δυνατὸς to the participle δυναμενος by such uncials as Sinaiticus and Ephraemi Rescriptus (C), some later uncials, and one Vulgate edition. This seems to be an effort to smooth out the abrupt δυνατὸς, which is introduced with a conjunction.

Context

In 3:1–2 a new topic is introduced—namely, the great role played by teachers in the assemblies of Jesus-believers and their subsequent great responsibility. This responsibility relates to the teacher's obvious use of the tongue as the instrument for speaking and teaching. This topic of speech is described first by vividly illustrating both the powerful and positive effects of such a small member in one's body (3:3–5a). The negative influence of the tongue—great in relation to its tiny size—is illustrated in 3:5b–12. In both of these sections, some quite colorful rhetorical figures are drawn from both the animal and natural worlds in the created order. In addition to these colorful analogies drawn from the world of nature, James also utilizes a rich intertexture by drawing from both Jewish wisdom literature and also from the sayings of Jesus, both of which he adapts for his own purposes. The following commentary will illustrate how he effectively argues that his readers should give serious consideration before assuming the responsible "job" of becoming a teacher.

Sentence Flow and Translation

1

Μὴ πολλοὶ διδάσκαλοι γίνεσθε, ἀδελφοί μου,
Not many of you should become teachers, my brothers,

εἰδότες ὅτι μεῖζον κρίμα λημψόμεθα.
for you know that we who teach will receive a stricter judgment.

2

πολλὰ γὰρ πταίομεν ἅπαντες.
For we all stumble in many ways.

εἴ τις ἐν λόγῳ οὐ πταίει,
If anyone does not stumble in what he says,

οὗτος τέλειος ἀνὴρ
he is a perfect man,

δυνατὸς χαλιναγωγῆσαι καὶ ὅλον τὸ σῶμα.
able also to bridle his whole body.

Exegetical Comments

3:1 Μὴ πολλοὶ διδάσκαλοι γίνεσθε, ἀδελφοί μου: In the opening complex clause of 3:1, James employs another second person imperative (γίνεσθε) combined with his now familiar nominative of direct address (ἀδελφοί μου). The recurrence of these forms indicates that James is initiating a line of thought different from the preceding context. As a section, 3:1–12 grounds and develops ideas introduced in 1:19–21, 26 about the importance of controlling the tongue and the decisive role of speech in reflecting man's inner nature.

The combination of the negated particle μή with an imperative appears in only seven of the nearly sixty imperative expressions in the book. The actions that are discouraged in this way are those of being deceived (1:16), showing partiality (2:1), boasting and lying (3:14), slandering (4:11), complaining (5:9), and swearing an oath (5:12). The present imperative should not be overread to assume that James is commanding the cessation of a practice that is taking place (contra Adamson, 146). The present imperative can express that idea, but the context must bear that out, and it is difficult to clearly determine if that is the case here. It expresses a general command that is always appropriate. The present imperative of γίνομαι conveys a dynamic action of "becoming" teachers, rather than a more stative idea that would be conveyed if he had used the imperative of the verb εἰμί, as he did with the present imperatives ἔστω/ἤτω in 1:19 and 5:12. His use of πολλοί recognizes that there must be teachers in the assemblies but stipulates that this should not be a role that many aspire to because of the great responsibility that comes with the role.

The noun διδάσκαλος was read in Attic Greek in the sense of a "schoolmaster" (Thucydides 3.82; Lysias 12.78). It keeps this meaning in the "Jewish Greek" of Philo, who records the νήπιος Moses as having διδάσκαλοι of different kinds (*Mos.* 1.2), and Abraham as having both διδάσκαλοι and παιδαγωγοί (*Migr.* 116). In Josephus (*Ant.* 15.373), there is a reference to servants as διδάσκαλοι. In the LXX, διδάσκαλος occurs in Esther 6:1, where it refers to the slave who was entrusted with the education of the eunuchs, and in 2 Macc 1:10, where it refers to the διδάσκαλος of King Ptolemy, and it is at this point that the word begins to describe the more professional role of "the teacher."

This διδάσκαλος has also a developing role in in the NT. The cognate verb διδάσκω appears in the NT ninety-seven times, while the substantive διδάσκαλος appears fifty-nine times. In the Gospels, one must distinguish between the teacher being addressed, which corresponds to the common Jewish address *rabbi,* and the noun used with the article which designates Jesus absolutely as "The Teacher" (Matt 23:8; Mark 14:14; John 13:13). Jesus also functioned as a teacher (the verb) in Matt 4:23; 9:35; Mark 10:1; and Luke 4:15. His sermon in the synagogue in Nazareth provides an example of his teaching. The address to Jesus as διδάσκαλε corresponds to this fact (Mark 4:38; 9:17, 38; 10:17, 35; Matt 19:16; 22:16), and this title corresponds to the Hebrew/Aramaic term *rabbi,* which was common in Judaism. In John 1:38, the address to Jesus as *rabbi* is translated διδάσκαλε (cf. John 20:16). Nicodemus used this term for Jesus in John 3:2 and Jesus also used it of Nicodemus in 3:10.

In the Gospels, the verb and the noun describe a distinctive function within the church only in Matthew (5:19; 23:8; 28:20), but there is a wider distribution of the verb and noun in Acts and in the Epistles. Teachers were prominent in the Jewish-Christian assemblies (Heb 5:12; Acts 13:1) and were ranked just below apostles and prophets by Paul (1 Cor 12:28; Eph 4:11). They were associated with the prophets but higher than the ἐπίσκοποι and διάκονοι in the first-century Jewish-Christian document, the *Didache* (13:2; 15:1, 2).

A scene similar to that which James refers in 3:1 is preserved in Acts 13:1, where five prophets and teachers are mentioned. It is possible that the "Christians" at Antioch were among the first to hear James' warning read aloud to them in the presence of these teachers! It appears clear in our text that James is warning about ethically, not doctrinally, subversive teachers—those who say one thing and do or live another.

Teachers in Jewish and Christian contexts were highly esteemed and revered (Matt 13:52), and Paul affirmed the legitimacy of individuals desiring to be an "overseer" (1 Tim 3:1), whose role included teaching (3:2). It was thus both natural and normal for many aspiring "teachers" to desire to exercise this highly desired function; but since the role was also considered one of the *charismata* (Eph 4:11 and Rom 12:7), there would be few who could rightly exercise this gift.

εἰδότες ὅτι μεῖζον κρίμα λημψόμεθα: This subordinate causal clause introduced by the perfect active participle εἰδότες (from οἶδα) provides the reason why there are few who should pursue the role of teacher: teachers in the assemblies will undergo a stricter divine examination due to the seriousness of the role. James uses the causal participle elsewhere only in 1:3, where he also appealed to information that his readers should already know: "... because you know [γινώσκοντες] that the testing of your faith produces endurance."[1] With the future middle indicative verb λημψόμεθα James switches, for the first time, to the first person plural "we." This usage becomes a characteristic in this overall section, appearing twice in 3:2–3 and twice in 3:9. James employs a first person plural verb elsewhere only in 5:11 (cf. 4:13, 15, not James' usage). Efforts to explain this by the editorial or literary "we" fail to see that this first person plural is our author expressing a self-designation. In other words, James considers himself also as a "teacher." "The author clearly considers himself among the teachers. James 3:1–2a is thus the only passage in which we learn something about the author himself" (Dibelius, 183; plus most other commentators).

In the following paragraph (3:13–18), some virtues of a "sage" (σοφός) are listed. In ancient Israel, the term "teacher" (Hebrew רַבִּי) and the term "sage" (Hebrew חָכָם) described the same person. Thus

---

[1] A suggested fine semantic distinction in "knowing" between the verbs γινώσκω and οἶδα, maintained by a few of the older commentators, does not seem to be linguistically justified. See Mayor, 34, for a good discussion.

this entire chapter, while still maintaining in a general sense an application to all Jesus-believers, conveys a particular application to those who function as teachers and sages—and one of those teacher/sages was James himself. If we have been accurate in the idea that his self-designation of δοῦλος (1:1) described the noble and honored role of one in the line of Israel's prophets (see the comments there), then the identity of James as a prophet/teacher/sage seems supported both in 1:1 and 3:1. But this is only the implication of the verse, since his readers are the ones who are his main focus.

Few should consider becoming teachers because "we who teach will receive a stricter judgment" (κρίμα). The sense of this expression is not that teachers will be punished more severely than laypeople, but that teachers will be more strictly examined because of the effect, both for good and bad, which their speech will produce. An eschatological motivation for this type of exhortation was issued earlier in 1:12, where the one who is faithful can anticipate that he will receive (same verb λήμψεται) the crown of life. The patient believer in 5:7–8, like the patient farmer, receives (same aorist verb λάβῃ) the fruit from his labors. The term normally refers to the result of judgment rather than the judgment itself (Mark 12:40; Luke 23:40; Rom 2:2; 3:8; 5:16), and this is also indicated by the -μα ending of the noun. It appears that James is again adapting another Jesus *logion* (or more than one) to argue his point. This could be in a general sense drawn from the teaching of Jesus about the inconsistency between saying and doing, which was also issued in a context of judgment (Matt 7:15–20). More specifically, this verse is an echo of Jesus' warning about the baneful teaching of the scribes (who were Israel's teachers!) in Mark 12:38–40 and Luke 20:45–47. Note particularly the verbal similarity between the sayings: οὗτοι λήμψονται περισσότερον κρίμα (Mark 12:40 and Luke 20:47). If James is referencing the teaching of Jesus, it also provides an explanation why James can appeal to both his knowledge and that of his hearers/readers ("because *we* know"). They are expected to be familiar with the teachings of the Master.

The degree to which this imperative may reflect any specific situation is difficult to discern. "This exhortation presupposes a social situation much like that in the synagogue, where almost anyone who was able to speak in public could come forward and do so (1 Cor 14:26, 31), but we are a long way from ordained rabbis or teachers in this imperative" (Witherington, 485). I am sure that he intended to apply this also to the believing synagogues among the dispersed Jesus-communities.

3:2 πολλὰ γὰρ πταίομεν ἅπαντες: This subsection (3:1–2) concludes with two clauses, one causal and the other declarative. The first is a primary clause that introduced γάρ in its postpositive position. This clause asserts an additional supporting reason for his warning in the opening imperative command of 3:1. James often utilizes a similar pattern to develop his argument. First, he will issue an imperative command. Then he will set forth an example of how that command can be broken. Then he will support his point by a further argument and finally conclude with an apothegm, or wise saying, that rounds off and seals his argument. This pattern can also be discerned in the previous chapter (2:1–13) where he first issues a command against partiality (2:1), and then introduces an example from the synagogue (2:2–4, introduced by γάρ). Then he offers further scriptural support for his command (2:5–12), and finally concludes with an aphoristic saying that seals the exhortation (2:13). In this paragraph, he also issues a command (3:1), then provides a reason (3:2), then offers extended support by analogies echoing Scripture (3:3–11), and finally concludes with a wise saying (3:12).

The accusative neuter plural πολλά functions not as a direct object but as an adverb, expressing "how" we stumble. However, the declaration is not simply a reiteration of the charge made in Rom 3:23: "For all have sinned." The use of the first person plural verb expresses a realistic anthropology on the part of the author. This shared failing does not disqualify James from being a teacher, but rather alerts his readers to the urgency of the challenge that faces those who desire to become teachers. Some commentators reference similar statements in the Hellenistic moral treatises where the verb πταίω certainly does appear. It is my contention, however, that we do not need to venture outside traditional Jewish wisdom literature to discover statements which James might be echoing by his use of the verb in 3:2. In those same Jewish wisdom documents, there appear metaphorical uses of this verb in relation to speech (e.g. *T. Job* 38.1 and similar uses in Deut 7:25 and Sir 2:8). Furthermore, there are the additional quite similar ideas found in many of the Jesus *logia* concerning speech ethics (e.g., Matt 12:37). James may also have another and nearer reason for using this word—namely, that he already has used it in 2:10: "For whoever observes the whole law but stumbles (πταίσῃ) at one point has become accountable for all of it." Finally, since James will soon illustrate his concerns about the abuse of the tongue with an analogy from a horse (in 3:3, to keep it from stumbling), his use of the verb πταίω in this verse can be explained by its use in the immediate literary context rather than by its appearance in non-Jewish material.

εἴ τις ἐν λόγῳ οὐ πταίει: This section (3:1–2) concludes with a conditional sentence, with the protasis repeating the verb πταίει from the previous sentence (3:2a). This first class conditional statement with εἴ does not imply anything about its necessary fulfillment or its impossibility, nor is it a future more probable condition (third class). So one may take it in its immediate context to imply that it is not likely to happen at present, but it is expected to happen. James clearly desires that believers bridle their tongues, though presumably he does not expect them to do it perfectly or without relapse. James has not yet used the word "tongue" nor will he do so until 3:5a. The use of ἐν λόγῳ confirms what becomes evident in the following clause with the infinitive χαλιναγωγῆσαι, recalling 1:26 which referred to bridling the tongue. While there is a small transition in thought from 3:1, λόγος is probably chosen because of this word's appropriate application to teachers. "It is not limited to error in teaching (Dibelius, 184) but includes all speech in general, a synonym for γλῶσσα of 3:5" (Davids, 137).

οὗτος τέλειος ἀνὴρ: The apodosis begins with the demonstrative pronoun οὗτος, which is not grammatically improper but is characteristic of James' style. He employed this demonstrative in the same way in 1:23 and also used it following a participle in 1:25. This might be called a "redundant" or pleonastic use of the demonstrative, and is the author's style of emphasizing the prominence of the role that this "perfect man" fulfills.[2]

Our author's semantic style is witnessed in the expression "perfect man," using the word ἀνήρ. This noun usually refers to a male, while ἄνθρωπος is utilized in a more generic sense as "person." In his letter, James employs ἀνήρ on six occasions (1:8, 12, 20, 23; 2:2; 3:2) and uses ἄνθρωπος seven times (1:7, 19; 2:20, 24; 3:8, 9; 5:17). Is this diversity simply another example of his stylistic variation, or is there a pattern that emerges in these passages? Consider the following important observation:

> St. James commonly uses ἀνὴρ with some characteristic word, as μακάριος 1:12, κατανοῶν 1:23, χρυσοδακτύλιος 2:2, τέλειος 3:2, keeping ἄνθρωπος for more general expressions, ἐκεῖνος, πᾶς, οὐδείς, etc. This agrees fairly with the use in the LXX and Gospels: in the other epistles ἀνὴρ is almost exclusively used in opposition to γυνή (Mayor, 42).

This affirmation in 3:2b also recalls the important word τέλειος in 1:4, where it embodies the goal of becoming a mature believer.

δυνατὸς χαλιναγωγῆσαι καὶ ὅλον τὸ σῶμα: A special stylistic feature is the asyndeton utilized in his description of the perfect man with the abrupt use of the adjective δυνατός: "able also to bridle the entire body." One might anticipate a conjunction or at least a relative pronoun ("which is able"). The abundant use of asyndeton is also

---

[2] Wallace refers to this as the "pleonastic" or "redundant" use of the pronoun (329–30). He adds that the redundancy is only from the English perspective.

characteristic of his style.

The apodosis of the sentence functions both anaphorically, by its use of the verb χαλιναγωγῆσαι previously used in 1:26, and cataphorically, by anticipating the literal use of the noun χαλινούς in 3:3. James' comment prepares the reader for his colorful analogies in the following verses. The complementary aorist infinitive χαλιναγωγῆσαι ("to bridle") will immediately lead to an equestrian analogy in 3:3 with clear references to horses and their "bridles" (χαλινούς). The expression ὅλον τὸ σῶμα is repeated in 3:3 and 3:6. James sees one's tongue or speech as crucial because of the potential harm or good it can also do to the "body." Could this be a reference to the body of Christ, as some commentators affirm (Reicke 37; Martin 110)? While attractive, this view suffers from an anachronism that imports a later Pauline metaphor into this context with little justification. "James has not prepared his readers for any such theological application of the word body" (Moo, 2000, 153).

Small but Powerful (3:3–5)

Context

James calls attention to three examples of small things in nature that have large effects. The bit/bridle, the rudder, and the tongue are here mentioned as being alike in one thing: they are *multum in parvo* in their power. Each is comparatively small, but each produces great effects (see Adamson, 142–43). To help visualize the structure of this section, notice the following analysis and the prominent role of the orienters ἴδε and ἰδού.

Greek Text

3 εἰ δὲ^a (or ἴδε) τῶν ἵππων τοὺς χαλινοὺς εἰς τὰ στόματα βάλλομεν εἰς τὸ πείθεσθαι αὐτοὺς ἡμῖν, καὶ ὅλον τὸ σῶμα αὐτῶν μετάγομεν. 4 ἰδοὺ καὶ τὰ

πλοῖα τηλικαῦτα ὄντα καὶ ὑπὸ ἀνέμων σκληρῶν ἐλαυνόμενα, μετάγεται ὑπὸ
ἐλαχίστου πηδαλίου ὅπου ἡ ὁρμὴ τοῦ εὐθύνοντος βούλεται, 5 οὕτως καὶ ἡ
γλῶσσα μικρὸν μέλος ἐστὶν καὶ ᵇμεγάλα αὐχεῖ. ἰδοὺ ἡλίκον πῦρ ἡλίκην ὕλην
ἀνάπτει·

Textual Notes

3.a. Confusion due to the itacism (confusion of sound) between ει and
ι was common among ancient scribes, and it is possible that a copyist
wrote ιδε but meant ει δε, or vice versa. "The editor must therefore
choose the reading that, in his judgment, is most appropriate in the
context. A majority of the UBS4 committee preferred εἰ δέ as the more
difficult reading, and explained the rise of ἴδε partly as the result of
itacism and partly in harmonization with ἰδού in verses 4 and 5. The
Textus Receptus assimilates to ἰδού, with 36 483 1874 1877." However, it
should be remembered that it was a *majority* of the committee (3-2)
and the ἴδε reading has some strong manuscript and contextual
support and should not be discounted. See the end of this paper for an
extended note defending the ἴδε reading over against the NA/UBS
texts.*

5.b. In 3:5, the critical texts read μεγάλα αὐχεῖ ("boasts great things"),
with the support of P⁷⁴ A B C P 33. TR has one word μεγαλαύχει, a result
of crasis (the combination of two words), which means the same thing
(P20 ℵ C Ψ 1739 Byz).

Sentence Flow and Translation

3
ἴδε
Look!

τῶν ἵππων τοὺς χαλινοὺς εἰς τὰ στόματα βάλλομεν
We put bridles into the mouths of horses

εἰς τὸ πείθεσθαι αὐτοὺς ἡμῖν,
so that they obey us

καὶ ὅλον τὸ σῶμα αὐτῶν μετάγομεν.
and we guide their whole bodies.

4
ἰδοὺ
Look!

καὶ τὰ πλοῖα τηλικαῦτα   SUBJECT
The ships also,

> ὄντα καὶ ὑπὸ ἀνέμων σκληρῶν ἐλαυνόμενα,   CONCESSIVE
> though they are so large and are driven by strong winds,

> > μετάγεται ὑπὸ ἐλαχίστου πηδαλίου   PREDICATE
> > are guided by a very small rudder

> > > ὅπου ἡ ὁρμὴ τοῦ εὐθύνοντος βούλεται,   WHERE
> > > wherever the will of the pilot directs.

5
οὕτως καὶ ἡ γλῶσσα μικρὸν μέλος ἐστὶν καὶ μεγάλα αὐχεῖ.
So also the tongue is a small member, and yet it boasts of great things.

ἰδοὺ
Look!
ἡλίκον πῦρ ἡλίκην ὕλην ἀνάπτει·
Such a small fire sets ablaze such a great forest!

Exegetical Comments

The sentence flow display above demonstrates that this section consists of five crisp, primary clauses, held together this time by a καί in each verse. There are also three embedded clauses in 3:3–4 (one governed by an infinitive and two by participles) with a secondary relative clause that concludes verse 4.

3:3 ἴδε τῶν ἵππων τοὺς χαλινοὺς εἰς τὰ στόματα βάλλομεν εἰς τὸ πείθεσθαι αὐτοὺς ἡμῖν, καὶ ὅλον τὸ σῶμα αὐτῶν μετάγομεν: I have altered the wording of the critical NA[27]/UBS[4] texts at the beginning of 3:3. I prefer the reading ἴδε instead of εἰ δέ, and this preference alters the verse from being a conditional clause to becoming two primary clauses. The first of the primary clauses consists of an imperative command, "look," which has been translated traditionally as "behold." In this reading, therefore, the protasis and apodosis in the conditional sentence are rendered as follows: "Look! We put bridles into the mouths of horses so that they obey us and we guide their whole bodies." In an Appendix to this commentary, I have provided an extended note that discusses this variant reading in depth. At this point, I will simply summarize the evidence for the adopted reading.

Although normally reticent to dissent from the readings of the two critical texts of NA27 and UBS4, I have nevertheless chosen to adopt the ἴδε reading for the five following reasons, each of which is based on what textual scholars call internal evidence. (1) In every other case in which the conditional εἰ δέ appears in James, the δέ clearly expresses an idea that is adversative to what he has just stated (1:5; 2:9, 11; 3:14; 4:11). Such an adversative idea is *not* the case if there is a conditional sentence beginning in 3:3. (2) If 3:3 is a conditional sentence, the καί that initiates the proposed apodosis seems to be out of place. Although English translators have recognized this by rendering it as "also," it is not the normal role of an apodosis in a conditional sentence to add new information to the protasis, but rather to show the result of fulfilling the hypothetical condition in the protasis. (3) Because James uses the aorist middle imperative of ὁράω (ἰδού) to call attention to the ship/rudder in 3:4 and to the fire/forest in 3:5a, the parallelism is more evident if he uses the aorist active imperative of ὁράω (ἴδε) in 3:3. This parallelism can be seen in the above sentence flow analysis by bolding the paralleled imperatives. (4) The καί in its postpositive position in 3:4 appears to refer back to the preceding illustration in a way that is consistent with the idea that James desires to call attention to the previous command to "look" at something in the natural processes of life. (5) Although Metzger informs us that a majority of the UBS committee members preferred εἰ δέ as the more difficult reading, the same point can be made about ἴδε, because it breaks the parallelism with ἰδού in 3:4 and 5. If someone objects that it would be inconsistent to utilize both ἴδε and ἰδού in such a close context, it should be noted that the following passages have these two different imperative forms utilized together in quite close context: Mark 3:32, 34; Matt 25:6, 20, 22, 25; John 16:29, 32; and Gal 1:20; 5:2.

The external evidence of manuscript age and quality seems to be an open question in this case, but the internal evidence of context and even of discourse considerations ought also to be given serious consideration. In my opinion, the function of the discourse markers ἴδε and ἰδού call attention to the three examples from natural life—the horse/bridle, the ship/rudder, and the fire/forest—and also effectively combine to make a powerful rhetorical argument for the unexpected power of the tongue, both for good and for evil. Therefore, he asks us, yea commands us, to "look" at them with serious attention!

τῶν ἵππων: The genitive for "horses" is fronted in an emphatic position in the sentence to lend more prominence to the comparison. "Look! In regard to the horses—we put ..." (Robertson, 418). "In other words, if the principle in view works with horses, how much more with humans" (Blomberg-Kamell, 155, n 27). The ἵππων belongs both to χαλινούς and to στόματα, probably more to the former as distinguishing it from the human bridle.

τοὺς χαλινούς: Rather than "bits" I have purposely chosen "bridles" for the accusative noun χαλινούς in 3:3, the less often used translation among the versions. This translation brings out more accurately the

obvious verbal link with the verb χαλιναγωγῆσαι in 3:2, which also
appears in 1:27, and which was our author's reason for choosing the
example of a bridle in the first place. The bit actually does not control
the horse, since the bit is the part of the bridle controlled by the rider.
The usage of the verb and noun thus support the translation "bridle."

εἰς τὰ στόματα: "This is an appropriate word; for the tongue is in the
mouth" (Bengel, 24). The closest scriptural parallel to this image is
found in Psa 32:9, where horse and mule must be controlled by both a
bit and a bridle. No such control should be necessary for a person.
James is using language familiar to first-century hearers/readers. We
should resist, however, the idea that these and the following
illustrations necessarily imply that the author has extensive
experience in horsemanship or the maritime arts. The vivid analogy
depends on the importance the tongue has because of the control that
can be exercised through it over the whole creature as through the
horse's mouth. The smallness of the member does not yet come into
consideration at this point.

εἰς τὸ πείθεσθαι αὐτοὺς ἡμῖν: This purpose clause could be translated
literally, "in order that they may be persuaded by us." The subject
(αὐτούς) of the infinitive is specified, as it is also in 1:18 (εἰς τὸ εἶναι ἡμᾶς
ἀπαρχήν); 4:2 (διὰ τὸ μὴ αἰτεῖσθαι ὑμᾶς); and in 4:15 (ἀντὶ τοῦ λέγειν
ὑμᾶς). The illustration also may suggest a rhetorical question. If we do
this with such strong animals as horses, a mere touch of the rein
turning them around, shall we not do this with ourselves, who are
much more than horses? We should be careful not to think that it is
the bridle/bit or the rudder that ultimately control the horse and the
ship. The rider controls the horse (alluded to in the purpose clause of
3:3: εἰς τὸ πείθεσθαι αὐτοὺς ἡμῖν) and the pilot controls the ship (clearly
mentioned in the relative clause of 3:4: ὅπου ἡ ὁρμὴ τοῦ εὐθύνοντος
βούλεται). The body of the horse follows his mouth, which is guided by
the bridle, which in turn is controlled by the rider. The same is true of
the ship controlled by the rudder, which is controlled by the captain.

This move from the "object of control" to the one who "steers" that control is also consistent with James' recognition elsewhere that the forces that drive our actions are our inner hearts and motives (1:14, 15; 2:2; 18; 3:13–17; 4:1, 2). Our deeds are simply the outward expressions that emerge from within. In other words, our tongue is controlled by our heart.

3:4 ἰδοὺ καὶ τὰ πλοῖα τηλικαῦτα ὄντα καὶ ὑπὸ ἀνέμων σκληρῶν ἐλαυνόμενα, "Look! The ships also, though they are so large and are driven by strong winds." The two present participles (ὄντα and ἐλαυνόμενα) are clearly concessive in force. The τηλικαῦτα is used elsewhere only in 2 Cor 1:10; Heb 2:3; and Rev 16:18. In those passages it is great in relation to importance, whereas here it is great in relation to size (BDAG, 1001–02; GE, 2112). Grammarians also note that this is an example of the NT practice of using the classical "superlative" for the "elative" (Wallace, 303; Turner 3, 31). Some have thought that James is calling attention to the size of the wind that large ships require in order to sail (see McKnight, 278), but it is better to see him calling attention to strongly violent winds tossing a ship controlled by a small rudder (Johnson, 257; Moo, 153–54). The two clauses describing the ships (all in the nominative plural) point to a big one tossed by violent winds and favor the second reading. The emphasis here and throughout the passage is the influence of the small on the large.

μετάγεται ὑπὸ ἐλαχίστου πηδαλίου ὅπου ἡ ὁρμὴ τοῦ εὐθύνοντος βούλεται: Not surprisingly, the word "rudder" (πηδαλίου) is used elsewhere in the NT only in the one sea voyage account (Acts 27:40). It is the "impulse, inclination, or desire" (ὁρμή, BDAG, 724) of the helmsman that is the ultimate factor in the guiding of the ship. The word ὁρμή is used of the origin of motion in either the moral or physical sphere. In the NT, it only occurs here and in Acts 14:5 (of a "rush" or "onset" of the people). What do these vivid analogies in 3:3, 4 convey? One might conclude that the idea of perfectly controlled speech is attainable since the beneficial power of a controlled tongue is positively portrayed;

however, what they highlight is only the general power of a controlled tongue resulting in a controlled body. They do not imply that the human tongue (yet to be specifically mentioned by name) can be controlled as completely as a horse's tongue or a ship's rudder. When a horse's mouth is made to obey, so does its whole body.

The more elaborate description in 3:4 adds some critical facets to this depiction. In his treatment of speech ethics, both in the Bible and in the ancient world, Baker has summarized these facets well.

> First, the inclusion of ἀνέμων σκληρῶν ἐλαυνόμενα brings to notice the fact that the tongue is not powerful in itself. Secondly, the accentuation of the smallness of the rudder (ἐλαχίστου) in contrast to the great size of the ship (τηλικαῦτα) draws attention to the importance of the tongue to the body which is vastly out of proportion to its relative size. Thirdly, the addition of ὅπου ἡ ὁρμὴ τοῦ εὐθύνοντος βούλεται enhances the fact that the tongue does not control itself. It should be controlled by the person, more specifically by his own desire, his choice of direction. Thus, ultimately he is responsible if his tongue is powered into bad speech by bad influences. All three of these points are drawn upon in the next two verses, the third being already established in 1:13.[3]

3:5 οὕτως καὶ ἡ γλῶσσα μικρὸν μέλος ἐστὶν καὶ μεγάλα αὐχεῖ: The consequential function of οὕτως, with the repetition of ἰδού initiating a new sentence in the middle of this verse, has led some commentators to see this subsection ending with 3:5a (NA[27]/UBS[4] end the paragraph with this clause; Davids, 140). But 3:6 seems to launch a new train of thought, so we will follow the traditional versification and view 3:5b as the concluding member of the ἴδε—ἰδού—ἰδού trilogy in 3:3–5. The phrase οὕτως καὶ draws the previous comparisons (bit/horse and

---

[3] William R. Baker, *Personal Speech-Ethics in the Epistle of James* (WUNT 2.68; Tübingen: Mohr, 1995), 124–25.

rudder/ship) to their specific application. James has used the same construction in 1:11, 2:17, and 2:26.

μικρὸν μέλος ἐστίν: James' fondness for alliteration is shown by the threefold repetition of an initial μ- (μικρὸν / μέλος / μεγάλα). The noun μέλος here and in the next verse has its ordinary meaning of a part of the body (1 Cor 12:12). Its appearance in 4:1 also appears to be consistent with its usage here.

καὶ μεγάλα αὐχεῖ: James uses the verb αὐχεῖ with the accusative direct object μεγάλα. The verb is unattested in the LXX or elsewhere in the NT, but similar usages of the verb αὐχέω can be found in Hellenistic literature (BDAG, 154; GE, 350) and exemplifies the level of the author's Greek. Some have suggested that boasting with the tongue is not denounced by James because the tongue's claims are in reality quite correct (Hort, 70; Mayor, 112; Johnson, 258). It is better, however, to see his description of the tongue as negative, since his use of analogies in this passage indicates that all of them are destructive to the community. The next passages follow this example of the negative use of the tongue (3:14–16; 4:1-6). This boasting, therefore, is a description of the arrogant speech that engenders strife, not peace (Davids, 140; McKnight, 279).

ἰδοὺ ἡλίκον πῦρ ἡλίκην ὕλην ἀνάπτει: This final clause of 3:5 completes the triad of attention-getters (see ἴδε in 3:3 and ἰδοὺ in 3:4). A good case can be made that it should begin 3:6 because it introduces the figure of "fire" that is the subject of that verse. However, the clause may simply have both an anaphoric and a cataphoric function in the paragraph, referencing the previous examples of small things having large effects and preparing the reader for the next reference to fire. The verb ἀνάπτω with the prefix ἀν- appears only here and in an eschatological Jesus logion (Luke 12:49). The noun ὕλη often appeared as a "forest" (Josephus, Ant. 18:357; Sir 28:10; Philo, Decal. 173; see BDAG, 1027).

The doubled adjectives ἡλίκον/ἡλίκην, differing only in gender, are used to describe an initially small fire that can eventually consume a huge forest. This apparently contradictory usage is resolved by recognizing that this word simply expresses alarm at the size of something ("such a," "what a," "how!", BDAG, 436; "of quantity [large or small]", GE, 907). The context then will supply the clue as to whether the size of the noun described is small or large, or both small and large! It is a word which comments on the relative size of something, whether big or small. The use of this word across the corpus of Greek literature is consistent with this meaning of the adjective.[4] The wordplay in 3:5 would then be in the close combination of the modifier ἡλίκην and the noun ὕλην. This becomes clearer when one recognizes that the words not only share rough breathing marks but also share the same initial sound. In the ancient pronunciation, to be contrasted with the Erasmian pronunciation, the η and υ were probably pronounced the same way (i.e., "ee").[5]

The tongue is not merely powerful, but it is also evil and destructive. The clearest parallel outside the canon is in Philo, *On the Decalogue* 173: "For nothing escapes desire ... like a flame in the forest, it spreads abroad and consumes and destroys everything." The description of the tongue as a fire certainly has some OT parallels (Prov 16:27; Isa 9:18). His thought is rooted in OT teaching, so even if the combination of images found in 3:3–5 are attested in Greek literature, James has not wandered from his OT sources.

Dibelius remarks on James' Greek: "The neat arrangement which is indicated here does not quite obtain in the treatise (i.e. vv 1-12). Instead we observe how the ideas bump against or even clash with one another—evidence that the author is transmitting school material" (Dibelius, 182). Luther also voiced this criticism. However, when we recognize the style of James' writing—e.g., such stylistic matters as his fondness for asyndeton, as well as his avoidance of secondary clauses and inferential particles—it should keep us from criticizing his

---

[4] LSJ, 768; Representative examples of this usage are in Josephus, *War* 1.626; *Ant.* 8, 208; Antiphanes, *Com.* 166, 6; and Epictetus, *Diatr.* 1, 12, 26.

[5] L. E. Elliott-Binns, "The Meaning of ὕλη in James iii.5," *NTS* 2 (1955) 48–50.

language in this way. When we recognize the rhetorical tropes that he uses, we can appreciate better the direct and often "clipped" language that he uses to urge his hearers to choose now to live an undivided life. Furthermore, by recovering his original text through both the external and the internal evidence supplied by textual criticism (as is the case with the ἴδε in 3:3), we can often succeed in softening those supposed bumps and clashes that bothered Dibelius so much.

Writers attuned to the rhetorical analysis of ancient texts have noticed a number of rhetorical touches in this passage, some of which we have already noted. To sum up a few thus far: (1) the catchwords πταίω and χαλινός linking several thoughts in James 3:2-3; (2) the alliteration of μικρὸν - μέλος - μεγάλα in James 3:5; and (3) the word ἡλίκον balancing its cognate ἡλίκην in James 3:5 in the highly rhetorical phrase ἡλίκον πῦρ ἡλίκην ὕλην ἀνάπτει, therefore providing a nice contrast: "how small a flame ignites so great a forest." The word used here, ὕλην, can indicate "wood" not a "forest," so it is possible that a Judean touch may be in view, since large forests were not plentiful in James' world. In the extremely dry conditions of Judea and Galilee, a forest fire becomes almost immediately out of control. The rhetorical effectiveness of James' language is also marked by a strange but effective combination of both grace and awkwardness in the passage: "Whereas vv. 2-3 presented the positive side that bridling the tongue indicated mastery of the body, v. 6 presents the negative side that in fact the tongue stains the whole body."[6]

Any reader of James 3:3-5 must agree that the common theme connecting the three analogies is the great effect that a small component wields within a larger system. It should be noted, however, that the particular emphases vary within the three. The emphasis with the bridle and horse analogy is the small size and the great impact. The emphasis of a small rudder on a large ship also stresses guidance. The small flame and large forest also emphasizes great destructiveness.

---

[6] D. F. Watson, "The Rhetoric of James 3:1-12 and a Classical Pattern of Argumentation," *NovT* 35 (1993) 60.

A Wild Fire and a Wild Beast (3:6-8)

Context

Because the rhetorical thrust and the message of this smaller pericope within the larger 3:1–12 are so intertwined and intended to be experienced as a whole, it is difficult to micro-analyze every individual word and clause. Therefore, the "message" of this section and the next section (3:9–12) clearly overlap. Therefore, any attempt to lay out the message of 3:6–8 must also clearly coincide at times with what follows in the next section.

Greek Text

6 ᵃκαὶ ἡ γλῶσσα πῦρ. ὁ κόσμος τῆς ἀδικίας ἡ γλῶσσα καθίσταται ἐν τοῖς μέλεσιν ἡμῶν, ᵇἡ σπιλοῦσα ὅλον τὸ σῶμα καὶ φλογίζουσα τὸν τροχὸν τῆς γενέσεωςᶜ καὶ φλογιζομένη ὑπὸ τῆς γεέννης. 7 πᾶσα γὰρ φύσις θηρίων τε καὶ πετεινῶν, ἑρπετῶν τε καὶ ἐναλίων δαμάζεται καὶ δεδάμασται τῇ φύσει τῇ ἀνθρωπίνῃ, 8 τὴν δὲ γλῶσσαν οὐδεὶς δαμάσαι δύναται ἀνθρώπων, ᵈἀκατάστατον κακόν, μεστὴ ἰοῦ θανατηφόρου.

Textual Notes

In an interesting departure from its general agreement with the Alexandrian family, Sinaiticus (א) has some unique readings in this passage, especially in verse 6.

6.a. Along with only a handful of Vulgate mss, א omits the καί at the beginning of 3:6.

6.b. Along with only a few Coptic Bohairic mss, א inserts a καί before ἡ σπιλοῦσα.

6.c. After the challenging expression, ἡ σπιλοῦσα, א makes the expression personal by adding the pronoun, probably to bring it into harmony with the previous expression: "our members" (μέλεσιν ἡμῶν).

8.d. Later textual witnesses (C Ψ minuscules) characterize the tongue as an "uncontrollable (ἀκατάσχετον) evil" rather than as a "restless (ἀκατάστατον) evil" (ℵ A B K P 1739). Because this reading appears to be a more common type of description, it probably arose through a later scribal adjustment.

Sentence Flow and Translation

6
καὶ ἡ γλῶσσα πῦρ·
And the tongue is a fire.

ὁ κόσμος τῆς ἀδικίας ἡ γλῶσσα καθίσταται ἐν τοῖς μέλεσιν ἡμῶν, The tongue is set as the unrighteous world among our members,

ἡ σπιλοῦσα ὅλον τὸ σῶμα
staining the whole body,

καὶ φλογίζουσα τὸν τροχὸν τῆς γενέσεως
and setting on fire the entire course of life,

καὶ φλογιζομένη ὑπὸ τῆς γεέννης.
and is itself set on fire by Gehenna.

7
πᾶσα γὰρ φύσις θηρίων δαμάζεται καὶ δεδάμασται τῇ φύσει τῇ ἀνθρωπίνῃ,
For every kind of beast can be tamed and has been tamed by mankind,

τε καὶ πετεινῶν,
and also birds,

ἑρπετῶν τε καὶ ἐναλίων
of reptile and sea creature,

8
τὴν δὲ γλῶσσαν οὐδεὶς δαμάσαι δύναται ἀνθρώπων,
but no human being can tame the tongue.
ἀκατάστατον κακόν, μεστὴ ἰοῦ θανατηφόρου.
It is a restless evil, full of deadly poison.

Commentary

3:6 καὶ ἡ γλῶσσα πῦρ: Picking up the catchword πῦρ from the last clause of 3:5, James openly applies the metaphor in this verbless clause. He then describes the awful power of that metaphor in the rest of the verse. For the general sense of this statement, compare Prov 16:24–30, especially verse 27: "he gathers fire on his own lips" (see also Sir 28:8–12 and *Pss. Sol.* 12:2–4). As the earlier references to the helmsman and the charioteer are typical illustrations of the power of reason, so fire is a favorite metaphor in Greek diatribal literature to represent the rule of the passions and desires. Philo depicts the growth of the flame in the wood. "Desire ... imitates the force of fire working on an abundance of fuel which it kindles into a blaze and devours until it has utterly consumed it" (Philo, *Spec. Leg.* 4.83). Thus the effect of the tongue was occasionally compared to a fire, as were other excesses of passion. The allusion to this application of the metaphor found in late Jewish witnesses (like *Midrash Rabba*) could go back to the models in Proverbs or in the Sirach and *Psalms of Solomon* passages mentioned above.

ὁ κόσμος τῆς ἀδικίας "[The tongue] is set as the unrighteous world among our members." The noun-genitive expression ὁ κόσμος τῆς ἀδικίας is the complement of the following verb καθίσταται, rather than being in apposition to the previous statement. The sentence flow analysis above attempts to convey this function. Along with some other recent versions, the Net Bible captures well the sense of the expression: "The tongue represents the world of wrongdoing among the parts of our bodies."[7] The fronting of the expression emphasizes its prominence in the clause—a further argument that it is a complement to the verb rather than simply an appositional renaming of "the world is a fire." It is in the nominative case, rather than in the accusative case, because it serves as a "nominative of appellation" (Wallace, 61). This usage conveys a title or a name given to the controlling verb's subject, ἡ γλῶσσα, often with a passive verb (as here) rather than as a direct object in the accusative case.

ἡ γλῶσσα καθίσταται ἐν τοῖς μέλεσιν ἡμῶν: The present passive verb καθίσταται of the verb καθίστημι means "to appoint, to set in order" (Abbott-Smith, 224). Now added to the figure of fire is that of the unrighteous world set within one's members. As in 3:5 and 4:1 the noun μέλος refers to a bodily member with no need to make it metaphorical for a "church member." Here the preposition ἐν bears the sense of "among" rather than "in" (BDAG, 326.1). There is no elucidation for this expression gained from anywhere but in Jewish sources and was self-evident to Jews as well as to Christians, namely the evil world. In *1 Enoch* 48.7 there is a very similar expression: "They have hated and despised this world of unrighteousness." 1 John 5:19 says, "... the whole world is in the power of the evil one" (ὁ κόσμος ὅλος ἐν τῷ πορηρῷ κεῖται).

ἡ σπιλοῦσα ὅλον τὸ σῶμα καὶ φλογίζουσα τὸν τροχὸν τῆς γενέσεως καὶ φλογιζομένη: The occurrence of three vivid attributive present participles (σπιλοῦσα, φλογίζουσα, φλογιζομένη) modifying γλῶσσα describe the destructive fiery power of the tongue and has led some commentators to offer detailed explanations of varying word

---

[7] The oldest English versions (Tyndale, Geneva and the KJV), as well as contemporary versions like the NASB and ESV, translate the expression as in apposition to the preceding statement. The ASV, RSV, NIV, NRSV, NLT, CSB, and NET translate it as a complement to the following verb.

meanings. Further explanations of the unique expression τὸν τροχὸν τῆς γενέσεως ("the entire course of life") often delve into the areas of Stoic philosophy or some of the other Greek naturalists.[8] It is my sense that such efforts are searching in the wrong place, because the language is so metaphorical that readers are meant to experience the rhetorical impact of these fiery figures rather than to discover some clear analogy found in nature. It is highly unlikely that James knew anything about Orphic reincarnation or about a cyclical life that was not going anywhere, or that he would be afraid of the changes in the cycle of life. The expressions here and throughout the paragraph are rooted not in the writings of Stoic philosophers but can be discovered in various expressions in both canonical and Second Temple Period Jewish literature (Ps 32:9; Prov 10:19; Eccl 5:1; Sir 14:1, 20:1–8; *1 En.* 48.7; see also some similar fiery expressions in Luke 16:9, 11; 18:6).

τὸν τροχὸν τῆς γενέσεως: This is literally *the wheel of nature*, or more functionally, *the entire course of life* (BDAG, 1017-18). Probably no translation will convey the precise impact the phrase had on the original hearers and readers. Most commentators agree that it refers to all of human existence on the broadest scale—past, present, and future (Ropes, 235; Mayor, 117; Laws, 150; Johnson, 261). This expression by itself is probably best understood as describing the whole circle of inner passions (hence the translation: *the entire course of life*). The image of the wheel as a symbol for life's cyclic circumstances was widely recognized in the pagan, Jewish, and Christian world. The fathers Theophylact, Bede, and Oecumenius took it to mean the round of human life with its temporal changes. The wheel's being set on fire means that this wrong use of the tongue engenders jealousy, faction, and every vile deed throughout the whole of one's life (cf. 3:16).[9]

---

[8] Dibelius has an extended note titled "The Cycle of Becoming" in which he attempts to trace these references in Hellenistic, primarily Stoic, literature (Dibelius, 196–97).

[9] See also NIDNTTE, 1, 573: "James is using the expression in a nontechnical sense, 'the whole course of one's life' (NIV). The term had probably lost its Orphic

ὑπὸ τῆς γεέννης: The Greek word γέεννα is drawn from the valley (*Ge Ben Hinnom,* גֵּי בֶן־הִנֹּם) to the west and south of ancient Jerusalem. The noun does not occur in this specific spelling in the LXX, although Γαιεννα appears in Josh 18:16, which is the transliterated Greek spelling of the Hebrew above for the "Valley of Hinnom" (also Josh 15:8; Neh 11:30). The gate in the south of Jerusalem has always been called the "dung" or "refuse" gate (Neh 3:13-14) because garbage was probably dumped outside the city into this valley. In an earlier era, there had also been child sacrifices there in a specific site in the valley known as "Tophet" (Jer 7:32; 19:11-14; 32:35), where the child was passed through fire into the hands of Molech. The place appears in some Jewish and Christian apocalyptic literature as the "fiery gehenna" (see BDAG, 191), as well as in later Christian literature (*2 Clem.* 5.4). In the NT, it occurs only in the Gospels as a place of punishment (Matt 5:22, 29, 30; 10:28; 18:9; 23:15, 33; Mark 9:45, 47; Luke 12:5). It is associated with *fire* also in Matt 5:22 and 18:9. James is the only NT writer outside the Gospels to use the noun γέεννα. This is further intertextual evidence of his use of Jesus *logia* (see above). *Gehenna* was near the home of James and the earliest followers of Jesus, immediately below the western hill of Jerusalem known today as Mount Zion. This is another indication of the "ring of truth" that characterizes his writing.

3:7 πᾶσα γὰρ φύσις θηρίων τε καὶ πετεινῶν, ἑρπετῶν τε καὶ ἐναλίων δαμάζεται καὶ δεδάμασται τῇ φύσει τῇ ἀνθρωπίνῃ: The submission of nature to humans is another commonplace of Hellenistic moral teaching (Seneca, *Benef.* 2.29.4; Philo, *Decal.* 113). The reference to animal creation in relationship to human nature and the tongue is picked up later by the *Shepherd of Hermas*, who adapts the language and thought of James in a number of his chapters. He writes of "the evil desire," that, "... you shall bridle and direct it as you wish. For the

---

character and had become a current phrase for the ups and downs of life, perhaps as today the term 'struggle for existence,' which belongs to the evolutionary theory of Darwin, is generally applied to social conditions rather than to particular aspects of biology." This is documented also in GE (423 and 2160).

evil desire is wild and only tamed with difficulty" (*Hermas* 44.2), and later argues that since God has subjected all his creation to man, so that he is its master, so man ought to be able to master God's commandments (*Hermas* 47.2).

3:8 τὴν δὲ γλῶσσαν οὐδεὶς δαμάσαι δύναται ἀνθρώπων: James now contrasts the unruly nature of the tongue with an adversative clause (δέ) that fronts the direct object τὴν γλῶσσαν for emphasis. Even if a person can tame wild beasts, the same individual (οὐδεὶς ... ἀνθρώπων) may not be able to control his tongue. The serious anthropological skepticism that is expressed in 3:7, 8—wild beasts can be tamed, but not the tongue—conveys an almost contradictory theme. This is the idea that we are supposed to control the tongue, but we actually are not able to do so! "The logical inconsistency with v. 2b, which assumes that there may be a man who can avoid sins of speech, shows that the language here as in v. 2a is that of hyperbole, with an understood exhortation to strive to do precisely what is said to be impossible" (Laws, 153–154). Furthermore, James' use of hyperbole and paradox is not meant to be pessimistic. The rhetorical language is intended to graphically challenge his readers to the difficult task of managing this small member.

ἀκατάστατον κακόν: What James describes as "unruly" here in vivid metaphor he will assign as a characteristic of the wisdom that is *not* from above in 3:13 (ἀκατάστατον here; ἀκαταστασία there). It is evil behavior that is marked by "instability." It is the chief characteristic of the individual who is so strongly exhorted in this book: the "double-souled" person (1:8).

μεστὴ ἰοῦ θανατηφόρου: The tongue is also full of "death-dealing poison" (the idea conveyed by the compound θανατηφόρου, BDAG,). Ps 140:3 (LXX 139:4) contains a similar idea, and may be the origin of this vivid metaphor (so also Rom 3:13). The idea was quite widespread in Jewish literature (1QH^a 5.26–27; Sir 28:17–23; 10:11; *T. Gad.* 5.1; cf. Job 5:15; Ps

58:4, 5). In the NT, ἰός can mean either a poison or rust/corrosion. In 5:3, it clearly means rust, and in the present case it refers to poison (Rom 3:13). In *T. Reu.* 5.3, ἰός is used for female seductiveness, but in LXX Ps 13:3, as also here, the word refers to the "poison on the lips" that leads to violence between people.

Observation

The strong language here may lead to pessimism, since it would be a mockery to attempt the perfection that James expects (1:4). It should be kept in mind, without attempting to mollify James' message here, that perfection here and elsewhere in the NT does not convey a kind of sinlessness but "wholeness"—a moral integrity that avoids doubleness. This in turn leads to the final subsection of this paragraph, where the dangers of inconsistency and the importance of wholeness are stressed even more.

A Strange Mixture (James 3:9-12)

Introduction and Clausal Analysis

The structure of 3:9–12 can be visualized by the following annotated clausal outline. In addition to isolating the various clauses, the annotation on the left margin identifies the grammatical function of each clause in the sentences.

main verb [9] ἐν αὐτῇ εὐλογοῦμεν τὸν κύριον καὶ πατέρα
main verb καὶ ἐν αὐτῇ καταρώμεθα τοὺς ἀνθρώπους
attributive participle τοὺς καθ' ὁμοίωσιν θεοῦ γεγονότας,
main verb [10] ἐκ τοῦ αὐτοῦ στόματος ἐξέρχεται εὐλογία καὶ κατάρα.
conclusion οὐ χρή, ἀδελφοί μου,
impersonal infinitive ταῦτα οὕτως γίνεσθαι.
negative question [11] μήτι ἡ πηγὴ ἐκ τῆς αὐτῆς ὀπῆς βρύει τὸ γλυκὺ καὶ

τὸ πικρόν;
negative question [12] μὴ δύναται, ἀδελφοί μου, συκῆ ἐλαίας ποιῆσαι ἢ ἄμπελος σῦκα;
(*main verb*) οὔτε ἁλυκὸν γλυκὺ ποιῆσαι ὕδωρ.[10]

James continues his practice of employing asyndeton by means of a series of primary clauses. There are eight of them in 3:9–12, and only two of the clauses are linked by a conjunction (καί in 3:9). The only participle in the passage (γεγονότας) introduces an embedded attributive clause, also in 3:9b. The admonition against being double in the use of one's tongue (3:9–10) is then followed by three rhetorical questions, each drawn from the nature of springs and vineyards (3:11–12a). The paragraph is concluded with an aphorism in 3:12b: "A salt pond cannot yield fresh water." The obvious use of ellipsis (omitted words that are implied) in these last verses indicates that James is drawing his argument to a rhetorically intensive and effective conclusion. He understands that his readers will identify the missing words and that they will know the obvious answer to the questions that are articulated with the negative particles μήτι and μή. That answer to these questions is: "No, these things can't be true!" Likewise, this tongue cannot be employed for contradictory purposes—namely, to bless God and others while also to curse God and others. The expression ἀδελφοί μου in 3:10 and 12 does not function to introduce new information at this point, but it intensifies his appeal that readers should apply what he has exhorted them to do. The expression also helps to span the entire paragraph (see also this use ἀδελφοί μου in 2:5 and 5:19).

Original Text

9 ἐν αὐτῇ εὐλογοῦμεν τὸν [a]κύριον καὶ πατέρα καὶ ἐν αὐτῇ καταρώμεθα τοὺς ἀνθρώπους τοὺς καθ' ὁμοίωσιν θεοῦ γεγονότας, 10 ἐκ τοῦ αὐτοῦ στόματος

---

[10] D. Deppe, *The Lexham Clausal Outlines of the Greek New Testament* (Logos Research Systems, Inc., 2006; 2009), *in loc.*

ἐξέρχεται εὐλογία καὶ κατάρα. οὐ χρή, ἀδελφοί μου, ταῦτα οὕτως γίνεσθαι. 11 μήτι ἡ πηγὴ ἐκ τῆς αὐτῆς ὀπῆς βρύει τὸ γλυκὺ καὶ τὸ πικρόν; 12 μὴ δύναται, ἀδελφοί μου, συκῆ ἐλαίας ποιῆσαι ἢ ἄμπελος σῦκα; b cοὔτε ἁλυκὸν γλυκὺ ποιῆσαι ὕδωρ.

Textual Notes

9.a. Instead of κύριον, the Textus Receptus reads θεόν, with K L, most of the minuscules, and the Vulgate, Syriac, and some Coptic versions. The reading κύριον is to be preferred because (1) the combination "Lord and Father" is unusual, occurring nowhere else. It would more likely be changed to "God and Father" than vice versa, and (2) the external evidence supporting κύριον is decidedly superior (‭א‬ A B C P, Old Latin, some Vulgate mss, and the Palestinian Syriac).

12.b. Many witnesses, including ‭א‬ C² K L P, Old Latin and Vulgate, add οὕτως before the negative. Since, however, it is absent from such early and important witnesses as A B C* and the Syriac and Coptic versions, the shorter reading is preferred.

12.c. From later manuscripts is traced the expansion in the Textus Receptus, which after an inserted οὕτως (see above) continues with οὐδεμία πηγὴ ἁλυκὸν καί.

Translation

9 With it we bless our Lord and Father, and with it we curse people who are made in the likeness of God. 10 From the same mouth come blessing and cursing. My brothers, these things ought not to be so. 11 Does a spring pour forth from the same opening both fresh and salt water? 12 Can a fig tree, my brothers, bear olives, or a grapevine produce figs? Neither can a salt pond yield fresh water.

Exegetical Comments

3:9 ἐν αὐτῇ εὐλογοῦμεν: The fronted prepositional phrase ἐν αὐτῇ looks back anaphorically to the tongue in the previous verse. The instrumental preposition plus noun is a Hebrew usage (בְּ-) (see the expressions εἰ πατάξομεν ἐν μαχαίρῃ [Luke 22:49] and ἀποκτεῖναι ἐν ῥομφαίᾳ [Rev 6:8]). James continues his identification with his readers by using a first person plural verb, εὐλογοῦμεν. Both in speaking and writing, ancient and modern Jews often add the words בָּרוּךְ הוּא ("Blessed is He") after the name of God. (See Mark 14:61, where ὁ εὐλογητός (the blessed One) is used in reference to God.) While we may be more accustomed to the word "praise," the practice of "blessing" God is prominent in both the OT (Gen 9:26; Exod 18:10; Ruth 2:20; 1 Sam 25:32; 2 Sam 6:21; 1 Kgs 1:48; 1 Chr 29:10; Pss 40:14; 68:19–20; 71:18) as well as in the NT (Luke 1:68; 2:28; Rom 1:25; Eph 1:3; 1 Pet 1:3). The action expressed in the component parts of the Greek verb εὐλογέω is to "say good" or "pronounce well of" (BDAG, 408.1). It can be used of both God's blessing man and vice-versa. God blesses people by conferring good on them. People bless God by praising the good that is in Him.

τὸν Κύριον καὶ πατέρα: This is a clear example of the Granville Sharp Rule, that when two substantives joined by καί are preceded by one article, the second noun refers to the same person as the first noun (Wallace 274).[11] Although Κύριος does refer to Jesus in 1:1; 2:1; and 5:7, its use with πατήρ here rules out a reference to Jesus. The combination of Κύριον καὶ πατέρα is in accordance with ordinary Jewish usage, but this exact expression does not occur elsewhere in the Bible (note, however, Isa 63:16: σὺ Κύριε πατὴρ ἡμῶν; and 1 Chr 29:10: εὐλογητὸς εἶ, Κύριε, ὁ Θεὸς Ἰσραήλ, ὁ Πατὴρ ἡμῶν). Careless comments that Jews did not refer to God as Father before Jesus' teaching the Lord's Prayer are corrected by this fact. Although Jews frequently speak of God as "Father," it is

---

[11] See also D. B. Wallace, *Granville Sharp's Canon and Its Kin: Semantics and Significance* (SBG 14; New York: Lang, 2009).

usually in a different combination, probably the most usual being "Our Father" alone, or "Our Father and King." Πατήρ is used with reference to God in order to emphasize His divine love. In 3:9, there is a strong contrast expressed between the love of the Father toward all His children and the contradictory mutual hatred among the latter.

καὶ ἐν αὐτῇ καταρώμεθα τοὺς ἀνθρώπους, "and with it we curse people." The continued first plural editorial "we" in καταρώμεθα shows that the special sin of the tongue which is here referred to is not slander or backbiting or lying, but personal abuse, such as results from loss of temper in a heated controversy (Rom 12:13). The verb καταράομαι means to "call curses down" or "execrate someone" (BDAG, 525) and is found frequently in the LXX (Gen 12:3; 27:29; Lev 24:15; Num 22:6; Deut 21:23; Ps 36:22). There is a remarkable parallel passage in T. Benj. 6.5: ἡ ἀγαθὴ διάνοια οὐκ ἔχει δύο γλώσσας εὐλογίας καὶ κατάρας ("the good mind does not have two tongues, one of blessing and one of cursing").

τοὺς καθ' ὁμοίωσιν Θεοῦ γεγονότας: The perfect attributive participle γεγονότας modifies ἀνθρώπους. James quotes or freely adapts Gen 1:26, where the LXX reads κατ' εἰκόνα ἡμετέραν καὶ καθ' ὁμοίωσιν. The Hebrew דְּמוּת (LXX ὁμοίωσις) is synonymous with צֶלֶם (LXX εἰκών). The belief that men are made in the material likeness of God was taught in some postbiblical Jewish literature, but platonically influenced writers, such as Philo and others, would naturally seek to modify this (Philo: "The resemblance is spoken of with reference to the most important part of the soul, namely, the mind" [Opif. 69]; see also Sir 17:3; Wis 2:23). The analogical point conveyed in 3:9 should not be missed. Just as a murderous attack on a man is an attack on God (Gen 9:6), so cursing one's fellow man amounts to cursing God. Although ὁμοίωσις appears often in the LXX (Muraoka, 496), this verse is its only occurrence in the NT. In the creation accounts it is used with the semantically similar word εἰκών (Gen 1:26), while only εἰκών is in the postdiluvian, "re-creation" account (Gen 9:6). The view that the "image" relates to the human's spiritual similarity to God is illustrated by the Pauline

238

statement using εἰκών in Col 3:10: "Put on the new man who is being renewed in knowledge after the image of its creator" (κατ᾽ εἰκόνα τοῦ κτίσαντος).

3:10 ἐκ τοῦ αὐτοῦ στόματος ἐξέρχεται εὐλογία καὶ κατάρα: James again fronts a prepositional phrase to highlight the source of the words, changing from the tongue to the mouth. The verb ἐξέρχεται (what comes out) recalls the ἐξέρχεσθαι of Matt 15:19, where Jesus taught that what comes out of a person is what defiles that person (Matt 15:11, 20). Like his brother, James understands that a person's speech is a barometer of their spirituality (Matt 12:33–37). One's speech cannot hide, but expresses what is in one's heart. In keeping with his approach on wholeness, James would describe the τέλειος ἀνήρ as one who both praises God and speaks well of persons. If someone is disposed toward deceit and hypocrisy, this will inevitably come out in speech. An example of "blessing and curse" coming from the same source is Moses in Deut 11:26. There it was a choice that he was placing before the people, but here it is inconsistency of speech that is the problem, when one blesses God but curses humans. Paul exhorts the same thing and adds a positive alternative (Eph 4:29).

οὐ χρή, ἀδελφοί μου, ταῦτα οὕτως γίνεσθαι: "The only use of this old impersonal verb (from χράω [*chraō*]) in the N.T. It is more like πρέπει [*prepei*] (it is appropriate) than δεῖ [*dei*] (it is necessary)" (Robertson, 44–45). One could paraphrase it as: "This is just not right." James continues his exposure of the "double-souled" person, and here "double-mindedness" (1:8) is revealed in being "double-tongued." Early Christian writings that were often inspired by James echo the same theme (*Did.* 2.4; *Barn.* 19.7). The powerful message of James here cannot be explained merely in academic terms. Many individuals at one time praise their Maker, and then with the same tongue slander and revile their brothers. After solemn worship in the house of God, the professed worshiper can go forth with feelings of malice in his heart, and the language of praise can turn quickly to that of provocation.

3:11 μήτι ἡ πηγὴ ἐκ τῆς αὐτῆς ὀπῆς βρύει τὸ γλυκὺ καὶ τὸ πικρόν; "Does the spring pour forth from the same opening both fresh and salt water?" The interrogative particle μήτι indicates that the question expects a negative answer and prepares the way for additional rhetorical questions. Because these things do not happen in nature, if a similar thing happens in human life with the tongue, it must be regarded as an enormity, a monstrosity. Separate articles with the substantival adjectives (τὸ γλυκὺ ... τὸ πικρόν) help to sharply distinguish the two different tastes. As is so often the case with analogical language, the figure can be easily misunderstood and therefore sound inconsistent. It is obviously true that some springs can produce a mixture of fresh and salty or "bitter" (πικρόν) water. The point is that the same spring does not emit sweet water one minute and then bitter water the next minute. Its water may be good or bad, but it is consistent in producing the same kind of water. The tragedy of a divided tongue is its tendency to bless God with one opening of the mouth, and yet to curse men with the next opening! With these figures, James is probably alluding to the Dead Sea, which was (and is) exceedingly bitter and had both salt and fresh springs on its shores, but not a spring that produced both![12] He will return to this illustration in 3:12b. Other examples of bitter waters are Marah (Exod 15:23), "the water that causes the curse" (Num 5:18–27), and the water in Rev 8:11. These reflections of Judean nature scenes continue in 3:12.

3:12 μὴ δύναται, ἀδελφοί μου: A second negative μή attends a question that again not only expects a negative answer, but is almost absurd in its query. "Μή is the negative of will, wish, doubt. If οὐ denies the fact,

---

[12] For an insightful study of the way in which James utilizes his Palestinian background to effectively communicate these metaphors and similes, see the largely overlooked volume by a Palestinian resident: E. Bishop, *Apostles of Palestine: The Local Background to the New Testament Church* (London: Lutterworth Press, 1958), 177–94.

μή denies the idea" (Robertson, 1167). Perhaps James uses it instead of the stronger μήτι as in the previous verse because of the verb here (δύναται) and the following softer address, "my brothers." While even a spring might pour forth a mixture of sweet and bitter water (see the previous clarification), no fruit tree produces mixed fruit! Seneca opined: "Good does not spring from evil any more than figs grow from olive trees" (*Moral Epistles* 87.25).

συκῆ ἐλαίας ποιῆσαι ἢ ἄμπελος σῦκα: Figs, olives, and grapes (vines) were some of the most abundant "staple" fruits in the land of Israel. They are considered as part of the "seven varieties" of agricultural products in the promised land (Deut 8:8). The absurdity of the question asked is so patent that it does not need much comment. The point is that such inconsistent speech is also absurd.

οὔτε ἁλυκὸν γλυκὺ ποιῆσαι ὕδωρ, "Neither can a salt pond yield fresh water." The lone negative οὔτε, normally used as part of an "either ... or" sentence, is a bit odd.[13] Perhaps it functions as a striking signal that this is the concluding point of the discourse (i.e., 3:1–12). The negation assumed by the previous question probably assumes the need of an additional, corresponding negative like οὔτε (Mayor, 125; Hort, 79–80). "The Salt Sea" (ἡ θάλασσα ἡ ἁλυκή) is the LXX name for the Dead Sea (Num 3:12; Deut 3:17). The use of the infinitive ποιῆσαι may appear unusual, but the word is used for trees "bearing" fruit in the LXX of Gen 3:11 and in Matt 3:10. The message is still clear. It is impossible for the evil tongue to "make" itself good. We should also recognize again the echoes of various Jesus *logia* in these graphic word pictures (see esp. Matt 7:16 and Luke 6:44).

Conclusion

This concise and realistic negative appraisal marks an appropriate

---

[13] The adverb "οὔτε can scarcely be correct, and perh. the text is faulty" (BDAG, 740).

close to the treatise (3:1-12) by retaining the negative emphasis on the tongue, which has been its consistent theme. It confirms the very first point in 3:1—namely, that teachers, who deal in words more than many others, place themselves in a position of facing a more difficult time at judgment.

8

FOLLOW THE WISDOM OF GOD (3:13-18)

Thematic Peak

The Prominent Role of 3:13-18 in the Letter

In the Introduction, we argued that this paragraph has the most prominent role in the overall structure of the Letter from James. This is because of its special linguistic features that set it apart from other paragraphs along with its semantic function of conveying the essential message of the entire letter. The paragraph has verbal ties with both previous and subsequent material, thus serving as a transitional section but also functioning as a summation of the entire discourse. Here we attempt to expand further our argument that this crucial paragraph justly deserves being called the thematic "peak" of the entire book.

Martin Dibelius believed that 3:13-17 did evidence internal unity but had no substantive thematic or linguistic links either with what precedes or with what follows it. He also considered 3:18 as an isolated saying that does not belong with the previous paragraph and that is distinct from 4:1-10. It can be demonstrated, however, that Dibelius was wrong in this observation. It is my estimation that he allowed his form-critical approach that James is composed of loosely arranged and isolated pieces of paranetic material to adversely influence his judgment. A number of commentators both before and after Dibelius have clearly affirmed the essential linguistic unity of 3:13–18 as well as its verbal and semantic connections both to its immediate context and also to the more remote sections of the book. Near the beginning of the twentieth century, two other German scholars contended for the central semantic role of 3:13–18. C. F. G. Heinrici, in a monograph on the literary character of the NT writings, acknowledged that the writing attributed to James, like previous proverbial OT books, was composed of a large number of distinct sections of familiar wisdom material. There was something, however, that held together all these apparently isolated sayings.

> Der zusammenhaltende Gedanke ist die Einsharfung der rechten Weisheit, die von oben kommt (3:13–18). Alle einzelnen Warheiten sind ihre Fruchte. [The connecting thought is the emphasis on the true wisdom, which comes from above (3:13–18). All of the other individual truths are its fruits.][1]

In an even earlier article, Herman Cladder also presented an effective argument for a recognizable measure of literary coherence that he found in the book. He even suggested that 3:13–18 also operated as both the linguistic and semantic "center" of the writing.[2]

The views of Dibelius almost completely overthrew this opinion in Germany and elsewhere and greatly influenced later generations of writers. Recently, however, a number of writers not only have found a coherent structure in James, but also have argued for the overarching structural and semantic role that 3:13–18 plays in the entire composition. James Reese, for example, regards 3:13–18 as "the heart of the letter," where its "core message" (the teacher's serious

---

[1] C. F. G. Henrici, *Der literarische Charakter der neutestamentliche Schriften* (Leipzig: Durr, 1908), 75, my translation.

[2] H. Cladder, "Die Anlage des Jakobusbriefes," *ZKT* 28 (1904): 37–57.

responsibility) is situated and developed.[3] In a large number of both books and articles, the Jesuit scholar, Patrick Hartin, has "... argued that this (3:13–18) is the central pericope in the epistle, the other pericopes forming an embrace around it."[4] In his published dissertation, Luke Cheung argued that 3:13–18 performed a fundamental function as a link passage in the book and that both the previous and the subsequent paragraphs contain both thematic and linguistic echoes of the passage.[5] In another published dissertation that utilizes a method of discourse analysis, Mark Taylor sets forth the idea that this passage encapsulates the entire message of the letter thus far and also prepares the reader for the strong rebuke in 4:1–10. "Functionally, 3:13–18 gathers key concepts raised in 1:2–3:12 and anticipates the next major movement in the discourse. Contextually, the passage reveals grounding in Jewish concepts of wisdom, emphasizing the practical obedience of a life marked by the possession of wisdom as a gift of God."[6] These anaphoric and cataphoric roles of the passage lead Taylor to affirm a similar conclusion as the previous writers. A significant number of recent scholars have also determined that 3:13–18 is the key to pulling together what may appear at first to be the seemingly unrelated pericopes of James into some sort of coherent structure.

Such a conclusion cannot be based simply on the linguistic surface features in what we have called the structural "peak" of the discourse. The semantic content of this paragraph must also express the main

---

[3] J. M. Reese, "The Exegete as Sage: Hearing the Message of James," *BTB* 12 (1982) 83.

[4] P. J. Hartin, "Who is wise and understanding among you?" *SBLSP* (1996) 483. See also P. J. Hartin, *James and the 'Q' Sayings of Jesus* (JSNTSup 47; Sheffield: Sheffield Academic Press, 1991), 29–32; and P. J. Hartin, *A Spirituality of Perfection* (Collegeville: Liturgical Press, 1999), 72–75.

[5] L. L. Cheung, *The Genre, Composition and Hermeneutics of the Epistle of James* (Paternoster Biblical and Theological Monographs; Milton Keynes: Paternoster Press, 2003), 75–85, 138–147.

[6] M. E. Taylor, *A Text-Linguistic Investigation into the Discourse Structure of James* (LNTS 311; London: T&T Clark, 2006), 116.

themes of the book for it to play its prominent role as the thematic peak of James. He expresses here the essence of his overall message that his readers must embrace a lifestyle that is based on the wisdom that descends from God above, and that consequently they must reject any forms of antiwisdom that arises from human viewpoint only. It is my argument that each distinct paragraph of the book displays the recognizable stamp of that overall message. The intensely imperatival paragraph that follows (4:1–10), for example, ascends to a hortatory peak by exhorting the reader to welcome the friendship of God, and therefore to discard any friendship with the world. In the very words of that previous thematic peak, this practically demands that we reject the antiwisdom emanating from this world "below" and then to embrace the true wisdom that emanates from the world "above."[7]

Greek Text

13 Τίς σοφὸς καὶ ἐπιστήμων ἐν ὑμῖν; δειξάτω ἐκ τῆς καλῆς ἀναστροφῆς τὰ ἔργα αὐτοῦ ἐν πραΰτητι σοφίας. **14** εἰ δὲ ζῆλον πικρὸν ἔχετε καὶ ἐριθείαν ἐν τῇ καρδίᾳ ὑμῶν, μὴ κατακαυχᾶσθε καὶ ψεύδεσθε κατὰ τῆς ἀληθείας. **15** οὐκ ἔστιν αὕτη ἡ σοφία ἄνωθεν κατερχομένη ἀλλὰ ἐπίγειος, ψυχική, δαιμονιώδης. **16** ὅπου γὰρ ζῆλος καὶ ἐριθεία, ἐκεῖ ἀκαταστασία καὶ πᾶν φαῦλον πρᾶγμα. **17** ἡ δὲ ἄνωθεν σοφία πρῶτον μὲν ἁγνή ἐστιν, ἔπειτα εἰρηνική, ἐπιεικής, εὐπειθής, μεστὴ ἐλέους καὶ καρπῶν ἀγαθῶν, ἀδιάκριτος, [a]ἀνυπόκριτος. **18** καρπὸς δὲ δικαιοσύνης ἐν εἰρήνῃ σπείρεται τοῖς ποιοῦσιν εἰρήνην.

Textual Notes

While there are some variations in spelling and a few additions of particles and articles to smooth out the syntax, mainly limited to later Byzantine mss, there are no *significant* variant readings that affect the translation and interpretation of any verses in this section.

---

[7] I have distilled much of the argument for Jas 3:13–18 as the peak of James from my discourse analysis commentary on James (Varner, 28–38; 134–36).

17.a. Westcott and Hort mention in 3:17 the addition of a καί after ἀδιάκριτος by some Byzantine manuscripts. They fail to mention, since they wrote before the discovery and publication of the papyri, that P¹⁰⁰ from the third century also includes the καί.

Translation

13 Who is wise and understanding among you? He should demonstrate by his good conduct, his actions done with the gentleness that wisdom brings. 14 But if you have bitter jealousy and selfish ambition in your heart, stop boasting and being false to the truth. 15 This is not the wisdom that comes down from above, but is earthly, unspiritual, demonic. 16 For where jealousy and selfish ambition exist, it is there that will be disorder and every vile practice. 17 But the wisdom that comes from above is first pure, then peaceable, gentle, open to reason, full of mercy and good fruits, impartial and sincere. 18 And a harvest of righteousness is sown in peace by those who work for peace.

Wisdom is Shown by Behavior (3:13)

Sentence Flow and Translation

3:13
Τίς σοφὸς καὶ ἐπιστήμων ἐν ὑμῖν;
Who is wise and understanding among you?

δειξάτω ἐκ τῆς καλῆς ἀναστροφῆς τὰ ἔργα αὐτοῦ ἐν πραΰτητι σοφίας.
He should demonstrate by his good conduct, his actions done with the gentleness that wisdom brings.

Exegetical Comments

3:13 Τίς σοφὸς καὶ ἐπιστήμων ἐν ὑμῖν: This paragraph opens with a rhetorical question addressed to those "among you" (ἐν ὑμῖν)—the first of six occurrences of this expression, all in the latter half of the book. The next paragraph opens with another challenging rhetorical question asked of those "among you" (ἐν ὑμῖν; 4:1). The remaining four times that this expression occurs are in the closing paragraph (5:13, 14, 19, 20). This indicates that James, at this point, begins to close in on the challenges of congregational lives in the Diaspora.

An important question that must be faced is this: who are the ones being addressed—teachers or believers in general? It is obvious that 3:1 concerns teachers. Some commentators think that James' question in 3:13, therefore, is directed particularly to the teachers who were mentioned in verse 1 (Adamson, 149; McKnight, 299–303). It is preferable, however, to consider the address as more general for the following reasons: (1) Neither σοφός ("wise person") nor ἐπιστήμων ("full of understanding") is regularly used as a title for a teacher. They do occur together several times in the Septuagint, once with reference to the qualities leaders should possess (Deut 1:13, 15), but also with application to all of Israel (Deut 4:6). (2) It is obvious from 1:5 that "wisdom" is a virtue available to all who request it. (3) 3:1 is not actually addressed to teachers, but to those who would *become* teachers. Therefore, James' exhortation is better taken as directed to all believers, but especially to those who pride themselves on their superior understanding.

The use of σοφός in the opening question of 3:13 strengthens the point that wisdom is the topic which will be explained. As has been briefly noted, coupled with σοφός is an added characteristic: "and understanding" (καὶ ἐπιστήμων). This word does not convey the semantic overtones of a "sympathetic understanding," but is more in the semantic field of its partner, σοφός. Louw and Nida define this field as "... pertaining to being able to understand and evaluate— 'intelligent, insightful, understanding.'" This is the only occurrence of the word in the NT, but it did appear occasionally in classical literature, and also in contemporary moral literature (Epictetus, *Diatr.* 2.22.3) and the papyri (*P. Oxy.* 1469), where it, "... carries with it a certain idea of expert knowledge." Although this specific combination of words does not appear elsewhere in the NT, the collocation would be familiar to those who honored the wisdom traditions of Israel and the wise men of that tradition. When Moses wondered how he could bear the burden of leading the people, he decided by issuing the following command: "Assign for yourselves men, wise and discerning [σοφοὺς καὶ ἐπιστήμονας] and prudent [συνετούς] for your tribes, and I will appoint them as your leaders" (Deut 1:13). The response of the people was to do just that; therefore, such wise and understanding men were so appointed (Deut 1:15). In Deut 4:6, Israel was told that if they kept the statutes, they would be a "wise and understanding [σοφὸς καὶ ἐπιστήμων] people"—the exact pair of wisdom words found in James 3:13. Daniel, at both an early age and in his older years, was referred to by the same two coupled adjectives (Dan 1:4; 5:11). The two words are also associated in Sir 21:15.

The sage played an important role in ancient Israel. Jeremiah even classed the sage with the priest and the prophet in an often-overlooked verse: "The law shall not perish from the priest, nor counsel from the wise man [חָכָם] nor the word from the prophet" (Jer 18:18). It is interesting to observe that in ancient Israel the primary function of the priest was to teach the Torah, while the primary function of the sage was to offer counsel on how to obey the Torah. Therefore, attending to the intertexture of James suggests that he is inquiring about any individual [τίς] who desires to be a "sage" among the reconstituted tribes of Israel, who are centered on their ultimate Sage-Teacher, Jesus Messiah. This connects the paragraph to the opening of the previous one, where a warning was issued against too many desiring to be teachers (3:1). It is not necessary to identify the sage in 3:13 solely with the teachers that James spoke about in 3:1. It is certainly important that a teacher be wise, but it is also possible that a wise person may not be a teacher in the formal sense. He may be an advisor or counselor. The teacher was a "rabbi," while the "sage" was one who advised with wisdom and skill. The requirement for the rabbi was to be perfect in the use of his tongue (3:2–12), while the requirement for the sage was that he should demonstrate by his behavior the gentleness that comes from heavenly wisdom (3:13, 17).

δειξάτω ἐκ τῆς καλῆς ἀναστροφῆς τὰ ἔργα αὐτοῦ ἐν πραΰτητι σοφίας: The question in 3:13a is answered immediately by an imperative (δειξάτω) clause that echoes an earlier use of this specific imperative form (twice in 2:18). It also echoes the same semantic message, namely that the one aspiring to be wise must demonstrate it by attractive (καλῆς) behavior displayed through his works of faith (2:18) and through his gentleness (3:13b). More specifically, it is that gentleness that has its origin in wisdom (σοφίας as a genitive of source). Although this is only the second occurrence of σοφία in James (see 1:5), it also appears twice in 3:15 and 17, and introduces the topic of "wisdom" which will then be defined and described in the rest of the paragraph. The phrase *good conduct*, or the good "way of life" (καλῆς ἀναστροφῆς), denotes the entire manner of one's life. Paul used it to describe his entire manner of living before conversion (Gal 1:13). The two-word expression is a theme picked up and developed in 1 Pet 2:12 (also 1 Pet 1:15; 3:1–2, 16; 2 Pet 3:11). The adjective καλῆς means more than the English word "good," for it has ideas of excellence and beauty (cf. Jas 2:7 and 4:17).

πραΰτητι: "gentleness." Finding an exact definition of the πραΰ- word group can be a challenge due to the modern associations that "meekness" often implies, that is, some aspect of "weakness." Some commentators and a host of preachers have occasionally mentioned that the word was used in Classical Greek to describe a horse that has been broken, although the source for this usage is never mentioned. It was used by the great Athenian philosophers to describe a calm disposition (Plato, *Symp.* 197), as well as moderation (Aristotle, *Eth. Nic.* 1125). Philo did use the word of Moses to describe his calmness (Philo, *Mos.* 1, 328) and the moderation that comes with age (*Op.* 81). Not surprisingly, therefore, it is attributed to Moses in Num 12:3 (see also Sir 45:4; Josephus, *Ant.* 3.97), as well as to David (Ps 132:1), to the godly person (Ps 37:11), and to the Messiah (Zech 9:9). The noun is also often associated with the "fear" of the Lord in wisdom literature (Prov 15:33; 22:4). Therefore, in light of this previous usage, James is talking about the same godly wisdom—or the wisdom that comes down from God—to which he has previously referred, and about those who humble themselves to receive it can have it.

The example of Jesus actually defines the word for the rest of its use in the NT. Jesus presented Himself as meek and lowly of heart (πραΰς εἰμι καὶ ταπεινὸς τῇ καρδία)—a trait in the literature that is to be characteristic of teachers. This brief review of the word's usage does at least convey that it does not mean "weakness," and removes it from being denied consideration as a "masculine" virtue. The following definition seems balanced: "the quality of not being overly impressed by a sense of one's self-importance, *gentleness, humility, courtesy, considerateness, meekness*" (BDAG, 861). It is the lowly attitude of heart that is full of gentleness and mildness toward others, the opposite of arrogant self-assertion and of ruthless domination. It was used to denote the attitude with which the implanted word is to be received (1:21), which also implies being "teachable." This gentle attitude is claimed for the Messiah and commended for His followers (Matt 5:5; 11:29; 21:5). It is commended as a moral virtue also in 1 Cor 4:21; 2 Cor 10:1; Gal 5:23; 6:1; Eph 4:2; Col 3:12; 2 Tim 2:25; Titus 3:2; and 1 Pet 3:15.

σοφίας: The genitive is usually taken as expressing source, but it could also be an attributed genitive: "gentle wisdom." But since the following verses describe what "gentleness" looks like, we should probably keep it as the head noun in the expression: "gentleness from wisdom." The believer is exhorted to be characteristically gentle, particularly during conflicts (Gal 6:1; Eph 4:2; 2 Tim 2:25; Titus 3:2; 1 Pet 3:15). Hellenistic writers occasionally viewed meekness and humility as a vice (Laws, 160–161). The biblical faith, on the other hand, is countercultural, and just as Moses (Num 12:3) and Jesus (Matt 11:29; 21:5; 2 Cor 10:1) did not defend themselves, so also the Christian is exhorted to be characteristically gentle, and that particularly in potential conflict situations. This cardinal virtue in other NT vice and virtue lists (e.g.

Gal 5:23) is one clear result of wisdom. "Therefore, this verse functions as a topic sentence to a paragraph which is itself a list of virtues and vices" (Davids, 150).

The attempt to offer a more precise definition of σοφία is also a challenge. As "the capacity to understand and function accordingly," it can refer to natural wisdom that belongs to this world, such as the σοφία Αἰγυπτίων (Philo, *Mos.* 1.20; Josephus, *Ant.* 2.286; and Acts 7:22). It can also refer to a transcendent capacity that is imparted by God, and the most obvious example would be Solomon (2 Kgs 5:9; Prov 1:2; Josephus, *Ant.* 8.168; Matt 12:42). We have seen how the substantive σοφός was the designation applied to the sages of ancient Israel (see LXX Prov 9:8–12; 13:10; 19:20; Wis 7:15; Sir 1:8; 9:17; 21:13). In the NT, the term is used negatively for those with "worldly wisdom" who are blind to God's revelation (Matt 11:25; Luke 10:21; Rom 1:22; 1 Cor 1:19–20, 25–27; 3:18–19, 20). It can on occasion be used as a designation for leaders (Matt 23:34) and as a quality to be desired among believers (Rom 16:19; 1 Cor 3:10; 6:5; Eph 5:15). There is some basis for tying into the definition of wisdom the concept of "skill," a meaning that can be found in both testaments (Exod 36:1, 4, 8—of Bezaleel and other skilled workers; and 1 Cor 3:10—of a skilled architect). The fact, however, that wisdom is divine in nature and origin in this passage and in 1:5 points to a possible additional nuance. It is "understanding that results in wise attitudes and conduct" (BDAG, 935). In the end, it is best to conclude that "wisdom" is better described than defined. And that is exactly what James attempts to do in the following verses, both negatively—what it is not (3:14–17)—and positively—what it is (3:17–18).

Unwise Behavior That Comes from Below (3:14–16)

Context

The next three verses (3:14–16) introduce a negative tone, because

James loves portraying the oppositions of actions through his ethical exhortations. The Jewish "two ways" tradition could also be invoked here, as he describes the characteristics of antiwisdom by means of a vice list. He never calls this behavior a type of wisdom, but he does state, "this is not the wisdom that comes down from above, but is earthly, unspiritual, demonic" (3:15).

Sentence Flow and Translation

3:14

εἰ δὲ ζῆλον πικρὸν ἔχετε καὶ ἐριθείαν ἐν τῇ καρδίᾳ ὑμῶν,
But if you have bitter jealousy and selfish ambition in your heart,

μὴ κατακαυχᾶσθε καὶ ψεύδεσθε κατὰ τῆς ἀληθείας.
stop boasting and being false to the truth.

Exegetical Comments

3:14 εἰ δὲ ζῆλον πικρὸν ἔχετε καὶ ἐριθείαν ἐν τῇ καρδίᾳ ὑμῶν: James commences his portrayal of antiwisdom with a first class conditional sentence. Young offers a helpful approach in framing a rhetorical and functional approach to conditional clauses in light of speech-act theory.[8] This approach to grammar focuses on what an author is attempting to actually *do* through the use of a conditional clause. In light of this approach, James here is not simply making an indicative statement but is rather issuing a strong exhortation. Notice the apodosis: "stop boasting and being false to the truth" (μὴ κατακαυχᾶσθε καὶ ψεύδεσθε κατὰ τῆς ἀληθείας). The exhortation is heightened by the presence of the δέ that introduces the protasis and also contrasts so vividly with, "the gentleness that wisdom brings" at the end of the previous clause.

Wisdom that comes from above will avoid any fanatical or envious

---

[8] R. A. Young, "A Classification of Conditional Sentences Based on Speech Act Theory," *GTJ* 10 (1989) 29–49.

ideas that can dominate one's heart. The word ζῆλος was clearly defined by Aristotle as a feeling that one has because someone else possesses something that you do not (paraphrased from Rhet. 1387–88). Positively, it can convey the desire to emulate a good quality, but negatively a desire to take something away from another. In this latter sense it is "jealousy," often coupled with "envy" (φθόνος) and also condemned by Hellenistic moralists (Epictetus, *Diatr.* 3, 22, 61). Likewise, in the NT it can refer to a person who is zealous in a good sense (2 Cor 7:11; Titus 2:14), or jealous in a negative sense. The modifier πικρόν ("bitter")—a word already used in 3:11 to refer to bitter water that is of no use—makes clear what the sense is here: "bitter jealousy" refers to envy (Acts 5:17; 13:45; Rom 13:13; 1 Cor 3:3; 2 Cor 12:20).

The word ἐριθεία occurs earlier only twice in Aristotle (*Pol.* 5.3.1302ᵇ4; 1303ᵃ14) and once in Philo (*Leg.* 68), in the latter referring to a party spirit or a "narrow partisan zeal of factional, greedy politicians in his own day" (Moo, 2000, 171). In the NT, it is associated with attitudes that destroy community life (Rom 2:8; Gal 5:20; Phil 1:17; 2:3). It will appear again as part of the "demonic" vices that are listed in 3:16. In biblical tradition, the "heart" (καρδία) is the seat of the affections and desires (Gen 6:5; Exod 4:21; Deut 6:6; Ps 11:2; see also Jas 1:26 and especially 4:8). James uses a singular noun with a plural possessive pronoun (καρδία ὑμῶν), and a few manuscripts desired to "improve" his grammar by putting "hearts" in the plural.[9]

μὴ κατακαυχᾶσθε. The apodosis clause of the conditional sentence warns in the imperative mood to *stop boasting*. This verb κατακαυχᾶσθε was used previously in 2:13 with a genitive to denote the triumph of one principle (mercy) over another (judgment). So it does also in the only other passage where it occurs in NT: Rom 11:17 (μὴ κατακαυχῶ τῶν κλάδων). It appears three other times in the LXX (Zech 10:12; Jer 27:11, 18), where the verb is used absolutely, with κατά having

---

[9] ℵ 323 945 1241 1739 2298 and a few Latin mss.

an intensifying force. This warning against boasting by being connected to wisdom indicates that James probably has in mind the warning from Jer 9:23–24: "Let not the wise man boast in his wisdom ... but let him who boasts boast about this: that he understands and knows Me."

καὶ μὴ ψεύδεσθε κατὰ τῆς ἀληθείας: "If you have bitterness you cannot be truly wise, for wisdom is shown by gentleness; your profession therefore is a lie" (Mayor, 123). 1 John 1:6 has a similar expression: ψευδόμεθα καὶ οὐ ποιοῦμεν τὴν ἀλήθειαν. The reference to lying against the truth sounds almost redundant, but the ancient tendency to personalize what we view as abstract concepts helps us to better "see" what James is doing here. Consider the parallel idea in Acts 5:3, where Ananias' deed of "lying against the Holy Spirit" means something like "falsifying the Holy Spirit," or counterfeiting the life guided by the Spirit. In 3:14 therefore, "lying against the truth" must mean living in a manner contrary to that "word of truth" (1:18) which was planted in them and which they were to receive "with meekness" (1:21). This dynamic, rather than purely conceptual, idea of "truth" is supported as well by James' final use of this important word in 5:19.

Sentence Flow and Translation

3:15
οὐκ ἔστιν αὕτη ἡ σοφία ἄνωθεν κατερχομένη
This is not the wisdom that comes down from above,

ἀλλὰ ἐπίγειος, ψυχική, δαιμονιώδης
but is earthly, unspiritual, demonic

Exegetical Comments

3:15 οὐκ ἔστιν αὕτη ἡ σοφία ἄνωθεν κατερχομένη: Verses 15–17 comprise a vice-virtue list. First come the vices—but not from heaven! It is unexpected and surprising that the negated being verb (οὐκ ἔστιν) should come first in the sentence. Of the ninety-eight occurrences of οὐκ ἔστιν in the NT, only nine times does it initiate a sentence. Four of those are in Synoptic sayings of Jesus (Matt 10:24/Luke 6:40 and Matt 28:6/Luke 24:6) and two of them are in OT quotations (Rom 3:11, 18). While most commentators ignore the issue, such a rare choice must be for a reason. This relates to another grammatical question in the verse—whether the participle κατερχομένη is part of a periphrastic construction (functioning like the indicative expression οὐ κατερχομέται) or if it expresses a new idea about wisdom. The placement of οὐκ ἔστιν—five words distant from the participle— makes it unlikely that it is periphrastic. This impacts interpretation, because if it is periphrastic, James is describing the vice list that follows as a type of wisdom: "The wisdom is not coming down from above." Rather, he affirms that, "this is not the wisdom that comes down from above." While "worldly wisdom" may be a valid implication of his language, James is careful not to apply the word σοφία in any way to the vices he is about to describe.

The NIV rendering "from heaven" is functionally equivalent to the Greek ἄνωθεν, which is formally rendered as "from above." James has used this word in 1:17 to identify the direction from which all good gifts come. This is the realm of God, who delights to grant His children what they request—especially wisdom (see 1:5). The wisdom that James commends does not come to the believer through intellectual effort or study, but as the wisdom literature has clearly taught, it is God's gift (Prov 2:6).

ἀλλὰ ἐπίγειος, ψυχική, δαιμονιώδης: The adversative conjunction ἀλλά clearly conveys the radical difference between the way of life that reflects wisdom from above and that way of life that reflects this counterfeit philosophy. "James describes it with three adjectives, each of which takes its meaning from its implied opposite" (Moo, 1985, 138). The adjectives are relatively rare and gain their specific sense from the context in which the writer uses them. Notice that they move semantically in a negative progression (Ropes, 248).

The first adjective is ἐπίγειος, "earthly" instead of heavenly. This is the most widely attested of the three, reaching back to the fifth century B.C., again in the sense of earthly (e.g., Plato, *Rep.* 546A). It contrasts with heavenly realities in Philo (*Praem.* 51; *Cher.* 101) but is not found in the LXX. Although in the five NT occurrences of the word it can have a neutral significance (John 3:12), it often takes on a negative meaning, describing that which is transitory, weak, and imperfect. It is that domain in which all that is essentially human dominates (BDAG, 368.1.b). Note the contrast between "earthly" and "heavenly" bodies in 1 Cor 15:40 (cf. 2 Cor 5:1). Its negative sense is obvious in Phil 3:19, where "... it provides a parallel moral application" (Hort, 84) when Paul says that the enemies of Christ have their minds "set on earthly things." The translation "earthbound" is an attempt to capture James' perspective—namely, that a wisdom excluding consideration of God is in reality not simply "earthly" in a neutral sense but represents a kind of closure (Johnson, 272).

The second adjective is ψυχική, "sensual" rather than spiritual. This adjective (from the noun ψυχή) is a bit more difficult. It often meant "of the soul," as opposed to "of the body" (σωμάτικος, as in 4 Macc 1:32). In the NT, it is opposed to πνεῦμα ("spirit"), thus suggesting a condition that is devoid of the Spirit, and always has negative associations. In every other occurrence, it is explicitly contrasted with πνευματικός, "spiritual" (1 Cor 2:14; 15:44, 46; Jude 19). Thus it is most often translated as "unspiritual" (BDAG, 1100; NIV). "We might cautiously translate it as 'selfish,' that is, focused on the advancement of one's own earthly personal welfare" (McCartney, 201). James' vivid characterizations are consistent with Pauline language about the "wisdom of the world" in 1 Cor 1:20; 2:6, and a "fleshly wisdom" in 2 Cor 1:12. See the excellent theological treatment of the ψυχή word group in NIDNTTE, 4.725-33.

The third adjective is δαιμονιώδης, "demonic" (lit. "pertaining to demons"), rather than godly. This word is a true *hapax legomenon* since it occurs only here in the both the LXX and the NT. It points clearly and frankly to the fact that this antiwisdom is demonic in nature or, more probably, in origin. It might be described as the kind of "wisdom" retained by fallen angels (demons), who were undoubtedly intelligent but utilized their "wisdom" to advance themselves. The use of "demonic" gains significance from the reference in 3:6 to the evil force of the tongue as "set on fire by *gehenna* (γεέννης)," and the later exhortation in 4:7 to "flee the devil." The similar language in *Hermas* 39.11 ("double-mindedness is an earthly spirit from the devil") may well be dependent on James. This climactic term is clearly the most pejorative of the three. It comes from demonic influences arising from a focus on "the things below," as opposed to the wisdom that comes from "the things above" (see Col 3:1–5).

An oft-repeated triadic paradigm for the enemies that a believer encounters is (1) the world, (2) the flesh, and (3) the devil. It is striking how similar to this triad is this collection of vices, even listed in the same traditional order! "Nowhere is the keen knowledge of human nature, which is so characteristic of the writer, more strikingly displayed than in these vv. 15, 16" (Oesterley, 455).

Sentence Flow and Translation

3:16

ὅπου γὰρ ζῆλος καὶ ἐριθεία,
For where jealousy and selfish ambition exist

ἐκεῖ ἀκαταστασία καὶ πᾶν φαῦλον πρᾶγμα.
it is there that will be disorder and every vile practice.

Exegetical Comments

3:16 ὅπου γὰρ ζῆλος καὶ ἐριθεία, ἐκεῖ ἀκαταστασία: Whereas 3:16 listed the vices by means of adjectival descriptors, here James turns to nouns to describe the *results* of those vices—jealousy, selfish ambition, and

258

disorder. When this type of attitude is displayed ἐχεῖ (the adverbial idea is, "it is there") will be found "disorder" (BDAG, 392).

In 1:8, James called the double-minded person "unstable" (ἀκατάστατος), and in 3:8 he described the tongue as a "restless [ἀκατάστατον] evil." Now ζῆλος and ἐριθεία are associated with this idea of "restless disorder." This disorder is semantically linked closely with the following section (4:1) by the word πόλεμοι ("wars"). Whatever be the immediate cause, the result of this is "anarchy" (Ropes, 248; Adamson, 153). While this word has inherited the concept of instability from its related adjective (1:8), this noun focuses more on the results of instability and restlessness. While ἐριθεία and ἔρις are different nouns, there is an obvious cognate and semantic connection between them.[10] Interestingly, the semantic linkage also appears in Luke 21:9 (πολέμους καὶ ἀκαταστασίας) and with ἔρις in 2 Cor 12:20 (ἔρις, ζῆλος ... ἐριθεῖαι ... ἀκαταστασίαι). Likewise, ζῆλος occurs in NT vice lists with ἔρις and φθόνος ("envy") and ἔχθρα ("enmity," see Jas 4:4): Rom 1:29; 13:13; 1 Cor 3:3; 2 Cor 12:20; Phil 1:15; 1 Tim 6:4; 1 Pet 2:1; Titus 3:3, and especially Gal 5:20–21.

καὶ πᾶν φαῦλον πρᾶγμα: The πᾶς ("all") is inclusive and means "every kind." The noun πρᾶγμα is used for any deed or thing, and the adjective φαῦλος connotes lowliness, cheapness, and meanness even more than moral wickedness (Prov 5:3; 22:8). The noun can also be used specifically for a "lawsuit" (see 1 Cor 6:1).[11] Occasionally, a commentator will mention the possible "non-evil" usage of the adjective. In other words, it "... expresses not so much moral evil as worthlessness" (Hort, 85). Yet it is also true that there are other NT

---

[10] Regarding ἐριθεία that is used here: "A derivation fr. ἔρις is not regarded w. favor by recent NT linguistic scholarship ... yet for Paul and his followers, the mng. *strife, contentiousness* ... cannot be excluded" (cp. Phil 1:17; BDAG, 392). Regarding ἔρις: "Engagement in rivalry, esp. w. ref. to positions taken in a matter, *strife, discord, contention*" (BDAG, 392).

[11] "In the light of James 2:6, which depicts the rich dragging the poor into *kriteria*, such an understanding is just possible here. Certainly, lawsuits are among the clearest demonstrations of envy and causes of *akatastasia*" (Johnson, 273).

occurrences of φαῦλος that stress the moral aspect of the term (John 3:20; 5:29; Rom 9:11; 2 Cor 5:10; Titus 2:8), and that is certainly the case here.

How was this litany of foul deeds relevant to James' readers? Davids captures the possible communal situation that James is addressing by applying socially some of the meanings that we have noted.

> One knows from observation that James has a burden of communal unity, so he would expect communal unrest to be a chief vice. This was true not only for James, but also for Paul (2 Cor. 12:20) and other groups (cf. 1QS 4:10). God, as Paul says, is a God of order and peace, not of unrest and disorder (1 Cor. 14:33). Furthermore, unrest is a characteristic of demons, and as such fits well with the accusation made in the previous verse (cf. the comments on 3:8 and 1:8 where the adjective ἀκατάστατος appears), and unrest is also paired with war (Luke. 21:9), which will appear in 4:1. Thus the term functions as a link-word which names another anti-Christian vice while bridging from the citation of the demonic to the coming citation of community disturbance (Davids, 153).

Sometimes a linguistic effort is attempted by some commentators to closely nuance the shades of semantic differences between these words in 3:15–16. This, of course, can be profitable if done correctly, and we have made some effort to do so in the previous comments. More valuable, however, than any attempt to closely define and contrast each of these negative terms is the effort to see (and to hear) the total disorder and unstable characteristics that are emerging from the carefully chosen words in these verses. As was mentioned, the word "disorder" (ἀκαταστασία) recalls the description of a double-minded man in 1:8 as "unstable" (ἀκατάστασος) and an uncontrolled tongue in 3:8 as "restless" (ἀκατάστασον). There are also evident verbal links to other sections with the references to "bitter jealousy" (ζῆλον πικρὸν) as they appear in 3:11 and 4:2. This list of seemingly disparate vices could be summed up simply by the confusion and disorder described in 3:16 as being the inevitable results of the sinful behavior described in 3:15. With that description of disorder and cacophony resulting from anti-wisdom firmly communicated, James now turns to the order and harmony that is to characterize lives that are based on heavenly wisdom.

Sentence Flow and Translation

3:17
ἡ δὲ ἄνωθεν σοφία πρῶτον μὲν ἁγνή ἐστιν,
But the wisdom that comes from above is first pure,

ἔπειτα εἰρηνική, ἐπιεικής, εὐπειθής,
then peaceable, gentle, open to reason,

μεστὴ ἐλέους καὶ καρπῶν ἀγαθῶν,
full of mercy and good fruits,

ἀδιάκριτος, ἀνυπόκριτος.
impartial, sincere.

Exegetical Comments

3:17 The striking contrast of the following list of virtues in 3:17 is evident by its emphasis on the harmony and peace that is conveyed by the words that characterize behavior that descends from "above." These attributes of heavenly wisdom perhaps are intended to recall the personification of wisdom in Prov 8:22–36, although there are even greater linguistic and semantic links to such a personification in Wis 7:7–30. The reader limited to a translated text is unable to appreciate the rhetorical flourishes that can be heard in the oral reading of the book to its original hearers. Six consecutive words beginning with epsilon appear in rapid sequence: ἡ δὲ ἄνωθεν σοφία πρῶτον μὲν ἁγνή ἐστιν, ἔπειτα εἰρηνική, ἐπιεικής, εὐπειθής, μεστὴ ἐλέους. Furthermore, the second, third, and fourth words rhyme by ending with a similar sound: -ή, -ῆς, -ῆς. This is followed by three words that are initiated by an alpha: καὶ καρπῶν ἀγαθῶν, ἀδιάκριτος, ἀνυπόκριτος. This intentional alliteration contrasts aurally in a graphic manner with the preceding vice list, which has no such alliteration. The contrast of the sounds conveys an oral message about the difference between the behavioral disharmony that comes from below and the harmonious order of the behavior that descends from above. This rhetorical impact of their collective sounds, to the ancient auditor, also conveyed meaning.[12]

ἡ δὲ ἄνωθεν σοφία πρῶτον μὲν ἀγνή ἐστιν: This positive note answers to the negative one in 3:15: οὐκ ἔστιν αὕτη ἡ σοφία ἄνωθεν. We should not necessarily expect to encounter a corresponding δέ in 3:18a to the μέν here, because sometimes μέν is found alone "... in enumerations, either if they are broken off or if they are continued in some manner that is irregular in form: πρῶτον μέν *in the first place* Rom 1:8; 3:2; 1 Cor 11:18. πρῶτον μὲν ... ἔπειτα ... James 3:17" (BDAG, 630).

In the LXX ἀγνός is found eleven times, of which three instances in Prov 15:26; 19:13; 20:9 refer to pure things, while Prov 11:7 refers to a chaste maiden, and instances in 4 Macc 18:7–8 refer to "pure" virginity (Muraoka, 7). The diversity of these references seems to coalesce around the idea of "being without moral defect or blemish" (L-N, 88.28). The adjective ἀγνός occurs eight times in the NT, especially in the Pastorals (1 Tim 5:22; Titus 2:5) and the General Epistles (Jas 3:17; 1 Pet 3:2; 1 John 3:3). It does not occur either in the Gospels or in Acts. Ἁγνεία is found only in 1 Tim 4:12 and 5:2, ἁγνότης only in 2 Cor 6:6 and 11:3, and ἁγνῶς only in Phil 1:17. The related words ἁγνίζω and ἁγνισμός occur seven times and one time, respectively. Thus ἀγνός ranks behind καθαρός and related words (sixty-five occurrences) in the NT as a designation for purity. This corresponds with the usage in the LXX,

---

[12] We call these features alliteration and rhyming, while the rhetoricians called it *epiphora* (επιφορα). A commentator who gives adequate attention to James' use of rhetoric in this passage is Witherington, 503.

where ἁγνός occurs eleven times, but words more closely associated with ritual are more frequent, such as καθαρός and related words, which appear approximately 170 times. This data supports the idea that its meaning is related more to moral and ethical purity rather than to ritual purity. The word in the NT depicts that which is "unmixed" or "unalloyed," as in the expression "pure gold." This is consistent with James' overall emphasis on wholeness contrasted with double-mindedness, as in Kierkegaard's famous work, *Purity of Heart Is To Will One Thing*.[13]

The priority (πρῶτον) given to "pure" (ἁγνός) at first does not seem to fit well with the progression of thought, for "pure" in this case sounds very general. It is only after this word that the adjectives emphasizing the peaceable character of wisdom appear: peaceable, gentle, tractable. Perhaps James intends by this ranking to teach that someone can be peaceful and gentle, etc., but unless these virtues arise from a genuine Christian faith, they prove to be meaningless from the divine perspective.

ἔπειτα εἰρηνική: The adverb ἔπειτα can mean "next in order of time, then, thereupon" (Luke 16:7; Gal 1:21; Jas 4:14; Gal 1:18; 2:1; 1 Cor 15:46; 1 Thess 4:17; Heb 7:27; 1 Cor 15:23; or as it is here, in Heb 7:2, and 1 Cor 12:28, "next in position of an enumeration of items, *then*" [BDAG, 361]). It seems to contain no special semantic significance, but does further the alliteration (the second in a string of ε- words).

The adjective εἰρηνική ("peaceable, peaceful, ready for peace") was combined with truth and wisdom in Ps 85:10: Prov 3:17; Isa 32:17, 26:3; Jer 33:6; and Mal 2:6. This specific word appears elsewhere in the NT only in Heb 12:11: καρπὸν εἰρηνικὸν ... ἀποδίδωσιν δικαιοσύνης— discipline "yields the peaceful fruit of righteousness" (i.e. which, after much suffering, brings peace with it). The parallel with its use here

---

[13] Richard Bauckham illustrates extensively the Danish theologian's fondness for the Book of James (Bauckham, 1–10, 159–74).

will become even clearer in 3:18, with its reference to "peacemakers."

ἐπιεικής: The second ἐ - adjective, ἐπιεικής, can mean, "... *yielding, gentle, kind, courteous, tolerant,* but is defined as being that attitude which is "not insisting on every right of letter of law or custom" (BDAG, 371). The Greek world valued this virtue for its being reasonable and fair-minded (Aristotle, *Eth. Nic.* 1137B; Plato, *Symp.* 210B). The adjective appears four other times in the NT (Phil 4:5; 1 Tim 3:3; Titus 3:2; 1 Pet 2:18). The noun ἐπιείκεια appears twice (Acts 24:4; 2 Cor 10:1), and is often translated as "forbearance."

εὐπειθής, "open to reason." The next adjective, εὐπειθής, is attested in Philo as the opposite of "obstinate" (*Virt.* 3), but appears only once in the LXX (*4 Macc* 12:6). It appears with the sense of "willing to yield" or "compliant" in a number of personal and legal documents among the papyri (M-M, 263–64.). This is also another of James' *hapax legomena.* The KJV renders it as "easy to be entreated." In light of the above meanings of "compliant" (CSB) or "obedient," it could be possible to render it as "open to reason" (ESV).

μεστὴ ἐλέους καὶ καρπῶν ἀγαθῶν: The breaking of the strict alliteration by inserting the word μεστή may be consciously to contrast the virtue "full of mercy" with the tongue that is "full [μεστή] of deadly poison" (3:8). "The next two virtues fit together in that ἐλέους is the practical mercy or concern for the suffering that manifests itself in alms (ἐλεημοσύνη), i.e., bears "good fruit" (cf. 1:26–27; 2:18–26). These certainly are virtues close to the author's heart" (Davids, 154). The choice of the adjective ἀγαθός to describe the "fruits" may be dictated by two reasons. (1) The fruits are "good" inwardly (ἀγαθός) rather than "good" outwardly (as in 3:13, καλῆς ἀναστροφῆς). They are the "good gift" (δόσις ἀγαθή) that also comes down from the "Father of lights" (1:17). (2) The adjective is strategically placed after the noun and thus becomes the first of three words beginning with the letter ἀ - that conclude the verse. Perhaps both a semantic and a rhetorical function are served by the word choice and order!

ἀδιάκριτος, ἀνυπόκριτος: BDAG (19) mentions that the meaning of the hapax, ἀδιάκριτος, can "... pert. to not being judgmental or divisive, *nonjudgmental, not divisive, impartial"* or "pert. to not being uncertain, *unwavering.*" It adds, however, that, "... the literary structure, with climax 4:11f, points strongly in this (first) direction." Recent commentators prefer "impartial" (Blomberg-Kamell, 176; McKnight, 315) or "unwavering" (McCartney, 202). Earlier commentators see it as expressing "simple," "harmonious," "of a single outlook" (cf. δίψυχος, Dibelius, 214; Adamson, 156; Laws, 164). There may be a fullness of meaning at work here, especially when related to the following ἀνυπόκριτος. "These meanings are relatively close to one another: the person with true wisdom is apparently nonpartisan: instead he is pure and absolutely sincere in his opinions and actions. This description fits with ἀνυπόκριτος, 'without hypocrisy,' 'sincere' (1 Pet 1:22; Rom 12:9; 2 Cor 6:6; 1 Tim 1:5; 2 Tim 1:5), for such a person could not pretend or playact in order to influence people, but would act alike toward all" (Davids, 154–55). These two final terms anticipate the simplicity and honesty toward which James will exhort his readers in 4:8: "purify your hearts, you double-minded."

To summarize the details of this verse, it is "wise" to note that ἡ δὲ ἄνωθεν σοφία is the supreme excellence of life. Even the apocryphal *Book of Enoch* cried out about it: "Wisdom did not find a place on earth where she could inhabit. Her dwelling therefore is in heaven" (*1 En.* 42:1. See also Bar 3:37: "And afterward He [wisdom] appeared on earth and dwelt among men").[14] Wisdom did physically come down, and was exemplified in the child Jesus who kept advancing in it (Luke 2:52). It was manifested in His adulthood (Matt 13:54) and guided His life (Matt 11:19). It continues to come down from above as a gift to those who ask for it and choose it over the earthly option (3:14–16).

---

[14] Baruch 3:36–37 was a passage often cited in early Jewish-Christian debates. See W. Varner, *Ancient Jewish Christian Dialogues* (Lewiston, ME: Edwin Mellen Press, 2004), 33, 35, 37, 95, 153, 160–61, 213, 253.

Sentence Flow and Translation

3:18
καρπὸς δὲ δικαιοσύνης ἐν εἰρήνῃ σπείρεται
And a harvest of righteousness is sown in peace

τοῖς ποιοῦσιν εἰρήνην.
by those who work for peace.

Exegetical Comments

3:18 καρπὸς δὲ δικαιοσύνης ἐν εἰρήνῃ σπείρεται τοῖς ποιοῦσιν εἰρήνην: This final verse in this section performs a strategic role in the book, since it rounds off the points that James has made in 3:13–17 and also is thematically connected to 4:1–10. It is close enough in sense to be properly placed but different enough to indicate its separate origin (note the δέ). It rounds off an effective argument and transitions the thought to the following section. Righteousness and peace are both mentioned, and these "fruits" are often associated in the OT (Ps 85:10 [LXX 71:7]; Isa 32:17). The "fruit of righteousness" (καρπὸς δικαιοσύνης), is a phrase familiar in the LXX, though usually without an exact equivalent in the Hebrew text (Prov 3:9, 11:30; Amos 6:12).

A close parallel to the language and ideas of James is found in Heb 12:11: "… discipline … yields the peaceful fruit of righteousness" (καρπὸν εἰρηνικὸν … δικαιοσύνης). The genitive δικαιοσύνης can be read either as one of source or as appositional. In other words, the fruit is either that which springs from righteousness or is the fruit that consists in righteousness. Many commentators adopt the former interpretation and see *peace* as the fruit from which righteousness will be produced as a contrast with anger, which in 1:20 provides a situation in which righteousness cannot be effected (e.g. Ropes, 250–51). The genitive is more probably appositional—namely, the fruit that is righteousness (Johnson, 275; Blomberg-Kamell, 177; McCartney, 202–03; McKnight, 317). This is supported by James' insistence that righteousness be revealed or demonstrated in deeds (2:20–23) and the logic of the aphorism itself: the *deed* is the doing of peaceful acts, while the *result* is justice or righteousness. Laws prefers the genitive of source. "The solution to this exegetical difficulty, and to the place of the verse in this section of the epistle, may be found in terms of OT allusion. In Prov 11:30 the 'fruit of righteousness' is described: it is 'a tree of life.' But in Prov 3:18 it is wisdom herself who is 'a tree of life'. It is not difficult to make the connection that the 'fruit of righteousness' is in fact wisdom. James' argument, assuming this connection, would then run as follows: there is no wisdom where there is divisiveness, for wisdom is peaceable (cf. Prov 3:7, 'her paths are peace'); it is the peacemakers, then, who possess wisdom, which is the *fruit of righteousness.* James draws on Prov 3 elsewhere in his epistle (4:6), and such an allusive use of the OT is characteristic of him (cf. on 1:10, 3:9, 5:4). The promise of *the fruit of righteousness* will then be a coherent and satisfactory conclusion to this section, because it is implicitly a promise of the true wisdom from above" (Laws, 165–166).

James 3:18 serves as a bridge to the following passage (4:1–3) describing conflicts by its reference to peacemaking as a fruit of the wisdom from above and in contrast with the "conflicts" that characterize that coming passage. The participle τοῖς ποιοῦσιν most probably is a dative of agency. "And a harvest of righteousness is sown in peace *by those who make* [or work for] peace."[15] The appropriate intertextual echo undoubtedly reflects the famous *logion* of Jesus: "Blessed are the peacemakers, for they shall be called sons of God" (Matt 5:9).

It is also possible that James is referencing the Holy Spirit when he refers to the wisdom "from above." Apart from the disputed reference to τὸ πνεῦμα in 4:6, James has no explicit reference to the Holy Spirit. This has prompted some to suggest that, for James, "wisdom" effectively functions as the Holy Spirit does in other NT writings. A simple comparison of the characteristics of the wisdom "from above"

---

[15] Wallace, 163–66. See also 3:7: καὶ δεδάμασται τῇ φύσει τῇ ἀνθρωπίνῃ.

in 3:17–18 with the Pauline "fruit of the spirit" in Gal 5:22–23 illustrates clearly this possible identity of wisdom with the Spirit.

J.A. Kirk cites not only the above description of wisdom in 3:17–18, but also other references where the language that James uses about the gift of wisdom (1:5–8) is paralleled by references to the gift of the Spirit in Paul (1 Cor 1:18–31; Eph 1:17; Rom 8:9–11, 14–15; Col 1:28).[16] He then traces references to God's Spirit and wisdom in the OT and in Second Temple Period Literature, including the writings from Qumran. He concludes that there are a limited but significant number of passages in which wisdom and Spirit are directly identified, or have the same functions, and that wisdom is the supreme gift of the Holy Spirit. In the end, the internal evidence of the epistle itself is the strongest. There is the clearly ethical role given to wisdom (3:13–18) plus the fact that wisdom is a moral force to help overcome testing and temptation (1:5–8)—ministries all related to the Spirit elsewhere.

If these comparisons are valid, then we do not have a writing that omits the Third Person of the Trinity, and James may simply have been unfamiliar with the terminology that later theologians utilized with reference to the divine Spirit.

---

[16] J. A. Kirk, "The Meaning of Wisdom in James: Examination of a Hypothesis," *NTS* 16 (1969–70) 24–38. A number of recent commentators are positive toward Kirk's suggestion (Davids, 55–56, 71–72; Blomberg-Kamell, 178–79). For a cautious approach, see McCartney, 289–90; and McKnight, 85, fn 85.

9

BECOME A FRIEND OF GOD (4:1-10)
Hortatory Peak

A War in the Members(hip) (4:1-3)

Literary Connection between James 4:1–10 and 3:13–18

James 4:1–10 has features that both connect it closely with the previous paragraph and also distinguish it as the next separate paragraph in the book. Connecting it with 3:13–18 are the following features: (1) 4:1 begins with a rhetorical question like in 3:13. (2) Its initial question ends with the phrase ἐν ὑμῖν in 4:1 as in 3:13. (3) The query about why peace is not present in the community is semantically tied, by contrast, with the reference to peacemaking that ends 3:18. (4) The verb ζηλοῦτε in 4:2 echoes its cognate noun ζῆλον in 3:14, as evidence that the behavior that is condemned in 4:1–3 comes not from above but from below. (5) The vice φθόνος (jealousy) in 4:5 shares the same semantic field with a number of the vices that are listed in 3:14–16, particularly the ζῆλος that is condemned in 3:14, 16. Because of these lexical and semantic connections between the passages, some commentators view them as comprising one continuing unit rather than two separate ones.

While the links between 3:13–18 and 4:1–10 are quite numerous, there are a number of ways in which each passage is distinct and which justify treating the latter as a separate paragraph with its own integrity and coherence. Consider the following differences: (1) While each of the sections begins with a rhetorical question, each also ends with an aphorism that looks very much like an adapted Jesus *logion*. This is a shared characteristic of other separate paragraphs in James. (2) The topic introduced in 3:13 (wisdom) is different than the topic introduced in 4:1 (conflicts). (3) The tone of the two sections is quite different. While both passages describe behaviors that are to be avoided, the second passage is harsher and more hortatory in nature. There are three commands in 3:13–18 with no harsh accusations addressed to the implied readers. On the other hand, there are ten commands concentrated in 4:7–10 plus a sequence of severe indicative charges in 4:2, 3, as well as a series of direct questions that function rhetorically as condemnations of the reader's behavior (4:1, 2, 4–6). This difference in style leads to the conclusion that James could be described as functioning like one of the *sages* of Israel in 3:13–18 while he functions like one of the *prophets* of Israel in 4:1–10.

I argued in the Introduction that 3:13–18 is the *thematic peak* of the book while 4:1–10 is the *hortatory peak* of the book. While both passages clearly reflect the "two ways" approach to ethics in wisdom literature, 3:13–18 does so by contrasting the two ways of heavenly viewpoint versus earthly viewpoint. On the other hand, in 4:1–10, those two ways are elaborated as describing a person who is either God's friend (and thus the world's enemy) or who is God's enemy (and thus the world's friend). In these two passages, James brings together both traditions of OT wisdom literature and the OT prophetic corpus. While James is "*the* wisdom writing of the NT," a more nuanced description would be that it is the NT writing that best exemplifies the concept of "prophetic wisdom."

Because 3:13–18 and 4:1–10 serve as the thematic and hortatory peaks of the discourse, James' call to reject human wisdom (that makes one God's enemy) in favor of divine wisdom (that makes one

God's friend) underlies the dual nature of each of his other paragraphs. This is true regardless of how specifically the exhibition of those behaviors is exemplified. Furthermore, if someone attempts to live one's life both ways, it will only result in that person becoming "double-souled" (4:8; see also 1:8). On the other hand, to follow the Lord fully without yielding to rival loyalties will result in a whole, complete, and "perfect" life.

Greek Text

1 Πόθεν πόλεμοι ªκαὶ πόθεν μάχαι ἐν ὑμῖν; οὐκ ἐντεῦθεν, ἐκ τῶν ἡδονῶν ὑμῶν τῶν στρατευομένων ἐν τοῖς μέλεσιν ὑμῶν; 2 ἐπιθυμεῖτε καὶ οὐκ ἔχετε, φονεύετε καὶ ζηλοῦτε καὶ οὐ δύνασθε ἐπιτυχεῖν, μάχεσθε καὶ πολεμεῖτε, οὐκ ἔχετεᵇ διὰ τὸ μὴ αἰτεῖσθαι ὑμᾶς, 3 αἰτεῖτεᵇ καὶ οὐ λαμβάνετε διότι κακῶς αἰτεῖσθε, ἵνα ἐν ταῖς ἡδοναῖς ὑμῶν δαπανήσητε.

Textual Notes

There are no significant textual variants in these verses, as evidenced by no variants being listed in the UBS[5] text.

1.a. Byzantine manuscripts and Codex Alexandrinus have a slightly different word order in 4:1, with the former also eliminating the second πόθεν.

2.b. 3.b. A few manuscripts also insert the conjunction δε in 4:2 and 4:3 (e.g., p[74]) to add more of an adversative force to the argument.

Translation

1 What causes quarrels and what causes fights among you? Is it not from this, from your pleasures that are at war in your members? 2 You desire and you do not have. You murder and you covet and are not able to obtain. You fight and quarrel. You do not have because you do

not ask. 3 You ask and do not receive, because you ask wrongly, to spend it on your pleasures.

Context

We have now entered a section of that differs from both chapter one and also from the three so-called "treatises" that precede it (2:1–12; 2:13–26; 3:1–12). Not only is the tone more severe in this section, but James has introduced the expression ἐν ὑμῖν (3:13 and 4:1) which he will continue to use in 5:13, 14, and 19. He also begins to use the consequential conjunction οὖν at this very point (4:4, 7, 17; 5:7, 16). He is now dealing more with specific situations within the communities he is addressing. It is in this last half of the book that he focuses in on the specific behavioral problems that are being exhibited within the communities that he is addressing. Even the use of the οὖν is for transitioning to the expected ethical application rather than for logical development of his argument—the way it often appears in the writings attributed to Paul.

Recognizing this new way of addressing his readers can also help explain why James waits until 3:13–4:10 to expound the thematic and hortatory peaks of his discourse. While everything that has preceded this passage can be also viewed in light of the polar opposite behaviors he portrays, from this section onward he exposes that wrong behavior even more closely and fervently than he has done before. One could be asked to imagine a preacher initially discoursing about general issues that affect all congregations, but then becoming more fervent and specific as he moves into problems that he knows are prevalent in his own parishioners' lives.

Exegetical Comments

4:1 Πόθεν πόλεμοι καὶ πόθεν μάχαι ἐν ὑμῖν: James often employs the interrogative mood in direct questions, usually to address serious breaches of behavior (2:4, 5, 6, 7, 14, 15, 16, 19, 20, 21, 25; 3:11, 12, 13; 4:4, 5,

12, 14; 5:6?). This also is characteristic of his diatribal style, of which 4:1–10 plays a prominent role. This section, therefore, opens with two verbless rhetorical questions (4:1). The second question functions as the answer to the first question. One could state the result indicatively, "The outward conflicts that exist among you arise from the selfish pleasures that are at conflict inside of each one of you." The recurrence of πόθεν, especially when it is not needed to ask the question, conveys the force of the questions that function as an indictment.[1] The entire rhetorical effect is intensified by both his employing a triple alliteration (πόθεν πόλεμοι καὶ πόθεν) and a triple homoioteleuton (πόθ<u>εν</u> πόθ<u>εν</u>, ἐντεῦθ<u>εν</u>). James does not utilize these rhetorical features simply for ornamentation, but to convey the intensity of his charges, which can only be appreciated fully by the oral culture in which the writing was first heard when it was read out to the congregations.

The words πόλεμοι and μάχαι are used in contrast with εἰρήνην, the last word of 3:18. This point would be even more obvious to the original hearer/readers who would not be hindered by modern chapter divisions. General wars (πόλεμοι) and specific battles (μάχαι) are standard activities of armies. The first, πόλεμος, pictures a continual campaign or "war." The second, μάχη, describes the separate conflicts or battles in that war (Trench, 32). It may not be that helpful, however, to finely distinguish between the two words, since James' purpose in using the words is to be as comprehensive in his condemnation as he can. In other words, James covers the whole problem by using them both. The words can describe both literal battles (using weapons) and metaphorical battles (using words). The reference in this context is obviously to a personal and not a national context. The first word (πόλεμοι) is used only of military conflicts in the NT (1 Cor 14:8; and of apocalyptic war in Rev 9:7; 12:4; 16:14; 20:8). It is used, however, by Clement of conflicts within the Corinthian church (*1 Clem.* 3.2; 46.5). The latter word (μάχαι) is clearly used for personal

---

[1] The Byzantine scribes missed this point and omitted the second πόθεν in an attempt to smooth out the redundancy of the repetition. It is hard to explain why a scribe would have added the πόθεν.

strife elsewhere in the NT (2 Cor 7:5; 2 Tim 2:23–24; Titus 3:9).

The expression ἐν ὑμῖν functions with the same rhetorical force as it did in 3:13, and also is another indication that although they are separate paragraphs they function in the same manner, one as the thematic peak (3:13–18), while the other (4:1–10) as the hortatory peak. Some commentators have concluded that because of this language, the assemblies that James addresses must be actually undergoing serious divisions and fights comparable to what we might call "church splits" (Ropes, 252; Martin, 144). We do not believe that the language implies such, but will defer further comment until 4:3 with its condemnation of "murder."

οὐκ ἐντεῦθεν, ἐκ τῶν ἡδονῶν ὑμῶν: James continues his questions with one that this time expects a positive response (asked with an οὐκ). The ἐντεῦθεν is a demonstrative adverb, directing our attention ahead to the source of the conflicts that have been mentioned. James places the source of these outward conflicts of 4:1 on the inward "desires" or "cravings" (ἡδονῶν). James repeats the expression ἡδονῶν ὑμῶν in 4:3 where it describes the selfish desires that are satisfied by things one acquires. This repetition emphasizes those desires as the theme and is the real problem being addressed in this passage. This important word, ἡδονή, usually means "pleasure," but it can also carry the sense of a "desire for pleasure" (Xenophon, *Mem.* 1, 2, 23; *4 Macc.* 5:23).[2] It is mentioned by Philo in his discussion of the Ten Commandments where he writes of that which "arouses and awakes the soul when at rest and like a light flashing upon the eyes raises it to a state of great elation. This sensation of the soul is called passion (ἡδονή)" (Philo, *Dec.* 143).

τῶν στρατευομένων ἐν τοῖς μέλεσιν ὑμῶν. These desires are continually at war (attributive present participle of στρατεύομαι) within their bodily

---

[2] "The fact that James follows immediately with *epithymein* suggests that this is also the meaning here (compare Luke 8:14; Titus 3:3; 2 Pet 2:13; and see Cantinat, 196; Adamson, 166)" (Johnson, 276).

members (μέλεσιν). The verb was used in Attic for military expeditions and the serving of a soldier (GE, 1971) as also in the Apocrypha (Muraoka, 638) but not as a metaphor. Its metaphorical use here for the "strife" of the passions within our bodily members is with an eye to the "quarrels" and "fights" just mentioned. However, one is also reminded of Rom 7:23, where within a person's members the "law of sin" does battle with the "law of the mind," although it is probably not wise to argue dependence of one on the other. In using the words μέλεσιν ὑμῶν ("your members") in 4:1, does James refer to "members" of the physical body or to people who are "members "of the believing Diaspora communities, as some commentators have advocated (Davids, 157)? As has been noted, the parallelism with the ἐν ὑμῖν in the first question is only a formal one. More important is how James uses the word μέλος, which he clearly does elsewhere to refer to parts of the human body (3:5, 6). Parallels with Pauline metaphorical usage (e.g., Rom 12:5; Eph 4:25) miss the point if James' use of the word elsewhere is intended to be literal and not metaphorical. Furthermore, the cognate noun ἐπιθυμία in 1:14, 15 (see ἐπιθυμεῖτε in 4:2) clearly identifies the problem addressed here as one that arises from within their individual natures, not inside their individual communities. Of course, we know that whole people manifest these sinful urges, but that is not the point being made in 4:1–3. In using this term for members of the body—as his older Brother also did (Matt 5:29, 30)—James reveals that as he wrote, he had Jesus looking over his shoulder, not Paul.

4:2 ἐπιθυμεῖτε καὶ οὐκ ἔχετε, φονεύετε καὶ ζηλοῦτε καὶ οὐ δύνασθε ἐπιτυχεῖν, μάχεσθε καὶ πολεμεῖτε, οὐκ ἔχετε διὰ τὸ μὴ αἰτεῖσθαι ὑμᾶς: James' familiar and abrupt style continues in 4:2–3 with a series of short, second person plural statements, which alternate between the negative (ἐπιθυμεῖτε, φονεύετε, ζηλοῦτε, μάχεσθε, πολεμεῖτε, οὐ λαμβάνετε) and the positive. The sense of the καί that connects these alternating experiences is better understood as adversative, as in 4:3:

"You request but you do not receive" (αἰτεῖτε καὶ οὐ λαμβάνετε).3 Later scribes sought to strengthen the adversative nature of the καί by replacing it with δέ.

In untangling the complex syntax of these verses, it is also possible to detect a chiastic structure to them. If the three secondary clauses are removed, the primary clauses can be structured as follows:

A   ἐπιθυμεῖτε   καὶ οὐκ ἔχετε,
B   φονεύετε καὶ ζηλοῦτε   καὶ οὐ δύνασθε ἐπιτυχεῖν,
B' μάχεσθε καὶ πολεμεῖτε   οὐκ ἔχετε
A' αἰτεῖτε   καὶ οὐ λαμβάνετε

The A clause parallels the A' clause and the B and B' compound clauses also are parallel, structurally as well as semantically. While this commentator is hesitant to overly stress the role of chiasms (especially long ones), such an arrangement as found here can be helpful to discern the overall flow of the author's densely expressed portrayal. The addition of the secondary clauses in lines B' and A' completes the charge by explaining both the causes (4:2) and the result (4:3) of requests that are driven by selfish desires.

Another way to discern the chiastic structure of 4:1–2b is offered by William Brosend, who displays the structure of the sentences in English as follows:

A where comes war and where comes fighting among you?
    B from your desires warring in your bodily members
        C you long for something and have not
        C' you murder and covet
    B' but you are unable to obtain
A' you fight and make war (Brosend, 108).

φονεύετε καὶ ζηλοῦτε: The association of envy/covetousness and

---

³ See Wallace, 668–73, for examples of the "contrastive" or "adversative" usage of καί.

murder is often found in the Septuagint tradition, canonical and otherwise (Wis 2:24: "through the devil's envy death entered the world"; Josephus, *Ant.* 2:10–18; Philo, *Jos.* 5–12, both about Joseph and his brothers). Christian writings make the same connection (Mark 15:10; Matt 27:18; Acts 5:17; 7:9; 13:45; 17:5; *1 Clem.* 4:9–5:2). Some commentators question how such severe behavior, including "murder" (4:2), could ever be envisioned as part of the community's experience. Note again the phrase ἐν ὑμῖν, which is repeated from 3:13. Some have even suggested that there was a Zealot faction within the community, either in the past (Martin, 144) or even in the present (Reicke, 46). It seems rather clear, however, that the terminology is being used in a metaphorical way. The attempt to see here a reference to Christians being the victims of Jewish zealots or themselves fighting alongside other Jews before or during the Jewish war from a.d. 66–70 is simply ignoring all of the rhetorical language being utilized, including the plain use of the phrase *within you* (Ropes, 252–53; Hort, 88; Davids, 156). This type of language no more literally refers to something that has already happened than does the exclamation "adulteresses," also found in this same context (4:4). When the rhetorical language is recognized, we must conclude that these expressions are hyperbolic and overstated for effect.

In his role as prophet, James is utilizing the hyperbolic language that was often utilized by the canonical prophets and even in the hatred/murder statements by Him who was the ultimate prophet, Jesus. It is a distinct possibility that James is echoing the prophetic teaching of his Brother who equated hatred with murder (Matt 5:21–22). The recognition that James is employing rhetorical and hyperbolic language should not lead to any lessening of the seriousness of his words. This internal source of community friction and factions and selfish behavior could possibly lead to blows and even worse if sinful desires are allowed to play themselves out in human relationships. But the dramas are not only played out publicly, since some of the worse conflicts are allowed to see the people after they have gone home. The Pauline admonition is also appropriate here: "But if you bite and devour one another, watch out that you are not consumed by one another" (Gal 5:15).

οὐκ ἔχετε διὰ τὸ μὴ αἰτεῖσθαι ὑμᾶς. The construction of διὰ τὸ with an infinitive is clearly causal (BDF, 207; Wallace, 597, 662). But people do ask! Why then do they not "have"? This statement cannot be isolated from its context. By choosing pleasure as their goal, people cut themselves off from the source of good things (1:17), and they find that their prayers, aiming at their own pleasures and not His service, are unacceptable. If you make God's service your supreme goal, then your desires will be such that God will answer your prayer. There are possible echoes again of teaching like Matt 6:31–33. The result will be cessation of this current strife. The verb αἰτέω ("ask") here is also an echo of Jas 1:5. If persons do not live according to the "wisdom from above," it is not likely that they will turn to God with their requests.

4:3 αἰτεῖτε καὶ οὐ λαμβάνετε: In the contrasting indicative statement αἰτεῖτε καὶ οὐ λαμβάνετε, the καί is also adversative, as it was in 4:2. The opening words of 4:3 do not hold up as a contrast of a group of Christians who are different from those of 4:2b. There are not some who fail to ask and then others who ask wrongly. Rather, those who sometimes fail to ask God at other times ask Him in the wrong spirit (Martin, 147). Note that the verse does not say that God does not hear, but that we *do not receive*. The problem is on our end of the communication act.

διότι κακῶς αἰτεῖσθε: The grammatical structure of the verse makes it clear that this causal clause (with διότι) explains the reason why they do not receive the request for which they are praying. The purpose ἵνα clause ending the sentence explains their sinful purpose that leads to that cause.

αἰτεῖτε καὶ οὐ λαμβάνετε	CHARGE
διότι κακῶς αἰτεῖσθε,	REASON
ἵνα ἐν ταῖς ἡδοναῖς ὑμῶν δαπανήσητε	PURPOSE

The adverb κακῶς is not as mild as the softer sounding "amiss" in the KJV. It means "basely" or "in a wrong way," or "with wrong motives" (BDAG, 502.2). It is not merely a matter of using the wrong words but of approaching God with evil motives. Their prayer itself is "evil" in the way that the tongue is characterized as a "world of wickedness."

A sometimes overlooked issue is our author's shift in voice from the middle αἰτεῖσθαι in 4:2 to the active αἰτεῖτε in 4:3 and then back to the middle voice αἰτεῖσθε at the end of the verse. The change in voice has had a number of suggested solutions. These range in scope from seeing no significance in the differences in voice (Dibelius, 219) to Mayor's suggestion that the middle expresses the spirit of prayer while the active expresses only the words (Mayor, 138). Hort suggested that the active indicates the asking of a person, while the middle connotes asking for something (Hort, 90). Others have suggested simply that αἰτεῖτε reflects a conscious assimilation to the Jesus *logion* in Matt 7:7 (Davids, 160).[4]

Perhaps another explanation worth considering lies in the use of a negative adjunct accompanying the middle voice in the first and third occurrences and the absolute use of the active voice in the second verb. In both 4:2 and 4:3, the middle voice is accompanied in both occurrences by a causal clause (expressed by διά τό plus infinitive in 4:2 and διότι plus indicative in 4:3). This does not suggest that the middle voice always expresses some negative aspect of prayer, but it may imply that when there is some significant accompanying action,

---

[4] The warning of this grammarian is important. "It is true that the middle has a commercial or contractual flavor where the active serves for requests to God." But "there is often no principle either here or in the NT" and no rule applies to their use in Jas 4:2 (Turner, 55).

the subject's greater involvement in the predicator may be expressed by the middle voice. In any case, the switch to the active αἰτεῖτε probably does specify another use of the Jesus *logion* mentioned in Matt 7:7–10. James is balancing Jesus' prayer promise by stressing that asking should be accompanied by right motives, not with the goal of simply spending the answer to satisfy one's own pleasures. In Jas 1:6–8, prayer is not successful if it is the prayer of a doubter. In 2:16, the "prayer" fails because it is not accompanied by appropriate action. Here in 4:2–3, prayer is unanswered because it is for the wrong purpose.

ἵνα ἐν ταῖς ἡδοναῖς ὑμῶν δαπανήσητε: The ἵνα plus subjunctive (δαπανήσητε) clause expresses the purpose for the wrong type of "asking." The verb δαπανάω means simply to spend any kind of resource (BDAG, 212.1) but can also imply extravagance (see Luke 15:14, of the prodigal). People ask to acquire the resources to enable them to obtain the objects of their desire and craving. The key to understanding why this is wrong is this purpose clause and the negative ideas conveyed by the ἡδοναῖς. How important is this word in the overall message conveyed by this passage? Johnson has argued that James in 3:13–4:10 is discoursing on the "Topos περὶ φθόνου" ("the topic about envy") due to its reference in 4:5 along with semantically related words for "envy." However, I suggest that Johnson has too strictly limited the *topos* to envy and bases his argument too much on the use of that word in the highly controversial "quotation" in that verse. James certainly is speaking on a *topos* of concern to Jewish moralists, as well as Greco-Roman ones. If we must choose such a parallel, I suggest that it is the "Topos περὶ ἡδονῶν" ("about pleasures"). This word, while it can refer to the legitimate desires and pleasures of life, is used only in its sinful and selfish meaning in the NT. James locates the foundation of these conflicts in these ἡδοναί in 4:1 and then puts the blame for unanswered prayer on selfish ἡδοναί in 4:3. "Selfish pleasures" appears to be the focus of his concern rather than envy, which of course is a manifestation of selfish pleasure.[5] While it is possible to recognize this inner tendency with the "evil inclination" (יֵצֶר הָרָע) of Jewish tradition, the late documentation for that leaning in Jewish sources counsels caution in this regard.[6]

Adultery and Bad Friendships (James 4:4–6)

Introduction

There are a large number of textual and hermeneutical issues in this brief passage, so the treatment will be more detailed. The message that the passage conveys, however, is readily understandable by the average reader. That message is that the world and what it stands for are the enemies of the believer and we should be unswervingly loyal to God as we face this enemy of our souls.

Original Text

4 ᵃμοιχαλίδες, οὐκ οἴδατε ὅτι ἡ φιλία τοῦ κόσμου ἔχθρα τοῦ θεοῦ ἐστιν; ὃς ἐὰν οὖν βουληθῇ φίλος εἶναι τοῦ κόσμου, ἐχθρὸς τοῦ θεοῦ καθίσταται. 5 ἢ δοκεῖτε ὅτι κενῶς ἡ γραφὴ λέγει· πρὸς φθόνον ἐπιποθεῖ τὸ πνεῦμα ὃ ᵇκατῴκισεν ἐν ἡμῖν;

6 μείζονα δὲ δίδωσιν χάριν; διὸ λέγει· ὁ θεὸς ὑπερηφάνοις ἀντιτάσσεται, ταπεινοῖς δὲ δίδωσιν χάριν.

---

[5] Johnson expresses the thought well. "The gift-giving God is here manipulated as a kind of vending machine precisely for purposes of self-gratification (see 1:26, *apatōn kardian*). In this case, 'prayer' is a form of idolatry and, as we shall see, expressive of 'friendship with the world'" (Johnson, 278).

[6] J. Marcus, "The Evil Inclination in the Epistle of James," *CBQ* 44 (1982), 606–21.

Textual Notes

4.a. There are two significant textual variants in this passage, each suggesting the habits of later scribes. When Byzantine copyists understood the word μοιχαλίδες ("adulteresses") only in its literal sense, they were puzzled why only women were mentioned and therefore added a reference to men as well (μοιχοὶ καὶ). The shorter reading, however, is strongly supported by both Alexandrian and Western witnesses (ℵ* A B it vg syr cop arm eth). In scriptural imagery, μοιχαλίς ("adulteress") is used figuratively of Israel as the unfaithful spouse of Yahweh (Ps 73:27; Isa 54:5; Jer 3:20; Ezek 16 and 23; Hos 9:1). This is also the case in the New Testament (Matt 12:39; 16:4; Mark 8:38).

5.b. In 4:5, κατῴκισεν is better attested (P[74] ℵ A B, e.g.) than κατῴκησεν (Byzantine and versions). The first verb, from κατοικίζειν, is causative ("the spirit which He has made to dwell in us"), whereas the second, from κατοικεῖν, is intransitive ("the spirit which dwells in us"). Since κατοικίζειν occurs nowhere else in the NT, copyists were more likely to replace it with the much more common κατοικεῖν than vice versa.

Translation

4 You adulteresses! Do you not know that friendship with the world means enmity with God? Therefore, whoever decides to be the world's friend becomes God's enemy. 5 Or do you suppose that the Scripture speaks to no purpose? Does the spirit that He has caused to dwell in us long enviously? 6 But He gives more grace. Therefore, it says,

"God opposes proud people, but gives grace to humble ones."

Context

In the second of the three sections in 4:1–10, the serious charges introduced in 4:1–3 by the "prophet" James reach a rhetorical crescendo. By a series of questions concluded with a scriptural citation, his diatribe powerfully portrays the central thrust of his argument—namely, that one must finally decide whose friend he actually is: the world's or God's. In keeping with the idea that 3:13–18 contains the thematic peak of the book (following wisdom from above and not from below), this passage equates the choosing of heavenly wisdom with being God's friend. Making the opposite choice, however, will result in being opposed and resisted by God, who will actually become the enemy. This charge leads in the third section (4:7–10) to a series of imperatives that press even further for a decisive choice between these two contradictory philosophies of life, one based on pleasing self and the other based on pleasing God.

Exegetical Comments

4:4 μοιχαλίδες: The familiar and affectionate ἀδελφοί μου has been radically altered to the harsh nominative of address, μοιχαλίδες. James actually does not return to the consistent use of the affectionate address until 5:7. The apparent anomaly of using the more affectionate ἀδελφοί μου in 4:11 right in the middle of this diatribe will be addressed in the comments on that verse.

The use of the feminine noun must have annoyed some later literal-minded scribes, who added μοιχοί καὶ before μοιχαλίδες to include a reference to adulterous men as well (see previous Textual Notes). The type of adultery addressed, however, is not the sexual act but is a figure of speech used by the prophets of Israel's frequent infidelities (LXX Ps 72:27; Jer 3:6–10, 20; 13:27; Isa 54:5–8; 57:3; Hos 3:1; 9:1; Ezek 16:38; 23:45; see Muraoka, 466). This collective figure was also utilized by Jesus (Matt 12:39; 16:4). The shorter and earlier readings of the Alexandrian and Western texts support this "Israel as wife of Yahweh" understanding of James' analogy.

This metaphor that characterized the people as a whole came to be used of individual people. Philo interprets the mystery of the "sacred marriage" (ἱερὸς γάμος) as an image of God and the soul. "But when

God begins to consort with the soul, He makes what before was a woman into a virgin again, for he takes away the degenerate and emasculate passions by which it was made womanish and plants instead the native growth of unpolluted virtues" (Philo, *Cher.* 50). James' use of it to apply to individuals, however, is not borrowed from the Philonic usage, for he applies it to behavior and does not attempt to allegorize further the figure of speech.

There have been commentators who have seen a reference to physical adultery in this word (e.g., Hort, 91). He thinks that at this point, James has broadened his appeal to unbelievers. The other figurative language in the passage (wars, etc.), however, certainly rules out this option, as the vast majority of commentators agree (e.g., Witherington, 2007, 523; McKnight, 330–31). Despite the widespread recognition that the better reading is the feminine μοιχαλίδες, it is surprising that a large number of modern English versions from across the spectrum still retain the masculine "adulterers" rather than the more literal feminine "adulteresses." The following chart lists the three main translations of the address in 4:4 and thirteen representative versions that support one of the three translations.

"adulterers and adulteresses"	KJV, NKJV
"adulterers"	NRSV, NJB, ESV, NIV, NET, NLT
"adulteresses"	ASV, NASB, CENT, HCSB

The CSB now has "adulterous people," while RSV has "unfaithful creatures," and the Vulgate has the masculine *adulteri* or "adulterers." It is not surprising that the KJV/NKJV have the two words since they are both based on the later Byzantine textual tradition. Only four other versions render μοιχαλίδες as it is in the original. Perhaps the other versions that use "adulterers" desire to avoid a possible feminine "put down," but in doing so they obscure the clear OT allusion to the unfaithfulness of the people of God to their covenanted divine

Husband.

οὐκ οἴδατε: This alarming address is followed by a rhetorical question in 4:4a that lays out the stark cosmological binary opposition between friendship with God and friendship with the world. This is the clearest example in James of the diatribal rebuke for not acting upon a recognized store of shared knowledge (see also 1 Cor 3:16; 5:6; 6:2; 9:13; Rom 6:16; 11:2). Their behavior rejects what they know but refuse to live by. He then completes his attack with a "therefore" in the verse plus two more rhetorical questions in 4:5 (in my view the last clause is a question).

ὅτι ἡ φιλία τοῦ κόσμου: The ὅτι clause functions as the complement of the verb οἴδατε. The construction is a clear example of the objective genitive, as is also the case later in the verse (φίλος ... τοῦ κόσμου; ἐχθρὸς τοῦ θεοῦ). "The genitive substantive functions semantically as the *direct object* of the verbal idea implicit in the head noun" (Wallace, 116). James has referred to the "world" three times previously (1:27; 2:5; 3:6), and this reference must be consistent with those occurrences. It is important to recognize that the κόσμος is not the world of the physical universe, which was created by God and is still good because it reveals Him (Gen 1:31; Ps 19:1–3). Nor is it the human beings in that world who are made in the image of God and are loved by Him (3:9; John 3:16). It is that "system of human existence in its many aspects," (BDAG, 562; GE, 1165) especially those aspects of the desires and influences that are in opposition to God or disregard Him. For James, however, the κόσμος is always a negative designation. It is the place where the lowly are held in dishonor (2:5) and it is characterized by unrighteousness (3:6). The κόσμος is the opposite of God's order and is actively hostile to Him. "Thus the problem for God's people is neither delight in the physical world nor love for humanity in its fallenness, but an attitude toward either the physical or the social world that puts it in the place of God" (McCartney, 209).

The abstract noun φιλία (friendship) appears only here in the NT, but it is used thirty-six times in the LXX. The personal noun φίλος (friend) occurs twenty-nine times in the NT, including this verse. The concept of "affectionate regard" or simply "friendship" dominates its meaning, but the semantic field both of the word itself and certainly of the word group can include sexual friendship/love (Prov 5:19; 7:18). One might conclude that James even implies that flirting with the world is as serious as unfaithfulness to one's spouse.

The more difficult question is why James should assume his readers would know this. This is a clear example of the typical rebuke in a diatribe for not acting upon an assumed knowledge (Epictetus, *Diatr.* 1.12.24–26). There is, however, "no such proverb in the Greco-Roman moral literature or in Hellenistic Jewish writings" (Johnson, 279). Efforts to locate the source within the sayings of Jesus seem to fall short of certainty. Probably there is no better commentary on Jas 4:4 than that familiar admonition from another of the three "pillars" of the apostolic church: "Do not love the world or the things in the world. If anyone loves the world, the love of the Father is not in him. For all that is in the world—the desires of the flesh and the desires of the eyes and pride in possessions—is not from the Father but is from the world. And the world is passing away along with its desires, but whoever does the will of God abides forever" (1 John 2:15–17). The passages are close enough to suggest the existence of some common Christian tradition to which both John and James could appeal, or the appeal is to a general knowledge based on implications form other statements.

ἔχθρα τοῦ θεοῦ ἐστιν: the substantive noun ἔχθρα is the predicate nominative, agreeing with φιλία. The genitive τοῦ θεοῦ is objective, receiving the verbal action implied in ἔχθρα. The entire expression is the semantic counterpoint to ἡ φιλία τοῦ κόσμου.

ὃς ἐὰν οὖν βουληθῇ φίλος εἶναι τοῦ κόσμου: The transitional οὖν leads to a powerful affirmation that both applies what has been stated about world-friendship and advances his point to God-enmity. The ἐὰν ... βουληθῇ introduces the protasis of the third class conditional sentence.

The infinitive εἶναι is its complement. The verb βούλομαι should be read in light of its previous use concerning God's decision to birth us (1:18) as well as the decision of the ship's pilot (3:4). It is stronger than the "wish" expressed by a word like θέλω (2:20). This is a settled "desire" that has decided to be friendly with the world.

ἐχθρὸς τοῦ θεοῦ καθίσταται: Those who dare to engage in this world-order are out of harmony with God's order and become (καθίσταται) God's enemies rather than His friends. As in James 3:6 (where the tongue becomes "the unrighteous world"), this verb takes a complement that is in the nominative case (the world's friend becomes "God's enemy" ἐχθρός). This could be called the *nominative of appellation*, which is treated as a proper name. In light of what has been affirmed earlier, it is now clear to see that as Abraham was given the name, "Friend of God" (2:23), the friend of the world is given the title, "Enemy of God."

Friendship in the ancient world implied far more than a causal acquaintance; it involved commitment and fidelity to that friend. In the biblical context, friendship operates in the mode of binary opposition to enmity, and the world is in opposition to God. The ἐχθρός is the opposite of the φίλος (Prov 15:28; also Sir 5:15; 6:9). The expressed statements about these two loyalties and their clear implications can be displayed simply as follows:

Friendship with God means enmity with the world.

Friendship with the world means enmity with God.

While it is true that James 4 does not explicitly mention the phrase "friendship with God" in this context, attention to the earlier part of the book where Abraham is a "friend with God" (2:23) renders the implication here a valid one. "Like Abraham's friendship with God (2:23), friendship with the world is a deliberate choice; as in 1:18, the Greek (βούλομαι) means not mere will, but will with premeditation. He who *determines* to be a friend of the world becomes an enemy of God, not because God hates him but because he hates God" (Adamson, 170).

The importance of this statement about friendship and enmity cannot be stressed enough, since this verse appears in the very heart of the "hortatory peak" of James' discourse. Other authors have recognized the pivotal role of these concepts at this point in the book.

> Among the spiritual values that James's community is encouraged to embrace is the call to maintain friendship with God. This expresses the very identity of the community. James 4:4 is one of the central verses of the entire letter; it captures the main thrust of the letter's argument.[7]

The effectiveness of James' use of friendship language here becomes even more apparent when the modern reader recognizes the nature of friendship in the ancient world. Jas 4:4 states that the believer is to be a friend of God (something previously affirmed in 2:26 about Abraham), although it is stated in reverse with the world being God's enemy. As James has placed special emphasis on testing and the one who withstands great tests becomes that friend of God, the person who withstands the trials placed before him by the world can possess this friendship with God. Friendship language is quite powerful, for friends show unparalleled loyalty to one another; they are of "one soul," not double-souled (1:8); and they should share all things and even die for one another (John 15:13). As God's friend, one must share that same vision. "If the community members are to be friends with God, like Abraham and Rahab, they will manifest the great characteristics, through good works, which true friends are expected to have."[8]

---

[7] P. J. Hartin, *A Spirituality of Perfection: Faith in Action in the Letter of James* (Collegeville, MN: Liturgical Press, 1999), 110.

[8] A. J. Batten, *Friendship and Benefaction in James* (Emory Studies in Early Christianity 15; Blandford Forum, U.K.: Deo Publishing, 2010), 75.

The world has been portrayed in James as evil and marked by unrighteousness (1:27; 3:6). In 4:4 it is now opposed to God. To be friends with it is to embrace its values, which do not come from God. This devotion to God is not marked by isolation in a desert but by not living according to the values of the world.

4:5 ἢ δοκεῖτε ὅτι κενῶς ἡ γραφὴ λέγει· πρὸς φθόνον ἐπιποθεῖ τὸ πνεῦμα ὃ κατῴκισεν ἐν ἡμῖν, "Or do you suppose that the Scripture speaks to no purpose? Does the spirit that he has caused to dwell in us long enviously?" I have included the entire verse and translation again so the reader can know where we are going with my suggestion. The confrontational questioning of 4:4 continues in 4:5a and finally culminates in 4:6 with a scriptural quotation accompanied by a citation formula from Prov 3:34. The second rhetorical question in 4:5a is introduced by the meta-comment ἢ δοκεῖτε.[9] Such questions are not meant to search for an answer but to function as a more powerful statement. That statement would be, "The Scripture does not speak to no purpose!" Some linguists call this type of inquiry a "queclarative"— a question that is intended to make a declaration.[10] This combination of a meta-comment and a queclarative serves to raise the prominence of this diatribal thrust. The meta-comment ἢ δοκεῖτε is also used to question a false opinion in Matt 26:53, and the verb introduces a false opinion elsewhere in 1 Cor 3:18; 8:2; 10:12; 14:37; Mark 6:49; Luke 12:51; and 24:37. James has already used it this manner in 1:26.

This question also leads into one of the most difficult interpretive challenges in the book. Are the words that follow the question a quotation from the OT or from some other sacred writing? If so, where in "the Scripture" (ἡ γραφή) are they to be found? There certainly is no passage in the OT containing such a verse as we find here in 4:5. Or is James referring to a "lost" passage or one otherwise unknown to us

---

[9] A *meta-comment* is "when a speaker stops saying what they are saying in order to comment on what is being said" (Runge, *Discourse Grammar*, 131).

[10] G. Thompson, *Introducing Functional Grammar* (2nd ed.; London: Arnold, 2004), 80, 240–41.

(Marty, 159; Davids, 162)? Or is he making a broad allusion to the "sense" of Scripture as a whole (Bede, 50; Mayor, 140–41; Ropes, 262; Dibelius, 222)? Or should these words be taken in an entirely different way than as a quotation from some previous source? The problems of where to place the punctuation and the identity of that "Scripture" have generated more discussion than any other issue in James, with the possible exception of 2:14–26. The answers that have been offered by commentators are legion. See Davids (162–64) and McCartney (210–12) for convenient summaries of the various alternatives. I offer the following simplified charts to explain the issues to be addressed and the interpretations that have been suggested for Jam 4:5. They have been drawn from a number of commentaries and articles (see a Selected Bibliography following 4:10), but are adapted mainly from McCartney, 210–12.

Various Grammatical and Exegetical Questions in James 4:5

1. How should the prepositional phrase Πρὸς φθόνον ("for envy") be taken? Can God ever be said to do anything Πρὸς φθόνον?
2. Is the "yearning" (ἐπιποθεῖ) a virtuous longing or a sinful lusting?
3. Is the "spirit" (τὸ πνεῦμα) the human spirit, viewed either neutrally or negatively, or God's Spirit?
4. Did the original read either κατῴκησεν (he dwelt) or κατῴκισεν (he caused to dwell)?
5. If causative, is God or the Spirit/spirit the subject of "yearns/longs for"?
6. How should the verse be punctuated? Does πρὸς φθόνον begin a separate sentence, or delineate what Scripture says?

The answers to the above questions still lead to a number of translations and interpretations of the verse. The following chart lists the varying approaches to the verse with some versions that adopt them.

Various Translations/Interpretations of James 4:5

1. "The Spirit that God has caused to dwell in believers yearns jealously" (the Holy Spirit does not tolerate His people trying to be friends with the world – KJV).
2. "God yearns jealously over the Spirit that He has caused to dwell in us" (the threat of withdrawing the Spirit hangs over those who want to be friends with the world – NASB).
3. "God yearns jealously regarding the breath of life that He has put within us" (i.e., God vehemently desires loyalty from His creatures generally – NRSV, ESV).
4. "When the human spirit that God has caused to dwell in us yearns (for pleasures of the world), envy (and conflict) is the result" (cf. CSB).
5. "The human spirit that God has caused to dwell in us yearns (for the world) enviously" (NIV).
6. "Do you suppose that the Scripture speaks to no purpose? Does the spirit that he has caused to dwell in us long enviously?" Thus Jas 4:5a and 4:5b are two questions. See the following discussion.

Caution should be exercised in any dogmatic approach to solving the questions raised by this verse, and one should be careful about deciding a doctrinal point based on this verse. I offer below what I believe is the best approach to the translation and interpretation of this *crux interpretum*. I will do this in light of both the grammar and also the rhetoric of the passage. We will strive to discover the function of this verse in moving forward the discourse. In other words, how does this statement best serve the book as a whole?

I find the interpretation offered by Sophie Laws very helpful with a slight variation that I believe actually strengthens her view. Laws' conclusion is that the so-called quotation from "Scripture" is best viewed as a question about the human spirit's longing toward envy. "Does the spirit that He has caused to dwell in us long enviously?"

(Laws, 176–79).[11] Thus, the unmentioned "God" or the "Spirit" is not the subject of the verb ἐπιποθεῖ, a verb that never takes God or the divine Spirit as its subject anywhere else in Scripture. It is important to note that the only other reference to "the spirit" in James is to the human spirit (2:26). Most all commentators agree that the adjunct phrase πρὸς φθόνον functions adverbially ("jealously" or "enviously").[12] Finally, if we remove from our thinking that this is a citation from Scripture, canonical or not, and read it as a question that expects a negative answer, the answer to the question would be as follows: "No, the spirit which God has caused to dwell in us (κατῴκισεν) does not long enviously." In other words, God did not create man this way, i.e., with a spirit that longs enviously.[13] This is because God is the source of only good (1:13–18).

But what is the scriptural origin of this "quotation"? What "Scripture," OT or otherwise, is its source? Laws suggests such passages as the LXX of Ps 83:3 or 40:2, but it is difficult to see the sentiment in 4:5 clearly expressed in those passages. I believe that the best approach is that ἡ γραφή in 4:5 is *not* referring to the words immediately following in the verse, but rather anticipates the clear scriptural quotation in 4:6. The thought proceeds as follows. Having disposed of the fact that Scripture does not speak "vainly" or "wrongly" in assigning envy to the spirit created within mankind, James now turns to what Scripture actually does say. This would better explain the contrastive δέ introducing 4:6a and the διὸ λέγει introducing 4:6b, which is not "he says" but "it says." The sense would be as follows:

---

[11] This view was also presented in an article by Laws, "Does Scripture speak in vain? A reconsideration of James iv.5," *NTS* 20 (1973–74) 210–15.

[12] The noun appears regularly in the "vice lists" of the NT (Rom 1:29; Gal 5:21; 1 Pet 2:1) and as the motive for the high priests in handing over Jesus (Matt 27:18). This militates against its being used for God's strong desire that is not necessarily evil (contra Blomberg-Kamell, 191).

[13] "Since James has Genesis 1–2 in view in James 3, this may also be the case here. If so, then it refers to God's creating humanity in his image—causing his breath (spirit) or animating principle to dwell in the body he formed" (Witherington, 2007, 514).

While Scripture does not say *this*—namely, 4:5b—it does say *this*—namely, 4:6b (Prov 3:34).

From the wider perspective of the book as a whole (i.e., the discourse), an additional rhetorical question like this fits better with the thrust of the diatribal style that James is using. James does away with any justification for the human conduct he is condemning and states that God offers not only an alternative to prideful self-seeking but also the grace to enable humble people to choose Him as their friend.[14]

4:6 μείζονα δὲ δίδωσιν χάριν; διὸ λέγει· ὁ θεὸς ὑπερηφάνοις ἀντιτάσσεται, ταπεινοῖς δὲ δίδωσιν χάριν: The difference between what he denies in 4:5 and what he affirms in 4:6 is strengthened by the δέ that contrasts the promise of God with what he has just denied (see comments on previous verse). Again, the sense of the verse would be: "On the other hand, He gives all the more grace" (μείζονα δὲ δίδωσιν χάριν). James already had in view the OT passage he quotes afterward from which these words are taken. The subject is the same as in the former sentence. The adjective μείζονα (comparative of μέγας) again contrasts the divine grace that follows with the worldly human attitude of the previous verse. This may, however, simply be a case of the Koine comparative form used for the positive ("great").

The quotation from the LXX of Prov 3:34 expands what he has affirmed and prepares the reader for what follows in 4:7–10. The first group, ὑπερηφάνοις ("proud ones"), is in the dative case and functions as the direct object of the verb "opposes" (ἀντιτάσσεται).[15] The second

---

[14] This interpretation is reflected in *Hermas* 28. The author there is urging his readers to love the truth "in order that the spirit which God caused to live (κατῴκισεν as in Jam 4:5) in this flesh may prove to be true." Later he states that we received in creation from the Lord an uncontaminated spirit (πνεῦμα). Both the thought and language of James are often reflected in *Hermas*. Thus, *Hermas* is an early witness to this interpretation of 4:5.

[15] Wallace, 142–44. The special cataphoric role of this same verb plus dative of direct object in 5:6 (οὐκ ἀντιτάσσεται ὑμῖν;) will be explained in the commentary on that verse.

group, ταπεινοῖς ("humble ones"), is the more common dative of indirect object. The lack of definite articles before each of the substantives (like the LXX but different from the MT; see Muraoka, 670) denotes not "the proud" and "the humble" as classes of people, but as a characteristic of anyone who can be one but become the other, which the following call to humility in 4:7–10 makes clear. The same ideas are found in Job 22:29 with the cognate verbs: "Because He has humbled (ἐταπείνωσεν) him, you will say, 'He has behaved proudly (ὑπερηφανεύσατο), but He will save the lowly.'"

Previously, we mentioned that this quotation from Prov 3:34 functions as a "structural lynchpin" for the entire paragraph of 4:1–10. Edgar explains both its anaphoric and cataphoric functions:

> The first line of the quotation 'God opposes the arrogant' looks back to the enemies of God, who stand over against God at the climax of vv. 1–4, while the second line of the quotation 'but to the lowly (ταπεινοῖς) he gives grace' anticipates the following verses, which culminate in the command: 'Humble yourselves (ταπεινώθητε) before the Lord and he will exalt you' (Edgar, 187).

More will be said about the comparison and the contrast that exists between 4:1–3 and 4:7–10 in the following section. Thus far the message conveyed by the intertexture of 4:4–6 has been plainly conveyed. That message is that arrogant and proud people do not acknowledge their dependence on God but choose to live according to the order of the world and as enemies of God. By contrast, God gives grace to lowly people (ταπεινοί) who are acknowledging their dependence on God.[16]

---

[16] That Jas 4:4–6 is a sort of midrashic commentary on the account of Noah in Gen 6–8, see L. J. Prockter, "James 4:4–6: Midrash on Noah," *NTS* 35 (1989) 625–27. Prockter examines the rabbinic notion of the הָרָע יֵצֶר (*evil inclination*), which Noah resisted and experienced grace from above. The linguistic parallels between James and the LXX of Gen 6 are simply not as clear as Prockter desires them to be.

Because James desires not only to be a negative condemner of arrogance but also a positive encourager of humility, he wants to assure his readers of divine grace and forgiveness. Therefore, he turns from the subject of God's opposition to the idea of God's approval with the second line of this quotation. This is a general statement and we should not automatically connect it to the poor who are so often included among the "humble" in the book. Those people who align themselves with the poor in spirit are they who receive this grace.

Richard Bauckham has noted that in his only clear citations of OT Scripture, James actually uses the word γραφή (2:8 and 4:5). In each of these two passages James is also revealing his own hermeneutical keys to the two main sections of OT literature. "Thus Leviticus 19:18b serves as James' hermeneutical key to the Torah and Proverbs 3:34 serves as James' hermeneutical key to the wisdom literature" (Bauckham, 155). In the case of the Leviticus reference in 2:8, he also follows Jesus in recognizing this verse as the summary of the entire Torah. The Proverbs reference here in 4:6 expresses most neatly the theme of "reversal in status" that is also quite prominent in Jesus' teaching (e.g. Matt 5:3–6; 10:23, 25, 31, 33–34).

Additional Bibliography on James 4:1-6

Jeremias, J. "Jac 4:5: epipothei." ZNW 50 (1959) 137–38.

Johnson, L. T. "Friendship with the World/Friendship with God: A Study of Discipleship in James." In Discipleship in the New Testament, ed. F. Segovia, 166–83. Philadelphia: Fortress Press, 1985.

———. "James 3:13–4:10 and the Topos PERI PHTHONOU." NovT 25 (1983) 327–47.

Keener, C. S. "Friendship." Pages 380–88 in Dictionary of New Testament Background. Ed. C. A. Evans and S. E. Porter, 380–88. Downers Grove: InterVarsity Press, 2000.

Konstan, D. Friendship in the Classical World. Cambridge: Cambridge University Press, 1997.

Marcus, J. "The Evil Inclination in the Epistle of James." CBQ 44 (1982) 606–21.

Perkins, P. "James 3:16–4:3." Int 36 (1982) 283–87.

Schmitt, J. J. "You Adulteresses! The Image in James 4:4." NovT 28 (1986) 327–37.

Townsend, M. J. "James 4:1–4: A Warning against Zealotry?" ExpT 87 (1978–79) 211–13.

Divine Submission and Humility (4:7–10)

Introduction

This third section (4:7–10) of the larger paragraph (4:1–10) includes some stylistic links with the first section (4:1–3). These links highlight how the quotation in 4:6 looks both backward and forward, as previously noted. There were eleven second person plural present indicative verbs in 4:2–3, while 4:7–10 contain nine second person plural aorist imperatives, one third person singular imperative, and one future indicative verb expressing the fulfillment of the preceding commands. These structured sets of eleven clauses both compare and contrast the reproach of the beginning section in 4:1–3 with the call to repentance at its end in 4:7–10. This evident contrast between the two passages is emphasized stylistically by these changes in tense and mood.

Greek Text

7 ὑποτάγητε οὖν τῷ θεῷ, ἀντίστητε δὲ τῷ διαβόλῳ καὶ φεύξεται ἀφ' ὑμῶν, 8 ἐγγίσατε τῷ θεῷ καὶ ᵃἐγγιεῖ ὑμῖν. καθαρίσατε χεῖρας, ἁμαρτωλοί, καὶ ἁγνίσατε καρδίας, δίψυχοι. 9 ταλαιπωρήσατε καὶ πενθήσατε καὶ κλαύσατε. ὁ γέλως ὑμῶν εἰς πένθος ᵃμετατραπήτω καὶ ἡ χαρὰ εἰς κατήφειαν. 10 ταπεινώθητε ἐνώπιον ᵃκυρίου καὶ ὑψώσει ὑμᾶς.

Textual Notes

The textual variants in this section are few, none of which affect the translation or interpretation of the passage.

8, 9, 10.a The SBLGNT mentions only the change in form of the future ἐγγίσει to ἐγγιεῖ in 4:8, the change in spelling of μετατραπήτω to μεταστραφήτω in 4:9, and the addition of the article τοῦ to κυρίου in 4:10. Each of these variants is supported by the later Byzantine text.

Changes in NA28

4:10 NA27: ταπεινώθητε ἐνώπιον κυρίου καὶ ὑψώσει ὑμᾶς.

4:10 MAJ: Ταπεινώθητε ἐνώπιον <u>τοῦ</u> κυρίου, καὶ ὑψώσει ὑμᾶς.

4:10 NA28: ταπεινώθητε ἐνώπιον <u>τοῦ</u> κυρίου καὶ ὑψώσει ὑμᾶς.

NA28 now agrees with MAJ. SBLGNT, NIV, and THGNT follow NA27.

Translation

7 Therefore submit yourselves to God and resist the devil, and then he will flee from you. 8 Draw near to God and He will draw near to you. Cleanse your hands, you sinners, and purify your hearts, you double-minded. 9 Be wretched and mourn and weep. Your laughter must be turned to mourning and your joy to gloom. 10 Humble yourselves before the Lord, and He will exalt you.

Context

The clauses in James 4:7–10 are not best served by an overly detailed and atomistic linguistic examination of the individual words in each separate command, although some linguistic observations will be certainly offered. An aggregate approach to their overall meaning is especially important when we recognize that the clauses are not just eleven discrete elements to be seen in isolation from one another. This can be illustrated by the following analysis of their overall structure. Three couplets of imperatives (7b–9) are framed by two other imperatives dealing with submitting oneself to God (7a, 10), thus forming a fivefold structure.

4:7
ὑποτάγητε οὖν τῷ θεῷ,   IMPERATIVE 1

ἀντίστητε δὲ τῷ διαβόλῳ καὶ φεύξεται ἀφ' ὑμῶν,   IMPERATIVE 2

4:8
ἐγγίσατε τῷ θεῷ καὶ ἐγγιεῖ ὑμῖν.

καθαρίσατε χεῖρας, ἁμαρτωλοί,   IMPERATIVE 3

καὶ

ἁγνίσατε καρδίας, δίψυχοι.

4:9
ταλαιπωρήσατε καὶ πενθήσατε καὶ κλαύσατε.   IMPERATIVE 4

ὁ γέλως ὑμῶν εἰς πένθος μετατραπήτω

καὶ

ἡ χαρὰ εἰς κατήφειαν.

4:10
ταπεινώθητε ἐνώπιον κυρίου καὶ ὑψώσει ὑμᾶς.   IMPERATIVE 5

An inclusio frames the passage (IMPERATIVE 1: "submit to God" and IMPERATIVE 5: "be humbled before the Lord"). Often overlooked are the syntactic parallels that are also obvious in the three middle couplets. In the second couplet, a command is issued in regard to the devil and to God with a response in movement described in both, if the command is fulfilled (the devil flees and God draws near). In the third couplet, the focus is geared toward body parts (hands and hearts), which obviously are metonymies for actions and attitudes. The "sinners" and "double-minded" are the ones who are to receive the commands. In IMPERATIVE 4, the focus is on the inward repentance that should accompany such cleansing and purification. The imperatives mount up in a rhetorical effect that is heightened by the *homoioteleuton* of 4:9a (ταλαιπωρήσατε καὶ πενθήσατε καὶ κλαύσατε) and the ellipsis of 4:9c (omitting μετατραπήτω). The final imperative with its intertextual echo of a Jesus *logion* closing the parable of the Pharisee and the publican (Luke 18:14) affirms the eschatological reversal of status that is so often evident in the letter (1:12; 2:5; 5:1–6, 9) as well as in many other Jesus *logia* (Matt 5:3–10). The forgiveness of sins that results from such humble repentance and cleansing must also be viewed in the light of the "lynchpin quotation" from Prov 3:34.

A detailed examination of the individual words in a passage is, of course, necessary. That analysis is the important step of working a passage from the bottom up. Now that we have made an overall analysis from the top down, we can proceed to the lexical analysis.

Exegetical Comments

4:7 ὑποτάγητε οὖν τῷ θεῷ: The "therefore" (οὖν) clearly indicates that these fervent imperatives are intended to expound the Proverbs 3:34 text, a passage that evidently served a number of other Christian authors as well. The verb ὑποτάσσω (ὑποτάγητε is an aorist passive imperative) is regularly used of submission to human authority in the NT (Luke 2:51; Rom 13:1; Eph 5:22; Titus 2:9; 1 Pet 2:13), but only here and in Heb 12:9 is it used of submission to God. This exhortation is addressed to the ὑπερηφάνοις (the proud) in the previous verse. Because God resists (ἀντιτάσσω) them, they are to submit (ὑποτάσσω) to God. The idea is that of complete and humble submission that is patterned after the example of Jesus (1 Pet 2:21–25), even though He had no need to submit to God because of pride!

ἀντίστητε δὲ τῷ διαβόλῳ καὶ φεύξεται ἀφ' ὑμῶν: The next aorist imperative is from ἀνθίστημι, a verb that appears fourteen times in the NT, and is used of resisting individuals (Acts 6:10; 13:8; 2 Tim 4:15) and quite dramatically of Paul resisting Peter to his face (Gal 2:11). Previous similar exhortations referring to the devil's fleeing can be found in the *Testaments of the Twelve Patriarchs*, such as: ἐὰν οὖν καὶ ὑμεῖς ἐργάσησθε τὸ καλόν ὁ διάβολος <u>φεύξεται ἀφ' ὑμῶν</u> (*T. Naph.* 8.4); and ταῦτα καὶ ὑμεῖς, τέκνα μου, ποιεῖτε, καὶ πᾶν πνεῦμα τοῦ Βελίαρ <u>φεύξεται ἀφ' ὑμῶν</u> (*T. Iss.* 7.7). In these passages, however, good conduct is the means by which the devil is driven off. James sees resistance to the devil as only possible through submission to God and His will. This idea was a commonplace of early Christian thought. The clearest semantic parallel is the command to resist the devil in 1 Pet 5:9, where the quotation of Prov 3:34 also precedes the command (see also Eph 6:11–17). *Hermas* 48.2 is closer to James and may even reflect dependence on him: "He cannot oppress God's servants who hope in Him with all their heart. The devil can wrestle with them, but he cannot throw and pin them. So, if you resist him (ἐὰν οὖν ἀντισταθῆτε αὐτῷ), he will be defeated and will flee from you (φεύξεται ἀφ' ὑμῶν)."

James affirms that Satan is not omnipotent but human beings can resist him and when they do, he will then flee in the face of such resistance (see also 1 Pet 5:8–9). Jas 4:7, however, is the only place in the Bible where Satan is said to flee if he is resisted. James suggests that the ultimate source of personal evil is supernatural—that is, the devil (so also Matt 4:1–11; Luke 22:31; John 13:2, 27). There is no better example of resisting Satan than that of Jesus during His temptation in the wilderness. However, it was not inner strength in that case that led to the departure of Satan, but dependence on a word from God (Eph

6:18).

4:8 ἐγγίσατε τῷ θεῷ καὶ ἐγγιεῖ ὑμῖν: The aorist imperative ἐγγίσατε, from the common verb ἐγγίζω (forty-two times in NT), recalls the OT imagery by which Israel's relationship with God is expressed in terms of "approaching." At Mount Sinai, the people were told not to "approach" God (Exod 19:21), whereas the priests and Moses could "approach" the mountain (Exod 19:22; 24:2). The verse also promises God's reciprocal response, a divine action regarded as exceptional when Israel's God approached His people: "What great nation is there to whom their god approaches (ἐγγίζων) as the Lord our God does for all those who call upon Him?" (Deut 4:7; also Hos 12:7). Similarly, in the LXX of Zech 1:3 we find: "'Turn to Me and I will turn to you (ἐπιστρέψατε πρός με καὶ ἐπιστραφήσομαι πρὸς ὑμᾶς)' says the Lord." This OT idea of approaching God was reflected in Hellenistic Jewish authors like Philo (*Mig. Abr.* 11) and the *Testaments of the Twelve* (*T. Dan* 6.2: ἐγγίσατε τῷ θεῷ, "draw near to God"). In the NT, however, only the heavily Jewish James and Heb 7:19 contain this specific linguistic way of describing "approaching God."

καθαρίσατε χεῖρας, ἁμαρτωλοί, καὶ ἁγνίσατε καρδίας, δίψυχοι: The aorist imperatives continue, but now, for the first time, they are addressed to the ones who need the cleansing and purifying—namely, the sinners and double-minded. The economic use of words, with no personal pronouns (cleanse hands, purify hearts), heightens the intensity and provides balance amidst the flurry of the other imperatives. With each of these verbs James uses Jewish language associated with OT cultic purity (Exod 19:10; 30:17–21; Num 8:21; 19:12; 31:23). From ritual washing that fits one for cultic religious duties, which was familiar to NT readers (Mark 7:3), there emerged a figurative use of language, which can be seen in the OT in such texts as Isa 1:16; Job 17:9; and 22:30. The combination of both verbs in the LXX of Isa 66:17 (ἁγνιζόμενοι καὶ καθαριζόμενοι) provides James with an additional OT context that deals, as he does here, with moral purification. The washing of hands was a symbolic ritual indicating the cleansing away of old impurities. When James says "draw near to God," he is addressing Christians and is not suggesting that acceptance by God or initial salvation for the unbeliever can be achieved by following these steps. James speaks too often of God's grace that is both given and received to suggest some sort of works-exchange by these expressions. He is talking about reconciliation between a wandering believer and his Lord. James speaks of the "sinner" (ἁμαρτωλός) once more in 5:20 as one who needs to be turned from his erroneous way.

These verses also echo Ps 24:3–4: "Who shall ascend the hill of the Lord? And who shall stand in His holy place? Those who have clean hands and pure hearts, who do not lift up their hearts to what is false, and do not swear deceitfully." The heart is the seat of both one's affections and decisions (Gen 6:5; Deut 8:2). The "pure heart" is the symbol for one who is in a right relationship with God (Ps 50:1–12; see also Matt 5:8). This balance between the outward "hands" and the inward "hearts" sounds another clear note in James that has been seen a number of times thus far. The problems with mankind, and the solution to those problems, lie deep within the inner person, not simply in reforming their outward behavior.

4:9 ταλαιπωρήσατε καὶ πενθήσατε καὶ κλαύσατε: The next three aorist imperatives are all intransitive (with no direct objects needed) because it is obvious who is being addressed. The first verb, ταλαιπωρέω, often meant hardship and harsh labor (Josephus, *Ag. Ap.* 1.237), but together all three verbs are filled with meaning in the OT prophets. The first is a NT *hapax* that in the LXX often described Israel's response to catastrophes (Hos 10:2; Mic 2:4; Joel 1:10; Zech 11:2–3; Jer 4:13, 20; 9:18; 10:20; 12:12). The second, πενθέω, appears in the prophets for punishment on Israel for apostasy from the covenant with Yahweh (Amos 1:2; 8:8; Joel 1:9–10; Isa 24:4; 33:9; Jer 4:28; 14:2; Lam 1:4; Ezek 7:27). It is also used in the NT for general mourning (Mark 16:10; Luke 6:25; 2 Cor 12:21). The most striking NT parallel is Matt 5:4, "Blessed are those who mourn (οἱ πενθοῦντες), for they shall be comforted." The third imperative, from κλαίω, describes Israel's sorrow at Yahweh's punishment (Hos 12:5; Joel 1:5; 2:17; Isa 22:4; 30:19; Jer 8:12; 13:17; Lam 1:1). It is a common verb in the NT for crying, but its combination with the previous verb πενθέω to describe the repentance of David (2 Sam 19:1) illustrates the intensity and vividness of James' commands.

ὁ γέλως ὑμῶν εἰς πένθος μετατραπήτω καὶ ἡ χαρὰ εἰς κατήφειαν: For the final two commands, James shifts to a third person aorist imperative (μετατραπήτω) for each of the subjects (γέλως and χαρὰ), but this does not lessen the imperatival force of the verb. The switch is due to James' desire to express the need for the "laughter" and "joy" of the sinners to be transformed into outward actions that manifest inner repentance, "mourning," and "gloom" (κατήφεια, another hapax not appearing in the LXX, although often in Hellenistic literature, BDAG, 533). "It describes the condition of one with eyes cast down (κατ-) like the publican in Luke 18:13" (Mayor, 142). This is once more illustrative of James' love for the language of reversal (see Jas 1:9–11; 2:5).

   This behavior is not intended to be a description of how Christians must always be solemn or puritanical. An earlier interpretation of this verse was that it is a call to voluntary asceticism (Dibelius, 227, citing Erasmus and Grotius). The intransitive nature of ταλαιπωρέω, however, has to do with something that is endured, not something that is practiced. It refers rather to the conduct that accompanies genuine repentance and acknowledgment of sin (Huther, 187; Witherington, 2007, 515). Turning "joy into gloom" might appear strange in light of a command such as "rejoice in the Lord always" (Phil 4:4). But the joy Paul describes is that joyfulness that comes when one realizes that sins are forgiven. "True Christian joy can never be ours if we ignore or tolerate sin; it comes only when we have squarely faced the reality of our sin, brought it before the Lord in repentance and humility, and experienced the cleansing work of the Spirit" (Moo, 196).

   The performance of weeping and wailing is worthless in itself, for it is inward penitence that matters. If that is present, then weeping and wailing will take care of themselves. The move from laughter to weeping (4:9) must also be understood in the context of wisdom literature. Fools take delight in doing wrong and laughter is often the sound of sinful revelry (Prov 10:23). James is not suggesting that the righteous should go about in a state of morbid depression over their sins. If such people turn to God, they discover that those activities and objects that previously gave them joy are evidence of the distance that separated them from God. An appropriate balance must be sought.

4:10 ταπεινώθητε ἐνώπιον κυρίου καὶ ὑψώσει ὑμᾶς: As was mentioned, this verse serves with 4:7 as an inclusio to the entire paragraph. We are to submit to God in 4:7 and then to be humbled before Him in 4:10. James picks up the reference in 4:6 to the "humble" (ταπεινοῖς) receiving divine grace by exhorting us in 4:10 to "be humbled" (ταπεινώθητε) before the Lord. This clearly indicates that their self-humbling will lead to God's lifting them up, but the converse follows if someone exalts themselves. This idea found previous expressions in Job 5:11: "He who makes the humble ones exalted (τὸν ποιοῦντα ταπεινοὺς εἰς ὕψος). It is better to see here echoes of such dominical sayings as Luke 6:25 (laughter turned to weeping) and 14:11 (the humbled being exalted). Peter is also probably indebted with his same quotation from Prov 3:34 in 1 Pet 5:5, which is also followed by the exhortation: "Humble yourselves therefore, under God's mighty hand, that he may lift you up in due time."

The ultimate outcome of the present time of repentance and suffering will be glory, but the exaltation promised to those who are humbled is not a lofty perch from which they can look down on others. It is the position of grace that James has described thus far as the undivided life. Perhaps that exalted position can be summarized by Jam 3:13: "Who is wise and understanding among you? He should show from his good life the deeds done in the gentleness of wisdom."

How can we best summarize the teaching of Jas 4:7–10? The core of this passage is repentance, and not many would disagree with that assessment. What is striking, however, about how James describes repentance is that he never uses the Greek word μετάνοια. Yet the passage succinctly describes repentance with an economy of words. What are its chief features? Scot McKnight answers that question as follows.

> First, repentance is about a person's relationship, mind, and behaviors before God: it is profoundly theological. This is why this section begins and ends with the face of God (4:7, 8a, 10). Second, repentance leads to forgiveness that can be described in terms of purification (4:8b). Third, repentance is both embodied and emotive—as 4:9 makes clear. And, fourth, repentance leads to grace that elevates a person not into envy but into peacemaking, love, and compassionate deeds (4:10) (McKnight, 358).

10

SPEECH ETHICS CONTINUED (4:11-12)

Greek Text

11 Μὴ καταλαλεῖτε ἀλλήλων, ἀδελφοί. ὁ καταλαλῶν ἀδελφοῦ ἢ κρίνων τὸν ἀδελφὸν αὐτοῦ καταλαλεῖ νόμου καὶ κρίνει νόμον· εἰ δὲ νόμον κρίνεις, οὐκ εἶ ποιητὴς νόμου ἀλλὰ κριτής. 12 εἷς ἐστιν [ὁ] νομοθέτης καὶ κριτὴς ὁ δυνάμενος σῶσαι καὶ ἀπολέσαι· σὺ δὲ τίς εἶ ᵃὁ κρίνων τὸν πλησίον;

Textual Notes

12.a. The only significant variant reading is in the closing question at the end of 4:12: σὺ δὲ τίς εἶ ὁ κρίνων τὸν πλησίον; evidently some later Byzantine scribes were uncomfortable with the syntax of the question which involved a "right dislocation" of the final clause (see the later analysis for an explanation of this construction). They substituted ὃς κρίνεις for the ὁ κρίνων represented in the earlier Alexandrian and Western manuscripts.

SBLGNT, NA28, and NIV omit the [ὁ] before νομοθέτης. THGNT retains it without brackets.

Translation

11 Do not slander each other, brothers. The one who slanders a brother or condemns his brother, slanders the law and condemns the law. But if you condemn the law, you are not a doer of the law but a judge. 12 The lawgiver and judge is one, the one who is able to save and to destroy. But who are you, you who are condemning your neighbor?

Introduction

The relationship between these two verses and the rest of the chapter and the book as a whole has not always been evident to commentators. More than one commentator has described it as a sort of free-floating admonition (Ropes, 273; Dibelius, 228). One reason for the apparent disjunction with their context is the more tender address directed to the ἀδελφοί (4:11) in the middle of a diatribal/condemnatory section (4:1–5:6), marked by a questioning about wars among you (4:1) with its subsequent harsh charges (4:2–4) plus the following strong condemnations in 4:13–17 and 5:1–6, each of which is initiated by the direct "come now" (ἄγε νῦν) imperatives. Verbal and semantic connections with what precedes, however, are not totally absent. For example, the sin that is condemned in 4:11–12, namely sinful slander, can be viewed as simply an outward result of those selfish motives that are the actual causes of those conflicts and divisions that are so strongly condemned in 4:1–3. While the passage does begin with an address to the "brothers," the exhortation is still quite a strong one, since it declares that the slanderer places himself at God's level and His law rather than submitting to both. How then and why does James combine this affectionate address with such a stern warning about slander?

Exegetical Comments

4:11 Μὴ καταλαλεῖτε ἀλλήλων, ἀδελφοί: The combination of a nominative of address (ἀδελφοί) with an imperative (καταλαλεῖτε) does indicate a new paragraph. I believe that there is a discernible reason that James carefully chooses the word ἀδελφοί at this point. He does employ the singular ἀδελφοῦ/όν twice in the very next clause, thus heightening the seriousness of the brothers' slanderous talk. Therefore, the slander that he condemns is not speech directed toward those who are outside the community, but it is speech that slanders other believers within the community of faith. This recognition provides the paragraph with a link to its previous context and also makes it distinct in its more specific application among brothers and sisters who share "the faith of Jesus" (2:1). Finally, the brief paragraph picks up again the prominent theme of speech ethics, which has been stressed in some of the earlier sections (1:26, 3:1–12). What is unique here is that James adds a specific concern about slanderous speech, which is the primary subject he addresses in 4:11–12.

The verb καταλαλέω in Classical writers has the sense of "speak against, to accuse, someone," with a suggestion of the false or exaggerated sense of "calumniate" (Polybius, *Hist.* 3, 90, 6). The word is not, however, very common in secular usage. Along with its cognate καταλαλιά, it does not occur at all in Josephus, and in Philo it is found only in two passages influenced by biblical usage: *Leg. All.* 3.66: Miriam κατελάλει Μωυσῆ, based on LXX Num 12:8; and in the same work (78) as a quotation from the LXX of Num 21:7. In the LXX καταλαλέω mostly (nine times) bears the emphasis on the hostility toward whoever is denoted by the prefixed preposition κατα-, whether against God (Num 21:5, 7; Hos 7:13; Mal 3:13); his servant Moses (Num 12:8), or frequently one's neighbor (Ps 49:20; 100:5; Prov 20:13). In the first instances the essential element in the hostility is contradiction and rejection, whereas in καταλαλεῖν κατὰ τοῦ ἀδελφοῦ the main idea is malice and slander. This sense of speaking evil against one's neighbor is the only sense conveyed by the cognate noun and adjective καταλαλιά ("slander"), and appears this way in the biblically influenced admonition of Wis 1:11: "Beware of useless grumbling, and keep your tongue from slander (καταλαλίας)."

The verb καταλαλέω appears three times in Jam 4:11, and in light of the LXX and Hellenistic usage, is best rendered as "to slander" rather than by the more generic translation, "speak against" (ASV, NET, NASB). This latter translation reflects an overly mechanical transference of the verb's component parts (κατα and λαλέω), and may be guilty of what has been called the "root fallacy."[1] The rendering "speak evil" in other translations like the AV, ESV, and NRSV is better, while the CSB uses "criticize." Only translations like the NIV and the NJB convey accurately the semantics of the word group by their "do not slander."[2] A person may actually speak against someone else or even criticize them and still speak the truth and not engage in slander. James himself, throughout his letter, is certainly *speaking against* his readers through his many pointed admonitions! The sin that is being condemned in 4:11, however, is the kind of speech that is both inaccurate and also damaging to someone's character and reputation ("bearing false witness"). The usage of the cognate noun elsewhere in the NT (1 Pet 2:1) and also in the Apostolic Fathers (*1 Clem.* 30.1–3; *Hermas* 27) further supports the rendering of the verb here as "to slander."

A negated present imperative (like μὴ καταλαλεῖτε) appears nine times elsewhere in James (1:7, 16, 22; 2:1; 3:1, 14 [2]; 5:9, 12). Some grammarians and commentators have taught that a negated present imperative commands the ceasing of an action that is already in progress. This approach is usually accompanied by the idea that a negated aorist imperative conveys the idea that the prohibited action should never even begin to take place.[3] The ceasing of an action that is already in progress is *not* the nature of the action addressed by the use of a negated present tense imperative. While this *could* be the case,

---

[1] The "root fallacy" is the practice of drawing a word's meaning from its component roots, rather than from its actual usage. D.A. Carson, *Exegetical Fallacies* (Grand Rapids: Baker Academic, 1996), 28–33.

[2] The word group includes the noun καταλαλία which expresses the more focused idea of "slander" (2 Cor 12:20). Both L-N, 433 and BDAG, 519, indicate "slander" as a meaning of both verb and noun.

[3] H. E. Dana and J. R. Mantey, *A Manual Grammar of the Greek New Testament* (Toronto: Macmillan, 1927), 301–02, is representative of this traditional view. See Wallace, 714–17 for an excellent critique of this older view.

such a kind of action (*aktionsart*) should be determined only from a close examination of the context in which the command is found. A better approach to this subject is in recognizing that the present tense of the imperative mood is intended to convey a general rather than a more specific prohibition. In the case of 4:11, therefore, it is the *practice* of slander that is forbidden (Porter, *Idioms*, 225). Further reflection on the specific use of imperatives by James reveals that when he does employ an aorist imperative, it is always accompanied by an adjunct expression that indicates the time of the command, or its reason, or its result (1:2; 21; 4:7–10; 5:1, 7, 8, 10). When James does employ a present imperative, the command is more general and the specifics of time or result or reasons will follow only in subsequent comments about that command (2:1, 12; 4:11; 5:9, 12). This approach to verbal aspect can also caution an interpreter from assuming that some sort of "mirror hermeneutic" is at work—namely, that the author is aware that a specific sin or behavior is prevalent among the community being addressed. Furthermore, the general nature of this letter as an "encyclical" also suggests that this is a general rather than a specific exhortation.

ὁ καταλαλῶν ἀδελφοῦ ἢ κρίνων τὸν ἀδελφὸν αὐτοῦ καταλαλεῖ νόμου καὶ κρίνει νόμον: In these clauses, the topic of slander is expounded and expanded by relating it to the semantic field of the words κρίνω/κριτής. These words appear six times in 4:11b, 12. The area of meaning of this word group includes the idea of "condemn." This meaning fits here and also is demanded by the use of the verb in 5:9 and the noun in 5:12. In both these appearances, the context indicates that it is an eschatological condemnation that is implied (L-N, 56.28, 30). Because the English verb "to judge" can also result in a judgment of "innocent," I suggest that the word "condemn" more accurately conveys the meaning of the action described here that always results in the judgment of "guilty." It is the attitude that is always condemning a brother that is forbidden here. "The Christian community also needed the unity which slander destroyed, so among Christians it also comes up frequently in vice lists (Rom 1:30; 2 Cor 12:20; 1 Pet 2:1; 2 Pet 2:12;

3:16; *1 Clem.* 30.1–3, which uses Prov 3:34 in the context; *Hermas* 27, with ἁπλότης; 38; *Sim.* 8.7.2, with δίψυχος; 9.23.2–3)" (Davids, 169).

As can be seen in the following sentence flow analysis of 4:11, the subject of the compound clause that ends the verse is "the one who slanders (ὁ καταλαλῶν) a brother or condemns (ὁ ... κρίνων) his brother."

ὁ καταλαλῶν ἀδελφοῦ

ἤ

κρίνων τὸν ἀδελφὸν αὐτοῦ   (Subjects)

καταλαλεῖ νόμου

καὶ

κρίνει νόμον·   (Predicates)

He who slanders and condemns his brother is the one who also "slanders (καταλαλεῖ) the law and condemns (κρίνει) the law." The person who deliberately breaks a law and does not repent thus slanders that law and also disrespects that law, since it is the essence of a law to require obedience, and he who refuses obedience, in effect, says it ought not to be a law. Thus the one who slanders a brother, in effect, also slanders the law. The law which the writer has in mind is certainly the "royal law of brotherhood" mentioned in 2:8, to which reference is also made by the word πλησίον in 4:12. This offense against a brother/neighbor is also an offense against God (see the comments on 3:9, as well as Prov 17:5, Ps 12:4; Matt 25:42–45; and 1 John 4:20).

The fact that "law" (νόμος) remains anarthrous (without an article) throughout this section suggests that James is speaking qualitatively here, seeing God's will *as* law. Indeed, instead of thinking of Torah by itself, he may be referring to the Torah as fulfilled in Jesus the Messiah, the gospel message, and the new covenant as the (qualitatively) royal law. This is the sense also of a previous reference to "law" in 2:8–13 (see Blomberg-Kamell, 158).

εἰ δὲ νόμον κρίνεις, οὐκ εἶ ποιητὴς νόμου ἀλλὰ κριτής: The verse ends with a first class conditional sentence. The use of the noun κριτής (judge) in the apodosis of the conditional clause may argue against my earlier suggestion about rendering its cognate verb as "to condemn" rather than the dominant translation of "to judge." But this is only a problem in English, since there does not exist, at least not widely used, a suitable English word like "condemner." Greek speakers would immediately link the similar semantic concept of "condemning" that is inherent in both the verb and the noun. The idea of "judging" here is not the action of "rendering an opinion." The more specific practice within the semantic field—namely, "condemning"—is the action that is forbidden by this passage. The irony involved is biting. We who should stand condemned by the law actually end up condemning the law when we utter slanderous speech! The conditional sentence actually declares (which is one rhetorical function of conditional sentences) that the person who condemns both his brother and the law becomes no longer a "doer" (ποιητὴς) of the law[4] but becomes a judge (κριτής) of the law. This hypothetical "judge" performs the ironic role of condemning the very law that he is supposed to uphold!

4:12 εἷς ἐστιν ὁ νομοθέτης καὶ κριτὴς ὁ δυνάμενος σῶσαι καὶ ἀπολέσαι, "The lawgiver and judge is one, the one who is able to save and to destroy." σὺ δὲ τίς εἶ ὁ κρίνων τὸν πλησίον;, "But who are you, you who are condemning your neighbor?" The first sentence of 4:12 is a declarative clause, while the second sentence in the verse is an interrogative clause. Both of them contain an embedded clause that is in apposition to the subject of the sentence (ὁ νομοθέτης and σύ). These clauses can be described as *dislocated*, because they each appear at the end of

---

[4] The expression involves a head noun (ποιητής) and a genitive functioning as its direct object (νόμου). See this earlier use of this construction in 1:25 (ποιητὴς ἔργου). For further explanation of the "objective genitive," see Wallace, 116–19.

their respective sentences.[5] A sentence flow display can better clarify this structure.

The lawgiver and judge is one,	he who is able to save and to destroy.
εἷς ἐστιν ὁ νομοθέτης καὶ κριτὴς	ὁ δυνάμενος σῶσαι καὶ ἀπολέσαι.

But who are you,	you who are condemning your neighbor?
σὺ δὲ τίς εἶ	ὁ κρίνων τὸν πλησίον;

These substantival participles (ὁ δυνάμενος and ὁ κρίνων) further define the subjects that are expressed earlier in each sentence. In any translation of the first sentence, it is important to maintain the order of the Greek words, in which the numerical adjective εἷς precedes the copula ἐστιν. A translation like "there is one lawgiver and judge" misses the significance of the order. The rendering "the lawgiver and judge is one" is better. By respecting the word order, the oneness of the lawgiver and judge is brought to a prominent position in 4:12a. It also clearly reflects the structure of Deut 6:4, the Torah statement which this verse undoubtedly echoes. "Hear O, Israel, the Lord our God, the Lord is one." The LXX rendering of the "Shema" also locates the numerical adjective before the verb (κύριος εἷς ἐστιν). Therefore, this order would be readily recognizable to a Jewish reader/hearer.

This specific title ("able to save and destroy") is not found in the OT. However, it is often stated throughout the OT that God is able to save (σῶσαι) His people (LXX Deut 33:29; Judg 2:16; 3:9; 6:14; 1 Sam 4:3; Pss 3:8; Isa 19:20; 33:2; Jer 15:20; 26:27; Zech 9:16) and that He is also able to destroy (ἀπολέσαι) them (Exod 19:24; Lev 17:10; Num 14:12; Deut 2:12, 21; Josh 24:10; Pss 5:7; 9:6; Isa 1:25; Jer 25:10; 26:8; Ezek 25:7, 16). The point of this last statement is that because there is only one who can "save and destroy," there can be only one judge of divine law who in this way carries out the sanctions of His own divine law.

---

[5] For the terminology and function of "left dislocations," along with additional examples, see Runge, *Discourse Grammar*, 287–313.

σὺ δὲ τίς εἶ ὁ κρίνων τὸν πλησίον; The last question (σὺ δὲ τίς εἶ) expresses and also advances the diatribal challenge that pulses throughout this passage. The question finds its closest verbal parallel in Rom 14:4: "You who are judging another man's servant, who are you?" The switch from condemning the "brother" (ἀδελφόν) in 4:11 to the condemning of the "neighbor" (πλησίον) at the end of 4:12 is another deliberate echo of the love command delivered in Lev 19:18. This allusion also evokes the surrounding context of Lev 19:11–18 in which the "neighbor" (πλησίον) is mentioned no less than six times.[6] James' desire, however, is to filter his use of Lev 19 through the very same love command cited by Jesus in Matt 22:39. Therefore, his use of Lev 19 here also echoes his use of the same passage in 2:8, where his purpose was to condemn the practice of partiality shown to the rich during gatherings in one's synagogue. The surrounding context of Jam 2:8–13 shares many verbal links with 4:11, 12, especially in its handling of various statements about the Torah (νόμος in 2:8, 9, 10, 11, 12).[7]

This is another example supporting the idea that James' various references to the law/Torah function in a similar way. When he refers to the law, there are different descriptors that convey careful nuances about that specific law (law of liberty, royal law, etc.). This "law" is the one delivered through Moses, but it is also the same law as it was understood, expounded, and applied through Jesus. When this unity is recognized, therefore, it is proper to also recognize in these references to slandering and condemning a brother another probable allusion to the Jesus-saying found in Matt 7:1, 2: "Do not condemn (κρίνετε), that you be not condemned (κριθῆτε). For with the condemnation you condemn you will be condemned (κρίματι κρίνετε κριθήσεσθε), and with the measure you use it will be measured to you."[8]

---

[6] See again the seminal article by L. T. Johnson, "The Use of Leviticus 19 in the Letter of James" *JBL* 101 (1982) 391–401.

[7] M. E. Taylor, *A Text-Linguistic Investigation into the Discourse Structure of James* (JSNTSup 311; London: T&T Clark, 2006), 109–11.

[8] For a good treatment of the use of the OT in James 4 and also throughout the book, see Carson, "James," 997–1013. See also the perceptive comments on the Jewish/OT background of this passage in McKnight, 362–65.

11

DO NOT PLAN PRESUMPTUOUSLY (4:13-17)

Greek Text

13 Ἄγε νῦν οἱ λέγοντες· σήμερον ἢ αὔριον πορευσόμεθα εἰς τήνδε τὴν πόλιν καὶ ποιήσομεν ἐκεῖ ἐνιαυτὸν καὶ ἐμπορευσόμεθα καὶ κερδήσομεν·14 οἵτινες οὐκ ἐπίστασθε ᵃτὸ τῆς αὔριον ᵇποία ἡ ζωὴ ὑμῶν· ᶜἀτμὶς γάρ ἐστε ἡ πρὸς ὀλίγον φαινομένη, ἔπειτα καὶ ἀφανιζομένη. 15 ἀντὶ τοῦ λέγειν ὑμᾶς· ἐὰν ὁ κύριος θελήσῃ καὶ ζήσομεν καὶ ποιήσομεν τοῦτο ἢ ἐκεῖνο. 16 νῦν δὲ καυχᾶσθε ἐν ταῖς ἀλαζονείαις ὑμῶν· πᾶσα καύχησις τοιαύτη πονηρά ἐστιν. 17 εἰδότι οὖν καλὸν ποιεῖν καὶ μὴ ποιοῦντι, ἁμαρτία αὐτῷ ἐστιν.

Textual Notes

Because of the quite difficult syntax in this passage, we should expect that variant readings might arise, embodying scribal attempts at smoothing out some of those difficulties. Metzger mentions three that particularly stand out in 4:14. I summarize the evidence for three readings which he defends in the UBS⁴/NA²⁷ text as follows.

14.a. Of several readings, τα της αυριον, though supported by several good witnesses (A P 33 81), is suspect as a scribal assimilation to Proverbs 27:1; and, in view of a certain tendency of B to omit the article, the reading τῆς αὔριον cannot be confidently regarded as original. The remaining reading, τὸ τῆς αὔριον, is supported by a wide diversity of witnesses (א K Ψ most minuscules vg syr^p arm).

14.b. Although the reading with γαρ is widespread (P^74 א^2 A K L P most minuscules vg syr cop), the conjunction appears to have been inserted in order to prevent ambiguity (ποία may introduce an independent question, or may depend upon ἐπίστασθε). The reading ποία is adequately supported by א* B 614 syr cop^ms.

14.c. The conjunction γάρ could be read as interrupting the sense after a preceding question, so it was omitted in A and 33. Several important manuscripts (B 1739) lack the article, so it could be that scribes would accidentally omit ἡ rather than add it. In ancient Greek αι and ε were often pronounced alike, so either ἔσται or ἔστε may have originated through an itacistic corruption of the other. The manuscript evidence for the two together far outweighs those that support εστιν. Not only does external evidence on the whole favor the second person ἔστε, but it is also probable that copyists tended to favor the third person ἔσται in the reply to a question.

Translation

13 Now listen, you who say, "Today or tomorrow we will go into such and such a city and spend a year there and trade and make a profit." 14 Actually you do not know what will happen tomorrow. What is your life? For you are a puff of smoke that appears for a little while and then vanishes. 15 Instead you ought to say, "If the Lord wills, we will live and do this or that." 16 But now you boast so arrogantly. All such arrogant boastings are evil. 17 Therefore, whoever knows the right thing to do and fails to do it, for him it is sin.

Introduction

Some commentators describe this passage as bursting uninvited onto the scene. "There is no connection between this passage and the preceding series of imperatives" (Dibelius, 230). However, a very real connection to the context can be discerned. The thought of one's own weakness and ignorance ought to keep a person from judging his fellows and thus finding fault with the law (4:11–12). This concern should also prevent him from declaring bold and confident assertions as to his future (4:13–17). The passage, however, is more directly related to the following paragraph due to their identical openings (Ἄγε νῦν 4:13; 5:1). Moreover, these sections are semantically connected also by the topic of wealth. To be sure, those strongly admonished in 4:13–17 are not explicitly said to be "rich," but their extensive travel plans mentioned in 4:13 imply that they are well-off, and their expressed intention certainly is to "make money." Both paragraphs, 4:13–17 and 5:1–6, do not condemn wealth as such, but they do criticize "people of the world" for simply leaving God and His values (heavenly wisdom) out of their course of life. However, while the rich in 5:1–6 are condemned, the merchants in 4:13–17 are exhorted to change their attitudes. It is not their wealth that James criticizes, but their boastful presumption.

The greatest interpretive challenge in 4:13–17 is not discovering its overall meaning, which is the foolishness of making confident plans apart from unforeseen circumstances. The vivid portrayal of "merchants" whose plans are altered by unknown developments can be appreciated even by unbelievers. The challenge to the interpreter is exactly how that topic is conveyed syntactically through clauses which are strangely complex in their structure. What is James attempting to do with his choice of words here, and how does his language function to fulfill his intended purpose?

Exegetical Comments

4:13 Ἄγε νῦν οἱ λέγοντες: The expression Ἄγε νῦν was found in Greek literature as far back as Homer (*Il.* 3.441) and was effectively used by the diatribal moralists (e.g., Epictetus, *Diatrib.* 3.24.40). While this exact expression here and in 5:1 does not appear elsewhere in the

Greek Bible, a similar use of the imperative verb alone can be seen in the B manuscript of Judg 19:6 (Ἄγε δὴ) and also in Isa 43:6 (Ἄγε καὶ). Every interpreter recognizes that a new paragraph has begun with this special expression. But even in this case, there is a difference because after he addresses "those of you who say" (οἱ λέγοντες) and mentions what they say (σήμερον ἢ αὔριον ... κερδήσομεν), he does not clearly issue a command like he does later with οἱ πλούσιοι in 5:1 (κλαύσατε ὀλολύζοντες ... "weep and wail"). While ἄγε is certainly an imperative (second person singular of ἄγω), it is "frozen grammatically as a particle" that derives its meaning by whatever verb that follows, as is the case of the imperative κλαύσατε following it in 5:1 (Dibelius, 231). Yet no such verb appears in the reported speech of 4:13b. This "anacoluthon" (BDAG, 9) is only the first of the grammatical anomalies in this passage. The overall message, however, is not hindered by James' apparent departure from grammatical strictness. After this "attention getter" or "orienter" that opens 4:13, James follows up with a challenging question in 4:14. Modern Bible readers forget the "orality" of ancient texts that for more than fifteen hundred years were read out to congregations more often than they were read by individuals in the audience. When we recognize this, we can understand how this makes perfect sense as an arresting message. We would never question the grammar of a speaker who exhorted a congregation in this manner.

Another grammatical anomaly lies in the fact that following the *singular* imperatives in both 4:13 and 5:1 there are nominative *plural* substantives (οἱ λέγοντες and οἱ πλούσιοι). As mentioned above, the frozen imperative Ἄγε νῦν serves more of a rhetorical rather than a temporal function, despite the νῦν. This explains, therefore, the role of the plurals and the parenthetic nominatives in both verses.[1] Therefore, a literal translation like "Come now" does not clearly communicate the urgency of the expression. The NIV captures the rhetoric nicely, "Now listen, you who say ..."

---

[1] See BDF, 80, for explanations of both of these grammatical terms. For the "parenthetic nominative," see Wallace, 53–54. More will be said about the function of this "orienter" (Ἄγε νῦν) in the comments on its use in 5:1.

σήμερον ἢ αὔριον πορευσόμεθα εἰς τήνδε τὴν πόλιν καὶ ποιήσομεν ἐκεῖ ἐνιαυτὸν καὶ ἐμπορευσόμεθα καὶ κερδήσομεν: After fixing on a launch date for his business venture, "today or tomorrow," the confident businessman lays out his future agenda by four important future verbs. The sentence flow analysis displays clearly the parallelism:

σήμερον ἢ αὔριον

πορευσόμεθα εἰς τήνδε τὴν πόλιν

καὶ

ποιήσομεν ἐκεῖ ἐνιαυτὸν

καὶ

ἐμπορευσόμεθα

καὶ

κερδήσομεν·

Some manuscripts change the mood of the verbs from the indicative to the subjunctive in order to convey a more hortatory intention: "Let us go ... let us spend ... let us make sales ... let us make a profit." In each case, however, the simple future indicative is better attested by older manuscripts. "One could also argue that the future indicative better expresses the fatuous sense of certainty implied by the speech" (Johnson, 295).

The picture that James draws is quite consistent with the mercantile society of the first-century Hellenistic world, which included Judea, Galilee, the Decapolis, and the surrounding areas.[2] Many Jews were quite active in these types of business enterprises, for large numbers had settled in cities throughout the Mediterranean world just for these very commercial reasons. "Let us go to such and such a city." The phrase εἰς τήνδε τὴν πόλιν ("into such and such a city") does not indicate that the merchants are targeting some specific well-known example, but neither is this a purely hypothetical example. James knows that even believing businessmen are not immune to this temptation to presumption. Some commentators have argued that the people addressed here are non-believers, usually from the parallel with those condemned in 5:1–6. But the rich condemned there face only judgment, while those here are offered an opportunity to change (4:15–17). The problem is the same one described in the parable of the rich fool in Luke 12:16–21, which may very well supply the background for this warning. The merchant forgets that his times are in God's hands, and seems oblivious to what God's will might be in regard to the details of his "going" and "doing." He works on the assumption that he can accomplish what he intends and he does not expect death or any other obstacle to stop him. He has the time and places all set and he does not think at all of how God might regard his plans. It is not that these people are engaged in a sinful or "secular" occupation. Their business may be entirely legitimate. "It is not their occupation, but their attitude, that has become secular" (Blomberg-Kamell, 207).

4:14 οἵτινες οὐκ ἐπίστασθε τὸ τῆς αὔριον ποία ἡ ζωὴ ὑμῶν· ἀτμὶς γάρ ἐστε ἡ πρὸς ὀλίγον φαινομένη, ἔπειτα καὶ ἀφανιζομένη: The anacoluthon in 4:14 consists of a secondary relative clause (οἵτινες οὐκ ἐπίστασθε τὸ τῆς αὔριον), then a question (ποία ἡ ζωὴ ὑμῶν), and finally a causal statement of why their boastful planning is wrong (ἀτμὶς γάρ ἐστε ... ἀφανιζομένη). Compounding the syntactical problem is the fact that the critical Greek texts punctuate 4:14a as an initial declarative clause,

---

[2] See M. Hengel, *Judaism and Hellenism: Studies in Their Encounter in Palestine during the Early Hellenistic Period* (trans. John Bowden Philadelphia: Fortress Press, 1974), 32–57.

ending just before the ἀτμίς. Thus it is translated this way by some versions as: "You do not know what your life will be tomorrow" (NASB, NLT). This creates some serious grammatical problems, however, because the required punctuation takes the interrogative pronoun as the object or complement of the verb even though it is in the nominative case (ἡ ζωή). In its thirty-four other NT occurrences, ποῖος almost always is either the subject of an interrogative clause or serves as an adjunct within such a clause. Matt 24:42 is the only verse where ποῖος is in the nominative case as a completer to an indicative verb. Its function here, therefore, is most probably as the initial inquiring in a question that follows the first clause.[3]

The following sentence flow illustrates this approach to the four clauses in 4:14:

οἵτινες οὐκ ἐπίστασθε τὸ τῆς αὔριον.   CHARGE

ποία ἡ ζωὴ ὑμῶν;   RHETORICAL QUESTION

ἀτμὶς γάρ ἐστε ἡ πρὸς ὀλίγον φαινομένη,   REASON

ἔπειτα καὶ ἀφανιζομένη.

The presence of a γάρ in the final statement that concludes the verse may appear to be a bit strange since we would not normally expect an answer to a question to begin with a causal conjunction. Perhaps we should recognize the rhetorical force of the question being asked, "What is your life?" as communicating sarcasm in its implied answer. The sense of the entire construction, therefore, would be as follows: "What is your life, really?" Then the explanation for the emptiness of such a life would be: "For your life is only a puff of smoke ..." This would deliver a powerful rhetorical punch. It is seen now, but

---

[3] As many versions take it (KJV, with a slight textual difference, and RSV, NRSV, NIV, ESV, NET, CEB).

soon will disappear forever. The word ἀτμίς denotes a swirl of smoke arising from a fire (Gen 19:28; Lev 16:13; Ezek 8:11).

Intertextual echoes from other Scriptures abound in this verse for those hearers whose ears are sensitive enough to hear them. Too much attention has been paid to the supposed links between James and the Greco-Roman ethical traditions. While it is obvious that parallel ideas can certainly be found, we should not automatically conclude that Greco-Roman writers are the sources for James's expressions. Consider, for example, what looks like a near parallel from another first-century writer. "Nobody knows what will be after tomorrow or after one hour. Death is heedless of mortals, and the future is uncertain" (Pseudo-Phocylides, *Sent.* 116–17). The context and purpose of both quotations, however, is different. "Here (i.e., in Phocylides) the saying is the motivation for the following admonition, 'Do not let evils dismay you nor exult in success.' In James 4 the saying grounds the concluding admonition addressed to social relationships of 4:13."[4]

There is no need, however, to conclude that James is consciously borrowing from these sources. There are many additional verbal and semantic links that his ethical advice shares with canonical wisdom literature and also with the sayings of Jesus. In this passage, for example, one can detect clearly an echo from Prov 27:1: "Don't boast [καυχῶ] about tomorrow [αὔριον], for you do not know [γινώσκεις] what the next day may bring forth." Hos 13:3 says that idolaters "shall be like the morning mist, or like the dew that goes away early." Yet these entrepreneurs were planning as if they were going to be here forever!

Consider also Jesus' teaching about the prosperous land owner:

> And he said, "I will do this: I will tear down my barns and build larger ones, and there I will store all my grain and my goods. And I will say to my soul, 'Soul, you have ample goods laid up for many years; relax, eat, drink, be merry.'" But God said to

---

[4] M. E. Boring, K. Berger, and C. Colpe, eds., *Hellenistic Commentary to the New Testament* (Nashville: Abingdon Press, 1995), 527.

him, "Fool! This night your soul is required of you, and the things you have prepared, whose will they be?" So is the one who lays up treasure for himself and is not rich toward God. (Luke 12:18–21)

These and numerous other textual links can be found within the ancient Jewish wisdom that nurtured James and other Jewish Christian teachers. They indicate that James is situated well within the tradition of the ancient Jewish sages as they were interpreted by Jesus the Sage.[5]

James has basically declared in compact form the very same things about the rich in Jas 1:10–11. We are probably intended, therefore, to see this paragraph as a preparation for his final diatribe about rich unbelievers in 5:1–6, where the rich who oppress the poor will look forward to nothing but judgment.

The complexity of the clauses, the use of anacoluthon and the abrupt style that begs for additional conjunctions for smooth transitions all combine to offer a serious challenge to anyone seeking to unpack their structure and meaning. The variant readings all seem to be due to the convoluted and abrupt sounding syntax of the verses. In reflecting on the rhetorical force of the language that James employs in this passage, the following possibility should be seriously considered. James often utilizes what can be called the surface features of his language to communicate semantic messages at a deeper level. We observed this practice in noting the alliteration and rhyming he uses to emphasize the *order* of the heavenly virtues in 3:17 that contrast with his language describing the vices that come from below in 3:14–16 and which result in *disorder* (ἀκαταστασία). Is it possible that the apparent disorder and lack of precision in the syntax of 4:13–14 are also intended to convey the resulting disorder that characterizes a life that is lived without God in its plans? Despite our

---

[5] B. Witherington III, *Jesus the Sage: The Pilgrimage of Wisdom* (Minneapolis: Fortress Press, 1998). Witherington also draws on sapiential traditions in his commentary on James (2007).

boastful planning, all our presumptuous plans about future results are uncertain because of our ignorance of what will even happen tomorrow! Therefore, even the language James uses to communicate this message seems to be uncertain and in disorder. On the other hand, the contrast evident by the simple and straightforward syntax in 4:15 may also be intended to convey the simplicity and order of a life that is lived in conscious awareness of God's will. Again, recognizing the original orality—and thus the consequent aurality of these texts—will help us to better appreciate their rhetorical thrust!

4:15 ἀντὶ τοῦ λέγειν ὑμᾶς: Jas 4:15–16 serves as a "point and counterpoint" to the preceding verses and their description of the presumptuous planners.[6] James 4:15 informs the readers what they should do to avoid the presumption so condemned in 4:13–14—i.e., to include God's plan in their plans. Then 4:16 returns to the original problem with the additional charge that the attitude he is condemning is not just one that is a poor choice. It is actually an example of "evil and arrogant boasting."

The contrasting character of the "two ways" tradition in James is effectively brought to the fore by the fronted articular infinitive construction in 4:15: ἀντὶ τοῦ λέγειν ὑμᾶς ("Instead, you ought to say"). The preposition ἀντί is one of the rarer prepositions, appearing only here in James and elsewhere in the NT only twenty-one times. This is the only time it appears with an articular infinitive. "In giving the correct viewpoint James again commits an anacoluthon, for while ἀντὶ τοῦ λέγειν is good Greek, it presumes that οἱ λέγοντες in 4:13 is a conjugated verb: 'You say ... instead of saying ...'" (Davids, 172). The use of the preposition ἀντί with an articular infinitive appears often in classical orators and historians. There is, however, only one appearance in the LXX: Ps 108:4: ἀντὶ τοῦ ἀγαπᾶν με ἐνδιέβαλλόν με ("Instead of my love, they slander me"), and in the NT only here.[7] The

---

[6] For a discussion of how NT authors utilize "point and counterpoint," see Runge, *Discourse Grammar*, 73–100.

[7] The standard NT Greek grammars (Wallace, Moule) offer no explanation of this construction, apart from simply listing the reference (BDF, 208; Robertson,

meaning, however, is clear: "just the opposite should be said." Indeed, this is the type of "anti-language" so typical of the counterintuitive contrast between earthly and heavenly behavior (3:13–18) that James impresses on every passage in his book.

ἐὰν ὁ κύριος θελήσῃ καὶ ζήσομεν καὶ ποιήσομεν τοῦτο ἢ ἐκεῖνο: The reported speech that then follows also is consistent with the pattern of the imagined speech in 4:13. The four future indicative verbs in that verse are balanced with two future indicative verbs here in 4:15 (ζήσομεν καὶ ποιήσομεν). The καί ... καί collocation indicates "both ... and." On the other hand, preceding these indicatives is a third class conditional protasis, "If (ἐὰν) the Lord is willing, then we will ..." The uncertainty conveyed by this form of the condition clause contrasts vividly with the boastful planning previously announced. But the condition is grounded in One who knows the details of a future that we do not know! This attitude reflects a humility that was earnestly commended in 3:13 and 17. It also clearly contrasts with the boastful pride that James condemned in 3:14–16. James urges these presumptuous merchants to add a key clause to their planning: "If it is the Lord's will." This expression of dependence on the Lord is known as the "Jacobean condition" (*conditio Jacobaea*). Such a sentiment is not absent from secular authors. Probably the most characteristic example is found in the following exchange: "'If you wish, Socrates.' 'That is not well said, Alcibiades.' 'Well, what should I say?' 'If God wills' [ἐὰν βούλῃ σύ, ὦ Σώκρατες. οὐ καλῶς λέγεις, ὦ Ἀλκιβιάδη. ἀλλὰ πῶς χρὴ λέγειν; ὅτι ἐὰν θεὸς ἐθέλῃ]" (Plato, *Alc.* 1.135d; see Hartin, 225). The attitude that it expresses, however, is thoroughly widespread among NT characters and authors. Most familiar is its inclusion in the Lord's Prayer (Matt 6:10; see also Matt 26:42; Acts 21:14; Rom 15:32; 1 Pet 3:17). Paul frequently verbalized his own submission to the Lord's will in his plans for missionary labors (Acts 18:21; Rom 1:10; 1 Cor 4:19; 16:7). Even

---

1070; Turner 3, 144). Stanley Porter calls it the "Substitutionary Infinitive": "The infinitive may specify a relation in which substitution occurs (that is, one item is substituted for another). This use is very rare, but one example can be ascertained (Jas 4:15)" (Porter, *Idioms*, 201).

more significant for James is that Jesus himself expressed this same submission to the Father's will at the great crisis in Gethsemane (Luke 22:42). Jesus, Paul, and the other apostles did not always clearly enunciate this condition when they planned for their future. What is most important is not their verbalization of a "mantra," but that they had this as a principle fixed in their minds—namely, that they would do nothing apart from the permissive will of God. "James takes a common expression of general religious sentiment and 'baptizes' it in the service of his distinctive biblical vision of a biblical worldview of history and its sovereign ruler" (Moo, 2000, 205).

4:16 νῦν δὲ καυχᾶσθε ἐν ταῖς ἀλαζονείαις ὑμῶν· πᾶσα καύχησις τοιαύτη πονηρά ἐστιν, "But now you boast so arrogantly. All such arrogant boastings are evil." With an effective rhetorical move, James now repeats the νῦν he had mentioned earlier, but he now turns it against the arrogant boaster. "But now (νῦν δὲ) you boast so arrogantly." James is certainly aware that the semantic field of the verb καυχάομαι can include "boasting" in a positive sense (Rom 5:2, 3, 11). He adds, therefore, a qualifying phrase (ἐν ταῖς ἀλαζονείαις ὑμῶν) that should be understood adverbially: "for how can you boast *in* your arrogant boastings?" By the word "arrogantly" the plans expressed in 4:13 are meant. A parallel to this use of the term can be found in *1 Clem.* 21.5: "Let us offend foolish and thoughtless people, who are exalted and boast *in the arrogance* [ἐν ἀλαζονείᾳ] of their words, rather than God." "The Greeks called this boastful pride *hybris,* and Homer in *The Iliad* depicted in imaginative detail the havoc it wreaked when Achilles succumbed to it" (Moo, 2000, 207).

The expression does not denote the subject of "glorying" (like ἐν τῷ ὕψει 1:9), but the manner in which glorying was shown. The adjective form is also found twice, each time joined with ὑπερήφανος, as in 4:6. Here the word implies an excessive confidence in one's own cleverness or skill. This attitude cannot simply be excused as part of man's frailty. It is a real and dangerous evil (πονηρά), only the second time James has employed this fairly common word (see 2:4). The copulative ἐστιν then ends the sentence, something he has also done in 2:20, 26 and again in 4:17, each of which are climactic statements. "This climactic ending suggests that James wants to emphasize that such behavior—presently a part of the scene—is inherently evil. The reason for this negative judgment is that, as with the godless in *Wis.* 5:7–10, the presence and providence of God have been left out of consideration" (Martin, 168).

We should not expect such "secular" thinking to emerge later, after the fervent early days of the faith. James warns that it is present at his time. Another witness to this attitude in the early Christian era is found in the *Shepherd of Hermas*. Hermas admits that he was entangled in shady business dealings (*Herm.* 7.1) and knew of restless schemers among the believers (*Herm.* 63.5), a witness of the development of what was feared by James, even if we recognize the difference between the specific personal experiences in *Hermas* and the more general admonition by James.

4:17 εἰδότι οὖν καλὸν ποιεῖν καὶ μὴ ποιοῦντι, ἁμαρτία αὐτῷ ἐστιν: Having exposed those who arrogantly boast (4:13, 14, 16), James seals his paragraph with another proverbial saying. This is no extraneous aphorism, however, because it further advances his point. The οὖν in 4:17, the third of its five appearances (see also 4:4, 7; 5:7, 16), provides a transition to the application of an effective proverb. An extended paraphrase: "Therefore, it is not only unsafe to openly disavow the Lord's control with boastful words, it is also wrong for the 'one in a state of knowing'[8] what is the right thing to do (i.e., acknowledging dependence on God's will) not to do it. This person's attitude is then sinful." The pronoun αὐτῷ is a good example of a dative of disadvantage. The infinitive ποιεῖν is complementary to εἰδότι and governs the complement adjective καλόν. "Examples of the infinitive after οἶδα in this sense are found in 2 Pet. 2:9, Matt. 7:11. The word καλόν is common with St. James (2:7, 3:13) as with St. Paul (Rom. 7:18, 7:19, 7:21, 2 Cor. 13:7, Gal. 6:9, where the phrase ποιεῖν τὸ καλόν occurs)"

---

[8] The perfect active participle εἰδότι [οἶδα] is fronted for special prominence.

(Mayor, 148).

The sentiment compares to the Jewish search for hidden guilt, in which every sin of omission is important. "This precept is quite certainly of Jewish origin, even if we cannot show specific evidence for it" (Dibelius, 235). The sentiment can be seen in the fervent prayer of Ps 19:12: "Who perceives his unintentional sins? Cleanse me from my hidden faults" (CSB). Thus Job, when examining himself for transgressions, expressly mentions sins of omission (Job 31:16–18), while Zophar had already hinted at the possibility of secret guilt (Job 11:6). Failing to do the good that one knows one can do is also viewed as a serious moral failure in other Second Temple Literature (*T. Sim.* 6.1; Philo, *Flacc.* 7).

12

WOE TO THE RICH (5:1-6)

Woe Because They Hoard Wealth (5:1–3)

Greek Text

1 Ἄγε νῦν οἱ πλούσιοι, κλαύσατε ὀλολύζοντες ἐπὶ ταῖς ταλαιπωρίαις ὑμῶν ταῖς ἐπερχομέναις. 2 ὁ πλοῦτος ὑμῶν σέσηπεν καὶ τὰ ἱμάτια ὑμῶν σητόβρωτα γέγονεν, 3 ὁ χρυσὸς ὑμῶν καὶ ὁ ἄργυρος κατίωται καὶ ὁ ἰὸς αὐτῶν εἰς μαρτύριον ὑμῖν ἔσται καὶ φάγεται τὰς σάρκας ὑμῶν ὡς πῦρ. ἐθησαυρίσατε ἐν ἐσχάταις ἡμέραις.

Translation

1 Now listen, you rich people, weep and wail because of the miseries that are coming upon you. 2 Your wealth is rotten, and your clothes are moth-eaten. 3 Your gold and silver are corroded, and their corrosion will testify against you and eat your flesh like fire. It is in the last days that you have hoarded your wealth.

Introduction

By opening this paragraph with the "frozen imperative," Ἄγε, James is undoubtedly linking it with the preceding passage (4:13–17) which begins in the same way ("Ἄγε νῦν). This expression appears only in these two locations in James. However, the passage also displays its own unique linguistic features and internal coherence, while also containing literary and semantic links to the near and far context. The orienter, "Ἄγε νῦν, again performs more of a rhetorical function than that of a specific command. The nominative plural of address, οἱ πλούσιοι, although not the familiar ἀδελφοί that initiates other paragraphs, is followed by an aorist imperative κλαύσατε. This combination of a group address plus an imperative appears at the beginning of many other paragraphs in James. The paragraph ends with a challenging rhetorical question in 5:6b, as is so often the case elsewhere in the book. While most translations have taken this clause as an indicative statement, there is good reason, as we shall see, to view it as a question. A new paragraph then follows in 5:7 with the transitional οὖν accompanied by the repeated combination of ἀδελφοί with another aorist imperative, Μακροθυμήσατε.

While these characteristics demonstrate that 5:1–6 is a self-contained unit, the paragraph also shares a number of formal and thematic links with what precedes. The most obvious link is the initial "Ἄγε νῦν which initiated the previous paragraph (4:13). A similar semantic theme also links these two paragraphs—namely, an address to a group of people who place too much emphasis on money, material possessions, and the desire to gain more of them. The specific exhortation, and thus condemnation, issued to each group differs. Furthermore, 5:1–6 shares many semantic ideas with 4:1–10, where the condemnation of greedy pleasures that divide believers (4:1–3) ends with a confrontational call to repentance (4:7–10) which is quite similar to the same hortatory thrust in 5:1, 2. This is particularly true in the case of the following cognate words shared between the passages: φονεύετε/ἐφονεύσατε; ταλαιπωρήσατε/ταλαιπωρίαις; κλαύσατε/κλαύσατε; πένθος, πενθήσατε/ὀλολύζοντες. This link between 5:1–6 and 4:1–10 is particularly evident when the semantic fields of the vocabulary used, rather than simply the same cognate words, are examined with the help of a work like the Louw and Nida lexicon. For example, the words ταλαιπωρήσατε, κλαύσατε, πένθος, πενθήσατε, and ὁλολύζοντες not surprisingly all belong to Field 25, 136–142 of the Louw and Nida lexicon: "Cry, Groan."

Notwithstanding their obvious linguistic similarities, these two passages evidence also some very real differences between them. The main difference is that the hopeful possibility of forgiveness is offered to the ones exhorted so strongly in 4:7–10. On the other hand, in 5:1–6 the weeping and crying that is commanded to the rich oppressors is because they will face a certain judgment that is to come (5:1), and no hope of repentance is offered.

The final verbal link between these passages is the rare verb ἀντιτάσσεται ("oppose"), which appeared earlier (4:6) with God as the clearly expressed subject, taken from the Prov 3:34 citation. The very same form of that verb in 5:6 is part of a sentence that I will argue is a question, likewise with God as the implied subject. While more will be said about that verb later, one must agree that its use at this point serves to bring the strong attack begun in 4:1 to its hortatory climax in 5:6. Thus 5:1–6, while maintaining its own integrity, ends a subdivision in the discourse that many see as the main body of the letter. This leads directly, with the use of οὖν, to the concluding remarks of the letter (5:7–20). We will consider 5:1–3 and 5:4–6 separately, because the interjection/orienter ἰδού at 5:4 signifies a slight transition in the thought progression at that point.

James issues a series of rapid-fire condemnations (as is his style) against the rich. But these are not simply rich people as such—they are rich oppressors of their own day laborers. An imperative clause followed by a call to mourn is then followed by a series of six indicative clauses describing the results of mislaid trust in riches. The three perfect verbs describe the state in which the rich find themselves, while they are attempting to enjoy their riches. Then two future clauses describe what will take place during their judgment, while a final clause looks back to what they have done to deserve this condemnation. This rhetorical move from their present to their future back to their past can be illustrated by the following sentence flow analysis of 5:1–3.

5:1

Ἄγε νῦν οἱ πλούσιοι,	ORIENTER
Κλαύσατε	IMPERATIVE
ὀλολύζοντες ἐπὶ ταῖς ταλαιπωρίαις ὑμῶν ταῖς ἐπερχομέναις.	MANNER

5:2

ὁ πλοῦτος ὑμῶν σέσηπεν	PERFECT
καὶ τὰ ἱμάτια ὑμῶν σητόβρωτα γέγονεν,	PERFECT

5:3

ὁ χρυσὸς ὑμῶν καὶ ὁ ἄργυρος κατίωται	PERFECT
καὶ ὁ ἰὸς αὐτῶν εἰς μαρτύριον ὑμῖν ἔσται	FUTURE
καὶ φάγεται τὰς σάρκας ὑμῶν ὡς πῦρ.	FUTURE
ἐθησαυρίσατε ἐν ἐσχάταις ἡμέραις.	AORIST

Exegetical Comments

5:1 Ἄγε νῦν: As in the previous paragraph (4:13–17), 5:1 opens with the second person imperative plus a temporal adverb. Most English translations render it as "Come now." This overly literal translation ignores what is obvious in the original Greek—namely, that the imperative is singular in form (ἄγε) while the ones being addressed are plural in form (οἱ πλούσιοι) as is the following imperative (κλαύσατε). This was the same pattern in 4:13, except there the plural group (οἱ

332

λέγοντες) is addressed but is not issued any direct command, and the sentence there is not even really completed. This disjunction between the singular and plural imperatives underscores the fact that it is the rhetorical function of Ἄγε νῦν that is again in view here, not some literally expressed command to "come." This meaning is in reality only one of the possible meanings of ἄγω.[1] It is what some call an orienter, a word that is used to direct the reader's attention to the importance of what is to follow. The expression is also called a "meta-comment," a statement by the speaker/writer that is not necessary to the structure of the following clause, but is an added expression that calls attention to the importance of what is about to be said.[2] The NIV is one of the few English versions that recognize this rhetorical function of Ἄγε νῦν by rendering it "Now listen!"—the translation I also adopt.

οἱ πλούσιοι: While not the first time that the rich have been addressed (see 1:10–11; 2:6; and 4:13–16 by implication), this is the first time that no hope is held out for them—only judgment. Why would James address unbelieving rich Jews who would not be found in the congregations of Jesus-believers? Some commentators still see these rich as among the intended recipients thinking themselves to be believers in Jesus (2:1), albeit inconsistent believers (Witherington, 2007, 524–29). The intense rhetoric of invective in this passage permits the rich being addressed as a class (Robertson, 57) or "apostrophized" (Adamson, 183–84), even as the prophets often addressed the rich as a class in ancient Israel (e.g., Amos 4:1–3; 6:1–7). The direct mode of address—a nominative accompanied by the article—shows that the rich are probably apostrophized as an (ungodly) social caste. This phraseology would be similar to what Paul also does with "the rich" in

---

[1] BDAG states that ἄγε is used as an "interjection" (16). The rhetorical function of the little imperative arresting the attention of those to whom it is addressed is the same as in its three OT occurrences: Judg 19:6; 2 Kgs 4:24; and Isa 43:6.

[2] Other linguists refer to this as a "meta-lingual comment," e.g. G. Brown and G. Yule, *Discourse Analysis* (Cambridge Textbooks in Linguistics; Cambridge: Cambridge, 1983), 132.

1 Tim 6:17 (τοῖς πλουσίοις). The message that immediately follows is not directed toward their reform, but is a warning of certain judgment (5:1–6). The following words directed to believers (5:7–11) constitute "a certain grim comfort in the hardships of poverty" (Ropes, 282), although there is more comfort offered than Ropes seems to grudgingly allow.

Many of these ideas about the rich were expressed in Wisdom 2:6–20, where the arrogance and selfishness of the rich as a class, the transitory nature of their prosperity, and their ill-treatment of the righteous are clearly described. Similar ideas about rich and poor can also be found in *1 Enoch* 94.7–11; 96.4–8; 97.3–10; 98.4–16; 99.11–16, although these passages, dating to the late centuries B.C., simply reflect earlier Hebrew prophetic denunciations.

κλαύσατε ὀλολύζοντες: The aorist imperative plus an embedded clause commands the rich to "cry by wailing," utilizing an aorist imperative followed by a present "participle of manner describing the crying."[3] Their wailing is because of the miseries that are coming upon them. The idea conveyed by the vivid combination of the imperative and participle is something like: "burst into weeping [aorist active of κλαιω as in 4:9] by howling with grief." The participle is the onomatopoetic verb ὀλολυζω, which appears only here in the NT (BDAG, 704). The verb had often been employed in the Greek world for women crying out to the gods, usually in joy (Aeschylus, *Eum.* 1043; Euripides, *Bacch.* 689; GE, 1447). The LXX, in contrast, uses the verb exclusively as laments for disasters visited on the people by the Lord for their apostasy (Isa 10:10; 13:6; 14:31; 15:2–3; 16:7; 23:1, 6, 14; Hos 7:14; Amos 8:3; Zech 11:2). A NT verb that can be compared to this *hapax legomenon* is ἀλαλαζω. "They came to the house of the synagogue official; and He saw a commotion, and people loudly weeping and wailing (ἀλαλάζοντας)" (Mark 5:38). The action expressed is like that of the Latin verb *ululare* (*ululantes* in the Vulgate), from which we derive the

---

[3] C. L. Rogers, Jr. and C. L. Rogers III, *The New Linguistic and Exegetical Key to the Greek New Testament* (Grand Rapids: Zondervan, 1998), 563.

English word *ululate*. The deep feelings expressed in this action can only be appreciated if one has witnessed Middle Eastern people like Sephardic Jewish women wailing at the Western Wall or Bedouin Arab women wailing in grief.

ἐπὶ ταῖς ταλαιπωρίαις ὑμῶν ταῖς ἐπερχομέναις: The vivid present attributive participle (ταῖς ἐπερχομέναις) places the judgment clearly in an eschatological context. The apocalyptic writings have a good deal to say about the "miseries" (ταλαιπωρίαις) "that were coming" (ταῖς ἐπερχομέναις) upon them (Joel 2:10–14; Zech 14:12–15; Dan 12:1). The Gospels connect them also with the Day of the Lord (Matt 24–25; Mark 13:14–27; Luke 21:9–19). Some of these prophecies delivered by Jesus were fulfilled in the destruction of Jerusalem. In 5:1, however, this is not the case due to the present tense form and because the context is clearly eschatological (5:3b: ἐν ἐσχάταις ἡμέραις). The cognate adjective is in the anguished cry of Paul in Rom 7:24: "O wretched man that I am" (ταλαίπωρος) but is illustrated even better by the cognate imperative verb ταλαιπωρήσατε in James 4:9: "Be wretched."

James is fulfilling the role of an OT prophet with this language of crying and wailing, as can be seen in such additional passages like Isa 13:6; Zech 11:2; Amos 8:3; and Lam 1:1–2. "Thus, associations with passages like Joel 1:5–11 would come to mind for those who knew the history of Jewish prophecy" (McKnight, 384). Furthermore, weeping in the NT often follows some earthly disaster (Matt 2:18; 26:75; Mark 5:38–39; Luke 6:21, 25; John 11:33; 20:11, 13; Rev 18:9, 11). While wailing is sometimes in the context of repentance (Luke 7:38), it is also displayed at the prospect of judgment, as when Jesus wept over what must happen to Jerusalem (Luke 19:41; see also Luke 23:28; Acts 21:13). This extensive OT and NT usage of weeping would make clear to readers of this Jewish-laden letter that the eschatological judgment of the Day of the Lord awaits these selfish rich who have hoarded rather than shared their riches. The attributive participle ἐπερχομέναις, modifying ταλαιπωρίαις, is heightened in its vividness by its present tense and imperfective aspect. The verb, used of judgment 'coming upon' sinners on the 'Day of the Lord,' was mentioned in Luke 21:26 and Acts 13:40. [4]

5:2 ὁ πλοῦτος ὑμῶν σέσηπεν καὶ τὰ ἱμάτια ὑμῶν σητόβρωτα γέγονεν: The vividness of the present tense verbs in 5:1 is now amplified by the series of perfect verbs that follow in 5:2–3. These verbs raise to a higher level the prominence of the condemnation that James is delivering. The following six primary clauses in these two verses are anchored by three perfect verbs (σέσηπεν, γέγονεν, κατίωται), each of which conveys the current state of the rich person's possessions. Their hoarded wealth decays in a state of rottenness. Their fine clothes are useless because they are in a moth-eaten condition. Their precious money lies in a state of corrosion. The traditional explanation of the perfect as describing an event that took place in the past with its present effects does not offer an adequate explanation of James' vivid language. An aspectual approach to the perfect tense verb offers a better explanation. Even earlier commentators recognized that the perfect serves to create a vivid sense of the imminence of the miseries (Ropes, 284). More recent commentators have acknowledged that a greater prominence is delivered through these perfects by the deliberate use of prophetic diction (Johnson, 299; Adamson, 185).

The plural of the noun πλοῦτος is best rendered collectively as "wealth." The word can be used for any sort of wealth or treasure, whether they are precious metals or other possessions. While not using this specific word, Sir 14:19 expresses well the same sense of wealth wasting away: "Every product decays and ceases to exist, and the one who made it will pass away with it." It is not wealth in general, but finding security in it that concerns James. The tendency of wealth to offer false security is also targeted in other NT passages like Mark 4:19; Matt 13:22; Luke 8:14; 12:21; and 1 Tim 6:9. It is the fragility of wealth that is exposed. The verb σήπω is a NT *hapax* which in the active voice means "cause to rot" (BDAG, 921-22), but the perfect active

---

[4] "The words of Zophar in the LXX of Job 20:28 illustrate the use of this term: 'The possessions of his house will be taken away completely when the day of wrath *comes* to him' " (McKnight, 385).

tense is sometimes used as equivalent to the passive state of affairs ("is rotten"). The verb is used by LXX translators in Job 19:20; 33:21; Ps 37:6; and Sir 14:19. The word σητόβρωτα is a "late and rare compound from σης, moth, Matthew 6:19ff and βρωτος, verbal adjective of βιβρωσκω to eat John 6:13. This compound is found only here, Job 13:28, and Sibylline Oracles *Proem.* 64. Rich robes are heirlooms, but moth-eaten" (Robertson, 58). The destruction of clothes by moths echoes such passages as Isa 51:8: "For the moth will devour them like a garment, and the worm will eat them like wool," or Job 13:28: "Man wears out like something rotten, like a moth-eaten garment" (see also Sir 42:13). The closest parallel, however, is again found in the words of Jesus promoting the value of a "treasure in heaven" that is resistant to moths, or worms, or thieves (Matt 6:19–20; Luke 12:33).

5:3 ὁ χρυσὸς ὑμῶν καὶ ὁ ἄργυρος κατίωται: The verb κατίωται is the perfect passive indicative of another hapax legomenon, κατιόω, *"become rusty, tarnished, corroded"* (BDAG, 534). Readers recognize the danger of corroding silver, but what about the same "corrosion" applied to gold? James was not alone in utilizing the figure, for it is found also in the *Epistle of Jeremiah* 11–12, which says of silver, golden, and wooden gods that they "cannot save themselves from rust and corrosion" (see a similar idea in Sir 29:10). The problem concerns the rusting of a metal which does not actually "rust," but is a problem only if someone desires to make it so. In an insightful discussion of the noun ἰός, Louw and Nida suggest the following:

> Pure gold is not affected significantly by oxidation, but much of the gold of the ancient world was not pure, and therefore oxidation and resulting tarnish did take place. However, in most languages it is inappropriate to speak of "rust" as occurring with gold and silver. If there is no satisfactory term to indicate the deterioration in gold and silver resulting in extreme tarnish, it may be possible to translate James 5:3 as "your gold and silver will be ruined and this will serve as a

witness against you" (L-N, 27).[5]

The apparent conflict has continued to intrigue commentators. "The word 'rust' (ἰός) also proves intriguing, because it can mean both rust and poison or venom (as in 3:8). In some ways the latter definition fits best with the flesh-eating fire of the second half of the verse" (Blomberg-Kamell, 221). With all the discussion about the "rust" or "corrosion," we should not lose sight of the rhetorical punch that is being effectively delivered. We should also, again, not overlook that Jesus warned the rich in similar words (Matt 6:20, after mention of the "moth"!) that their treasures (undoubtedly of "gold and silver") would rust.

καὶ ὁ ἰὸς αὐτῶν εἰς μαρτύριον ὑμῖν ἔσται καὶ φάγεται τὰς σάρκας ὑμῶν ὡς πῦρ: These perfect verbs in 5:2–3a are then followed here in 5:3b by two future tense verbs (ἔσται and φάγεται) as those metals of silver and gold are personified as both testifying and eating. The corrosion of the precious metals belonging to the rich will be (ἔσται) a witness against them, and their money will actually turn back against them and will eat (φάγεται) their flesh like fire. This theme of an eschatological reversal—alluded to briefly in 1:11–12—is now elevated to the prominent context of an entire paragraph.

The idea that the corrosion (ἰός, elsewhere in NT only in Rom 3:13 as "venom" – BDAG, 477) will serve as a witness (εἰς with accusative) against the hoarding rich echoes a common idiom expressed, for example, by Jesus' instruction to the cleansed leper in Matthew 8:4: "Go, show yourself to the priest and offer the gift Moses commanded, as a testimony (εἰς μαρτύριον) to them." The ὑμῖν is a dative of disadvantage as in Mark 6:11 (εἰς μαρτύριον αὐτοῖς). In the parallel passage to the ones above (Luke 9:5), there is a similar expression: εἰς μαρτυριον ἐπ' αὐτους.

---

[5] Some commentators stress that there is no problem since a supernatural judgment implies a supernatural calamity. "Like Chaucer, James knows that gold does not rust. 'If golde ruste what shal iren do?' (*Canterbury Tales*, line 504)" (Adamson, 185).

The gruesome comment that the corrosion will also consume their flesh with fire is an obvious mixing of metaphors that is intended to convey the horror of the eschatological fire reserved for the selfish rich. The reference to "flesh" is similar to Jdt. 16:17: "The Lord Almighty will take vengeance on them in the day of judgment; he will send fire and worms into their flesh; they shall weep in pain forever." The apocalyptic language here is spoiled and even becomes contradictory if we read it with a narrow literalism that is not intended. The language again is metaphorical, although describing something only too real, and is designed to provoke a response—namely, repentance. By adding "like fire" (ὡς πῦρ) James may be recalling 3:5–6 where fire was not only destructive but its source was hell. This language emerges from a strong OT tradition that connects God's judgment with fire (Isa 30:27, 30; Jer 5:14; Ezek 15:7; Amos 1:12, 14), but we find a similar use of "fire" by Jesus (Matt 13:42; Mark 9:47–48). Although it postdates James, the language of the Apocalypse, where "fire" is used no fewer than twenty-five times, is also a recollection of the very same OT figures (Rev 8:5; 14:10; 18:8).

ἐθησαυρίσατε ἐν ἐσχάταις ἡμέραις: The eschatological reversal (a "turning of the tables") is dramatically portrayed by the condemnation of the aorist verb that ends 5:3: "You have hoarded [ἐθησαυρίσατε] your wealth in [ἐν] the last days." The powerful impact of this closing statement is best conveyed in English by switching the order of the components. The sense would be: "Although you have amassed all this wealth (and have not adequately shared it as the following passage states), what you have hoarded so selfishly for the future will all be lost because 'it is in the last days that you *have* hoarded it'!" This vivid eschatological reference thus prepares a reader for the following specific condemnation that is charged against the fraudulent employers who have deprived their day-laborers of their pay (5:4). They will face, not a present day for feasting, but a future day for slaughter (5:5), because it is God himself who resists their selfish deeds (5:6).

OT echoes again resound throughout the intertexture of this entire passage. Isaiah's fierce condemnation of Babylon—which, like James, also includes some economic aspects—utilizes very similar language. The expression, "wail [ὀλολύζετε] for the day of the Lord is near and a destruction will come from God," echoes prophetic oracles like Isa 13:6. Condemnation of the wealthy due to their selfish hoarding of silver and gold was also mentioned in Isa 13:12, 17. In the next section (5:4), James will clearly recall "the Lord of *Sabaoth*" (Lord of Hosts) who was also mentioned by that same title in Isa 13:4, 13. When NT authors cite these seemingly isolated texts from the OT, like James does here, they do not neglect to invoke the larger context of those passages. More will be explained about this reference to the "Lord of *Sabaoth*" in the explanation of James 5:4.

James 5:2-3 sounds like an abbreviation and adaptation of Jesus' words in Luke 6:24, 25: "But woe to you who are rich (πλουσίοις), for you have received your consolation. Woe to you who are full now, for you shall be hungry. Woe to you who laugh now, for you shall mourn and weep [κλαύσετε]." Direct verbal connections and semantic similarities both resonate between these texts. Jesus also warned against the selfish hoarding of treasures in passages like Matt 6:19-20: "Do not *lay up for yourselves treasures* [θησαυρίζετε ὑμῖν θησαυροὺς] on earth, where *moth* [σὴς] and *rust* destroy and where thieves break in and steal, but lay up for yourselves *treasures* in heaven, where neither moth nor *rust* destroys and where thieves do not break in and steal." James, therefore, is simply condemning the rich for practicing those same things that Jesus so vividly condemned.

ἐν ἐσχάταις ἡμέραις: The question that arises from the use of James' final expression in 5:3 is whether ἐν ("for") means that the last days are already here or that James is referring to a future day of judgment. The best approach is to see James as being consistent with the thinking of his other NT colleagues. "In line with other NT writers and in the light of his use of ἐν (lit., "in") it appears that James reflects the belief that the last days have already begun to dawn upon the world (Acts 2:17; 2 Tim 3:1; Heb 1:2; 2 Pet 3:3; 1 John 2:18; Jude 18)" (Martin, 178). In this approach, the rich are described as laying up treasure in the last days, which are imminent to the point of actual arrival. Some have thought that James may be ironic at this point (Davids, 127; Moo, 1985, 162), with the treasure in mind not being their riches but rather the misery that awaits them. While they think that their accumulated wealth is held as a permanent possession, they actually will face severe judgment not only because their wealth is temporary, but also because it is the witness whose testimony condemns them. Such irony may be like what Paul had in mind when he spoke of the wicked "storing up" wrath (ὀργή) for God's judgment (Rom 2:5). Instead of sharing their wealth with the needy (already spoken of as a sign of a saving faith in 2:14–16) they hoard it. While the last days represent the period before the coming of the Lord (5:8) to vindicate his own, this same period also highlights the nearness of the judgment reserved for those who oppose the Lord and also oppress His "poor ones." James is implying that the day may come at any time. Thus, with such an ominous event on the horizon, the misuse of wealth by those who hoard it is taking place as a prelude to the coming of the Lord.

Woe Because They Steal and Murder (5:4-6)

Introduction

The linguistic and semantic characteristics of Jas 5:1–3 apply also to 5:4–6, but even more intensely. The "meta-comment" Ἄγε νῦν opened 5:1, while 5:4 opens with a similar "orienter" (ἰδού) that directs the reader to the words that follow. The strong accusatory tone directed toward the rich in 5:1–3 is actually heightened in 5:4–6. The personification of their corroded riches by their "testifying" and "eating" flesh in 5:3 is developed further by the day laborers' defrauded wages crying out against their heartless employers (5:4). Eschatological themes were earlier expressed by future tenses (5:3), allusions to Isaiah (5:1, 3), and reference to the "last days" in 5:3b. These themes are stressed in the same ways in 5:4–6 by references to a future judgment and a clear allusion to the "day of slaughter" by Jeremiah. In approaching the unique features in this section, therefore, we will briefly: (1) survey the clauses and tense usages; (2) mention an important textual variant; (3) examine appropriate allusions to the OT; and (4) defend the view that the final clause in 5:6c is a question rather than a statement.

Greek Text

4 ἰδοὺ ὁ μισθὸς τῶν ἐργατῶν τῶν ἀμησάντων τὰς χώρας ὑμῶν ὁ ᵃἀπεστερημένος ἀφ᾽ ὑμῶν κράζει, καὶ αἱ βοαὶ τῶν θερισάντων εἰς τὰ ὦτα κυρίου σαβαὼθ εἰσεληλύθασιν. 5 ἐτρυφήσατε ἐπὶ τῆς γῆς καὶ ἐσπαταλήσατε, ἐθρέψατε τὰς καρδίας ὑμῶν ᵇἐν ἡμέρᾳ σφαγῆς, 6 κατεδικάσατε, ἐφονεύσατε τὸν δίκαιον, οὐκ ἀντιτάσσεται ὑμῖν.

Textual Notes

4.a. The reading of ἀπεστερημένος in 5:4 is supported by the manuscripts A B² Ψ 33 and the Majority Text. Considered to be an Alexandrian refinement by the editors of our modern critical text, ἀφυστερημένος nevertheless has strong textual support from ℵ B*. The difference in meaning between the two readings is not all that significant, nor does it necessarily affect the meaning of 5:4. Most likely the earliest reading is ἀφυστερημένος, but was later emended to match Mal 3:5, to which James alludes. Metzger demurred from the UBS committee's decision and preferred this reading (Metzger, 614).

SBLGNT prefers ἀφυστερημένος. THGNT prefers ἀπεστερημένος.

5.b. In 5:5, the "Majority" of the later Byzantine manuscripts, as well as the corrector of Sinaiticus, insert ὡς before ἐν ἡμέρᾳ σφαγῆς. This variant is an attempt to clarify the expression and make it a simile, but such assistance is not needed to perceive the figurative imagery.

Translation

4 Look! The wages which you defrauded from the laborers who mowed your fields are crying out against you, and the cries of the harvesters have reached the ears of the Lord of *Sabaoth*. **5** You have lived on earth in luxury and self-indulgence. You have fattened your hearts for the day of slaughter. **6** You have condemned; you have murdered the righteous person. Does He not oppose you?

Sentence Flow

5:4
ἰδοὺ   ORIENTER

ὁ μισθὸς τῶν ἐργατῶν τῶν ἀμησάντων   AFFIRMATION PRESENT
τὰς χώρας ὑμῶν ὁ ἀπεστερημένος
ἀφ’ ὑμῶν <u>κράζει</u>,

καὶ αἱ βοαὶ τῶν θερισάντων εἰς   AFFIRMATION PERFECT
τὰ ὦτα κυρίου σαβαὼθ <u>εἰσεληλύθασιν</u>.

5:5
<u>ἐτρυφήσατε</u> ἐπὶ τῆς γῆς   ACCUSATION AORIST

καὶ <u>ἐσπαταλήσατε</u>,   ACCUSATION AORIST

<u>ἐθρέψατε</u> τὰς καρδίας ὑμῶν ἐν ἡμέρᾳ σφαγῆς,   ACCUSATION AORIST

5:6
<u>κατεδικάσατε</u>,   ACCUSATION AORIST

<u>ἐφονεύσατε</u> τὸν δίκαιον,   ACCUSATION AORIST

οὐκ <u>ἀντιτάσσεται</u> ὑμῖν;   QUESTION PRESENT

After the initial orienter ἰδού, 5:4–6 conveys its message through eight primary clauses characterized by asyndeton (lack of conjunctions). Two of those clauses contain brief secondary participial clauses (5:4). In both of these, the subject of the clause is fronted, calling our attention to the cries of the defrauded laborers (present κράζει) and how these cries have entered (perfect εἰσεληλύθασιν) God's ears. This threefold combining of (1) an imperative orienter; (2) the initial placement of the subjects; and (3) the present/perfect tenses combine to convey a greater degree of prominence for these cries expressed to God and for His willingness to hear.

Exegetical Comments

5:4 ἰδού: The function of this cataphoric "orienter" in the book is to draw attention to an illustrative example of a principle just enunciated or to call the reader to look at the subject in more of its details. In 3:4–5, the word points to examples in life of small things that have inordinately larger effects. In 5:4, it calls attention to the farmer, who is an example of patience. In 5:9, it calls attention to the divine judge, who is an example of correct judging. In 5:11, it points to Job, who is an example of endurance. Here in 5:4, it also calls attention to the defrauding of wages by employers, an example of the selfishness of some rich people.

ὁ μισθὸς τῶν ἐργατῶν τῶν ἀμησάντων τὰς χώρας ὑμῶν ὁ ἀπεστερημένος ἀφ' ὑμῶν κράζει: The Greek syntax in the first clause of 5:4 can appear to be a bit complex, so translators have struggled to express the thought clearly while not straying too far from its formal structure and word order. The attributive participle clause ὁ ἀπεστερημένος ("which is kept back") clearly references the wages (μισθὸς τῶν ἐργατῶν) since both are singular and in the nominative case (despite the plural English translation "wages"). The intervening attributive participle clause τῶν ἀμησάντων τὰς χώρας ὑμῶν ("who have mowed your fields") provides a challenge for rendering a faithful but smooth translation, because the predicate is at the end of the sentence and the subject is at its beginning. For purposes of clarity, it is advisable to avoid using the passive voice and express the ideas by two coordinate clauses: "You have defrauded the workers who mow your fields and their missing wages are crying out against you to the Lord of *Sabaoth.*"

The word that is translated as "kept back" by a number of translations, the participle ἀπεστερημένος, is not present in the two fourth-century uncials ℵ and B, which contain the similar participle ἀφυστερημένος. The Westcott and Hort text does contain this last word, but a majority of the editors of NA[27] and UBS[4] preferred the first word. Bruce Metzger was probably part of the minority decision because he writes the following: "The earliest reading appears to be the rare word ἀφυστερημένος, which copyists emended to a more familiar word" (Metzger, 614). This is a good assessment, although the meaning that is finally conveyed by the expression is not seriously affected by whatever is the ultimate word choice.[6]

Should we take the prepositional phrase ἀφ' ὑμῶν as completing the preceding participle ("kept back *from* you,") or as completing the main verb κράζει ("are crying out *against* you")? The first choice has been advocated by later commentators (e.g., Dibelius, 238; Laws, 202; Martin, 178–79), while the second approach is advocated by some earlier commentators (e.g., Alford, 322; Lange, 129–30; Huther, 205). The usual meaning of the preposition ἀπό ("from") supports the first translation, but that reading requires that the people being addressed are the laborers, when it is obvious that the landowners are being addressed in the context. On the other hand, the idea of opposition ("against") is a rare use of this word, if ever existing at all! I suggest that a functional rather than a formal translation be followed. The wages are kept back by the greedy landowners, and it is because those wages are with the landowners, that they are personified as crying out "from" them formally, but against them functionally. Thus a functional translation like "they are crying out *against* you," in the sense of a

---

[6] Louw and Nida do not finely distinguish the meanings of the words (L-N, 563, 576).

witness against you, is similar to the thought already expressed in 5:3.[7] The personification of the defrauded wages "crying out" echoes the figure of Abel's blood that was described as crying out to God (Gen 4:10). The verb κράζει echoes the "crying out" of the Israelites to Yahweh when they were in distress (Exod 5:8; Num 11:2; Judg 1:14; 3:9; 4:3; Pss 3:5; 18:42; 21:3; 27:1; Isa 19:20; Mic 3:4).

The entire issue addressed in this paragraph is a NT application of the Torah commands found in such parallel passages as Deut 24:14/Lev 19:13 ("Do not oppress a hired hand who is poor and needy"). James 5:4–6 is another indication that James is developing a midrashic treatment of Lev 19 for many of his concerns (see comments on 2:1–9).

καὶ αἱ βοαὶ τῶν θερισάντων εἰς τὰ ὦτα κυρίου σαβαὼθ εἰσεληλύθασιν: This is another OT allusion, even a quotation, and it is indicated that way by the italicized form of those words in NA²⁷ (see above) and by the footnote in UBS⁴. It describes how the cries of the workers defrauded of their wages "have entered into the ears of the Lord of *Sabaoth*" (εἰς τὰ ὦτα κυρίου σαβαὼθ εἰσεληλύθασιν). I suggest that we use the English transliteration of the Hebrew צְבָאוֹת, rather than attempt the traditional translation of "Lord of Hosts." My reason is that James also chose not to translate it but to use the Greek transliteration as it is found in the LXX (Muraoka, 616). The quotation is from either Isa 5:9 or 22:14 (in the LXX), and becomes obvious when we realize that these two verses are the only other places where the figurative expression, "the ears of the Lord of Hosts," is utilized before James employs it. The citation is even more obvious when we recognize that the context of Isa 5:9 is also about the oppression of the poor while the context of Isa 22:14 describes the extravagant lives of the rich, both of which are echoed in the language of James in the context of 5:1–6. In a similar scene of suffering, the "cries" (βοαί) of the defrauded Israelites in Egypt ascended to God (Exod 2:23).

---

[7] The following versions agree with this functional translation: ESV, NLT, NET, NIV. The NASB has it both ways with the second "against you" in italics!

5:5 ἐτρυφήσατε ἐπὶ τῆς γῆς καὶ ἐσπαταλήσατε, ἐθρέψατε τὰς καρδίας ὑμῶν ἐν ἡμέρᾳ σφαγῆς: The five consecutive clauses in 5:5–6b, each anchored by an aorist indicative verb, deliver in rapid-fire style the accusations against the rich defrauders. They have engaged in gross self-enrichment, which James conveys by the colorful alliteration of the aorist verbs (ἐτρυφήσατε, ἐσπαταλήσατε, ἐθρέψατε). They have led prodigal lives and at the same time have inflicted such terrible hardships on their poor employees. The aorist tenses convey that idea from the perspective of the future judgment, and these wealthy sinners are confronted by the enormous sins they have committed during their lives. "On earth" means "during your lifetime." While the cries of their victims ascended to *heaven*, they were living in luxury on *earth*, oblivious of the wrath to come.

The "day of slaughter" (ἡμέρᾳ σφαγῆς – genitive of description) also recalls the prophetic denunciation (as it does throughout this passage) of a passage like Isa 22:12–13. The expression thus balances "in the last days" in 5:3. The wealthy landowners, like well-fed oxen, were unconsciously fattening themselves for the slaughter. The "day of slaughter" echoes Jer 12:3, where a prophetic word threatens evildoers with similar threats: "pull them out like sheep for the slaughter and set them apart for the day of slaughter." While the context does appear to be eschatological, could the threats ominously anticipate a soon-to-be accomplished judgment of the rich oppressors that serves as a harbinger of the eschatological judgment? An occasional commentator has mentioned that the destruction by Rome in a.d. 70 was just such an event. "Did any of those whom St. James here condemns remember his words when, a few years later, thousands of the Jews of the Dispersion were once more gathered together at Jerusalem for the sacrifice of the Passover, and there they became unwilling sacrifices to God's slow but sure vengeance? It was the wealthy among them who especially suffered (*Bell. Jud.* V. x. 2)" (Plummer, 285).

5:6 κατεδικάσατε, ἐφονεύσατε τὸν δίκαιον: The actions of the rich and greedy landowners also included judicial acts of condemnation (κατεδικάσατε) and even murder (ἐφονεύσατε). The verb καταδικάζω is often found in a forensic context, as a sentence of condemnation given against someone for committing a crime (Job 34:29; Josephus, *Ant.* 7.271; Matt 12:37; Acts 25:15). The judicial nature of 5:6 recalls the earlier, vividly described court scene in 2:1–4. In that passage, it was said that the rich drag the poor believers into court and deal with them unjustly (2:6–7). It is a description of the abuse of power by the powerful against the powerless. The only other appearance of this verb in the NT offers an interesting parallel: "If you had known what this means, 'I want mercy and not sacrifice,' you wouldn't have *condemned* [κατεδικάσατε] the innocent." Psalm 10 describes such a scene all too familiar in ancient Israel. "He sits in ambush in the villages; in hiding places he murders the innocent. His eyes stealthily watch for the helpless; he lurks in ambush like a lion in his thicket; he lurks that he may seize the poor; he seizes the poor when he draws him into his net" (Ps 10:8–9 ESV).

The murder accusation (ἐφονεύσατε τὸν δίκαιον) may be hyperbolic in its rhetoric or juridical in its language (Huther, 207; Martin, 181). Rhetorical "murder" seems to be the charge, for example, in Sir 34:25–27: "The bread of the needy is the life of the poor; whoever deprives them of it is a murderer. To take away a neighbor's living is to commit murder; to deprive an employee of wages is to shed blood." We cannot, however, confidently reject outright the idea that this should be taken in a very literal sense, and that the Sirach passage should also be taken literally. If laborers who depend on receiving their pay at the end of the day (Matt 20:1–16) are thus defrauded, the loss of their promised daily bread may actually lead to the deaths of family members. These heartless employers, therefore, are directly to blame for their sufferings and possible deaths (Moo, 2000, 219).

An impressive amount of scriptural evidence can be assembled for the idea that the substantive τὸν δίκαιον, which serves as the direct object of the predicate ἐφονεύσατε, actually refers to the Righteous One—namely, the Messiah. "The righteous one" was a title applied to Jesus by such early sermonizers as Peter (Acts 3:14), Stephen (Acts 7:52), and Paul (Acts 22:14). Linguistic roots for this messianic title can also be found in such OT texts as Isa 3:10 and 53:11. Wisdom 2:10–20 may also be influencing the language here, and if it does, it is probably best to view the substantive adjective as a collective term for the righteous poor, who are the subjects of the oppression described in the context.

οὐκ ἀντιτάσσεται ὑμῖν, "Does He [God] not oppose you?" I include my suggested translation and will attempt to defend it. The concluding clause in 5:6c suddenly reverts to a present tense when making a statement about someone (singular) who resists or opposes (ἀντιτάσσεται) these oppressors. Identifying the subject of this verb has been one of the biggest grammatical and hermeneutical issues in James. Is the subject the "righteous one" just mentioned, whoever that might be? Furthermore, is the clause a statement or is it a question? Good commentaries list the various views about this clause and offer the reasons for each view.

(1) The sentence is indicative and the subject is the Righteous Messiah (a few commentators, who identify "the righteous one" as messianic). The reference is to the submissive nonresistance of Jesus to His rich, Sadducean interrogators (patristic commentators such as Bede, Oecumenius, and Theophylact).

(2) The sentence is indicative and the subject is the collective righteous sufferers (the majority of commentators, such as Adamson, 188; Mayor, 160; Dibelius, 240; Martin, 182; Moo, 219–20).

(3) The sentence is interrogative and the subject is the Messiah. This would imply a future sense given to the present verb. "He will resist you" in the eschatological judgment already mentioned (Ropes, 292).

(4) The sentence is interrogative but has a rhetorical twist that implies that the poor *are* resisting their treatment with protests before God's throne (Davids, 180; McKnight, 400).

It is best to view the sentence as a question. Westcott and Hort punctuate their text in this way. But who exactly is the questioner who is the subject of the verb ἀντιτάσσεται? I believe that God should be considered as the subject of this rhetorical question: "Does He [God] not oppose you?" One of the keys to this approach is the sudden switch in tense from the series of aorist verbs to this single present verb, ἀντιτάσσεται, and the appearance of that same form of the verb in 4:6: ὁ θεὸς ὑπερηφάνοις ἀντιτάσσεται.

Luis Alonso Schökel first suggested this interpretation of James 5:6c in 1973, and listed fifty previous authors who had *not* recognized the important connection between Jas 5:6 and Jas 4:6.[8] A vital implication of recognizing this connection is that 5:6c then becomes a question, with God the one who is doing the opposing. Schökel's simple argument is that ἀντιτάσσεται has appeared earlier in this exact tense form in 4:6, where it is part of a quotation from LXX Proverbs 3:34: "God opposes [ἀντιτάσσεται] the proud, but gives grace to the humble." Jas 5:6c, therefore, concludes the subsequent commentary by James on that quotation. "This explains the surprising present ἀντιτάσσεται and the lack of a specific subject."[9] This proposal also helps to explain the lack of a conjunction that would connect the clause to what precedes. For example, some have suggested that the sense of the verse is: "You murdered the righteous one, *but* he does not oppose you." The asyndeton, however, supports the idea that someone other than "the righteous one" who was just mentioned is the actual subject of ἀντιτάσσεται.

This approach is best because of the following additional reasons. The passage (5:1-6) has moved alternatively between a discussion of the behavior of the rich to their promised judgment, and the reading given here forms the logical response to their final murderous act. The use of a rhetorical question here certainly fits James' diatribal style. If we acknowledge the discourse unity of James, then the use of ἀντιτάσσεται in proximity to 4:6 is not accidental. In 4:6, God is said to

---

[8] L. A. Schökel, "James 5, 2 [sic] and 4, 6," *Bib* 54 (1973) 73–76.
[9] Schökel, 74.

oppose (ἀντιτάσσεται) *the arrogant*. James has now given three such examples of arrogance, climaxing with the just-mentioned accusation of judicial murder. That God *opposes* them makes a fitting conclusion. That discourse unity of the book continues with the following verse. If 5:6 concludes not with a statement about the righteous person's lack of opposition, but with an assurance of God's opposition to the arrogant, then the οὖν ("therefore") that follows in 5:7 makes much more sense.[10]

We suggest that the call to repentance in 4:7–10 expounds the latter part of Prov 3:34 ("He gives grace to the humble"). The role of God as judge, beginning in 4:11 and continuing through the harsh words of 4:13–17 and 5:1–6, further develops the first half of the quotation ("He opposes the proud"). The powerful conclusion to James' prophetic attack, therefore, comes in the final clause of 5:6: "God opposes the arrogant. You rich oppressors have behaved arrogantly. *Should He not oppose you?*"[11]

---

[10] Luke Johnson was evidently the first major commentator who espoused the view that God is the subject of the verb (Johnson, 305). Some recent monographs have also recognized the wisdom of Schökel's suggestion about the verse: T. C. Penner, *The Epistle of James and Eschatology: Rereading an Ancient Christian Letter* (JSNTSup 121; Sheffield: Sheffield Academic Press, 1996), 155–58; D. H. Edgar, *Has God Not Chosen the Poor? The Social Setting of the Epistle of James* (JSNTSup 206; Sheffield: Sheffield Academic, 2001), 203; M. E. Taylor, A Text-Linguistic Investigation into the Discourse Structure of James (JSNTSup 311; London: T&T Clark, 2006), 67–68.

[11] While other commentators have recognized the clause as a question, they either take the subject to be the righteous poor person or Jesus the righteous Messiah. If we again assume the possibility that Wis 2:6–20 could be a source for Jas 5:6, it is interesting to note that when the righteous person in that passage, who is clearly a term for the collective righteous poor, is said to "oppose" those oppressing and condemning him, the verb in Wis 2:12 is ἐναντιοῦται—not a NT word and definitely not the verb ἀντιτάσσεται of 4:6 and 5:6.

13

PATIENCE AND ENDURANCE (5:7-11)

Introduction

James 5:7–11 shares a number of thematic connections with its context while it also indicates its own distinct role as a separate paragraph. The postpositive οὖν in 5:7, in one of its few appearances (see 4:4, 7, 17; 5:16), signals a transition from the description of the suffering of the laborers in 5:1–6 to the exhortation delivered to them in 5:7–11. This admonition could be summarized as follows: "Be patient in your sufferings because the Lord will recompense both you and your unfair employers." Those who were condemned in 5:5 were described as feeding their hearts for a *day of slaughter*, while the brethren are encouraged in 5:8 to establish their hearts for the *Day of the Lord*.

The transitional particle οὖν is combined with the aorist imperative μακροθυμήσατε and the nominative ἀδελφοί, together indicating a new paragraph. This transition is also confirmed by the introduction of the new semantic topic of patience/endurance (μακροθυμία/ὑπομονή). There is a thorough discussion among commentators about the issue of whether 5:12 concludes this paragraph, starts a new one, or even stands alone. By examining a semantic chain in 5:7–11, the argument will be made that these verses form a stand-alone unit. Furthermore, the repetition of ἀδελφοί in 5:9–10 does not indicate new paragraphs at those points but the use of ἀδελφοί serves to further stress the topic that is introduced in 5:7. This observation can be justified also by recognizing that same semantic chain.

The internal structure of 5:7–11 indicates that a slight transition occurs between 5:7–9 and 5:10–11. The passage is introduced by the imperatival clause in 7a: Μακροθυμήσατε οὖν, ἀδελφοί, ἕως τῆς παρουσίας τοῦ κυρίου. Two following sub-sections each share the following features. Both utilize the imperative ἰδού (5:7b, 9b/5:11), as was the case in the previous paragraph (5:4), where this "orienter" called attention to the cries of the day laborers. Here, James three times employs it to call attention to the patience of the farmer, the role of the judge, and the blessedness of the prophets. The exemplar of patience in the first section is the farmer, while two exemplars of patience/endurance in the second section are the prophets and Job. Finally, two similar descriptions are made about the Lord's coming in the first section (His coming is near and He is at the door), while in the second section two factual statements are added about the Lord's character (He has a purpose and He is compassionate/merciful). The following sentence flow analysis illustrates this structure.

5:7

Μακροθυμήσατε οὖν, ἀδελφοί, ἕως τῆς παρουσίας τοῦ κυρίου.

ἰδού

ὁ γεωργὸς ἐκδέχεται τὸν τίμιον καρπὸν τῆς γῆς μακροθυμῶν ἐπ' αὐτῷ ἕως λάβῃ πρόϊμον καὶ ὄψιμον.

5:8

μακροθυμήσατε καὶ ὑμεῖς, στηρίξατε τὰς καρδίας ὑμῶν, ὅτι ἡ παρουσία τοῦ κυρίου ἤγγικεν.

5:9

μὴ στενάζετε, ἀδελφοί, κατ' ἀλλήλων ἵνα μὴ κριθῆτε·

<u>ἰδοὺ</u>

ὁ κριτὴς πρὸ τῶν θυρῶν ἕστηκεν.

5:10

ὑπόδειγμα λάβετε, ἀδελφοί, τῆς κακοπαθίας καὶ τῆς μακροθυμίας τοὺς προφήτας οἳ ἐλάλησαν ἐν τῷ ὀνόματι κυρίου.

5:11

<u>ἰδοὺ</u>

μακαρίζομεν τοὺς ὑπομείναντας·

τὴν ὑπομονὴν Ἰὼβ ἠκούσατε

καὶ τὸ τέλος κυρίου εἴδετε, ὅτι πολύσπλαγχνός ἐστιν ὁ κύριος καὶ οἰκτίρμων.

How does the paragraph convey this theme? Two concepts of *patience* that are represented by the word groups μακροθυμέω/μακροθυμία and ὑπομένω/ὑπομονή control the theme of the paragraph. Some older commentators, who were possibly influenced by their Classical Greek training, attempted to consistently discern a fine distinction between these two word groups, with μακροθυμία often viewed as describing *forbearance* with people while ὑπομονή often handled as describing *patience* with circumstances. While in some passages this distinction may serve to be a helpful one, the two words often have such a degree of semantic overlap that it is probably best not to maintain such a consistently fine distinction in meaning. Other uses of these words simply do not bear out such a clear distinction. A better approach to this question is to view these word groups along with similar word groups as composing what one writer has called a "semantic chain." The Louw and Nida lexicon, by grouping words according to their semantic domains, is a useful tool in this regard.

When James 5:7–11 is analyzed in this manner, we are enabled to see that in addition to the six occurrences of these two words, the passage contains four additional words that can also be included in the very same semantic domain. Following is a table with the letters of the chained words in bold type and the number of its L-N semantic domain below each word.[752]

Semantic Chain of "Field 25" Words in James 5:7-11

Μακροθυμήσατε οὖν, ἀδελφοί, ἕως τῆς παρουσίας τοῦ κυρίου. 25.168
ἰδοὺ ὁ γεωργὸς

ἐκδέχεται τὸν τίμιον καρπὸν τῆς γῆς **μακροθυμῶν** ἐπ' αὐτῷ 25.168
ἕως λάβῃ πρόϊμον

καὶ ὄψιμον. **μακροθυμήσατε** καὶ ὑμεῖς, στηρίξατε τὰς καρδίας ὑμῶν, 25.168
ὅτι ἡ

παρουσία τοῦ κυρίου ἤγγικεν. μὴ **στενάζετε**, ἀδελφοί, 33.384/25
κατ' ἀλλήλων ἵνα μὴ

κριθῆτε· ἰδοὺ ὁ κριτὴς πρὸ τῶν θυρῶν ἕστηκεν. ὑπόδειγμα λάβετε,
ἀδελφοί, τῆς

κακοπαθίας καὶ τῆς **μακροθυμίας** τοὺς προφήτας 24.89/25 25.167
οἳ ἐλάλησαν ἐν τῷ ὀνόματι

κυρίου. ἰδοὺ **μακαρίζομεν** τοὺς **ὑπομείναντας**· 25.120 25.175 25.174
τὴν **ὑπομονὴν** Ἰὼβ ἠκούσατε καὶ τὸ

τέλος κυρίου εἴδετε, ὅτι πολύσπλαγχνός   81/25
ἐστιν ὁ κύριος καὶ οἰκτίρμων ...

Figure 5: Semantic Chain of "Field 25" Words in James 5:7-11

Discerning the existence of such a semantic chain helps also to justify two observations previously made. The first is that 5:7–11 is a self-contained and discrete section with "patience" as its theme. The second is that this analysis helps to answer why both 5:1–6 and 5:12 are separate paragraphs. This is because the semantic chain is contained entirely within 5:7–11. Having attempted a macro-analysis of the passage, we will now proceed to the micro-analysis of its words and clauses.

Original Text

7 Μακροθυμήσατε οὖν, ἀδελφοί, ἕως τῆς παρουσίας τοῦ κυρίου. ἰδοὺ ὁ γεωργὸς ἐκδέχεται τὸν τίμιον καρπὸν τῆς γῆς μακροθυμῶν ἐπ' αὐτῷ ἕως λάβῃ[a] πρόϊμον καὶ ὄψιμον. 8 μακροθυμήσατε καὶ ὑμεῖς, στηρίξατε τὰς καρδίας ὑμῶν, ὅτι ἡ παρουσία τοῦ κυρίου ἤγγικεν. 9 μὴ στενάζετε, ἀδελφοί, κατ' ἀλλήλων ἵνα μὴ κριθῆτε·ἰδοὺ ὁ κριτὴς πρὸ τῶν θυρῶν ἕστηκεν. 10 ὑπόδειγμα λάβετε, ἀδελφοί, τῆς κακοπαθίας καὶ τῆς μακροθυμίας τοὺς προφήτας οἳ ἐλάλησαν ἐν τῷ ὀνόματι κυρίου. 11 ἰδοὺ μακαρίζομεν τοὺς ὑπομείναντας· τὴν ὑπομονὴν Ἰὼβ ἠκούσατε καὶ τὸ τέλος κυρίου εἴδετε, ὅτι πολύσπλαγχνός ἐστιν ὁ κύριος καὶ οἰκτίρμων.

Textual Notes

7.a. The reading as contained in the critical text has strong support from p[74] B 048 1739 vg cop[sa]. The variant readings in A P Ψ 33[vid] (υετον), and (ℵ*) syr[hmg] cop[bo] (καρπον) are a scribal attempt to supply the intended meaning of the phrase πρόϊμον καὶ ὄψιμον.

Translation

7 Be patient, therefore, brothers, until the coming of the Lord. Look! The farmer waits for the precious fruit of the earth, being patient about it, until it receives the early and the late rains. 8 You also, be patient. Establish your hearts, for the coming of the Lord is at hand. 9 Do not grumble against one another, brothers, so that you may not be judged. Look! The Judge stands before the gates. 10 As an example of patient suffering, brothers, take the prophets who spoke in the name of the Lord. 11 Look! We consider as blessed those who have endured. You have heard of the endurance of Job, and you have seen the outcome from the Lord, because the Lord is compassionate and merciful.

Exegetical Comments

5:7 Μακροθυμήσατε οὖν, ἀδελφοί:

> The storm of indignation is past, and from this point to the end of the epistle, St. James writes in the tone of tenderness and affection. The "therefore" shows that this sympathetic exhortation to the brethren is closely connected to the stern denunciation of the rich in the previous paragraph. The connection is obvious. These brethren are in the main to be identified with the righteous poor who are so cruelly oppressed by the rich; and St. James offers them consolation on two grounds: first, their sufferings will not last forever; on the contrary, the end of them is near at hand. Second, the end of them will bring not only relief, but also a reward (Plummer, 289–90).

The combination of an imperative with the nominative of address indicates a new paragraph. Everyone recognizes this because of the transitional particle οὖν, and because of the huge shift in tone from the previous passage, which was so vividly described by Plummer's quotation. It may not be wise to always posit a distinct difference between the two semantically associated words. It is easy to see, however, in this passage that there is an emphasis here on patience (μακροθυμέω/μακροθυμία) with other people (the Lord), while in 1:2–12 the emphasis was on the endurance (ὑπομένω/ὑπομονή) of difficult situations. This shift in words to a stress on endurance is also portrayed in the illustration of Job in Jas 5:11.[1] The word used here, μακροθυμέω, is rare in secular Greek, but the μακροθυμ-cognates are commonly used in the LXX, sometimes with reference to God's attribute of "longsuffering" (Ps 86:15) and sometimes in passages commending the virtue to people (Prov 19:11). Noncanonical Jewish texts also often utilize these words (e.g., Sir 29:8; Bar 4:25: τέκνα, μακροθυμήσατε τὴν παρὰ τοῦ θεοῦ ἐπελθοῦσαν ὑμῖν ὀργήν). See the summary of examples in Muraoka (439).

ἕως τῆς παρουσίας τοῦ κυρίου: The cognate verb πάρειμι can mean both "be present" and "become present (arrive)" (BDAG, 773). The substantive παρουσία can refer at times to the presence of persons (Jdt 10:18: "the noise of Judith's *presence* spread throughout the tents;" see also P. Oxy. 903.15: "He also swore in the *presence* [παρουσίᾳ] of the overseers"). It also sometimes can refer to an arrival or coming of someone, especially of a king (Thucydides, *Hist.* 1.128.5). In the Hellenistic period, it could describe the formal joyous visit of a sovereign to a city. An inscription from Tegea, the site of ancient Arcadia, is dated in "the sixty-ninth year of the first παρουσία of the god Hadrian in Greece."[2]

---

[1] Trench explains the difference between the word groups. "This distinction, I believe, will hold good wherever the words occur; namely, that μακροθυμία will be found to express patience in respect of persons, ὑπομονή in respect of things" (Trench, 198). This distinction may be useful at times, but it is difficult to dogmatically apply to their appearances in this chapter.

[2] *Bulletin de correspondance hellénique*, vol. 25, 1901, 275. "Beginning with the third century BC, there is the *parousia* of a Ptolemy (*P.Petr.* II, 39, *e* 18), then of Ptolemy Philometor and Cleopatra (*UPZ* 42, 18; cf. 109, 12), of Ptolemy II Soter (*P. Tebt.* 48, 13), of Ptolemy Philopator (3 Macc 3:17), of Germanicus (*SB* 3924, 34 =

In early Christian experience, the Greek word for "coming" or "arrival" (παρουσία) quickly became a technical term for Jesus' coming in glory and as judge. While there is a question about when in this chapter *Lord* is used as the title of God or of Christ, the use of παρουσία elsewhere in the NT refers to the return of Jesus—and that is undoubtedly the case here (Mayor, 182; Dibelius, 242–243; Laws, 208–9; Moo, 2000, 221). Therefore, this is the third explicit reference to Jesus in the book (see 1:1; 2:1). It assumes the function of a technical term in other NT documents from the earliest to the latest periods of their composition: Matt 24:3, 27, 37, 39; 1 Thess 2:19; 3:13; 4:15; 5:23; 2 Thess 2:1, 8, 9 (contrasting with the coming of Antichrist); 1 Cor 15:23; 1 John 2:28 and 2 Pet 1:16; 3:4. Believers are thus to remain resolute until Jesus returns and remedies their situation.

ἰδοὺ ὁ γεωργὸς ἐκδέχεται τὸν τίμιον καρπὸν τῆς γῆς μακροθυμῶν ἐπ' αὐτῷ ἕως λάβῃ πρόϊμον καὶ ὄψιμον: Between the fronted imperatives μακροθυμήσατε in 5:7a and 5:8a, James sets forth an illustrative example of that patience: the farmer's patient waiting (μακροθυμῶν) for the early and later rains in the autumn and spring seasons. The "early rain" was the rain of seed time and the "later rain" was the rain of ripening before harvest. The first rain still falls in the Levant about the beginning of November, after the seed is sown. The second comes around April, when the grain is ripening, and is thus prepared for the full harvest in the late spring. Without these two rains, the earth would be unfruitful. These "rains" were promised by God in the OT: "I will give you the rain of your land in due season, the first rain and the latter rain, so that you may gather in your grain, and your wine, and your oil" (Deut 11:14). For these seasonal blessings, they were not only to wait patiently, but also to pray (see Zech 10:1). While this agricultural analogy may not absolutely prove the point, it is at least consistent with a Palestinian, or at least a Levantine, provenance for

---

Chrest.Wilck., n. 413), and those of Hadrian" (references in this footnote cited from Spicq 3:55).

the letter.[3] The point of the illustration is that the situation is out of the farmer's hands because he must wait for the One who sends the rains. The believers addressed in this passage, therefore, must patiently wait for Him as well.

5:8 μακροθυμήσατε καὶ ὑμεῖς, στηρίξατε τὰς καρδίας ὑμῶν, ὅτι ἡ παρουσία τοῦ κυρίου ἤγγικεν: An eschatological theme that has been evident throughout the passage (5:1, 3, 5, 7) continues with another clear reference to the παρουσία. Three imperatives call for the readers to "be patient" and "establish their hearts" (5:8) and to "not grumble" against one another (5:9). In contrast with the rich who fatten their hearts for their own future judgment (slaughter) in 5:4, the aorist imperative here exhorts the believing poor to establish their hearts in anticipation of their future blessing at the Lord's coming. The verb στηρίζω with a direct object means to "set firmly" in the physical sense (Gen 28:12), and is used for "strengthening" oneself through food (Gen 27:37). Figuratively, it is used for "strengthening one's hands" (Exod 17:12) or "strengthening" others in their commitment (Acts 18:23; Rom 1:11; 16:25; 1 Thess 3:2; 2 Thess 2:17; 3:3). In the prophetic literature, "setting the face" denotes steadfastness of purpose (Amos 9:4; Jer 3:12; 21:10; 24:6; Ezek 6:2; 13:17; 14:8), a meaning carried over in Luke 9:51. James' language evokes the LXX idiom of "strengthen the heart," which connotes a courage that comes from trust in the Lord (Ps 111:8), or a firmness of intention (Sir 6:37; 22:16). It is one of these latter senses that James intends. The verb στηρίζω occurs thirteen times in the NT, and specifically appears in a similar "future" context in Luke 9:51; 22:32; and 1 Thess 3:13.

The other key question in this exhortation is how specifically it is true that this coming of the Lord "is at hand" or "is near" (perfect active ἤγγικεν). The word ἐγγίζω means "draw near" but describes something so near that its impact is starting to be felt. The word appears forty-

---

[3] D. Y. Hadidian, "Palestinian Pictures in the Epistle of James," *ExpTim* 63 (1952) 227–28; P. H. Davids, "Palestinian Traditions in the Epistle of James," in *James the Just and Christian Origins*, eds. Bruce Chilton and Craig A. Evans (NovTSup 98; Leiden: Brill, 1999), 47–48.

one times in the NT, and one of its occurrences that is significant for its usage in James is in Mark 11:1: "When they were approaching [ἐγγίζουσιν] Jerusalem, at Bethpage and Bethany, near the Mount of Olives, He sent two of His disciples." The point is that they were close but not yet there, but so close that Jesus sent two disciples ahead to get things ready. Other uses, such as Matt 21:34; 26:45–46; Luke 15:25; 18:35; 19:41; 21:8, 20; and 22:1 confirm that ἐγγίζω means to be very near—not yet arrived but still close enough for things to start happening. Scot McKnight has a useful illustration for the nearness of the Lord's coming in "the way a plane might be out into a holding pattern just before it arrives" (McKnight, 411–13). The state of affairs conveyed through the perfect tense of the verb is that God has heard the cries of the poor (perfect tense εἰσεληλύθασιν in 5:4), so that this hearing is now expressed in the "coming near" (ἤγγικεν) of the Lord's παρουσία as a "state of affairs."

Is the focus here of the coming for judgment on unbelievers or for blessing on believers? The nearness of the judgment may have reference to the destruction and sacking of Jerusalem in A.D. 70, and the next verse's reference to the Lord as "judge" (also expressed by a perfect tense) tends to support that view. The context in James, however, has stressed both judgment and blessing in the *eschaton* (see the previous verse for blessing) so the focus here is probably on both blessing and judgment.

5:9 μὴ στενάζετε, ἀδελφοί, κατ' ἀλλήλων ἵνα μὴ κριθῆτε: The three previous imperatives in 5:7–8 were positive and commended appropriate behaviors and attitudes to emulate. Here the imperative στενάζετε is fronted and negated and forbids the negative characteristic of grumbling. The verb is frequently used in the LXX for the utterance of various kinds of pain and grief (Exod 2:23; Jer 22:23; Lam 1:11; see Muraoka, 634). The following preposition κατ' increases the confrontational sense of the "groaning" (Martin, 192; Johnson, 316). The temptation to grumble may initially sound out of place, and appears at first to be imported inappropriately (Dibelius, 244). A farmer, however, may be tempted to grumble when the needed rains are delayed. In the same manner, the brothers may be tempted to grumble impatiently with each other when the Lord seems to delay His coming. The sense would be: "Don't blame one another for the distress of the present age." We ought to cultivate patience, and we ought not to blame one another for our undeserved distress, for it is part of the inevitable and temporary evil of the present age. For those who have ears to hear it, there is also a probable echo of the Dominical saying about judging in Matt 7:1. It is also appropriately employed here, especially with the similar use of the word group κρίνω/κριτής in the verse.

ἰδοὺ ὁ κριτὴς πρὸ τῶν θυρῶν ἔστηκεν. This eschatological tone, already negatively announced in the preceding paragraph (5:1–6), is repeated here as a positive reason to establish the hearts of the patient sufferers in 5:8c. The reminder that the judge is standing at the door in 5:9d (perfect stative ἔστηκεν) is emphasized because of the danger that believers face if they sinfully judge and condemn one other. The stative aspect of the perfect tense is employed in both these expressions (as well as in 5:4) to express the state of affairs that is associated with the Lord's *parousia*—namely that His coming is at hand and He is standing in front of the gates.[4] The urgency attending this admonition is emphasized by his calling the reader's attention (ἰδού) to the presence of the judge. With the reference to the judge being at the door, James utilizes a phrase which Jesus himself had used (Mark 13:29; Matt 24:33). Is this yet far into the future or as near as the realized eschatology of a.d. 70? The sense may be as much spatial as it is temporal, for James notes at once that "the judge stands before the gate," and he has said in 4:8, "draw near to God and he will draw near to you." The use of spatial and temporal categories with reference to

---

[4] Porter, *Verbal Aspect*, 358–59. Recent commentators, like McKnight (414–15), have been more sensitive to this function of the perfect tense, yet some still cling to older approaches to the perfect tense (e.g., Blomberg-Kamell, 228, who still have insightful comments on the entire passage).

God is necessarily metaphorical.[5]

5:10 ὑπόδειγμα λάβετε, ἀδελφοί, τῆς κακοπαθίας καὶ τῆς μακροθυμίας τοὺς προφήτας: James continues his practice of using asyndeton by means of using five primary clauses, two of which are supported by a relative clause (5:10b) and a causal clause (5:11e). The imperative λάβετε that initiates 5:10a is combined with the familiar address ἀδελφοί, as was the case in 5:9. This combination does not signal the beginning of a new paragraph because the following clauses continue the same semantic topic that was introduced in 5:7—that of patient endurance. The previous analysis displays a "double accusative" (ὑπόδειγμα ... τοὺς προφήτας) following the command to "take" (λάβετε). The initial ὑπόδειγμα functions as an accusative in apposition to the "prophets." Furthermore, it is in an especially prominent position preceding the predicate, something that James rarely does in this type of sentence (see 1:2). I have tried to point out this fronting by the translation, *"As an example of patient suffering, brothers, take the prophets ..."*

The reader's attention is thus drawn by this fronting of this second direct object ὑπόδειγμα in relation to the two prominent "exemplars" that follow—both the prophets in this verse and also Job in 5:11. The noun was used earlier in Jewish literature to call attention to the example of Israel's spiritual heroes (Sir 44:16; 2 Macc 6:28, 31). The prophets are exemplars of two characteristics that serve the purpose of this topic: τῆς κακοπαθίας καὶ τῆς μακροθυμίας. It is probably best to translate these doubled genitives as a *hendiadys* where one genitive modifies the other genitive ("patient suffering" or "patience in

---

[5] Witherington observes: "Paul is not talking about the temporal nearness of the return of Christ at all. He is reflecting on texts like Psalm 145:18–19 and Psalm 34:17–18 ('the LORD is near'), which goes on to speak of the righteous calling on the name of the Lord in a juxtaposition of the themes of perseverance, prayer and the nearness of God. Exactly the same thing occurs in James 5: James believes the Lord is spatially near the righteous in his audience, and he also believes that Christ could return at any time and so could be also temporally near. Some combination of the above (judgment, blessing and realized eschatology) thus best explains James' meaning here" (Witherington, 2007, 537).

suffering").[6] At least two English versions recognize here the use of hendiadys. "Brothers and sisters, as an example of *patience in the face of suffering*, take the prophets who spoke in the name of the Lord" (NIV). "For examples of *patience in suffering*, dear brothers and sisters, look at the prophets who spoke in the name of the Lord" (NLT). Both canonical and noncanonical Second Temple Period literature stressed the suffering of the prophets (Ezek 20:4, 5; 2 Chr 36:16; 1 Macc 2:59-64; Sir 44-50). Note especially 4 Macc 9:8: διὰ τῆσδε τῆς κακοπαθίας καὶ ὑπομονῆς ("through such patient endurance of hardship"). See also the prophets' suffering in NT references at Matt 5:12, 37; 23:34; Luke 11:49; Acts 7:52; Heb 11:33; and 1 Thess 2:15.

οἳ ἐλάλησαν ἐν τῷ ὀνόματι κυρίου, "who spoke in the name of the Lord." The relative clause refers back to the prophets. Were there specific texts that James had in mind? While we cannot know that for sure, it is striking that the Theodotian Greek text of Dan 9:6 reads: οἳ ἐλάλουν ἐν τῷ ὀνόματί σου. The LXX text says as much in Jer 20:9 and 44:16. This statement about what the prophets did may again appear to be extraneous, but it was undoubtedly added to point out that even the most eminent servants of God had been exposed to suffering and hardship. Therefore, the readers were not only to look to the message spoken by the prophets in the Lord's name (5:10b) but they were also to look to their example of patient suffering in the Lord's name. In other words, celebrated prophets had also experienced the same things that poor believers have suffered in 5:1-6! The wicked often oppressed the prophets because of the messages the prophets directed against them. In the same way, they oppressed the Son (see Matt 23:34), so even now they oppress the followers of those same prophets and the same Son! The responses of both Jeremiah the prophet as well as the One who was like Jeremiah, encourage present believers to be patient in their same type of suffering.

---

[6] B-D-F, 442, 16; D. A. Black, *Linguistics for Students of New Testament Greek: A Survey of Basic Concepts and Applications* (Grand Rapids, MI: Baker, 1988), 135.

5:11 ἰδοὺ μακαρίζομεν τοὺς ὑπομείναντας· τὴν ὑπομονὴν Ἰὼβ ἠκούσατε καὶ τὸ τέλος κυρίου εἴδετε: James then orders his readers to "look" at how we bless those who endure (5:11). That Daniel may be echoed in James' words appears possible due to the reference in 12:12: μακάριος ὁ ἐμμένων. The attempt to maintain an always sharp distinction between the separate word groups of μακροθυμία and ὑπομονή is questionable because they often overlap semantically. In this instance, however, it is important to recognize that James introduces the latter word, ὑπομονή, for the first time in this passage with his description of Job. He also appeals to the reader's knowledge about this patriarch and his ὑπομονή (ἠκούσατε). The verbal links with the OT character are quite evident, especially in the LXX. Job states in 6:11: "What is my strength that I should endure (ὑπομένω)?" In 14:14, he declares: "All the days of my service I would endure [ὑπομενῶ], till my renewal should come," and in 14:19 he states: "So You destroy man's endurance [ὑπομονὴν]," using the same noun as in Jas 5:11.

Contemporary readers of Job may be excused if they do not always recognize Job to be unfailingly *patient* in his dialogues with his friends that are recorded in Job 3–37! As a matter of fact, he often showed impatience with them, which we can appreciate by recognizing their ignorant charges of sinfulness as the reason for his suffering (Job 42:7). Job also was apparently impatient with God on some occasions (Job 9:27–35). If a careful nuanced distinction is recognized about the "endurance" (ὑπομονὴν) that Job displayed throughout his trials rather than his "patience" (μακροθυμίας), the problem of Job's improper response at times can be better appreciated.[7] Job was not always patient with his so-called friends, but he did begin his trial well (Job 1–2) and he also ended it well (Job 42). While struggling with the *why* of God's dealings with him, he never did curse God, although he was

---

[7] This approach is preferred to some occasional appeals to the *Testament of Job*, due to the lack of actual parallels to that work and also to its questionable dating. P. Gray, "Points and Lines: Parallelism in the Letter of James and the *Testament of Job*," *NTS* 50 (2004) 406–24. Thanks to Mariam Kamell for alerting me to this important article (Blomberg-Kamell, 230).

encouraged to do so by his wife (Job 2:9).[8] The unfortunate man did struggle because of his lack of knowledge of the entire situation, but despite that struggle, he endured until the final outcome.[9] The English word *outcome* is the best meaning of the word τέλος as well, and it is that outcome which he tells his readers "you have seen" (εἴδετε) by means of their hearing and/or reading the biblical text. This is an experience that James assumes on the part of his own hearers and readers! Rather than "purpose" the translation of τέλος as "outcome" better focuses on the end-events of Job's trials in Job 42 (GE, 2097 1.A).

ὅτι πολύσπλαγχνός ἐστιν ὁ κύριος καὶ οἰκτίρμων: The adjective πολύσπλαγχνος means "very kind" and has not been found in earlier Greek literature. Apart from much later patristic usage, it is found elsewhere only in *Hermas* 31, 57, and 60 (for nominal usage πολυσπλαγχνία, cf. *Hermas* 3, 6, 23, 39, as well as in Justin Martyr, *Dial.* 55). "It seems to be equivalent to LXX πολυέλεος. Like other words from σπλάγχνα (רחמים) it must be of Jewish origin. This group of words is rather more strongly represented in the NT than in the LXX, and seems to have come into free popular use in the intervening period" (Ropes, 299). The adjective οἰκτίρμων ("merciful") is frequently used in the LXX for רחמים, and nearly always used of God. In the majority of cases, it is combined with ἐλεήμων (see Luke 6:36).

The ὅτι that introduces these divine qualities and also the clause that concludes the paragraph provides the reason that leads to the outcome of the suffering, not only of Job but of the readers as well: "*because* the Lord is compassionate and merciful." This translation is preferred to viewing it as introducing a substantival clause and translating it as "that" in the sense of "namely, that the Lord is compassionate and merciful." The conjunction ὅτι appears sixteen

---

[8] The LXX's expanded rendering of the MT of Job 2:9 misses the intended meaning by rendering the Hebrew: "speak some word (εἰπόν τι ῥῆμα) to the Lord and die."

[9] C. R. Seitz, "The Patience of Job in the Epistle of James," in *Konsequente Traditionsgeschichte*, eds. R. Bartelmus, T. Kruger, and H. Utschneider (Orbis biblicus et orientalis 126; Göttingen: Vandenbrock & Ruprecht, 1993), 373–82.

times in James. Ten times it closely follows a verb and introduces a complement (1:3, 7, 13; 2:19, 20, 22, 24; 4:4, 5; 5:20). Six times it introduces an adverbial clause and is translated "because" (1:10, 12, 23; 3:1; 5:8, 11). James 5:11 follows this second pattern.

The message to James' readers is that they should focus on the ultimate outcome of their own trials, always with an eye to the Lord's certain coming. This is the only direct mention of Job in the NT, although the book bearing his name is likely quoted in 1 Cor 3:19 and in Phil 1:19. As the Lord was compassionate and merciful to Job, He will be the same to suffering and defrauded believers at the outcome of their own trials.

14

NO SWEARING (5:12)

Greek Text

12 Πρὸ πάντων δέ, ἀδελφοί μου, μὴ ὀμνύετε μήτε τὸν οὐρανὸν μήτε τὴν γῆν μήτε ἄλλον τινὰ ὅρκον· ἤτω δὲ ὑμῶν τὸ ναὶ ναὶ καὶ τὸ οὒ οὔ, ἵνα μὴ ᵃὑπὸ κρίσιν πέσητε.

Textual Notes

12.a. Byzantine scribes replaced ὑπὸ κρίσιν with εἴς ὑπόκρισιν and this reading appeared in the Textus Receptus. The translation then becomes, "So that you do not fall *into hypocrisy*." This reading was also in the text used by Oecumenius and Theophylact. However, since the expression ὑπὸ κρίσιν πέσητε is not found elsewhere, it is the more difficult reading and thus by the canon of *lectio difficilior*, it is to be preferred. All the early uncials and ancient versions also support the reading in the text.

Translation

12 But above all, my brothers, do not swear an oath, neither by heaven nor by earth nor by any other oath. Your "yes" should be yes and your

"no" should be no, so that you do not fall under judgment.

Introduction

There are some good reasons for considering 5:12 as marking a turn to the final section of this "homiletical letter." First is the use of the formula Πρὸ πάντων ("above all"). Whether or not it has specific contextual significance, such a phrase may serve in epistolary convention to signal a final series of remarks (see the later comments in this regard). Second, the negative command (μή) has initiated other major portions of James' composition (2:1; 3:1; 4:11). We will see if this proposal is valid, or if the verse has another overall role in the book at this point.

The following analysis reveals how James both addresses and arrests the attention of his readers, and then delivers two imperative commands, one that is negative and in the second person plural plus one that is positive and in the third person singular. The first command is elaborated by three neither/nor accusatives, and the second is elaborated by a purpose/result clause containing an implicit threat of judgment.

Πρὸ πάντων δέ, ἀδελφοί μου,

    μὴ ὀμνύετε μήτε τὸν οὐρανὸν

    μήτε τὴν γῆν

    μήτε ἄλλον τινὰ ὅρκον·

    ἤτω δὲ ὑμῶν τὸ ναὶ ναὶ καὶ τὸ οὒ οὔ,

        ἵνα μὴ ὑπὸ κρίσιν πέσητε.

I suggest that this passage should be viewed as standing alone. This is because of its special discourse markers and also because of its unique semantic content which is not linked directly to the surrounding paragraphs. The closing purpose clause in the verse does recall the coming of the Judge that was mentioned in 5:9. Therefore, this fact is against viewing the verse as a sort of free-floating piece of advice, either inserted here for no particular reason, or to loosely connect it to either what goes before or after. However, the great diversity among commentators as to whether it ends one section (Bengel, Alford, Alford, Mayor, Adamson) or initiates the next (Lange, Davids, Johnson) is a reason to stress its unique role in the flow of the book's argument.

The second person plural imperative (μὴ ὀμνύετε) in the first clause, combined with the nominative ἀδελφοί, is the way many other paragraphs open. In the second clause there is a shift to the third person imperative, which does not lessen the force of the command but is consistent with the Jesus *logion*, which will be examined shortly. The ellipsis in the coordinated third clause suppresses the predicator, which is also consistent with the *logion*. A secondary result clause concludes the verse and relates the exhortation to the coming of the judge mentioned in the previous paragraph (5:9).

Exegetical Comments

5:12 Πρὸ πάντων δέ, ἀδελφοί μου: The verse opens with the prepositional phrase πρὸ πάντων plus δέ, a postpositive conjunction that in some way relates the exhortation to the preceding paragraph. A distinctly new note is introduced by the adverbial expression πρὸ πάντων, which appears only here in the letter. An influential article by F. O. Francis contends that this is an indication that 5:12 begins the official conclusion to the letter.[1] Francis' arguments have been persuasive to many, but it should be noted that "introducing the conclusion" is not the function of the expression either in its other NT occurrence (1 Pet

---

[1] F. O. Francis, "The Form and Function of the Opening and Closing Paragraphs of James and I John," *ZNW* 61 (1970) 125.

4:8) or in its only use in the Apostolic Fathers (Did 10:4).[2] We have also previously noticed that this verse shares affinities more with its preceding than with its subsequent context. BDAG explains it as a "marker of precedence in importance or rank," translated as "above all," and appears to be quite accurate in that judgment (864). Louw and Nida note it as a "'marker of prime importance' tr. *more important than all else*" (627). Luke Johnson has effectively argued that Lev 19:12–18 is ever present in James' strategy, especially in chapter 5. He suggests that since Lev 19:12 is behind the command issued in 5:12, James refers to it as the *first* of those commands in Leviticus 19. According to Johnson the sense would be: "And the first of all [these commands], brothers, is not to swear."[3]

While Johnson's suggestion is creative, the use of πρό as first in a succession is not its meaning when used elsewhere with πάντων (e.g. Col 1:17). That the verse has a unique function that connects both to the preceding and to the subsequent passages is probably the best solution to the problem. In that regard, see the further comments on the next part of the verse.

μὴ ὀμνύετε μήτε τὸν οὐρανὸν μήτε τὴν γῆν μήτε ἄλλον τινὰ ὅρκον· ἤτω δὲ ὑμῶν τὸ ναὶ ναὶ καὶ τὸ οὒ οὔ: While the verb ὀμνύω occurs twenty-six times in twenty verses in the Greek NT, only in Jas 5:12 does it still take the accusative of that by which one swears, while it elsewhere is followed by ἐν or εἰς, which corresponds to the Hebrew preposition -ּבְ (e.g. Matt 5:34, 36; 23:12; BDF, 83; see also Wallace, 204–05).

While there are not many admonitions against oath-taking in earlier literature, an exception is the measured advice of Epictetus: "Refuse, if you can, to take an oath at all, but if that is impossible, refuse as far as circumstances allow" (Ench. 33). In Jewish ethical writings, there exists the clear prohibition only of frivolous swearing. For example, in Sir 23:9–11 the "man who swears many oaths"

---

[2] Polycarp, *Phil.* 5:3 uses the singular expression, πρὸ πάντος, not to conclude the letter, but rather to alert young men to be concerned with purity.

[3] Johnson, "Use of Leviticus 19," 133.

(πολύορκος) is reproached. A total prohibition of oaths did not prevail in Judaism, probably because the OT contained frequent oaths. The Essenes forbade oaths in general, but were required to take a solemn oath upon initiation (Josephus, J.W. 2.135, 139, 142). Philo has ethical advice of the most diverse nature on oaths. "To swear not at all is the best course and most profitable to life, well suited to a rational nature which has been taught to speak the truth so well on each occasion that its words are regarded as oaths" (Decal. 84). He also mentions swearing by the parts of the cosmos instead of by the Divine name (Spec. Leg. 2.5). However, "Rabbinic Judaism knows of such weakened substitute formulae" (Dibelius, 249).

Why does James consider his command not to swear to be of such primary importance? It is not necessary to think that James has placed this command above the royal law, which he has already enunciated in 2:12.[4] Perhaps James uses this expression because this command sums up all that he has said about speech ethics, which is undoubtedly a major theme in this letter. The absolute importance that he attaches to this command may also be related to the fact that this is the clearest example of a conscious reference to a Jesus logion that can be found anywhere in his letter. In the previous comments on 2:5, we explored in detail the use of the sayings of Jesus by his brother, James. The words of 5:12 bear striking verbal similarities to Matt 5:33–37, yet there are still differences between these sayings. While the differences are very real, they mostly are found in adjunct expressions or secondary clauses that explain or expand on the primary clauses. If we remove those secondary expressions, some striking verbal similarities emerge.

James 5:12	Matthew 5:34–37
μὴ ὀμνύετε	μὴ ὀμόσαι μήτε ἐν τῷ οὐρανῷ μήτε ἐν τῇ γῇ
μήτε τὸν οὐρανὸν	μήτε ἐν τῇ κεφαλῇ σου ὀμόσῃς

---

[4] The special function of this "law" in the ethics of James is stressed by Jobes, Letters, 203–11.

μήτε τὴν γῆν   ἔστω δὲ ὁ λόγος ὑμῶν ναὶ ναί, οὒ οὔ·

μήτε ἄλλον τινὰ ὅρκον·
ἤτω δὲ ὑμῶν τὸ ναὶ ναὶ καὶ τὸ οὒ οὔ
Figure 6: James 5:12 and Matthew 5:34-37

The purpose of this prohibition has to do with private assertions, so the two familiar substitute formulas for oaths are added simply as examples. Because it is not a question of uttering a specific formula for a specific occasion but rather a question of one's responsibility to be truthful, the second clause does not mean: "Let your affirmation be a simple 'yes,'" or, "Let your manner of affirmation be the double 'yes.'" Instead, the sense of the clause is: "Let your 'yes' be true and your 'no' be true." The problem that James addresses seems to be rash vows that were often broken, thus questioning the person's character and Christian testimony.

Does this strong imperative command forbid such things as national oaths of allegiance or oaths that are normally required when testifying in courtroom situations? Some Anabaptist groups and at least one cult have argued that it does. While oaths were not condemned in the OT, both Philo and the Essenes did limit them (see Philo, Decal. 17–19, 84; Spec. Leg. 2.1–6; Essenes: Josephus, J.W. 2.135). Jesus Himself, however, actually responded positively to what appears to be a legal call for an oath in the "courtroom" scene of Matt 26:63–64. It is difficult to see how this command forbids such public legal responsibilities as were just mentioned. The context, on the other hand, points to one's personal words used in everyday conversation. The meaning, therefore, is consistent with what James has been teaching about followers of Jesus being whole and complete and, therefore, single in all they do (1:8; 4:8). Those who follow Jesus should also follow the way of wisdom that is characterized by clear and honest talk. To feel that we must add an oath to what we are saying has the effect of debasing our words. The need for oaths makes it look as though our plain statement is not enough. Swearing should be necessary only in a society where the truth is not revered.

ἵνα μὴ ὑπὸ κρίσιν πέσητε, "so that you do not fall under judgment." James has in several other places connected his negative commands with statements concerning judgment (see 2:4, 12–13; 4:11–12; 5:9). Byzantine scribes replaced ὑπὸ κρίσιν with εἰς ὑπόκρισιν and this reading appeared in the Textus Receptus. As James has just clearly adapted a Jesus saying in the first part of the verse, it is likely that he also is echoing the judgment warning by Jesus found in Matt 12:36: "I tell you, on the day of judgment, people will give account for every careless word they speak, for by your words you will be justified, and by your words you will be condemned."[5]

---

[5] For a detailed and excellent analysis of this text, see W.R. Baker, "'Above All Else': Contexts of the Call for Verbal Integrity in James 5:12," *JSNT* 54 (1994) 57–71.

15

PRAYER, THE SICK, AND ELIJAH (5:13-18)

Greek Text

13 Κακοπαθεῖ τις ἐν ὑμῖν, προσευχέσθω· εὐθυμεῖ τις, ψαλλέτω· 14 ἀσθενεῖ τις ἐν ὑμῖν, προσκαλεσάσθω τοὺς πρεσβυτέρους τῆς ἐκκλησίας καὶ προσευξάσθωσαν ἐπ' αὐτὸν ἀλείψαντες [αὐτὸν] ἐλαίῳ ἐν τῷ ὀνόματι ᵃτοῦ κυρίου. 15 καὶ ἡ εὐχὴ τῆς πίστεως σώσει τὸν κάμνοντα καὶ ἐγερεῖ αὐτὸν ὁ κύριος· κἂν ἁμαρτίας ᾖ πεποιηκώς, ᵇἀφεθήσεται αὐτῷ. 16 ἐξομολογεῖσθε οὖν ἀλλήλοις τὰς ἁμαρτίας καὶ εὔχεσθε ὑπὲρ ἀλλήλων ὅπως ἰαθῆτε. Πολὺ ἰσχύει δέησις δικαίου ἐνεργουμένη. 17 Ἠλίας ἄνθρωπος ἦν ὁμοιοπαθὴς ἡμῖν, καὶ προσευχῇ προσηύξατο τοῦ μὴ βρέξαι, καὶ οὐκ ἔβρεξεν ἐπὶ τῆς γῆς ἐνιαυτοὺς τρεῖς καὶ μῆνας ἕξ· 18 καὶ πάλιν προσηύξατο, καὶ ὁ οὐρανὸς ὑετὸν ἔδωκεν καὶ ἡ γῆ ἐβλάστησεν τὸν καρπὸν αὐτῆς.

Textual Notes

14.a. The majority of witnesses contain the reading found in the critical text. The reading of 5:14 found in B oddly omits τοῦ κυρίου, giving only the phrase "in the name." Elsewhere in the NT this is a substitute for the fuller "the Lord Jesus Christ" (Acts 4:12, 17; 5:28; 1 Pet 4:16; 3 John 7). Already in James we see an occurrence of this (2:7). Furthermore, it is difficult to see how a scribe would have inadvertently omitted the longer reading of τοῦ κυρίου. In this regard, Metzger and his fellow editors agree.

15.b. The plural reading for the verb (ἀφεθήσονται) is supported by one later uncial (P), as well as some Byzantine mss along with Chrysostom and most of the Latin tradition. This "correction" of the grammar (to make the verb agree with the plural subject ἁμαρτίας), indicates that the singular verb in the text is both the earlier and the preferred harder reading.

Translation

13 Is anyone among you suffering? He should pray. Is anyone cheerful? He should sing praise. 14 Is anyone among you sick? He should call for the elders of the church, and they should pray over him, anointing him with oil in the name of the Lord. 15 And the prayer of faith will save the one who is sick, and the Lord will raise him up. And if he has committed sins, he will be forgiven. 16 Therefore, confess your sins to one another and pray for one another, that you may be healed. The prayer of a righteous person has great power as it is working. 17 Elijah was a person with a nature like ours, and he prayed fervently that it might not rain, and for three years and six months it did not rain on the earth. 18 Then he prayed again, and heaven gave rain, and the earth bore its fruit.

Introduction

It has been argued that 5:12 functions as a sort of stand-alone transition to the conclusion of this Diaspora encyclical, which now begins with 5:13. Conclusions of ancient letters often mentioned the recipients' health and a prayer, and this is consistent with the references to both health and prayer in 5:13–18. James, however, does not conform exactly to the way in which those matters are usually treated. He is concerned with internal and communal matters as is evidenced by his use of ἐν ὑμῖν in 5:13, 14, 19 and ἀλλήλοις and ἀλλήλων in 5:16. He introduces the topic of prayer in 5:13 and develops prayer as the main theme in the paragraph through 5:18. There are eight verbs— προσεύχομαι (5:13, 14, 17, 18), εὔχομαι (5:16), ψάλλω (5:13), προσκαλέω (5:14), and ἐξομολογέω (5:16)—and four nouns—ὄνομα (5:14), εὐχή (5:15), δέησις (5:16), and προσευχή (5:17)—that share the same semantic field (LN, 33.170–179). The paragraph first presents prayer as it is practiced in the community (5:13–16) and then describes the specific praying of Elijah as an exemplar (5:17–18).

Note the following sentence flow analysis of 5:13–14a:

5:13

Κακοπαθεῖ τις ἐν ὑμῖν,

    προσευχέσθω·

εὐθυμεῖ τις,

    ψαλλέτω·

5:14a

ἀσθενεῖ τις ἐν ὑμῖν,

    προσκαλεσάσθω τοὺς πρεσβυτέρους τῆς ἐκκλησίας

The above analysis of 5:13–14a illustrates how the paragraph begins with "Three Ecclesial Conditions and Three Responses" (McKnight, 432). The subparagraph thus opens with three rhetorical questions, each inquiring if there is any (τις) individual in the community with a special situation. Those who are found are then commanded to do certain acts in accord with their situations (5:13, 14a). How the elders are to pray over a sick one is described (5:14b) along with the results of such a prayer (5:15). A direct command is then issued to the entire community to confess their sins to one another (5:16a). The section is finally rounded off by an aphorism about the effectiveness of a righteous person's prayer (5:16b), which of course also leads to Elijah in 5:17 as the exemplar of a righteous person who prays.

Rather than opting for a moral utopian vision, James focuses on life and death within particular religious communities. "It is within knots of humanity that revolution is to occur: values, modes of thought about the divine, and their implications for how people live are to be transformed within tightly defined groups." Community members are to wait for the Lord to bring ultimate justice and purification of all human endeavors at the coming of the Lord. Now these members should endure any abuses from society and reject its way of life as an alien and polluting influence. Unlike the practices in the Dead Sea community (see 1QS), James issues no warrant for excommunication, since the letter ends with sinners being returned but not expelled.[1]

I have argued that the best antecedents to James' language and teachings are not found in the Greek moralists, but in the Jewish writers. James' concerns do tap into a moral discourse shared by a number of authors in antiquity, but James should be recognized as distinct in his particular Jewish communal concerns for the way through which morality is to be achieved and maintained.

The Suffering Should Pray and Sing (5:13)

Exegetical Comments

5:13 Κακοπαθεῖ τις ἐν ὑμῖν, προσευχέσθω: Of the three questions in 5:13–14a, only the third has an extended response (5:14b ff). "These short sentences, with question and answer, are characteristic of the diatribe" (Ropes, 303). This is still true even though this is in a positive and not a

---

[1] Strange has situated this letter within the Jewish world rather than in the Greek moralists. See J. R. Strange, *The Moral World of James: Setting the Epistle in its Greco-Roman and Judaic Environments* (SBL 136; New York: Peter Lang, 2010).

negative mood. As Ropes mentioned, this style of question and response is often found in the Greek diatribal literature (BDF, 262). There are other examples in the NT (e.g., 1 Cor 7:18: "Was anyone already circumcised when he was called? He should not undo his circumcision. Was anyone called while uncircumcised? He should not get circumcised); and in Philo (*Jos.* 144: "Have you great abundance? Share it with others. Have you but little? Do not envy those who have much. Are you in high reputation, and are you held in much honor? Be not insolent on that account. Are you lowly in your fortunes? Still let not your spirit be depressed. Does everything succeed with you according to your wish? Fear a change. Do you often stumble? Hope for good fortune hereafter").

James 5:13 highlights the two extremes of suffering and joy, and then outlines the two responses of praying and singing. The negative precepts for behavior in the previous verses (μὴ στενάζετε κατ' ἀλλήλων, μὴ ὀμνύετε), stressing the trials of earthly existence, are followed now by positive precepts for behavior in the community (ἐν ὑμῖν). In trouble and in joy and in sickness, the controlling thought should be prayer. The verb κακοπαθεῖ refers to calamity of every sort, and is not to be limited just as the opposite of εὐθυμέω (BDAG, 500, for κακοπαθέω; 316 for εὐθυμέω: "be cheerful"). See also the earlier use of the genitive noun κακοπαθίας in 5:10. The present tense forms of the imperatives are often viewed as expressing praying and singing continuously. A better approach is to recognize that the two present commands in 5:13 *generally* apply in all situations, while in 5:14 the two aorist commands apply *specifically* to severe illnesses (see Porter, *Verbal Aspect*, 359).

εὐθυμεῖ τις, ψαλλέτω: This verb can mean "to be cheerful" (LSJ, 715; Euripides, *Cyc.* 530; Plutarch, *Mor.* 465C). In the NT it can also mean "to take courage" (Acts 27:22, 25, 36). The English translation "be cheerful" (RSV) is accurate but should not be understood simply as describing someone as being in high spirits. It stands here in contrast to κακοπαθέω ("suffer") and ασθενέω ("be sick"), so the translation "feeling good" is more appropriate. The word group εὐθυμ- is not found in the canonical books of the LXX (the adjective εὔθυμος is only in 2 *Macc.* 11:26). In the NT, they are found elsewhere only in Acts 24:10 (εὐθύμως) and Acts 27:22, 25 (εὐθυμέω). "In both cases it is in passages of a distinctly Hellenic character" (Ropes, 303). The present imperative ψαλλέτω does not lessen the force of the imperative by being in the third person. Thus "let him sing a hymn" is probably better as "he should sing a hymn" or "sing praise" (see the verb in Eph 5:19; Rom 15:9; 1 Cor 14:15; and the noun ψαλμός in 1 Cor 14:26; Eph 5:19; Col 3:16). The verb was originally "play the harp" and is therefore used frequently in the OT, especially in Psalms (forty times) where it usually renders the verb זָמַר, "sing to the music of a harp" (Pss 7:17; 98:4). The use of the word in Hellenistic Greek, however, does not necessarily imply the use of an instrument (BDAG, 1096; GE, 2395-96).

It would be good to summarize overall what James has now said about what we should do when we "feel bad" due to suffering *and* also when we "feel good" due to positive experiences. The person who is suffering should not say, "I am being tempted by God" (1:13) or seek to retaliate against the source of his distress (5:7). Instead, he should direct his cries to "the ears of the Lord of *Sabaoth*" (5:4), for He is the one who "gives a greater gift" to the lowly (4:6). The person who is feeling good also should give expression to that truth by song, recognizing God as the generous giver (1:5) of every good and perfect gift (1:17), and as the one who is compassionate and merciful (5:11) and the source of genuine human happiness/blessedness (1:12; 5:11).

The Sick Should Call the Elders to Pray (5:14-16)

Exegetical Comments

5:14 ἀσθενεῖ τις ἐν ὑμῖν, προσκαλεσάσθω τοὺς πρεσβυτέρους τῆς ἐκκλησίας: The present active indicative of the verb ἀσθενέω means "is weak," as in a limb (Ps 109:29) or an organ (Ps 88:9). The NT also uses it in the sense of moral weakness (Rom 4:19; 1 Cor 8:7, 11–12), but the physical sense most often dominates the meaning (Matt 10:8; 25:36; Luke 9:2; John 4:46; 5:3; Acts 9:37; Phil 2:26). Physical weakness because of sickness is clearly the intended meaning here (cf. τὸν κάμνοντα in 5:15). How sick is "sick"? The answer to that question is in the verse itself—sick enough that the patient cannot go to the πρεσβύτεροι of the church but must have them come to his or her house.

The third appearance of ἐν ὑμῖν (the second is implied in the previous clause) clearly situates this and the entire set of actions *within* the believing community, an emphasis that dominates this last section (5:13, 14, 19). The first of two aorist imperatives, προσκαλεσάσθω, points to specific rather than general commands to be obeyed. It is interesting that it is the elders who are to be called—not apostles or someone else thought to have the gift of healing. Previously in Jas 2:2, the spiritual center of these believing communities is described as a building called a *synagogue*. Here the term that is used refers to a local worshiping community, an *ecclesia* (ἐκκλησία). In the Greek world, the ἐκκλησία referred to a gathered group of people (an "assembly") rather than to the place of meeting (Herodotus, *Hist.* 3.142; Aristotle, *Pol.* 1285A; Josephus, *Ant.* 12.164; *Life* 268). The reference here is also not to a building but to the communal gathering of believers.

The only other designation that James has used for church leaders was "teachers" (διδάσκαλοι) in 3:1. The term "elder" here (lit., "older one," πρεσβύτερος) is the comparative form of the classical πρέσβυς (LSJ, 1462) and occurs often in the papyri to describe a local town councilman or alderman (P. Oxy. 2121.4). The noun was also used in the LXX for local city council members (Josh 20:4; Ruth 4:2). The designation "elders of the people" or "elders of Israel," however, draws its meaning from Moses' appointment of seventy men to assist him in governing the people (Exod 19:7; 24:1; see also Lev 4:15; Num 11:16; 16:25; Deut 31:9; Josh 9:2; Judg 21:16; 1 Sam 4:3; 2 Sam 17:4). In the NT, the term is also used for the members of the Jerusalem Sanhedrin (Matt 15:2; 26:3; Luke 22:52; Acts 4:5; 6:12; 23:14; 25:15; see also Josephus, *Ant.* 11.83; 12.406). The word also describes leaders within the Christian movement both in Jerusalem and also in the daughter churches (Acts

11:30; 15:2, 23; 16:4; 1 Tim 5:1, 2, 17, 19; Titus 1:5; 1 Pet 5:1; 2 John 1; 3 John 1).

The expression "elders of the assembly" suggests something more than just older members in the community. The term πρεσβύτεροι describes official leaders who apparently are synonymous with the "overseers" (ἐπίσκοποι) in Acts 20:17, 28 and also in Pauline texts such as Phil 1:1; 1 Tim 3:1–7; and Titus 1:5–7. Note the similarity of language in 5:15 to Acts 20:17, where Paul "called to him the elders of the church" from Ephesus. It is impossible to always know how they were chosen at this stage, whether by an apostle (Acts 14:23) or simply recognized as worthy by the laypeople or by other elders. They certainly were respected spiritual leaders, probably very similar to the "elders" in other Jewish synagogues during the Second Temple Period.[2] That elders of Jewish communities would visit the sick is also attested in later rabbinic texts (*B. Bat.* 116a; *Ḥag.* 3a; and *Ned.* 41a).

καὶ προσευξάσθωσαν ἐπ' αὐτὸν ἀλείψαντες [αὐτὸν] ἐλαίῳ ἐν τῷ ὀνόματι τοῦ κυρίου: It is very important to recognize the syntactical structure of 5:14 because it affects the interpretation of the verse. Note that there are two primary imperative clauses that answer the question that was raised. Then there follows a subordinate participial clause describing an action that somehow accompanies the second of the main imperative command that precedes it. This can be seen in the following sentence flow analysis of 5:14.

ἀσθενεῖ τις ἐν ὑμῖν,	Question
προσκαλεσάσθω τοὺς πρεσβυτέρους τῆς ἐκκλησίας	Command
καὶ προσευξάσθωσαν ἐπ' αὐτὸν	Command
ἀλείψαντες αὐτὸν ἐλαίῳ ἐν τῷ ὀνόματι τοῦ κυρίου.	Action

The aorist middle imperative προσευξάσθωσαν commands the

---

[2] "It may very well be that the office of elder was taken over from the synagogue (drawn from the 'elders of Israel' in Exod 3:16; 24:1, 9; Deut 5:23; 19:12; Ezra 10:14; Matt 26:3) and given a Christian character (Bornkamm, *TDNT* 6:651–83; cf. Mussner, 219)" (Martin, 207).

elders to pray "over him" (ἐπ' αὐτόν). The elders were not summoned because they were especially skilled in medicine. There is not only no hint of that in the passage, but the context actually excludes that idea. If that were the writer's purpose, why does he not say at once, "Let him call for the physicians"? Physicians were available at this period, especially in the cities. If medicinal healing art is present at all in the passage, the case described is probably one in which medicine has already done all that it can. James would undoubtedly approve the advice given in Sir 38:9: "My son, in your sickness be not negligent, but pray unto the Lord, and He will make you whole." This agrees with the command, "Is anyone among you suffering? He should pray." The passage continues, "Then give way to the physician, for the Lord has created him. Let him not depart from you, for you have need of him. There is a time when in their hands there is good success" (Sir 38:12, 13). There is no exact equivalent in James, but he also says nothing that is inconsistent with it. Possibly something similar may have occurred in this situation in James, so that after the physician had done his part, and perhaps with no success, the sick person would summon the elders to offer prayer. "But it is simpler to suppose that the physician's part is left out of the account altogether" (Plummer, 326).

ἀλείψαντες αὐτὸν ἐλαίῳ: The participle is followed by the personal pronoun αὐτόν as an accusative of direct object with the "oil" (ἐλαίῳ) as an instrumental dative (Robertson, 64). The tense of the participle may express an antecedent action for the anointing, prior to the praying. This fine distinction in the timing of the aorist participle, however, is not inherent in the tense, and the action could simply be simultaneous (Davids, 193).[3]

Much detailed discussion among the commentators has arisen over the use of oil to anoint the sick, with Roman Catholicism drawing from this passage the sacrament of *extreme unction* (now called "the sacrament of the sick"). Only in the Middle Ages, however, did this

---

[3] Porter, *Idioms*, 187–90, lists a number of exceptions to the older idea of the "antecedent" function of the aorist participle.

sacrament develop for a dying person.[4] It is important to clearly note that the reference to the anointing with oil is part of a subordinate participle clause, with the primary clause describing the praying of the elders (see the above sentence flow analysis of 5:14). While this does not answer the remaining questions about the use of oil, it does place the subject in the larger context of prayer. What is clear is that the anointing is a secondary act that accompanies the most prominent action—namely, praying over the suffering one.

Was the application of oil intended to play a sacramental role (Mark 6:13), which somehow effects a spiritual result? Some commentators have also seen here a reference to demonic exorcism. "The whole procedure is an exorcism. A remedy from folk medicine was frequently applied in such miraculous healings, and such is the role of the oil here and in Mk 6:13. The intention is not to take advantage of its alleged or actual therapeutic effectiveness as a folk medicine, but rather to apply it as a medium of the divine power which is being conjured by means of the name" (Dibelius, 252). One of the most popular explanations is that the oil played a medicinal role (Luke 10:34). These two roles—sacramental and medicinal—are the two explanations most offered by commentators.[5] The sacramental explanation simply fails for lack of substantive evidence, apart from the possible function in the Mark reference. But there is also the difficult question that if the sacramental function is true, then why are there only two mentions of this "anointing" in the NT? In regard to the medicinal use of oil, the following extrabiblical references should be noted as representative examples. "For ointments what need was

---

[4] The decrees of the Council of Trent describe the "sacrament (as) insinuated indeed in Mark, but recommended and promulgated to the faithful by James the Apostle, and brother of the Lord" (Session 14, Chapter 1 on Extreme Unction). Later the result is described: "whose anointing cleanses away sins, if there are any still to be expiated, as also the remains of sins; and raises up and strengthens the soul of the sick person" (Chapter Two).

[5] There have been as many as ten explanations for the function of the oil in this passage, but most of these can be considered outright as inadequate (see McCartney, 253–55).

there to look for anything more than the fruit-juice pressed from the olive [ἀπὸ τῆς ἐλαίας ἐκθλιβομένου καρποῦ]? For indeed it produces smoothness, and counteracts physical exhaustion, and brings about good condition" (Philo, *Som.* 2.58). "When I finally calmed my stomach and refreshed my body with an *anointing* ..." (Seneca, *Ep.* 53.5). Herod was given an oil bath when he was ill (Josephus, *Ant.* 17.172; *J.W.* 1.657). It should be noted that these examples all are for refreshment, not for curing a sickness. Physicians probably made use of the derivative benefits of oils when rubbed upon the skin, or they used the oil as a medium for the application of other medicines. Shogren and others, therefore, have effectively ended the widespread assumption that oil as a curative medicine was universally recognized in ancient days.[6] Even if it was used as an external treatment (as in Luke 10:34), there is little, if any, solid evidence to back up its internal ingestion as a treatment for the ill.[7]

With these options (sacramental or medicinal), what is the best approach to its intended use in Jas 5:14? I agree with the suggestion that since the OT function of anointing with oil was to "consecrate" someone, the anointing here was intended to "consecrate" or "set apart" the sick one for concentrated prayer offered by the community (Moo, 241).[8] Anointing, therefore, was to remind the sick person that he belongs to God, as the anointed ones in the OT were so considered, and to remind the community (always as the main focus in this passage) that the sick one is now "set aside" for concentrated prayer.[9]

---

[6] G. Shogren, "Will God Heal Us? A Re-Examination of James 5:14–16a," *EQ* (1989) 99–108.

[7] Some mention a distinction between the "secular" word for anoint (ἀλείφω) and the "religious" word (χρίω) as indication here that this reference cannot have any religious connotation. The accompanying articles have again shown the fallacy of Trench's famous distinction between the words (Trench, *Synonyms*, 129).

[8] For a similar suggestion about this function of the oil, see Shogren, 99–108, as well as the excellent and thorough treatment by K. Warrington, "James 5:14–18: Healing Then and Now," *IntRevMiss* 93 (2004) 346–67. The latter article deserves serious consideration for its thorough handling of these issues.

[9] Is there a possible eschatological thrust related to the Anointed One in Isa 61 providing beauty and joy for those who grieve? "If James has this in mind, just as

5:15 καὶ ἡ εὐχὴ τῆς πίστεως σώσει τὸν κάμνοντα καὶ ἐγερεῖ αὐτὸν ὁ κύριος: In order for prayer to be effective, it must be offered out of a person's faith in trusting God. A cry out of desperation from an unbeliever will not prevail. "What James means by 'prayer of faith' is probably revealed in 1:5–6: praying without wavering or doubting. This is not a prayer that believes something *specific* about what God will do, although that is not excluded, but a prayer that is offered out of a basic unconditional trust that God knows what is best and can handle the situation" (Witherington, 2007, 544–45).

The verb σώσει does not likely refer to a person's spiritual salvation, but to the saving of the person from the sickness. James 5:15b is simply another way of expressing 5:15a, that is, if the person is cured, he has been raised up by the Lord from the sickbed. This is not a reference to the resurrection at the last day, but is a prayer of faith by others for the sick person, who has come to pray over the sick one (τὸν κάμνοντα, for the first time) (McKnight, 442). In other words, this verse cannot be used to suggest that healing depends on the degree of faith in the ill person, who must also pray for himself.

κἂν ἁμαρτίας ᾖ πεποιηκώς, ἀφεθήσεται αὐτῷ. The second half of the sentence forms a third-class condition, with a rare perfect active periphrastic participle (ᾖ πεποιηκώς) in the protasis.[10] The context of this conditional sentence makes it clear that there can be no confident assumption that there *must* be some sin committed by the sick person that needs divine forgiveness. One is reminded about the wrong assumption of Job's friends that lead to their repeatedly wrong

---

in 1:2, suffering is linked with eschatological joy" (McCartney, 255). This nuance may be an example of over-reading the text by forcing on it a theological construct arising from later reflection rather than from what actually is in the text.

[10] With the accompanying subjunctive ᾖ, this construction is called a "pluperfect periphrastic participle" (Robertson, 906; BDF, 252, 355; Wallace, 583–86, 649). Although the perfect active participle is quite common in the NT, appearing 122 times, its use as a periphrastic elsewhere is limited to five times in Lucan writings (Luke 5:1; 15:24; Acts 16:9; 21:33; 22:29) and once in Hebrews (2:13, quoting Isa 8:17) in a future perfect periphrastic construction.

admonitions delivered to him. The verse, however, also does not exclude the possibility that past sins may well have caused current illnesses.

The switch from the preceding plural "sins" to the singular verb should be noted (ἀφεθήσεται αὐτῷ, "it will be released/forgiven with respect to him"). The construction is, therefore, impersonal (Mayor, 174). It is problematic and a textual variant (ἀφεθήσονται) suggests that some scribes saw this as a "problem."[11] The singular verb ἀφεθήσεται should, however, be retained as the "harder" and the preferred earlier reading (cf. Matt 9:2–6; 12:31; Mark 2:5–11; 3:28; Luke 5:20–24; 7:47–48; 12:10).

Some writers have argued that these verses indicate a practice that was valid only in apostolic times, and that we should not have the right to expect supernatural healings any longer, thus Calvin and others, in both the Reformed and the Dispensational traditions. "But James does not place any restrictions on how long or to whom his command applies, and inasmuch as miraculous healings have occurred throughout the Bible and church history for good and godly ends, we dare not restrict such activity to any given time period" (Blomberg-Kamell, 244–45). Church leaders need to prayerfully consider how this ministry of mercy should be conducted in its details.

The Sinners Should Confess and Pray (5:16-18)

Exegetical Comments

5:16 ἐξομολογεῖσθε οὖν ἀλλήλοις τὰς ἁμαρτίας καὶ εὔχεσθε ὑπὲρ ἀλλήλων: The transitional particle οὖν leads to the overall lesson to be gained

---

[11] "It has the plural verb *aphethēsontai* ("they will be forgiven him"), clearly because *hamartias* in the previous clause is seen as an accusative plural rather than a genitive singular. The singular verb ('it will be forgiven him') appears to demand taking *hamartias* as the genitive singular: 'if he has become a doer of sin.' The plural form of *hamartia*, furthermore, appears in the very next verse!" (Johnson, 334).

from this instruction: the command to confess sins to one another. The verb ἐξομολογέω is used in the LXX both for professing the Lord and for praising Him (see Gen 29:35; 2 Sam 22:50; 1 Chr 16:4; 2 Chr 5:13; Ps 6:6; Jer 40:11; Dan 3:25). In the NT ἐξομολογέω is used mostly for "professing" (Matt 11:25; Luke 10:21; Rom 14:11; 15:9; Phil 2:11). With the exception of the present passage, ἐξομολογέω is used for "confessing sins" in the NT only in Mark 1:5; Matt 3:6; and Acts 19:18. The act of confessing one's sins is firmly rooted in Judaism, whether for individuals (Lev 5:5; Num 5:7; Ps 38:8; 1QS 1.23–2.1) or for groups (Lev 16:21; 26:40; Deut 9:4–10; Jdt 9:1–14; Tob 3:1–6).

In 5:16 the link between sin and illness, forgiveness and salvation is continued from the preceding verse. Here, however, it is not only the elders who are encouraged to intercede on behalf of the sick, because the whole assembly (ἐκκλησία) is to constitute a community of mutual prayer. Thus they (and we) are all exhorted to confess their sins to one another and to pray for one another. We see public confession of sins in other texts from the NT (Mark 1:5; Matt 3:6; Acts 19:18; 1 John 1:9). Other early Christian communities understood this in a communal sense (1 Clem. 51.3; 52.1; Did. 14.1; Barn. 19.12; Hermas 1; 9; 100; cf. also Did. 4.14, which commands the young convert to "confess [ἐξομολογήσῃ, same verb as in James 5:16] your sins in an assembly [ἐν ἐκκλησίᾳ])."

There is nothing in the text to support the practice of oracular confession to a priest or minister—unless the priest or minister is the one who has been sinned against! Since James describes his concern as *mutual* confession, no basis should be then found here for designating any elders as official hearers of confession and grantors of absolution. "Perhaps the most distinctive aspect of the practice advocated by James is its *mutual* character: they are to confess to each other, not only 'transgressions' of law, but 'sins'" (Bengel, 334).

How public should this confession be, and how can this practice avoid descending into airing publicly information, false or true, personal or public, that might be unedifying? Jesus did teach a private and personal confession to the person offended (Matt 18:15). Since the context of the passage is that of the worshiping community, however, this is intended to be a communal command, not limited to private confession to each other. "Communal confession of sin remains important for the life and health of the community, even if our own sins have not had obvious physical consequences in our lives" (Kamell-Blomberg, 245). Elders should of course be vigilant in overseeing such public practice, but fear of possible abuse of this public confessing should not cause us to avoid it. A study of the history of revivals shows that real revivals have been initiated with such public confessions! This practice is rarely witnessed today and is usually limited to the "general confession" in liturgical churches.[12]

ὅπως ἰαθῆτε: The plural verb again stresses the communal character of this passage, while the combination of ὅπως and the subjunctive can convey purpose but also result.[13] This verb (ἰάομαι) can refer to healing the diseases of the soul (Heb 12:1; 1 Pet 2:24; Matt 13:15; as well as LXX of Deut 30:3, "ἰάσεται Κύριος τὰς ἁμαρτίας σου"; 2 Chr 30:20; Isa 6:10; 57:19). If the word is understood literally of healing bodily diseases (examples too numerous to cite), then the connection is perhaps closer with the preceding thought. A miraculous cure, which is spoken of in the preceding verse, seems also to be referred to in the words that follow, which dwell on the miraculous power of Elijah's prayers.

Πολὺ ἰσχύει δέησις δικαίου ἐνεργουμένη: This indicative statement has the appearance of an aphorism, which James often appends to the end of his paragraphs (see 3:18). If so, it not only rounds off what he has just written, but also points forward to Elijah, the shining exemplar of the righteous praying person whom he will commend to his readers.

---

[12] "If an individual has sinned against the whole body, then confession to the whole body by way of its elders is appropriate, and sins that disrupt the harmony and peace of the community must be dealt with within the community, not by posting them in public, not even by putting them on display before everyone in the church, but by way of the elders who represent the body as a whole" (McCartney, 258).

[13] See the helpful discussion on this usage in Porter, *Idioms*, 232; Wallace, 473–74; and Moule, 138–39.

The use of the participle ἐνεργουμένη has caused some difficulty in getting a clear English translation of the sentence. The feminine participle says something about the feminine noun "prayer" (δέησις). This present middle participle of ἐνεργεω, as Paul apparently uses it in Gal 5:6; 2 Cor 4:12; and 2 Thess 2:7, probably has a temporal sense: "when it works." The passive is possible, as is the usual idiom elsewhere. Some older commentators did argue strongly for the passive here—namely, "when it is exercised" (Mayor, 171–73; and Ropes, 310). The ESV renders it like a periphrastic: "The urgent request of a righteous person is very powerful in its effect." The NASB: "The effective prayer of a righteous man can accomplish much." The CSB has: "very powerful in its effect." The NIV has a simple elegance: "The prayer of a righteous person is powerful and effective." I have opted for a circumstantial rendering conveying the manner of the prayer's working: "The prayer of a righteous person has great power as it is working." Anachronistic semantics, based on the modern English word *energy*, would see this as an "energetic" prayer! The participle more likely conveys that we should *exercise* or "work at" our approach to prayer more consistently.

In the Jewish tradition there was a strong belief in the powerful efficacy of the prayers of the righteous teachers/rabbis, known as the צַדִּיקִים (*tsaddikim*). Thus Abraham (Gen 18:25ff; 20:17); Moses (Exod 32:11–14, 31–35); prophets such as Amos (7:2–3, 5–6) and Jeremiah (Jer 7:16; 11:14; 14:2); and the Maccabean martyrs (2 *Macc.* 7) are all depicted as righteous individuals whose powerful prayers were heard by God. But James will focus on only one of these spiritual giants, Elijah the Tishbite.

5:17 Ἠλίας ἄνθρωπος ἦν ὁμοιοπαθὴς ἡμῖν, καὶ προσευχῇ προσηύξατο τοῦ μὴ βρέξαι: Following a simple but profound indicative affirmation about the human nature of the prophet, James follows with four additional indicative statements about his specific deeds related to prayer, and then concludes with two indicative statements about the results of his praying.

5:17

Ἠλίας ἄνθρωπος ἦν ὁμοιοπαθὴς ἡμῖν,
καὶ προσευχῇ προσηύξατο τοῦ μὴ βρέξαι,

καὶ οὐκ ἔβρεξεν ἐπὶ τῆς γῆς ἐνιαυτοὺς τρεῖς καὶ μῆνας ἕξ·

5:18

καὶ πάλιν προσηύξατο,

καὶ ὁ οὐρανὸς ὑετὸν ἔδωκεν

καὶ ἡ γῆ ἐβλάστησεν τὸν καρπὸν αὐτῆς.

As was noted, the previous verse ends with the general aphorism, "The prayer of a righteous person has great power as it is working." This rounds off the discussion of prayer in 5:13–16 and also leads into this concluding subparagraph. James holds up before his readers the one who is the prime exemplar of a righteous man whose prayers worked powerfully—Elijah the prophet. The nontypical (for James) parataxis of these six clauses, with five consecutive uses of καί, is the most prominent linguistic feature of this compact narrative section. It recalls, therefore, the narrative context of this exemplar, drawn entirely from the text of 1 Kings. Yet it is the very source for these actions that is sometimes called into question. It is common among commentators to posit a noncanonical source such as *4 Ezra* or *Lives of the Prophets* as influencing our author in the details of his description. The problem that they sense is twofold. The first problem is that the text of 1 Kings does not expressly mention that Elijah *prayed* for the rain to be withheld. Neither does the canonical text clearly state that he prayed for the rains to return. We clearly have the drought and we clearly have the rain, but strictly speaking, there is no mention of prayer in connection with the two miraculous conditions. The second problem is that the text of 1 Kings does not clearly mention that three *and a half* years was the length of the drought. Its author only generally refers to the "third year" of the drought before the climactic events at Mount Carmel (1 Kgs 18:1). What can be said about these issues?

This commentator has no problem with the possibility that James could employ a noncanonical source in his arguments, if that text conveys accurate information. Other NT authors like Jude, as well as the author of Hebrews, did as much. This suggestion, however, raises more questions than it answers. The current scholarly consensus is that both of the possible works mentioned earlier (*4 Ezra* and *Lives of the Prophets*) emerged no earlier than the late first century.[14] This would practically eliminate them as possible sources for James, unless one argues for its very late date, which is not the growing consensus about the date of the book. Furthermore, there is no reference in either of these sources to Elijah's first prayer. Finally, neither of them refers to the "three and a half year" period of drought.

Perhaps we should look closer at the most logical source for this information—within the canonical text of 1 Kings. The language of Elijah in 1 Kgs 17:1 at least implies a prayer: "As the Lord, the God of Israel, lives, *before whom I stand,* there shall be neither dew nor rain these years, except by my word." Thus his praying is an understandable inference from this statement. Evidently, other Second Temple Period authors drew the same inference (Sir 48:2–3; 2 Esd 7:109). Furthermore, the language used to describe the prelude to the long-awaited deluge in 1 Kgs 18:42 also implied an accompanying prayer: "And he bowed himself down on the earth and put his face between his knees." With this language so evident before us in the canonical text, why should we look elsewhere?

καὶ οὐκ ἔβρεξεν ἐπὶ τῆς γῆς ἐνιαυτοὺς τρεῖς καὶ μῆνας ἕξ: The three and a half year drought is also found in the words of Jesus in Luke 4:25, so the time period left some additional traction outside of James' writing.

---

[14] D. R. A. Hare, "Lives of the Prophets," *ABD* 5:502; M. E. Stone, "Second Book of Esdras," *ABD* 2:611–14.

A suggested source for this drought length usually is some unknown haggadic tradition, or it is explained as a supposed eschatological/apocalyptic reference (Daniel or Revelation). Of course, the suggestion of the Apocalypse as a source is quite anachronistic even again with a much later date for James and Luke. The author's familiarity with Palestinian traditions, which seems to permeate the writing, offers a better explanation. Earlier in the chapter, James displayed his knowledge of Palestinian agriculture with his reference to the early and later rains (5:7). It is well known among inhabitants of the Levant that after the later rains in the spring there is a six-month drought before the early rains commence in the autumn. Could the following, therefore, be a possibly similar scenario? If Elijah's announcement of the drought was at the end of the six-month dry season, the additional three years of drought would then provide the total length of three and a half years mentioned by James and Jesus. This explanation, also offered by a longtime Palestinian resident E. F. Bishop, has sadly been often overlooked by many commentators.[15]

ἄνθρωπος ἦν ὁμοιοπαθὴς ἡμῖν: We return to the first clause in this verse to remind ourselves of the nature of this man who prays. The message is that the great prophet was made of the "same stuff" of which both the readers and the author (ἡμῖν) were made. The difference is that Elijah prayed with faith and was not of a double mind (1:6–8). Furthermore, he "prayed with prayer," a cognate dative expression (προσευχῇ προσηύξατο) recalling the Hebrew infinitive absolute and expressing the idea "he prayed fervently." To intensify the action of the verb is the function of cognate datives (Wallace, 168). The praying of the great, although still human, prophet was held up to the readers as an example of what their prayers could accomplish if they prayed in faith out of the background of a righteous life. It is this type of single-minded praying, according to James, which is inspired by a wisdom from above.

The prayer of such a person is able to accomplish much when it is

---

[15] E. F. Bishop, "Three and a Half Years," *ExpTim* 61 (1949–50) 126–27.

in accord with God's plan, since there is no idea in the context or anywhere else in James about pressure being put on God for an answer. No one can persuade God to do something that is against His will, nor does prayer tell God about something of which He is ignorant. "Rather, it is our way of showing concern about something and gives us an opportunity to be a vessel through which God acts to heal and help, just as he used Elijah" (Witherington, 2007, 547).

5:18 καὶ πάλιν προσηύξατο, καὶ ὁ οὐρανὸς ὑετὸν ἔδωκεν καὶ ἡ γῆ ἐβλάστησεν τὸν καρπὸν αὐτῆς: The threefold repetition of καί in this verse serves as a signal that James is recounting the story in the biblical text, even following the narrative style in so doing (see the previous comments that explain this apparent allusion to 1 Kgs 18:42). The second clause, ὁ οὐρανὸς ὑετὸν ἔδωκεν, was a popular form of expression, as is seen in Acts 14:17. James then concludes his straightforward retelling of the Elijah saga with the following: καὶ ἡ γῆ ἐβλάστησεν τὸν καρπὸν αὐτῆς ("and the earth bore its fruit"). While that may be a safe conclusion to make from what we read in the biblical account, the OT text again does not state that in so many words. It is good to ask at this point why James would add this seemingly random statement. Has James "massaged" the canonical text of 1 Kings to make his points about the prophet? With an eye to the overall discourse strategy of James, it is easy to make two connections with previous material. The occurrence of καρπός, "fruit," recalls for an observant reader the description of wisdom from above in 3:17–18 with its promise there that the "fruit of righteousness is sown in peace for those who make peace." So the example of Elijah is used as a counterpoint to stress once again the need for a peaceful solution gained by prayer and submission to the divine will. There is also a possible connection with Jas 5:7, where we read that the farmer awaits the precious fruit of the earth (καρπὸν τῆς γῆς), which is always given after the first and then the second rain. The renewal of the earth by its fruit also establishes a parallel with the sick person also mentioned in this passage. There is a parallel with sickness/dry land and health/fruit-bearing land. The refreshing of the parched land through the praying of the righteous Elijah points to the refreshing of the weary and sick person through the praying of a righteous elder.[16]

Finally, the majestic greatness of Elijah that is stressed in other Elijah traditions (Sir 48:1–12) is not stressed here, because the interest of James in Elijah is precisely in his humanity. In other words, he is an example of the power of human prayer.

---

[16] "'Heaven gave rain' is idiomatic for 'God sent rain' (1 Kings 18:1 is in view), but there may also be a play on the two parts of creation (heaven and earth) as the means of God's provision: 'heaven gave rain, and the land [ἡ γῆ] brought forth fruit'" (McCartney, 261).

16

RETURNING A BROTHER (5:19-20)

Greek Text

19 Ἀδελφοί μου, ἐάν τις ἐν ὑμῖν πλανηθῇ ἀπὸ τῆς ἀληθείας καὶ ἐπιστρέψῃ τις αὐτόν, **20** ᵃγινωσκέτω ὅτι ὁ ἐπιστρέψας ἁμαρτωλὸν ἐκ πλάνης ὁδοῦ αὐτοῦ σώσει ψυχὴν ᵇαὐτοῦ ἐκ θανάτου καὶ καλύψει πλῆθος ἁμαρτιῶν.

Textual Notes

20.a. In 5:20, B and a few mss replace the third person imperative γινωσκέτω with the second person γινωσκετε, which can also be an indicative/imperative. The switch may be to help differentiate between the author and his readers.

20.b. The omission of αυτου in σώσει ψυχὴν αὐτοῦ ἐκ θανάτου in the Majority text is likely due to a scribal attempt to clear up the ambiguity as to whose soul will be saved: the converter or the converted.

Introduction

This brief passage is simple and structured clearly, as the following sentence flow analysis indicates:

5:19

Ἀδελφοί μου,

    ἐάν τις ἐν ὑμῖν πλανηθῇ ἀπὸ τῆς ἀληθείας

    καὶ ἐπιστρέψῃ τις αὐτόν,

5:20

    γινωσκέτω ὅτι

        ὁ ἐπιστρέψας ἁμαρτωλὸν ἐκ πλάνης ὁδοῦ αὐτοῦ σώσει ψυχὴν αὐτοῦ ἐκ θανάτου

        καὶ καλύψει πλῆθος ἁμαρτιῶν.

This final paragraph opens with ἀδελφοί—the fifteenth occurrence of this nominative of address and the tenth time that it inaugurates a new paragraph (1:2, 16, 19; 2:1, 14; 3:1; 4:11; 5:9, 12, 19). This address preceding the protasis of a conditional clause is combined with an imperative (γινωσκέτω) preceding the apodosis of the clause in 5:20. The imperative is not demanded in the syntax, so its function is as another meta-comment that calls attention to the prominent ὅτι content clause concluding the sentence and the book. Commentators have generally overlooked that this is only the second time that James fronts the ἀδελφοί μου, which normally is preceded by the imperative command. The placing of the address here and in 2:1 serve as an inclusio for the two paragraphs that open and close what a number of commentators view as the body of the letter with chapter 1 serving as "something of a table of contents" (Johnson, 15; Bauckham, 63).

There are also some interesting verbal connections with chapter 1. The imperative γινωσκέτω echoes the appeal to γινώσκοντες in 1:3. The subjunctive πλανηθῇ describes the erring that was warned against by the μὴ πλανᾶσθε command in 1:16. Larger semantic parallels with the entire work also emerge. The "two ways" tradition is the basis of the entire paranetic appeal and is evidenced by the peak paragraph in 3:13–18 with its comparison of the wisdom from above and that from below. This finds a clear illustration with the reference to the "erroneous way" in 5:20 and the "truthful way" in 5:19.

In addition to its connections at the macro-level of discourse, the paragraph's connection at the micro-level is evidenced by the τις ἐν ὑμῖν, which ties this paragraph with the preceding one which also opens with the repetition of the same expression three times (once implied) in 5:13–14. This expression also focuses the instruction on the internal life of the community rather than the general warnings to the faithless planners and the greedy rich in 4:13–5:6. The abrupt ending is absent of the typically Pauline greetings to particular churches. This is consistent with the catholic, or general, nature of this encyclical and is similar to the end of 1 John where the author abruptly ends with a warning against idolatry and an exhortation about a sinning brother (1 John 5:16–21). It is also no more abrupt than the conclusions in two other wisdom writings, such as *Sir.* 51:30 and *Wis.* 19:22:

Sirach: "Do your work in good time, and in his own time God will give you your reward."

Wisdom of Solomon: "For in everything, O Lord, you have exalted and glorified your people, and you have not neglected to help them at all times and in all places."

The canonical book of Proverbs also ends rather abruptly: "Give her of the fruit of her hands, and let her works praise her in the gates" (31:31; ESV).

Translation

19 My brothers, if anyone among you is led astray from the truth and someone brings him back, 20 let him know that whoever brings back a sinner from his straying will save his soul from death and will cover a multitude of sins.

Exegetical Comments

5:19 ἐάν τις ἐν ὑμῖν πλανηθῇ ἀπὸ τῆς ἀληθείας καὶ ἐπιστρέψῃ τις αὐτόν: Addressing them again as "brothers," James expresses concern about one of their "own" (ἐν ὑμῖν) who has been "turned" (note the passive πλανηθῇ) or "been led astray" from the truth. While we should not press the passive voice unduly, this is a hypothetical member of the community, considered to be among the "brothers," who was probably led astray by a false teacher.[1] Drawing from other references in the NT, this being deceived or led away by someone even to apostasy was a very real problem in the early church (Acts 20:29–30; 2 Tim 3:1–9; Heb 6:4–6; 2 John 7–8; Jude 3–4). Embedded in this verb's LXX usage are idolatrous ideas (Isa 9:5; Jer 23:17; Ezek 33:19; Prov 14:8). Satan is also portrayed as the ultimate deceiver and thus "the deceived one," like this individual, could be under just such satanic influence.

This attribution is borne out in much of the NT literature (see Matt 12:22–37; 24:4–5, 11; Mark 12:24, 27; 13:5–6; Rom 1:27; Eph 4:14; 2 Thess 2:11; 2 Tim 3:13; Titus 3:3; 1 Pet 2:25; 2 Pet 2:15, 18; 1 John 2:26; 4:6; Rev 2:20). James has already given attention to the warning that certain misbehavior is the work of the devil (3:15; 4:7; cf. 2:19). Thus, a person who deliberately forsakes the 'way of righteousness' is under the control of the devil and in need of a radical conversion. Otherwise, this person faces the risk of condemnation by God (Martin, 219).

---

[1] There is always the possibility that the aorist passive of the verb is a θη middle not intended to be translated as a passive voice: i.e. "turns."

"The truth" (τῆς ἀληθείας), at least in this context and most often elsewhere, does not refer to Christian doctrine in the theological sense but more broadly to all that is involved in the gospel and in its way of life. "This *truth* is something that is to be *done* as well as *believed* (Ps. 51:6; Gal. 5:7; 1 John 1:6). And for James, of course, correct doctrine cannot be separated from correct behavior" (Moo, 2000, 249). The expression does not mean theoretical correctness, although it assumes that as a base, but rather the proper "way" of behaving. We should perhaps think of a double-minded person like the one described in 1:8, to whom not only wrath is shown (4:8) but now also compassion and concern.

This responsibility of brothers who are following the way of wisdom to return an erring brother who has left "his way" (ὁδοῦ αὐτοῦ in 5:20) echoes Matthew's version of the parable of the lost sheep (Matt 18:12–14) and is incumbent on brothers in many other places in our literature (Gal 6:1–3; 1 Thess 5:14; 2 Thess 3:14–16; Jude 22–23; 2 *Clem.* 17.2; *Hermas* 38) and in relation specifically to sins committed against oneself (Matt 18:15–17; Luke 17:3–5). Those who have been led astray need someone to bring them back or to "turn them" (ἐπιστρέψῃ τις αὐτόν). This "conversion" language is well known in both testaments (Isa 6:10; Ezek 33:11; Acts 3:19; 9:35; 2 Cor 3:16). This command to motivate others to concern is rooted also in the OT (Lev 19:17; Ps 51:13; Ezek 3:17–21; 33:7–9) and echoed strongly elsewhere in the NT (Matt 18:12–15; 1 Thess 5:14; 2 Thess 3:15; 2 Tim 2:25; 1 John 5:16; Jude 1:23). As Paul also urged in Gal 6:1, James exhorts concerned brothers in the community who see a person in error to attempt in proper meekness and humility to turn him back to the way of the truth. This is the true way marked by wisdom from above that converts through firmness but gentleness (3:13, 17).

5:20 γινωσκέτω ὅτι ὁ ἐπιστρέψας ἁμαρτωλὸν ἐκ πλάνης ὁδοῦ αὐτοῦ σώσει ψυχὴν αὐτοῦ ἐκ θανάτου καὶ καλύψει πλῆθος ἁμαρτιῶν: There remains the question: Whose soul is saved and sins are covered? While there are text critical issues in these verses, the variant readings point to later scribes who desired to clarify a possible misunderstanding and the critical text probably does reflect the earliest and best readings (see the previous Textual Notes). I doubt if anyone would interpret this verse as referring to anyone else than the converted sinner unless commentators had suggested differently (Origen, *Hom. Lev.* 2.4, cited by Ropes, 315–16; Dibelius, 258; Adamson, 204). At first reading, that seems to be the sense, and, in my opinion, syntactical as well as theological reasons also support this interpretation. There is a distinct parallel construction between the following two clauses which is apparent when we rearrange the elements of the clauses.

Subject	Predicator	Adjunct
ὁ ἐπιστρέψας	ἁμαρτωλὸν	ἐκ πλάνης ὁδοῦ αὐτοῦ
σώσει	ψυχὴν αὐτοῦ	ἐκ θανάτου

It is clear from this construction that the soul who is saved in the second clause is the sinner in the first clause. If that is true, the parallelism of the final two clauses makes it clear that the sins that will be covered are also those of the sinner.

Predicator	Complement	Adjunct
σώσει	ψυχὴν αὐτοῦ	ἐκ θανάτου
καὶ καλύψει	πλῆθος	ἁμαρτιῶν.

Furthermore, the repetition of the pronoun αὐτοῦ in the complement connects to its use in the adjunct expression in the previous clause, where it clearly refers to the converted one. Finally, the future tense of καλύψει has in mind future sins. The sense would be that the action of converting the erring brother will also affect his future sins. This future focus on the "converted" or "loved" one is consistent with its usage both in Prov 10:12 and in 1 Pet 4:8 (Mayor, 177; Moo, 2000, 250–51; Johnson, 339; Davids, 201; Martin, 220; Hartin, 286–

87; Blomberg-Kamell, 249; McCartney, 264; McKnight, 459–60). It seems unlikely, therefore, that one's success in effecting the sinning believer's repentance would be the key to achieving one's own deliverance.

Mention should be made of a third option which sees the one "turned" as the sinner, but the sins that are covered are those of the "turner" (Dibelius, 258; Laws, 241). The same reasons just mentioned for adopting the more traditional reading apply also to this option, with this additional sober comment: "Such subtlety on the part of James would try his readers, which it still does!" (McKnight, 459).

That raises the final controversial hermeneutical issue in this verse and in the book. Is James citing, quoting, or alluding to Prov 10:12? Neither the LXX nor the Hebrew texts of Proverbs agree exactly with the wording in James, who also shifts to the future tense (καλύψει) and uses the noun πλῆθος to magnify the sins.[2] Those who argue that it is the restorer who saves his own soul see this also as a reference to having his own sins covered. While it is true that God tells Ezekiel that if he warns the wicked and they do repent, then he will save himself as well (Ezek 3:16–21; 33:9), is that the meaning here? We have seen previously that the most consistent grammatical way of approaching 5:20 is that the benefits mentioned accrue to the converted, not to the converter.

καλύψει πλῆθος ἁμαρτιῶν: In Jewish thinking, to "cover sin" means to procure forgiveness, both in biblical texts (Ps 32:1; 85:2) and in later Judaism (Sir 5:6). The concept of a multitude of sins has similar precedents (Ps 5:10; 85:2; Ezek 28:18). The future tense of καλύψει refers to the prevention of further sins being committed. It is best to conclude that James is *not* citing Prov 10:12 but is still influenced by its language. Perhaps he does not directly quote it because he applies it differently than the context of Prov 10:6–14, where the discussion is

---

[2] The LXX reads πάντας δὲ τοὺς μὴ φιλονεικοῦντας καλύπτει φιλία, "love covers all who do not love strife." The Hebrew is כָּל־פְּשָׁעִים תְּכַסֶּה אַהֲבָה, "love covers all transgressions."

about the effects of destructive versus helpful speech. What James does pick up on are the *effects* described in that passage. To James, the most *loving* act of all is to warn sinners from the error of their way and cover over their potential future sins.[3]

The final comment on this paragraph and on the homily as a whole concerns the intertextual echoes in these verses. In a book that has so often utilized the *logia* of Jesus as well as the canonical writings of the OT, those two sources again inform James' closing counsel on the restoration of wanderers. This could be an allusion to the parable of the lost sheep in Matt 18:12–14, or to the theme of restoring a sinning brother in Luke 17:3, 4. The last expression about the covering of sins probably alludes to a basic idea in Prov 10:12, even if the Proverbs text differs in its wording. The saying was later known in Jewish-Christian tradition (*1 Clem.* 49.4; *2 Clem.* 16.4), and this formulation was also regarded by Clement of Alexandria and others as an *agraphon* of Jesus (*Paed.* 3.91.3; see also *Did. Apost.* 4).

So the last words of a sometimes harsh and confrontational letter also become a reminder to its readers about the hope of forgiveness, restoration, and reconciliation.

---

[3] "This exhortation is of a piece with the recurring NT theme that evil is not overcome merely by refraining from doing it: we are to overcome evil with good. So too here at the end of James's epistle: it is not enough to try to be faithful ourselves; rather, it is essential to try to secure the faithfulness of others. We overcome evil with good" (Beale and Carson, *Commentary*, 1012).

FINAL THOUGHTS ON JAMES, THE MAN AND THE MESSAGE

What can we conclude about this book and its author? It has become obvious that it was written by someone who knew Jesus' words well and by someone who also knew the land of Israel well. In view of the lack of mention of the fall of Jerusalem in A.D. 70, it was likely written before A.D. 70 and as early as the A.D. 50s and possibly even earlier. Its main themes—endurance, impartiality, wisdom, good deeds, charity—are fundamental qualities that Christians need to be exhorted about on an ongoing basis. Its strong condemnation of rich oppressors should challenge us to examine our actions and lifestyles in how we relate to the poor around us.

Nothing here suggests a late theology or church situation, and much suggests an early or "primitive" stage of the early church period. The author is saturated in the OT and loves to tell small stories (parables) to illustrate his points. The letter is carefully constructed in a way that progresses around the theme of wholeness born from heavenly wisdom, not just a random set of moral axioms. It is a homily written in anticipation of a παρουσία that might come at any time. James exhorts us to not be double-minded, that is, not to waver. A person who is able to withstand trials and temptations and still be faithful to God in spite of circumstances is a τέλειος person who is complete or mature. That person does right both in his inner motives and in his outward actions with Divine help. As a general sermon, this document offers much of value to a church that is always undergoing trials and temptations.

And what about James the man? "Jacob" the Jewish believer stands at the very center of early Jewish Christianity—fixed as a rock in Jerusalem and not as an itinerant apostle. If the measure of a man is seen in those he influenced, then James is clearly a giant of a man. The intertextual echoes in 1 John and 1 Peter suggest that Peter and the Beloved Disciple—the major figures responsible for early Jewish Christians in the Greco-Roman world—were deeply indebted to the teaching and influence of James on the fledgling communities being birthed from Jerusalem to Rome. Together these three were the "pillars" of the growing spiritual temple. In this remarkable little document that we call "the Letter of James," James is firmly steering this ship of early Jewish Christianity, which in his lifetime was the only Christianity that existed!

From the beginning of his encyclical to its conclusion and then even to the conclusion of his life, we truly see "James at the Centre."[1]

---

[1] British spelling by an author whose writings on James the man and his letter have probably influenced my thinking more than any other: R. Bauckham, "James at the Centre," *EPTA Bulletin* (1995) 23–33.

APPENDIX ONE

Extended Note on James 3:3

I have omitted the footnotes that accompany the article on this subject published in *Graeco Roman Journal of Christianity and Judaism*, 2014. Please reference the article for those supporting footnotes.

I propose the adoption of a different textual reading in James 3:3a from what is found in the critical texts of NA27/28 and UBS4/5. These editions read as follows: εἰ δὲ τῶν ἵππων τοὺς χαλινοὺς εἰς τὰ στόματα βάλλομεν εἰς τὸ πείθεσθαι αὐτοὺς ἡμῖν, καὶ ὅλον τὸ σῶμα αὐτῶν μετάγομεν. "If we put bits into the mouths of horses to make them obey us, we can also turn the whole animal." I suggest that ἴδε instead of εἰ δέ has both older external evidence and a better argument from internal evidence for its adoption.

This preference alters the beginning of the verse from being the protasis of a conditional sentence to becoming the first of two primary clauses. In this suggested reading, the first clause then would consist of an imperative command ἴδε, i.e., "look," which has been translated traditionally as "behold." In this reading, therefore, the protasis and apodosis in the conditional sentence are changed to an orienter and two coordinate indicative clauses as follows: "Look! We put bridles into the mouths of horses so that they obey us and we guide their whole bodies." This is also the translation in the Authorized Version, although the reading of the *Textus Receptus* at this point (ἰδού) is based on only one late manuscript (1874), one Father (6th century Pseudo-Oecomenius), and one version (Old Church Slavonic). This ἰδού differs from the "Majority Text" reading of ἴδε which is found in C, P, and a large representation of Byzantine manuscripts. This singular reading in the *Textus Receptus* appears to represent an effort to assimilate with the two occurrences of ἰδού in 3:4 and 5:1. Other manuscript representatives of the Alexandrian, Western, and Byzantine families contain εἰ δέ. These readings are complicated, however, by the unique ΕΙΔΕ ΓΑΡ in Codex Sinaiticus. The presence of the consequential conjunction γάρ makes for a rather complicated clausal structure if the previous letters are read as the conditional particle εἰ and the conjunction δέ. The complication of these variant readings is better understood when the practice of itacism among scribes is recognized. It is well known among students of the discipline that the diphthong εἰ and the letter ι were both pronounced similarly in ancient times, and such is the case today in Modern Greek (the English sound "ee"). This situation gave rise to the occasional scribal practice of altering either εἰ to an ι or vice versa! Thus the seemingly odd ΕΙΔΕ ΓΑΡ in Sinaiticus may be intended to convey an original ἴδε! (See the end of the article for an image of James 3:3a in Codex Sinaiticus).

Due to the diversity of readings among the manuscripts and because of the distinct possibility of scribal itacism, the UBS committee gave a {C} rating to εἰ δέ in their text. Some of the committee members believed that εἰ δέ was the more difficult reading—an issue that we will address later. The diplomatic advice of Metzger is as follows: "The editor must choose the reading that, in his judgment, is most appropriate in the context." Although normally reticent to dissent from the readings of the two critical texts of NA27/28 and UBS4/5, I have chosen to follow Metzger's advice about context and suggest the adoption of the ἴδε variant for the five following reasons, each of which are based on what textual scholars call internal evidence.

(1) In every other case in which the conditional εἰ δέ appears in James, the δέ clearly expresses an idea that is adversative to what he has just stated (1:5; 2:9, 11; 3:14; 4:11). Such an adversative idea is *not* the

case if there is a conditional sentence beginning 3:3.

(2) If 3:3 is a conditional sentence, the καί that initiates the proposed apodosis (καὶ ὅλον τὸ σῶμα αὐτῶν μετάγομεν) seems to be out of place. Although English translators have recognized this by rendering it as "also," it is not the normal role of an apodosis in a conditional sentence to add new information to the protasis, but rather to show the result of fulfilling the hypothetical condition in the protasis.

(3) Because James uses the aorist middle imperative of ὁράω (ἰδού) to call attention to the ship/rudder in 3:4 and to the fire/forest in 3:5a, the parallelism is more evident if he uses the aorist active imperative of ὁράω (ἴδε) in 3:3. This parallelism can be seen as follows by bolding the paralleled imperatives:

ἴδε τῶν ἵππων τοὺς χαλινοὺς εἰς τὰ στόματα βάλλομεν εἰς τὸ πείθεσθαι αὐτοὺς ἡμῖν...

ἰδοὺ καὶ τὰ πλοῖα τηλικαῦτα ὄντα καὶ ὑπὸ ἀνέμων σκληρῶν ἐλαυνόμενα...

ἰδοὺ ἡλίκον πῦρ ἡλίκην ὕλην ἀνάπτει·

(4) The καί in its postpositive position in 3:4 appears to refer back to the preceding illustration in a way that is consistent with the idea that James desires to call attention to the previous command to "look" at something "also" in the natural processes of life.

(5) Although Metzger informs us that a majority of the UBS committee members preferred εἰ δέ as the more difficult reading, could not the very same point be made about ἴδε, because it breaks the parallelism with ἰδού in 3:4 and 5? If someone objects that it would be inconsistent to utilize both ἴδε and ἰδού in such a close context, it should be noted that the following passages have these two different imperative forms utilized together in quite close context: Sir 2:1 (LXX); Mark 3:32, 34; Matt 25:6, 20, 22, 25; John 16:29, 32; and Gal 1:20; 5:2.

J.B. Mayor also effectively defends the ἴδε reading at this point. He informs us that James also interchanges the active voice of αἰτεῖτε and the middle voice of αἰτεῖσθε in the same verse (4:3). This is the very same type of shift that I am proposing in 3:3. He even suggests that the difference between the voices in 3:3, 4 is that the middle voice calls for the subject to become more involved in the action that is commanded. "Look at the details of the ship and its rudder." Whether or not Mayor's explanation of the middle voice validates the variation in the voice of the imperatives elsewhere, these combined arguments for the preference of the ἴδε reading seem compelling enough to this writer to adopt it with less than the normal caution expected in a variant reading.

The singular insertion of the ΓΑΡ after ΕΙΔΕ in Sinaiticus also must have concerned a corrector since he placed four dots above the questionable word. The corrector may have assumed that ΕΙΔΕ should be read as εἰ δὲ and saw the grammatical difficulty of a conditional particle followed by two conjunctions. If the ΕΙΔΕ is understood as itacism for ἴδε, however, the original scribe of Sinaiticus intended for it to be read as "For look, we put bridles...". His intention then was probably to view the imperative in 3:3 as support for the point that he had just made in 3:2, namely that a mature man is able to bridle his whole body. James' fondness for asyndeton, however, does not demand such a connecting conjunction.

While some scholars obviously think that the weight of the external evidence of manuscript age and quality tilts toward the reading εἰ δὲ, the internal evidence of context and discourse considerations ought also to be given serious consideration in this passage. Furthermore, with the probable support for ἴδε from Sinaiticus, the reading does have some significant early manuscript support.

My conclusion, therefore, is that the function of both discourse markers ἴδε and ἰδού call attention to the three examples from natural life—the horse/bridle, the ship/rudder, and the fire/forest—and also effectively combine to make a powerful rhetorical argument for the unexpected (for its size) power of the tongue, both for good and for evil. Therefore, James asks us, yea even commands us, to "look" at them with serious attention!

The singular reading in Codex Sinaiticus:[1]

NOTE: I have utilized ideas from both the Metzger and the Comfort commentaries on Textual Criticism of the NT. Final judgments are my own.

---

[1] Image used by permission from the Center for the Study of New Testament Manuscripts (www.csntm.org).

APPENDIX TWO

Shepherd of Hermas References

Two different reference systems exist for the Shepherd of Hermas. The older one follows the division of the work into Visions, Mandates, and Parables (or Similitudes), while the newer system employs consecutive chapter numbers. Following a recent trend that also follows the commentary by Whittaker, the chapter numbers for Hermas in the text of this commentary follow the newer division.[1] The following table indicates the relation between the old and the new numbering.

Three Divisions	Old	New
Visions	1.1–4	1–4
Visions	2.1–4	5–8
Visions	3.1–13	9–21
Visions	4.1–3	22–24
Visions	5	25

---

[1] M. Whittaker, *Der Hirt des Hermas*, 2d ed. (Berlin: Akademie-Verlag, 1967).

Appendix Two: Shepherd of Hermas References

Mandates	1	26
Mandates	2	27
Mandates	3	28
Mandates	4.1–4	29–32
Mandates	5.1–2	33–34
Mandates	6.1–2	35–36
Mandates	7	37
Mandates	8	38
Mandates	9	39
Mandates	10.1–3	40–42
Mandates	11	43
Mandates	12.1–6	44–49
Parables	1	50
Parables	2	51
Parables	3	52
Parables	4	53
Parables	5.1–7	54–60
Parables	6.1–5	61–65

Parables	7	66
Parables	8.1–11	67–77
Parables	9.1–33	78–110
Parables	10.1–4	111–114

Figure 6: Shepherd of Hermas Reference Systems

GENERAL BIBLIOGRAPHY

Technical Monographs on James

Adamson, James B. *James: The Man and His Message.* Grand Rapids: Eerdmans, 1989.

Baker, William R. *Personal Speech-Ethics in the Epistle of James.* WUNT 2.68. Tübingen: Mohr, 1995.

Batten, Alicia J. *Friendship and Benefaction in James.* Emory Studies in Early Christianity 15. Blandford Forum, U.K.: Deo Publishing, 2010.

Bauckham, Richard. *James: Wisdom of James, Disciple of Jesus the Sage.* NTR. London: Routledge, 1999.

Cargal, Timothy. *Restoring the Diaspora: Discursive Structure and Purpose in the Epistle of James.* SBLDS 144. Atlanta, GA: Scholar's Press, 1993.

Cheung, Luke L. *The Genre, Composition, and Hermeneutics of James.* London: Paternoster, 2003.

Chilton, Bruce, and Craig A. Evans, eds. *James the Just and Christian Origins.* NovTSup 98. Leiden: Brill, 1999.

———. *The Missions of James, Peter and Paul: Tensions in Early Christianity.* NovTSup 115. Leiden: Brill, 2005.

Deppe, Dean B. *The Sayings of Jesus in the Epistle of James.* Chelsea, MI: Bookcrafters, 1989.

Edgar, David H. *Has God not Chosen the Poor?: The Social Setting of the Epistle of James.* JSNTSup 206. Sheffield: Sheffield Academic Press, 2001.

Eisenman, Robert. *James the Brother of Jesus.* New York: Viking, 1996.

Hartin, Patrick J. *James and the Q Sayings of Jesus.* JSNTSup 47. Sheffield: JSOT Press, 1991.

————. *A Spirituality of Perfection: Faith in Action in the Letter of James.* Collegeville, MN: Liturgical Press, 1999.

————. *James of Jerusalem: Heir to Jesus of Nazareth.* Collegeville, MN: Liturgical, 2004.

Henrici, C.F.G. *Der literarische Charakter der neutestamentliche Schriften* (Leipzig: 1908).

Johnson, Luke T. *Brother of Jesus, Friend of God: Studies in the Letter of James.* Grand Rapids: Eerdmans, 2004.

Painter, John. *Just James: The Brother of Jesus in History and Tradition.* Rev. ed. Columbia: University of South Carolina Press, 2004.

Penner, Todd C. *The Epistle of James and Eschatology: Re-Reading an Ancient Christian.* JSNTSup 121. Sheffield: Sheffield Academic Press, 1996.

Shanks, Hershel and Ben Witherington. *The Brother of Jesus: The Dramatic Story & Meaning of the First Archaeological Link to Jesus and His Family.* New York: Harper One, 2003.

Strange, James R. *The Moral World of James: Setting the Epistle in its Greco-Roman and Judaic Environments.* SBL 136. New York: Peter Lang, 2010.

Taylor, Mark E. *A Text-Linguistic Investigation into the Discourse Structure of James.* LNTS 311. London: T&T Clark, 2006.

Journals, Periodicals, Essays

Argyle, A. W. "Greek Among the Jews of Palestine in New Testament Times." *NTS* 20 (1973–74) 87–89.

Baasland, E. "Der Jakobusbrief als Neutestamentliche Weisheitsschrift." *ST* 36 (1982) 199–39.

Baker, William R. " 'Above All Else': Contexts of the Call for Verbal Integrity in James 5:12." *JSNT* 54 (1994) 57–71.

Bauckham, Richard. "James at the Centre." *EPTA Bulletin* (1995) 23–33.

———. "James and the Jerusalem Church." Pages 415–80 in *The Book of Acts in Its First Century Setting*, ed. Bruce W. Winter. Vol. 4: *The Book of Acts in Its Palestinian Setting*, ed. R. Bauckham. Grand Rapids: Eerdmans, 1995.

Bishop, E. F. "Three and a Half Years." *ExpTim* 61 (1949–50) 126–27.

Carr, Arthur. "The Meaning of Ὁ ΚΟΣΜΟΣ in James iii.6." *Exp* 7, 8 (1909) 318–25.

———. "The Patience of Job (St James v 11)." *Exp Series* 6, 8 (1913) 511–17.

Cladder, H. J. "Die Anfang des Jakobusbriefes." *ZKT* 28 (1904) 37–57.

Davids, Peter H. "The Meaning of ἀπείραστος in James 1.13." NTS 24 (1978) 386–92.

———. "Tradition and Citation in the Epistle of James." Pages 113–26 in *Scripture, Tradition and Interpretation: Festschrift for E. F. Harrison*, eds. W. Ward Gasque and William S. LaSor. Grand Rapids: Eerdmans, 1978.

———. "Theological Perspectives on the Epistle of James." *JETS* 23 (1980) 97–103.

———. "James and Jesus." Pages 63–84 in *The Jesus Tradition Outside the Gospels*, ed. David Wenham. Gospel Perspectives 5. Sheffield: JSOT Press, 1984.

———. "Palestinian Traditions in the Epistle of James." Pages 33–57 in *James the Just and Christian Origins*, ed. Bruce Chilton and Craig A. Evans. NovTSup 98 Leiden: Brill, 1999.

Elliott-Binns, L. E. "The Meaning of ὕλη in James iii.5." *NTS* 2 (1955) 48–50.

———. "James 1.18: Creation or Redemption?" *NTS* 3 (1956) 148–61.

Francis, Fred O. "The Form and Function of the Opening and Closing Paragraphs of James and 1 John." *ZNW* 61 (1970) 110–26.

Gray, Patrick. "Points and Lines: Parallelism in the Letter of James and the *Testament of Job*." *NTS* 50 (2004) 406–24.

Hadidian, Dikran Y. "Palestinian Pictures in the Epistle of James." *ExpTim* 63 (1952) 227–28.

Hartin, Patrick J. "'Come Now, You Rich, Weep and Wail ...' (Jas 5:1–6)." *JTSA* 84 (1993) 57–63.

———. "'Who is Wise and Understanding Among You?' (James 3:13). An Analysis of Wisdom, Eschatology, and Apocalypticism in the Epistle of James." Pages 483–503 in *Society of Biblical Literature Seminar Papers.* Atlanta: Scholars Press, 2005.

Haslehurst, R. S. T. "The Fifth Gospel." *Theology* XXXV (1937) 96–103.

Hengel, Martin. "Between Jesus and Paul." In *Between Jesus and Paul,* trans. J. Bowden. London: SCM, 1983, 1–29.

———. "Jakobus der Herrenbruder—der este 'Papst'?" Pages 71–104 in *Glaube und Eschatologie,* eds. E. Grasser and O. Merk. Tubingen: JCB Mohr, 1985.

———. "Der Jakobusbrief als Antipaulinische Polemik." Pages 248–78 in *Tradition and Interpretation in the New Testament. FS E. Earle Ellis,* eds. G.F. Hawthorne and O. Betz. Grand Rapids: Eerdmans, 1987.

Hymes, D. "The General Epistle of James," *IJSL* 62 (1986) 77.

Instone-Brewer, David. "James as a Sermon on the Trials of Abraham." Pages 250–268 in *The New Testament in Its First Century Setting: Essays on Context and Background in Honour of B.W. Winter on his 65th Birthday,* eds. P.J. Williams, A. D. Clarke, P. M. Head, D. Instone-Brewer. Grand Rapids: Eerdmans, 2004.

Jeremias, Joachim. "Paul and James." *ExpT* 66 (1954–55) 368–71.

———. "Jac 4:5: *epipothei.*" *ZNW* 50 (1959) 137–38.

Johanson, Bruce C. "The Definition of 'Pure Religion' in James 1:27 Reconsidered." *ExpT* 84 (1972–73) 118–19.

Johnson, Luke T. "The Use of Leviticus 19 in the Letter of James" *JBL* 101 (1982) 391–401.

———. "James 3:13–4:10 and the *Topos* PERI PHTHONOU." *NovT* 25 (1983) 327–47.

———. "Friendship with the World/Friendship with God: A Study of Discipleship in James." Pages 202–20 in *Discipleship in the New Testament,* ed. F. Segovia, 166–83. Philadelphia: Fortress Press, 1985.

———. "The Mirror of Remembrance (James 1:22–25)." *CBQ* 50 (1988) 632–45.

————. "Taciturnity and True Religion (James 1:26–27)." Pages 329–39
in *Greeks, Romans, and Christians: Essays in Honor of A. J. Malherbe*.
Ed. D. Balch et al. Minneapolis: Fortress Press, 1990

Keener, Craig S. "Friendship." Pages 380–88 in *Dictionary of New
Testament Background*. Ed. C. A. Evans and S. E. Porter, 380–88.
Downers Grove: InterVarsity Press, 2000.

Kirk, J. A. "The Meaning of Wisdom in James: Examination of a
Hypothesis." *NTS* 16 (1969–70) 24–38.

Laws, Sophie. "Does Scripture Speak in Vain? A Reconsideration of
James IV.5." *NTS* 20 (1973–74) 210–15.

Lightfoot, Joseph B. "The Brethren of the Lord." In *St. Paul's Epistle to
the Galatians*. 20th ed. London: Macmillan, 1896, 252–91.

Longenecker, Richard. "The 'Faith of Abraham' Theme in Paul, James,
and Hebrews: A Study in the Circumstantial Nature of New
Testament Teaching." *JETS* 20 (1977) 203–12.

Marcus, Joel. "The Evil Inclination in the Epistle of James." *CBQ* 44
(1982) 606–621.

McKnight, Scot. "James 2:18a: The Unidentifiable Interlocutor." *WTJ* 52
(1990) 355–64.

Myllykoski, Matti. "James the Just in History and Tradition:
Perspectives of Past and Present Scholarship." Parts I and II, *CBR* 5.1
(2006) 73–122; 6.1 (2007) 11–98.

Nietzel, Heinz. "Eine alte crux interpretum im Jakobusbrief 2.18." *ZNW*
73 (1982) 286–93.

Painter, John. "James as the First Catholic Epistle." *Int* (July 2006) 245–
59.

Perkins, Pheme. "James 3:16–4:3." *Int* 36 (1982) 283–87.

Porter, F. C. "The Yeçer Hara: A Study in the Jewish Doctrine of Sin." In
Yale Biblical and Semitic Studies. Yale Bicentennial Publications.
New York: Scribner's, 1901. 91–158.

Porter, Stanley E. "Is *dipsychos* (James 1, 8; 4, 8) a 'Christian' Word?" *Bib*
71 (1990) 469–98.

————. "Jesus and the Use of Greek in Galilee." Pages 123–54 in *Studying the Historical Jesus: Evaluations of the State of Current Research*, eds. Bruce D. Chilton and Craig A. Evans. NTTS 19. Leiden: Brill, 1994.

Prockter, Lewis J. "James 4:4–6: A Midrash on Noah." *NTS* 35 (1989) 625–27.

Reed, Jeffrey T. "Discourse Analysis." Pages 189–217 in *Handbook to Exegesis of the New Testament*, ed. S.E. Porter. NTTS 25. Leiden: Brill, 1997.

Reese, James M. "The Exegete as Sage: Hearing the Message of James." *BTB* (Aug 1982) 12:82–85.

Ropes, J. H. " 'Thou hast Faith and I have Works,' (James II.18)." *The Expositor*, 7th ser., 5 (1908) 547–57.

Schmitt, John J. "You Adulteresses! The Image in James 4:4." *NovT* 28 (1986) 327–37.

Schökel, Luis A. "James 5, 2 [sic] and 4,6." *Bib* 54 (1973) 73–76.

Scott, J. Julius. "James the Relative of Jesus and the Expectation of an Eschatological High Priest." *JETS* 25 (1982) 323–31.

Seitz, Christopher R. "The Patience of Job in the Epistle of James." In *Konsequente Traditionsgeschichte*, eds. R. Bartelmus, T. Kruger, and H. Utschneider, 373–82. Orbis biblicus et orientalis 126. Gottingen: Vandenbrock & Ruprecht, 1993.

Shogren, Gary. "Will God Heal Us? A Re-Examination of James 5:14–16a." *EQ* 61 (1989) 99–108.

Stagg, Frank. "An Analysis of the Book of James." *RE* 66 (1969) 365–68.

————. "Exegetical Themes in James 1 and 2," *RE* 66 (1969) 391–402.

————. "The Abused Aorist." *JBL* 91 (1972) 222–31.

Tollefson, Kenneth D. "The Epistle of James as Dialectical Discourse." *BTB* 21 (1997) 66–69.

Townsend, Michael J. "James 4:1–4: A Warning against Zealotry?" *ExpT* 87 (1978–79) 211–13.

————. "Christ, Community and Salvation in the Epistle of James." *EvQ* 53 (1981) 115–23.

Trudinger, L. Paul. "*Heteron de tōn apostolōn ouk eidon, ei Mē Iakōbon*: A Note on Galatians 1.19." *NovT* 17 (1975) 200–202.

Unger, Merrill F. "Divine Healing." *BSac* 128 (1971) 234–44.

Van Unnik, W. C. *"Diaspora* and *Church* in the First Centuries of Church History," In *Sparsa Collecta*. Vol. 3 Leiden: Brill, 1983, 95–105.

Varner, William. "The Main Theme and Structure of James." *TMSJ* 22 (Spring 2011) 115–32.

Verseput, Donald. "James 1:17 and the Jewish Morning Prayers." *NovT* (1997) 177–91.

————. "Wisdom, 4Q185, and the Epistle of James." *JBL* 117/4 (1998) 691–707.

Ward, Roy B. "The Works of Abraham: James 2:14–26." *HTR* 61 (1968) 283–90.

————. "Partiality in the Assembly." *HTR* 62 (1969) 87–97.

————. "James of Jerusalem." *ResQ* 16 (1973) 174–90.

Warrington, K. "James 5:14–18: Healing Then and Now." *IntRevMis* 93 (July/October 2004) 346–67.

Watson, Duane F. "The Rhetoric of James 3:1–12 and a Classical Pattern of Argumentation." *NovT* 35 (1993) 48–64.

Wilkinson, John. "Healing in the Epistle of James." *SJT* 24 (1971) 326–45.

Wiseman, Donald J. "Rahab of Jericho." *TynBul* 14 (1964) 8–11.

Wolmarans, J. L. P. "The Tongue Guiding the Body: The Anthropological Presuppositions of James 3:1–12." *Neot* 26 (1992) 523–30.

General Books

Aune, David E. *The New Testament in Its Literary Environment*. LEC 8. Philadelphia: Westminster John Knox Press, 1987.

————. *Westminster Dictionary of the New Testament and Early Christian Literature and Rhetoric*. Westminster: John Knox Press, 2003.

Barnett, Paul. *Jesus and the Rise of Early Christianity*. Downers Grove, IL: IVP Academic, 1999.

Beale, Gregory K., and Donald A. Carson, eds. *Commentary on the New Testament Use of the Old Testament.* Grand Rapids: Baker Academic, 2007.

Black, David A. *Linguistics for Students of New Testament Greek: A Survey of Basic Concepts and Applications.* Grand Rapids: Baker, 1988.

Blomberg, Craig. *Neither Poverty Nor Riches: A Biblical Theology of Material Possessions.* NSBT 7. Grand Rapids: Eerdmans, 1999.

Boring, M. Eugene, Klaus Berger, and Carsten Colpe, eds. *Hellenistic Commentary to the New Testament.* Nashville: Abingdon Press, 1995.

Bruce, Frederick F. *Peter, Stephen, James, and John: Studies in Early Non-Pauline Christianity.* Grand Rapids: Eerdmans, 1979.

Byron, John. *Slavery Metaphors in Early Judaism and Pauline Christianity: A Traditio-Historical and Exegetical Examination.* WUNT 2.162. Tübingen: Mohr Siebeck, 2003.

Casson, Lionel. *Ships and Seamanship in the Ancient World.* Princeton: Princeton, 1971.

———. *Travel in the Ancient World.* Toronto: Hakkert, 1974.

Chester, Andrew, and Ralph P. Martin, eds. *The Theology of the Letters of James, Peter, and Jude.* Cambridge: Cambridge, 1994.

Dodd, Charles H. *According to the Scriptures: The Substructure of New Testament Theology.* London: Nisbet, 1952.

Doty, William G. *Letters in Primitive Christianity.* Philadelphia: Fortress Press, 1973.

Fanning, Buist. *Verbal Aspect in New Testament Greek.* Oxford Theological Monographs. New York: Oxford University Press, 1990.

Harris, Murray J. *Slave of Christ: A New Testament Metaphor for Total Devotion to Christ.* NSBT 8. Downers Grove, IL: IVP Academic, 2001.

Hengel, Martin. *Judaism and Hellenism: Studies in Their Encounter in Palestine during the Early Hellenistic Period.* Trans. John Bowden. Philadelphia: Fortress Press, 1974.

———. *Property and Riches in the Early Church.* Trans. J. Bowden. London: SCM, 1974.

Hort, Fenton J. A. *Judaistic Christianity.* London/New York: Macmillan, 1904.

Jobes, Karen H. *Letters to the Church: A Survey of Hebrews and the General Epistles*. Grand Rapids, MI: Zondervan, 2011.

Klauck, Hans-Josef. *Ancient Letters and the New Testament: A Guide to Context and Exegesis*. Waco, TX: Baylor University Press, 2006.

Konstan, David. *Friendship in the Classical World*. Cambridge: Cambridge, 1997.

Levinsohn, Steven H. *Discourse Features of New Testament Greek*. 2nd ed. Dallas: SIL International, 2000.

Lightfoot, Joseph B. *Dissertations on the Apostolic Age: Reprinted from Editions of Paul's Epistles*. London: Macmillan, 1892, 3–44.

Louw, Johannes P., and Eugene A. Nida. *Greek-English Lexicon of the New Testament: Based on Semantic Domains*. 2 vols. New York: United Bible Societies, 1998.

MacArthur Jr., John F. *The Gospel According to the Apostles*. Nashville: Word, 2000.

Malina, Bruce J. *The New Testament World*. 3rd ed. Louisville: WJK Press, 2001.

Martin, Dale B. *Slavery As Salvation: The Metaphor of Slavery in Pauline Christianity*. New Haven: Yale University Press, 1990.

Metzger, Bruce M. *A Textual Commentary on the Greek New Testament*. 2nd ed. New York: United Bible Societies, 1994.

McKnight, Scot. *The Jesus Creed: Loving God, Loving Others*. Brewster, MA: Paraclete Press, 2004.

Neusner, Jacob. *Dictionary of Judaism in the Biblical Period*. Peabody, MA: Hendrickson, 1996.

———. *Rabbinic Literature and the New Testament: What We Cannot Show, We Do Not Know*. Eugene, OR: Wipf and Stock Publishers, 2004.

Porter, Stanley E. *Verbal Aspect in the Greek of the New Testament with Reference to Tense and Mood*. SBG 1. New York: Lang, 1989.

———. *Idioms of the Greek New Testament*. Biblical Languages: Greek 2. Sheffield: JSOT Press, 1992.

Porter, Stanley E. (ed.). *Handbook to Exegesis of the New Testament*. NTTS 25. Leiden: Brill, 1997.

Porter, Stanley E., and Craig A. Evans, eds. *New Testament Interpretation and Methods: A Sheffield Reader*. Biblical Seminar 45: Sheffield Reader. Sheffield: Sheffield Academic Press, 1997.

Porter, Stanley E., and D. A. Carson, eds. *Linguistics and the New Testament: Critical Junctures*. JSNTSup 168. SNTG 5. Sheffield: Sheffield Academic Press, 1999.

Robinson, John. A. T. *Redating the New Testament*. London: SCM, 1976.

Runge, Steven. E. *Discourse Grammar of the Greek New Testament*. Peabody, MA: Hendrickson, 2010.

Sevenster, Jans N. *Do You Know Greek? How Much Greek Could the First Jewish Christians Have Known?* NovTSup 19. Leiden: Brill, 1968.

Stowers, Stanley K. *Letter Writing in the Greco-Roman Antiquity*. Philadelphia: Westminster, 1986.

Turner, Nigel. *A Grammar of New Testament Greek*, eds. J. H. Moulton and W. F. Howard. Vol. 4: *Style*. Edinburgh: T&T Clark, 1976.

Wallace, Daniel B. *Greek Grammar Beyond the Basics*. Grand Rapids: Zondervan, 1996.

———. *Granville Sharp's Canon and Its Kin: Semantics and Significance*. SBG 14. New York: Lang, 2009.

White, John L. *Light from Ancient Letters*. FF. Philadelphia: Fortress Press, 1986.

Witherington, Ben. *The Indelible Image: The Theological and Ethical Thought World of the New Testament*, Volume 1: *The Individual Witnesses*. Downers Grove, IL: IVP Academic, 2010.

Printed in the USA
CPSIA information can be obtained
at www.ICGtesting.com
LVHW021336230823
756067LV00009B/286